The
Devil Is a
Gentleman

The

Devil Is a

Gentleman

Exploring America's Religious Fringe

J. C. Hallman

Random House
New York

Published in the United States by Random House, an imprint of The Random House
Publishing Group, a division of Random House, Inc., New York.

RANDOM HOUSE and colophon are registered trademarks of Random House, Inc.

LIBRARY OF CONGRESS CATALOGING-IN-PUBLICATION DATA
Hallman, J. C.
The devil is a gentleman: exploring America's religious fringe / J. C. Hallman.
p.   cm.
Includes bibliographical references.
ISBN 1-4000-6172-5
1. Cults—United States.   2. Sects—United States.   3. United States—Religion.
I. Title.
BL2525.H35   2006
200'.973'090511—dc22   2005050753

Printed in the United States of America on acid-free paper

www.atrandom.com

9 8 7 6 5 4 3 2 1

FIRST EDITION

Book design by rlf design

For B.H.C.

If one could be both poet, philosopher & historian,
one could write a pretty bully book.

    —William James

I do not know what I'm fishing for
   in these rivers, green   & not so,
but perhaps it's something   as ordinary
     as God   or the crease
separating the knowable and unknowable

    —Joseph C. Millar

Contents

King

1878–1890   97

Satan

1890–1898   141

Author

1898–1902   193

Godless

Prologue

The churches in Atlantic City weren't the biggest show in town anymore. Gaudy casinos stood like architectural braggarts next to stone temples crumbling and suffering the disgrace of graffiti. This was 1999, long before I conceived of *The Devil Is a Gentleman,* and mass was about to begin at Our Lady Star of the Sea, a shrub-fenced Catholic complex on Atlantic Avenue. I lived in Atlantic City for a time; this was my neighborhood. Mr. Lucky Barbershop, Alcohólicos Anónimos, a bail bonds joint, a funeral home, and my dinky apartment all shared a view of the church.

In the courtyard I headed for a statue I knew—I'd seen it before on walks, and returned to it sometimes. It was a Christ. The statue was all white except where it was streaked with city soot, and it stood in an open-armed Christ pose, as though you should look at its abdomen for some reason. It was the statue's eyes that I came back for. Someone had gouged out the concrete and inserted glass replicas. They weren't particularly lifelike, but they gave the statue an eerie presence because you could see that someone had tried to make it look alive. Much later, I would come to learn of the undulating definition of God: when things went bad, from war or exile or pestilence, people turned their backs on abstract conceptions of God and set off toward anthropomorphic visions. They resurrected a personal God, brought him back to life. They gave him eyes that looked real.

Atlantic City had a population of only about thirty thousand, but its blight had been world-class ever since commercial airlines diverted East Coast tourists to Florida. When I lived there I made a habit of exploring the city's tiny forgotten neighborhoods, the whole town sucked down into that special form of squalor available to places once grand. Corpses turned up pretty regularly in Atlantic City. Left in abandoned cars, dumped under bridges, once stuffed under the motel bed of an unsuspecting couple. One day, I watched two men load a body into a station wagon in broad daylight. They didn't have a stretcher, so they had rolled the stiff into a length of old carpet. The following summer there was a spate of suicides in the city: five in eight days, people throwing themselves off the casinos' huge parking structures. One of them was a friend of mine.

I had come to Atlantic City for a job, but I rationalized staying for a while with the observation that, like it or not, most of the world lived like this. Like a much larger metropolis, Atlantic City was divided into ethnic neighborhoods: Hispanic, African American, Vietnamese. This last drew me to Our Lady—the church held a weekly mass in Vietnamese, and on November 24, 1999, there was a special service for the Martyrs of Vietnam. More than a hundred priests, nuns, and believers in Vietnam had been murdered for their faith since Portuguese missionaries first arrived there in 1533. Pope John Paul II canonized all of them in 1988.

I've never really felt the need for faith, though I admire it in others. I'm told that as a boy I enjoyed mass and memorized hymns prodigiously so I could sing them at a little church by the ocean. But all that is beyond the horizon of my memory. What I remember is rejecting mass, despising it, hiding in closets to avoid the stucco suburban churches we attended once my family moved inland. I generally felt traumatized by mass, though not for any good reason. I became an altar boy for a time, back when the priest still placed the Eucharist directly onto the tongues of the congregation. One of my jobs was to hold a little metal disk—a paten, I think it was called—under people's chins. But at ten years old, I wasn't in the spirit: I imagined my paten as razor sharp, and I could cut all those throats if I wanted to.

Eventually our family stopped going to church altogether. I grew up, left home. Since then, I'd wandered into mass only a few times, and it wasn't until I heard about the Martyrs of Vietnam and connected them to the glass-eyed Christ that I considered taking the first step toward what would become *The Devil Is a Gentleman*. I just decided to go to the service. I'd sit in a pew, no one would look at me. It would be awkward to refuse Communion, but I didn't have to participate.

I stepped into Our Lady's foyer, where the little church had declared war on the casino hotels. Bingo flyers dabbed a pattern on a bulletin board of upcoming events. One sign read:

Stardust Annual Monthly Prizes:
Great Odds! Great Prizes!
Remember, there are no "losers" because you are donating to
the parish and that makes you a "winner" in our books!
(This is a New Jersey State legalized 50/50 raffle)

This wasn't such a surprise. Catholicism might have been alone among the Christian traditions to openly embrace gambling, but the wager concept has long played a prominent role in the philosophical wrangling over God. Once Western Christianity committed itself to an anthropomorphized Trinity—triplets perched on the fence between polytheism and monotheism—rational thinkers felt compelled to explain their faith with logic. More than one stumbled onto the metaphor of a bet. Luther described his faith as "a free surrender and a joyful bet on his unfelt, untried and unknown goodness." Pascal was more to the point: "Let us weigh the gain and the loss in wagering that God is. Let us estimate the two chances. If you gain, you gain all; if you lose, you lose nothing. Wager, then, without hesitation that He is." Kant was less explicit, but just as concerned with the wager's outcome: "The *speculative* interest of reason makes it necessary to regard all order in the world *as if* it had originated in the purpose of a supreme reason." The basic idea, much older than even these thinkers, was eventually shorthanded to "Pascal's wager," and divinity itself came to be understood with a principle familiar to the professional gambler: the expectation of loss. God was a good bet.

In Our Lady's sanctuary, religion, like Atlantic City, seemed like a bet already lost. It was all in decline. Below the pipe organ a camera oscillated meanly over the pews, and what sounded like the ocean a block away was really a malfunction in the public-address system. Casino dealers skulked into confessional stalls, dressed in their tacky uniforms. The votive candles were electric, and I watched a man sneak up and light six of the twitchy bulbs without leaving a donation. I was just about to abandon my adventure when the Vietnamese began to arrive. They came in neatly dressed waves, threading through the washboard pattern of pews. I took a seat behind a hunched old man with an ornate wooden cane, a flimsy white beard, inch-long thumbnails, and thin beautiful clothing like vestments.

I admit that I was baffled by the Martyrs of Vietnam. I could imagine dying for an idea, but I couldn't imagine dying for an imported idea, for someone else's idea. It was still a few years before I would go back to William James's *The Varieties of Religious Experience: A Study in Human Nature,* and it wasn't until I picked the book up again and took James as my patron that I began to understand how I could be curious about religion when some part of it still repelled me. "Our faith is faith in someone else's faith," James advised, "and in the greatest matters this is most the case." For James, religious experience—something quite different from going to mass—stood as a marker of both extremes of human potential: its fruits were the best that humanity was capable of, yet its distortions had resulted in the worst atrocities the world had ever seen. James was neither a strict believer nor a complete skeptic. His indecisiveness on this count has frustrated his biographers and serves as a fair introduction to the elasticity of his thinking. The same flexibility was why he wouldn't have been baffled by the Vietnamese. Nor by Pascal's wager:

> *It is like those gambling and insurance rules based on probability, in which we secure ourselves against losses in detail by hedging on the total run. But this hedging philosophy requires that long run should be there; and this makes it inapplicable to the question of religious faith.*

And here was where James began to get a little tricky. A certain kind of "risk," he went on, was not entirely without merit. We play the game of life not to escape losses, but to reap gains. Not wagering at all created its own problem: a society unwilling to risk "loss" in the form of error. The scientific world's "fear of loss" prevented it from entertaining that which *might* be true, and cut it off entirely from truth that came about as the *result* of commitment. Risk was not preferable, James said, but "the risk of being in error is a very small matter when compared to the blessings of real knowledge." Here he was gearing up for *The Varieties of Religious Experience,* in which he would explore and entertain a number of unusual religious beliefs and practices. It wasn't far into this book that he offered a defense of his method, a dictum that applied just as well to risk as to my uncertainty over attending a Vietnamese mass a century later:

The first thing to bear in mind (especially if we ourselves belong to the clerico-academic-scientific type, the officially and conventionally "correct" type, "the deadly respectable type," for which to ignore others is a besetting temptation) is that nothing can be more stupid than to bar out phenomena from our notice, merely because we are incapable of taking part in anything like them ourselves.

Varieties was distilled from a series of lectures James delivered in Scotland in 1901–02. In it, he quoted at length a broad range of testimonials and biographies of "religious geniuses," mapping out a few consistencies observable across the range of religious experience. The book was an act of generous synthesis. It was characterized by James's willingness to believe—not in the accuracy of any given testimony, but in the idea that patterns among them must hint at truths that science, for all its reliance on the observable and the repeatable, could not access. *Varieties* pioneered the study of comparative religions. In the book itself, James wrote, "We have the beginnings of a 'Science of Religion,' so-called; and if these lectures could ever be accounted a crumb-like contribution to such a science, I should be made very happy."

More seed than crumb, it turns out. *Varieties* helped to kick-start a field, just as *The Principles of Psychology* triggered the science of psychology and *Pragmatism* nearly spawned a religion. Yet now *Varieties* is remembered more for its methodology—comparing religions—than for what it said about them. Throughout his life, James expressed concern over the fragmentation of academic study and warned that science was threatening to become a religion no better than the faith it hoped to displace. Not long before he died he wondered whether all the dialogue had been worth it. Now James has been plastered with two labels: father of a psychology he would have despised, and adherent to a wacky Spiritualism long since discredited. His biographers pick at his bones, often seeming to dislike him even as they are fascinated by him. "James is our great philosopher of the cusp" is typical of the kind of backhanded compliment he is paid.

I took him differently. James kissed me awake with his work, his voluminous letters, a slew of haphazard biographies, and I carried him through the adventure of *The Devil Is a Gentleman,* his voice like a conscience as I wandered from monks to Druids to Satanists to Christian wrestlers and Scientologists and witches. What characterized James best was his spirit of participation. He had experimented with drugs to test alternate forms of consciousness, he had consorted with channelers and mind-curists. He was a hypnotist, and had studied "psychical" phenomena earnestly. He willingly embraced that which he could not explain but to which he would neither fully subscribe. It was intellectual generosity that saved him, shamelessness in the face of the academic scorn he sometimes suffered over the company he kept. James did not argue that one could or should will oneself to believe in anything. Instead, he entertained the fringe of belief and argued that all of us had a right to believe whatever chimed with our sensibilities. Part of James died in academia, yet some of his fruits have survived in the many new religious movements of the twentieth century.

Back at Our Lady, a spirit of participation was the lesson I was just about to learn as I realized the fallacy of sitting through mass without participating in it. *Varieties:* "One can never fathom an emotion or divine its dictates by standing outside of it." The service commenced and came to that moment of Catholic calisthenics when we all had to stand, to sing or be sprinkled. The Vietnamese turned toward me as one. I had never before been the tallest man in a room. In Jamesian language, Catholicism was a hypothesis that had died for me. But now I stood my ground through the awkward moment, and then we all faced forward to worship in a faith once mine but long since taken by the Vietnamese as their own.

The **Devil** Is a **Gentleman**

Infinite

—————◆—————

Yet how believe as the common people believe, steeped as they are in grossest superstition? It is impossible—but yet their life! Their life! It is normal! It is happy! It is an answer to the question!

—William James

The Andromedans hear your voice like distant amusement park
   music
converged on by ambulance sirens
and they understand everything.
They're on your side. They forgive you.

—Denis Johnson

1. Applewhite

I coasted my rental over Lake Hodges, on I-15 toward Del Dios Highway. The hills of California wriggled and waved like crumpled bedsheets. This was homecoming for me. I grew up on the messy suburban folds. The January warmth and the chaparral minimalism outside the car were offset by nostalgia, the scrutiny of personal faith attendant to voyages home.

When I was a boy, Lake Hodges had appeared overnight. The lake had dried long before I was born but the bridge had always been there, an anachronistic hulk, spanning a divot where cows roamed. One winter it rained for a month and there was the lake, proof that Noah had been right. I crossed the span and the road doubled back to follow the shoreline, pretty curves connecting the dry inland burb of Escondido to the coastal paradise of Del Mar. Del Dios Highway means "God's Highway." The twisting road jutted from steep canyon walls above the lake. Palatial estates rode the crest of the hills.

I left Del Dios well before the coast, turning in toward a residential neighborhood that ranked among the richest in the nation. I stopped the car to jot a note. I smelled the air outside for the first time since the airport and thought: *shampoo*. It was eucalyptus—that's how long I'd been gone. California, a state-sized mecca for new religious movements, was that place where plants didn't have leaves. Instead they had fronds, silver dollars, feather dusters, spines, the juicy tubules of ice plant, the thick gnarls of cacti.

I was looking for a house where thirty-nine adults had killed themselves in the name of seeking. The incident was five years old now, and I found that all my maps were wrong. The names of the nearby streets had been changed in the wake of the event. And that wasn't all. The house where the seekers took their poison had been razed. I learned all this by fumbling about, knocking on expensive doors and lying about my credentials as a journalist. I triangulated from a few sets of vague directions and found my-self on a sloping street with four driveways climbing away from a dead end. Each had an automatic gate and an intercom system. One of the driveways appeared abandoned, covered with pine needles blown into curvy drifts like sand. Everything was quiet. I jumped the gate and ascended.

If California was a draw for new religious movements, then San Diego, for some reason, drew UFO groups. I'd come home to visit two such groups, each founded by an unlikely couple. One was now a ghost; the other had just experienced the failure of the prophecy that had fueled their existence for twenty-seven years.

This was still early in my study of religion—in fact, it was my first step, taken on a whim—but even so it had a Jamesian goal. If you know nothing else about the thinking of William James on religion, you might still know of James's categories of the healthy-minded folk and the sick souls. The healthy-minded type were the world's optimists, cheerful almost to a fault, and the sick souls were the pessimists, the cynical intellectual brooders. That's about what I knew of James when I first went back to California— from a mostly forgotten course in psychology—but even with just that scrap of knowledge I'd had the thought that the two UFO groups I was there to visit might neatly express James's most basic human bifurcation.

Details on the first group were hard to come by. Marshall Applewhite and Bonnie Lu Nettles had been drawn together in the early seventies by mutual interest in pop metaphysics. Applewhite had checked into a Texas hospital where Nettles was employed as a nurse. She quickly became his Nightingale. The relationship was immaculate—Applewhite was a homo-sexual secure in his closet—and the belief they came to shape together combined Christian scripture, metaphysical teachings, and UFO lore.

The couple quickly turned prophet, pitching themselves as seers of a Revelation model. They took new names: Guinea and Pig, Bo and Peep, Ti and Do, or just The Two. Their first success at recruitment came in 1975 in Los Angeles. Twenty-four people abandoned their lives to fall in behind the message. An even more successful event followed in Waldport, Oregon. The earliest teachings of the group described the familiar Human Level of experience, and told of a cloud that was actually a spaceship that would take them all to the Next Level. Recruitment efforts continued through 1975 with meetings throughout the Midwest. Then they hit a snag. Two men from Oregon infiltrated the group in an attempt to find a friend who had vanished. The Two feared it was an assassination attempt, and vanished themselves.

The group struggled without them. They lost members as often as they attracted them and split into weak factions spread thin through the country. The Two reappeared in 1976, and gathered the hundred members who remained to initiate what sociologists have since called the group's "camping phase." Now the emphasis shifted toward deindividualization. Members wore uniforms and were assigned a variety of tasks, such as "fuel preparation" (cooking) and "brain exercises" (jigsaw puzzles). They were also encouraged to deny their sexuality (a number of members eventually underwent voluntary castration like early Christian ascetics). Nettles died around 1985. The camping phase continued until the early nineties, when Applewhite inherited $300,000. The group changed direction again, renting suburban homes and taking mainstream jobs. In 1994, they ran a full-page advertisement in *USA Today* announcing that civilization was about to be recycled. They rented a large home in Rancho Santa Fe and went high-tech, starting a webpage design company called Higher Source. The company's own webpage was called Heaven's Gate.

The Hale-Bopp comet, streaking past Earth in 1997, offered Applewhite the opportunity to claim that his spaceship-cloud had arrived. The Heaven's Gate website announced that a shadow in the wake of the comet was the ship that would carry them to the Next Level. The group had been heavily studied by sociologists in the seventies and eighties, but by the mid-nineties it had been years since anyone had paid any attention to them. It would take an anonymous phone call to the police to reveal that late in March 1997, the group had arranged their ascension to the comet by mixing phenobarbital with either applesauce or pudding and washing it down with vodka. The members were all dressed identically, and some had recorded video farewells. Each was found with five dollars and several quarters in one pocket.

Heaven's Gate was precisely the kind of group that William James's detractors have cited to criticize the voluntaristic system that James crafted to finagle his combination of belief and cynicism. But the criticism isn't fair. Not even James was willing to wipe away what he called the "wrong side of religion's account." Fanaticism, he said, was loyalty carried to a convulsive extreme, and to the charge "that religion and fanaticism are twins, we cannot make an unqualified denial." The problem, as James saw it, was fanaticism's conception of God. Extreme loyalty to a despotic deity lent itself to atrocity. "But as soon as the God is represented as less content on his own honor and glory," James said, "[fanaticism] ceases to be a danger." Better gods make for better religions.

But no one really knew what the Heaven's Gate followers' conception of God was in their final days, and in a world where James has mostly been set aside, the best choice seemed to be to forget the whole thing. The names of the streets in Rancho Santa Fe were changed to confuse pilgrims who would try to commune with land whose only memory was fear and latent guilt. And the house's owner bulldozed the place just in case it could remember, too.

Better to play it safe, I agreed, as I huffed up the driveway's incline past birds-of-paradise sheathed in violent weeds and flowering trees struggling for bloom. The estate sat near the top of one of those crimped California sheets, the steep grades made accessible with numerous sets of concrete stairs. Only the foundation of the house remained, a life-sized concrete blueprint spattered with weeds making a go of it in the cracks. A tennis court covered the flat at the peak of the hill, and only this and a brick gazebo had been left untouched. A swimming pool and a jacuzzi yawned empty and trapped lizards. Just before the suicides, the only contact Heaven's Gate adherents had with the outside world was a yard sale they held just before the spaceship was due to arrive. The members struck out-siders as colorless and robotic, but Applewhite himself was said to be lively, talkative, even friendly. Sociologists tend to dismiss brainwashing as the explanation for events like Heaven's Gate. It's too easy—like imagining that a haunted house can be exorcised with heavy machinery, or that history amounts to street signs. Besides, high rates of turnover suggested that membership in Heaven's Gate was entirely voluntary. As crazy as the move-ment seemed, there was something about the world that made *it* seem wackier than Applewhite's hybrid of beliefs.

I lingered for a time inside the foundation as a lonely trespasser, looking out across California. Afternoon mist threaded through a canyony maze of rises and gulleys, and the sun began to set between two stately palms. Great leaves had been falling from these trees—or not leaves, but huge man-sized fronds now scattered all about, conspicuous as corpses. I didn't have to talk myself *into* the sense that the land was haunted. I had to talk myself *out* of it.

A common enough explanation for unusual belief systems claims that people believe what they need to believe. But James never bought it. It was a fine enough theory, he said, until it was applied to what *you* believed, when of course you knew that your belief was a revelation of the living truth. At the same time, however, James acknowledged that different molds of people had different kinds of happiness available to them. There were varieties of religious experience precisely because people came in varieties. This was why he was willing, carefully, and with any number of caveats and exceptions, to distill categories of people, the sick souls and the healthy-minded type. Before this, however, James had published "Is Life Worth Living," an essay that defended any belief that helped make sense of the world:

> *We have a right to believe the physical order to be only a partial order . . . a right to supplement it by an unseen spiritual order which we assume on trust, if only thereby life may seem to us better worth living again.*

Of course, the problem with Heaven's Gate's unseen order was that it hadn't made life seem particularly worth living. Was the group made up of sick souls or the healthy-minded? James considered himself a sick soul, and had contemplated suicide, seemingly at length, as a young man. But Heaven's Gate members might just as easily have resembled the healthy-minded types who saw good in everything, even their own deaths. The difference between sick souls and the healthy-minded was precisely this: the healthy-minded individual blinked out the darker side of existence in favor of opti-mism and contentedness; the sick soul was more methodical and empirical, could not ignore life's shadows, and generally had to make sacrifices to cor-rect a world imperfectly built. Which group Heaven's Gate ultimately be-longed to didn't matter because either way something had gone awry. They were the wrong side of religion's account. James had taken as his purpose the defense of the flip side of the account, when religion did not descend into fanaticism. What this now meant for me was climbing back over the fence and driving my rental across San Diego to the second UFO group I had come to see.

I tried the neighbors before leaving. Two of them refused to speak to me through their intercoms, and the third was simply quiet. Just as I gave up the house's owner appeared, a woman in a Mercedes returning home. I slunk up beside the car as her gate pulled aside too slow for her to avoid me.

She looked out at me sadly. She knew what I would say, but pushed the button that lowered her window anyway.

I sort of lied about being a reporter.

"I don't talk about that," she said. "I wish I could help you, but it was just too horrible."

2. FAIRY GODMOTHER

By 2001, I had left Atlantic City behind, but not before my religious curiosity had taken another step toward religious study. I attended more services. They were not Vietnamese this time, not even Catholic. I tagged along with a girlfriend to another urban church. This one combined Baptism and Pentecostalism. There was a lot of music, and sometimes there were guest speakers whose talks were rapid-fire rants. My girlfriend and I tended to stay in the back, but up front people had their foreheads batted and there was some writhing around on the floor. I wanted to creep forward and take notes, but I worried what my girlfriend would think. Sometimes I loaned money to my girlfriend only to have her turn around and tithe 10 percent of it. It wasn't a relationship that would last. But even then, at the back of the church, craning my neck for a view, I had the thought that a study could be made of travel to America's more unusual forms of religious expression.

So perhaps that's how I found myself in December 2001, moved to a new town, tinkering around on the Internet, surfing for religious movements to read about. I stumbled across the Unarius Academy of Science. In 1974, Unarius's prophet, Uriel, Queen of the Archangels, made the prediction that in the year 2001 Muons from the planet Myton would land on a small plot outside San Diego, beginning for the planet Earth (a.k.a. the Insane Planet of the Robots) a spiritual renaissance of logic and reason. But now Uriel was dead and it was ten days before the thirty-year-old prophecy would officially fail. I had to decide whether to visit them quickly. I was about to fail myself. I'd left my job behind in New Jersey and my bank account was homing in on zero, and when I tallied the expenses of the trip it came to something like 70 percent of my net worth.

"So will this be a spiritual journey for you?" said Celeste Appel, a long-time member of Unarius, when I called to ask if I could attend their first meeting after the failed prediction.

"Sure," I said.

I researched both groups through the holiday, then flew to California halfway into January 2002, living large for the last few weeks before going completely broke.

Details on Unarius were a bit easier to come by.

The movement began in the fifties, when Ruth Norman (who became Uriel) met Ernest Norman at a psychic convention. As with Heaven's Gate, it was interpersonal chemistry that midwifed Unarius, the vision solidifying when Ernest began to hear voices from on high. He eventually channeled twenty books' worth of message. Again like Heaven's Gate, the Normans' philosophy melded Christian imagery with lay understandings of real science and pseudoscience, modernity offering up entire fields of rhetoric not yet exploited by mainstream spiritual thinkers. Special relativity was replaced with special spirituality (*Homo sapiens* was on its way to becoming *Homo spiritualis*), and bad karma was understood with cholesterol buildup analogies.

Ruth Norman didn't flower as a prophet until Ernest died, in 1971. He returned to inspire her, appearing as a fifteen-foot-high wall of flame somewhere in Escondido. Ruth became Uriel, and rented a mansion on top of a hill overlooking El Cajon. El Cajon was no Rancho Santa Fe; it was dirty and dusty and poor. But Uriel's neighborhood was as elevated as you could get in the area. Uriel underwent a kind of ascension herself, becoming a flamboyant, living fairy godmother, traipsing about in huge glowing gowns, wearing crowns and carrying roses. A couple of years later she made the prediction about the arrival of the Muons. She also converted Ernest's Cadillac into the Space Cad, basically the same car but with spaceships painted all over it and a four-foot-wide flying saucer attached to the roof. Uriel's genius, the Unariuns would later agree, was in marketing, as when she placed a bet with Lloyd's of London on whether the spaceships would be arriving. She lost the bet, but the advertising she got for her dollar was a grand swindle played on the media. Uriel channeled more than eighty books after Ernest died—lessons on how the flying saucers would arrive in 2001, stacking themselves one top of another on sixty-seven acres of land she had picked outside of town, shaping there a huge tower that would fill with Muon scientists and serve as both university and hospital. In the meantime the Unariuns, in the downtown El Cajon building that Uriel had leased on a rent-to-own agreement, set about creating, from scratch, with no training and volunteered time, a completely independent and entirely functional multimedia distribution network. They produced books and tapes and videos to spread their word. While Heaven's Gate went high-tech for the profit, the Unariuns wallowed in the comfortable waters of VHS, and, like the tortoise, they were still plugging along. They had their own movie studio, their own printing presses, their own recording studio. The building in El Cajon was called a Star Center. There was another Star Center in Canada, one in Nigeria, and a movement afoot in North Carolina.

A strange thing happens to sociologists who study new religious movements. They don't become members—they're never sucked in, and their work always reflects professional distance—but an affinity builds. You come to like the people, the poise belief lends them. Even James had felt it:

And it is equally certain that a resolute moral energy, no matter how inarticulate or unequipped with learning its owner may be, extorts from us a respect we should never pay were we not satisfied that the essential root of human personality lay there.

Just reading about the Unariuns brought me to admire them in a way I would never have admired Heaven's Gate. On my first night in California I met with a pair of sociologists who had studied Unarius. I feigned objectivity for a moment and asked after the Heaven's Gate connection. There were similarities between the two, weren't there? Hadn't they started out the same? What was the real difference?

The sociologists seemed miffed.

"How about the difference between night and day?" one of them said. "How about the difference between black and white?"

I took back roads from Rancho Santa Fe to El Cajon, veering through a dark stellar chill. Maybe there *was* something about the land that made Southern California a haven for UFO groups, something that had drawn settlers, lured gold diggers west and farther west, until the land ran out. Maybe UFO groups were like those plants with appendages for leaves, organisms that could survive only in a narrow temperate range.

The El Cajon strip leading to the Star Center crept past a fast-food joint, pizza distributorships, understocked pharmacies, a kung fu academy, and a place called 50,000 Books, the number trembling in red neon. The Star

Center was still open at seven-thirty. It had once been a furniture outlet, and the building had a deep, wide window space now decked out with book displays, murals of happy Unariun visions, and a life-sized seated mannequin of Nikola Tesla, the Hungarian-born pioneer of alternating current, whom the Unariuns had adopted as the kind of scientist that could get them past the whole problem of traveling faster than the speed of light. Despite the prominent Christian imagery in their teachings, the Unariuns insisted they were practitioners of a science, not a religion. The name itself was an ex post facto acronym: Universal Articulate Interdimensional Understanding of Science.

I had planned to attend, that night, the rehearsal of the Unarius choral singers, which included Celeste Appel, but the search for Heaven's Gate and dinner with the sociologists had made me late. An open house was scheduled for the next day, and there would be a special class session the following day to contend with the failed prophecy. I strolled into the Star Center. Inside, it was all Roman columns and plastic garlands. The right half of the room formed a small theater, twenty chairs lined up before a shallow stage. On the other side of the room stood a number of Greek statues, Zeus and Apollo, crouched in discus-throwing poses. Seventies-style portraits of Ernest and Uriel covered all the available wall space, and there was a Mona Lisa as well—with a permanent. Unariun books were everywhere, lined up on shelves or lodged in huge wooden carrels. Just to the right of the entrance was something like a miniature train set: a huge model of a city of the future, or perhaps just a principality of Myton. It was made of Christmas lights, seashells, and what looked like the colored gravel from the bottom of somebody's aquarium.

There was just one Unariun on duty, a chubby, balding man named Franklin. Franklin defined friendliness. The phone rang immediately after we shook hands, but it was a wrong number.

"Hello? Orthopedics?" Franklin said. "No, this is the Unarius Academy. We're a science, and it's the interdimensional science of physics! Orthotics? Orthopedics? I understand! Like bones. Your bones, my bones, your arm, my arm!"

Franklin had a large blue stain on his pants from having put an open pen in his pocket. When he finished getting the wrong number all straightened out, he gave me a tour of the Star Center and told me that he had worked as a sales rep prior to retirement. Physiological breakdown had made him a seeker, but that was all he would say of it. Then he said that death was not really death—it was going over.

"Okay," I said.

He took me all through their building, the movie studio (one hundred television shows, three feature films so far), and their book-storage facility, where there were huge crates of books stacked to the ceiling (120 titles in print). Franklin said that El Cajon was the perfect location for the Star Center because its dead soil and olive trees gave it a lot in common with Jerusalem. The sixty-seven-acre plot Uriel had purchased for the Muon landing site was a parallax, Franklin said, a place of strong energy. Franklin had something of a hard time maintaining a thread in conversation, but I liked him anyway. Unarius was practically an archetype for religions born in the twentieth century, a cobbling together of philosophy and trance states, a grassroots mesh of everything that had been blown apart by the explosion of future shock—in short, a simplified expression of a lot of what James had been interested in. Franklin was aggressively healthy-minded. And now, I reminded myself, he was simply speaking interdimensionally, channeling maybe, his words coming from the Muons, or from the fourth dimension (electricity), and who really cared anyway because he was just a friendly guy.

"It's so nice to have a focus," Franklin said when we parted.

Back outside, I paused before a broad mural cast across the exterior wall of the Star Center. The painting was of a bright city on a cove. A spaceship was on descent toward the shiny metropolis, coming out of something in the sky like a wormhole, a spirally galactic event. Everything twinkled in the painting, the spaceship easing to the ground like a frisbee toward a child's hand.

It was on the way back to my motel that it occurred to me that my idea of a pilgrimage through new religious movements had already been done, and by a name I was already familiar with. I stopped and bought a copy of *The Varieties of Religious Experience* from 50,000 Books, near the Star Center. The book was an old paperback, the cover long since out of style, and it began to disintegrate in my hands even as I paid for it. I started reading the old book again that first night in California. I didn't need faith, and I hadn't really been serious when I'd told Celeste Appel that my visit to Unarius was a spiritual journey, but almost at once James addressed the heart of my curiosity. My study of religion had already begun to morph into a study of James.

3. Homo spiritualis

Past lives were as important to Unariun philosophy as UFOs. The way Unariuns conceived of past lives wasn't so different from the way the rest of us conceived of history. Understanding your past lives was a way to avoid mistakes and cope with the present. It's perhaps worth noting that, historically, awareness of past life has been considered a power obtainable through certain yoga disciplines, and that traces of the transmigration of souls can be found in aspects of Sufism, Kabbalah, and early Christianity.

The open house hadn't quite begun when I arrived in the morning. I met Celeste, a thin pencil of a woman, and her husband, Jack. They were hard at work setting up the Star Center, so they sat me down in front of a television to watch *The Arrival,* one of the feature films the Unariuns had produced. The movie was about the first time the Muons came to Earth, 156,000 years ago. Uriel made a number of appearances, but not as a character. Sometimes the scenes just cut to her, all dressed in glittery finery, smiling wide and gesturing broadly like a game-show model, channeling wisdom in voice-over.

Just as I was noticing that the Muon spaceship looked a whole lot like a disposable razor, a man in a cardigan began to loiter behind me. He was well groomed, hands nervous in his pockets. Finally, he could stand it no longer and interrupted the movie to introduce himself. His name was Ron Breault, and his main concern seemed to be asking me whether I was familiar with Dr. Stephen Greer's Disclosure Project.

I was not, which apparently annoyed Ron. "You want to write about UFOs and you haven't heard of the Disclosure Project?"

Greer was collecting the testimony of former military and government personnel who had experienced phenomena they couldn't explain, Ron explained. There was a lot of this testimony, it seemed, and according to Ron everything that had happened since the project had kicked off—Bush's swiping of the 2000 election, 9/11, and the limitations put on the Freedom of Information Act—was an effort to prevent publicizing the established existence of UFOs.

Ron introduced me to his wife, Nanette, a French Canadian who was manning the welcome desk for visitors to the open house. So far there were just four visitors: three college kids with baseball caps and Vandykes, and a lithe fiftyish woman named Mona. Nanette was a contrast to Ron; she focused on the Unarius past-life therapy. It helped with her relationship with her daughter, she said. The girl's asthma, Nanette believed, was the result of her and her daughter burning each other at the stake in various past existences.

I didn't have a chance to respond to this before Dottie Millen teetered up, trailing herself along behind a persistent walker. Dottie was ninety-five years old. She was a sweet woman whose skull was clearly visible through her skin. Her hand was limp as kindling when I shook it. She had been a student of Unarius for thirty-five years, and she was the only Unariun left who had had personal experience with Ernest Norman. When she accidentally referred to someone dying—Ernest or Uriel—she stopped herself short.

"I shouldn't have said *died,*" she said. "Because, you know, there is no death. You know that, right? There is no death?"

"Okay," I said.

She got herself back on track and told me that many years ago Ernest had told her to write a book, her autobiography. "Me?" she had said. She was still writing it thirty years later. Dottie reminded me of her last name—Millen—and then told me the title of her book: *Once upon a Millennium.*

The El Cajon Star Center was the community gathering point for twenty-five active Unariuns. They all had troubled pasts, in this life. There was Lonnie, an attractive woman who had worked as a backup singer in Los Angeles and who had used Unarius to escape the entertainment industry's atmosphere of drugs and promiscuity; there was Becky, a recent recruit who had moved from North Carolina and whose only visible problem was shyness; there was Jack Appel, whose self-esteem problems matched Celeste's; there was Dece, who had beaten alcoholism and now owned her own hairdressing business; and there was Kevin Kennedy, today's designated open-house speaker, who had come to Unarius a quarter century before to escape a life left hollow by a dysfunctional family.

The Unariuns' catalog of personal trauma invited a second read of belief as a function of need. James would have had none of it, still. Early in *Varieties* he pointed out that Saint Paul was epileptic, George Fox and Saint Francis of Assisi were "hereditary degenerates," and Saint Teresa was hysterical. But there was no good reason to conclude that these dysfunctions, even if they were that, were the cause of their spiritual longing. When an atheist had a fit, James asked, did anyone ascribe his atheism to epilepsy? After refuting the need theory for a few pages, James concluded:

Let us play fair in this whole matter, and be quite candid with ourselves
and the facts. When we think certain states of mind superior to others, is
it ever because of what we know concerning their organic antecedents?
No! it is always for two entirely different reasons. It is either because we
take an immediate delight in them; or else it is because we believe them
to bring us good consequential fruits for life.

This was one of James's most basic tenets. Judging the present by analyzing the past did not reveal truth. To judge the value of a thing, we had best determine what good it might bring, what fruits it might bear. Even the Unariuns seemed disappointed when I asked questions about their pasts, as though they had borrowed this from James without even knowing it.

I sat next to Mona, one of the visitors, as the room began to organize. We smiled and nodded at each other, and stared off together at the Star Map, a celestial wall hanging with a spiral of lights representing the thirty-three planets of the intergalactic confederacy. Mona was a past-life believer. Her children thought she was crazy, she said. She laughed.

Kevin Kennedy stood up in front of us to begin the day's talk. "We are obsessed with negative information," he said. "We are not just physical beings." He gestured off to the celestial map: there were currently thirty-two planets with full membership in the celestial federation, and Earth was to be the thirty-third. "We are the laggard planet. We are the ash can." Kevin was adept with the language of Unarius, his sentences twisting smoothly over its non sequiturs. "We're speaking the language of progressive change here. We're speaking the language of love." His main point was something about Unarius's offhand approach to recruitment and missionary work. Basically, he said, they didn't need to do anything at all to spread their message of a unified consciousness. It would just happen. Mona pursed her lips when Kevin mentioned the Space Brothers for the first time, but the three other guests, the young men in baseball caps, leaned forward to listen, rapt as if for a play-off game. Kevin told the story of his alcoholic father and his own journey into Unarius. He was friendly and charming. Only late in his talk did he make reference to the failed prophecy. "The actual physical landing of a ship," he said, stumbling, "it won't happen until we're ready."

Kevin finished up and Franklin took a moment to fool with some AV equipment so we could watch tape of Uriel speaking. After that, there would be a break and then the Unarius choral singers.

"We have different vehicles to get where we're going," Mona whispered to me in the lull. "This is theirs. I'm not sure it's mine."

Then Uriel appeared on a screen, in grandmotherly grandeur, talking or channeling, part self-help litany of advice, part sunny encouragement and generic hope. The tape went on for twenty minutes to the gathered crowd.

> *There will be thirty-three thousand aliens, each ship has one thousand scientists and teachers. . . . There is no such thing as death. No such thing! Isn't that wonderful! It takes belief to see in an unconscious way. Life is never-ending. Life goes on. Isn't that wonderful? In 2001, you people will see. These spaceships are like our brothers and sisters, because it is our brothers and sisters who operate them.*

The three young men in baseball caps were gone before she finished.

Unarius had two kinds of gods. The first, the Infinite Creative Intelligence, borrowed heavily from nineteenth-century philosophy. James devoted a dismissive chapter of *Varieties* to philosophy's treatment of God. Philosophy had done little to help prove God's existence, he said, and what it had produced instead to describe the attributes of God (necessary, absolute, one, only, spiritual, immutable, immense, boundless, omnipresent, eternal, intelligent, infinite, and so on) was for James "a shuffling and matching of pedantic dictionary-adjectives, aloof from morals, aloof from human needs." Unarius's second god was the Space Brothers. These were the inhabitants of the other celestial planets, the *Homo spiritualis,* not human but not inhuman either, who were now officially late for their arrival on Earth. James had foreseen this as well. He had once noted that the demands of Western Christianity sent some in search of "humaner" gods—gods with eyes—and later he acknowledged that religion didn't need an infinite god at all:

> *Anything larger will do, if only it be large enough to trust for the next step. It need not be infinite, it need not be solitary. It might conceivably even be only a larger and more godlike self.*

Ron Breault approached me during the break. "Do you have a question?" he said. "Do you have a question about why they didn't land?"

He and Nanette and a woman named Carol surrounded me, and each of them offered a different explanation. The Space Brothers wouldn't land in a hostile environment, Ron said. Bush Sr. had been the head of the CIA, a force that was generally hostile toward UFOs. Nanette believed the spaceships had arrived, but they were still invisible or nonatomic. Carol said the spaceships were orbiting but couldn't land because it would be perceived as an invasion.

Off by one of the book carrels, Franklin demonstrated the Tesla coil for two young boys, a trick that made a fluorescent bulb light magically. He turned the bulb on and off and said, "May the force be with you!"

Dece, the hairdresser, sneaked up beside me and wanted to talk about the sixty-seven-acre landing site, Franklin's parallax.

"How sensitive are you?" she said.

"Pretty sensitive."

She nodded and described the first time she went to the land. At first she thought it was just regular land. Then one night she saw a giant hand sweep down out of the sky, spreading apart the stars. "I thought 'Wow,'" she said, "'this isn't just land! It's polarized land!'"

The chorus began to gather onstage, a half dozen Unariuns in gowns or blazers. Lonnie, the ex–backup singer, was their leader. "This has been like rubbing sandpaper together," she said, in her introduction. "But it's been getting smoother in the process."

The singing was shaky and unschooled. But no matter: the room simply took on the atmosphere of a forgiving karaoke parlor. There was something charming about them, untalented people trying anyway, people who had, all on their own, created a functional community with neither help nor instruction. They were happy.

I ate dinner that night with Celeste and Jack and Franklin. Franklin may have been a bit too aggressively friendly, but Jack seemed at peace with himself, and meeting Celeste appeared to have made them both more confident. Celeste was the most savvy of the three. She told me about a sociologist who had studied the Unariuns and predicted that they would vanish once Uriel's prophecy failed. Celeste wasn't happy that the Space Brothers hadn't landed, but she relished the fact that here it was, 2002, and they were still around.

I asked whether, as a group, they believed that they had figured life out, that they were basically right and everyone else wrong. They looked at me as though I were a child. They could clearly identify Unariun principles in other belief systems, yes, but being right was hardly a cause for celebration.

The landing of the Space Brothers, even if it was imminent, wasn't a reward—it was simply the next stage and meant a great deal of hard work.

Most sociologists argue that when a religious movement's prophecy fails, the group simply changes the terms of the philosophy to allow the teachings to continue. Christ died, Christ rose, Christ will come again. With Unarius, it was more complicated. The terms of the prophecy were changing, but so were the teachings. Uriel had become more mythical and godly, but at dinner the point was made again and again that they didn't need the physical landing of the Muons to be sure of themselves.

"There are people," Celeste said, "who are on the right track and who are doing the right kind of work to prepare for the landing. But they're not Unariuns."

"Is that how you see me?" I said.

She squinted as though she was worried about hurting my feelings. "Pretty much."

Jack turned our talk back to the prophecy, the class scheduled for the following day. It was the first meeting of the new year. "It may not be your normal class," he said. A couple of weeks before, Jack and another man, David, had teamed up to channel a new message from the Space Brothers, an explanation for why the landing hadn't taken place. Unariuns disagreed about the value of the message. Hopefully the meeting would move them all toward clarity.

4. SPACE CAD

Early next morning, before the class, Celeste, Dece, and a man named William took me to the polarized parallax in the Space Cad. The Space Cad had eighty thousand original miles on it. The landing site was painted on its hood. The flying saucer perched on the roof had lights around its rim, but the electrical connections in the trunk had slipped and weren't working.

People honked and stared at the Space Cad as we headed east out of El Cajon. The Space Cad's shock absorbers were as original as its miles. William had been the Space Cad's designated driver for some time. He said it had taken him a while to get used to the rude gestures the Space Cad sometimes got. But once he realized it was his insecurity that was bringing on the insults, he started getting smiles instead.

"My family is from back east and south, where you got the Bible Belt,"

William said. "I was raised on that. I went to church every Sunday, and if I didn't I was going to Hell, things of this nature. Even as a small child this seemed like a limitation to me. There was so much in the world. Why was I here? Why am I with the family I'm with? Why does things happen to me? Between then and the time I got into Unarius there were nights in my life, enigmas, negative reactions—I would cry in bed and blame Jesus and God for my problems. But the basic principle of Unarius is personal responsibility and knowing that when you're pointing a finger out at the world there's three fingers in your hand pointed back at *you*."

Now William was looking into getting the Space Cad entered into the Rose Parade in Pasadena. The Unariuns wanted the Space Cad in the Rose Parade because the rose was the symbol of love and because Uriel had often been photographed holding a rose.

"I imagine it being pulled by thirty-three white horses," William said, protective of those original miles.

The Space Cad levitated over the road, and Dece pointed out the window at things and talked about high frequencies. We made a turn that seemed to head directly off into the California quilt, and before long the Space Cad was smearing over looping switchbacks. William took a curve hard enough that the Space Cad's balding tires squealed in protest. In his two-handed grip on the steering wheel, at least eight fingers were pointed back at himself. Celeste shot him a glance of Unariun annoyance.

The Space Cad climbed higher and higher, twisting deep into rural California, until at last William swerved off onto an entirely unremarkable dirt path. The Space Cad rolled up to a tall locked gate. William hopped out to heave it aside. Two hundred yards more brought us to the cleared land, a few sheared-away acres where, twenty years before, the Unariuns had gone on location to shoot films like *The Arrival,* and where, back in September, they had held their Final Conclave in preparation for the landing. There had been a banner procession and a dove release.

WELCOME SPACE BROTHERS 2001 read a sign on a hill, high up, perhaps at eye level with whatever Muon craft would be the first to land. Across the empty lot stood a gazebo made entirely from glass. And that was it. There were a few benches, a few trails layered over with mulch, but that was all, that was the landing site, the promised land, the final destination for the thirty-three thousand Muon scientists, the Space Brothers, who would travel billions of miles to inaugurate a renaissance of earthly peace and harmony.

We stood around outside the Space Cad for a time, the Unariuns trying to feed me lines for whatever I would write of them. They seemed uncomfortable that I wasn't asking questions. Like Uriel, they were trying to make the best possible use of me, the media, but I wasn't playing along.

I asked to walk around the land by myself for a time, and the three of them gathered near the gazebo as I headed toward the barbed-wire fence a hundred yards out. I cut around the perimeter. Mostly it was just the hot dry shrubs of California, famous for going up in flames so quickly. There was some shade beneath a few yuccas, and I paused on a bench in a small moist pocket amid the arid thrum of the land.

Back up in the clearing, I saw that the glass of the gazebo was streaked with dirt and the scratches of windblown pebbles. Celeste admitted that the gazebo didn't really have a purpose, per se. No one was really sure why they had built it. William told a story about a UFO sighting that had occurred on the land, late one night. One of their neighbors—you could just see rooftops over close undulations—had spotted odd points of light on opposite horizons. "Then they started to move," William said, his hands describing the motion. "They slowly climbed into the sky, where they met. They stayed there for a while. Then, *zhoom!* They were gone!"

Dece laughed, not because she found the story funny, but because she found it joyous. The story was like every UFO story ever told: heavy on ambiguity, a dash of romance, and a journey to a better place. The UFOs weren't UFOs—they were angels. Or Space Brothers. Gods.

On the way back down to El Cajon, I scribbled out directions to the landing site in reverse.

5. Species of Inconsistency

James had summed up the nature of religion in *Varieties* as a two-stage process: uneasiness (a sense that there was something wrong with our natural state) followed by a solution (we were saved by contacting a higher part of ourselves, a *more*). Religious movements began with the conversion of an individual, who was invariably perceived as mad by his initial witnesses. If he managed to attract a few followers, the religion became a heresy. If he attracted enough, it became an orthodoxy. The dangerous moment came when the religion was passed on from its prophet to its followers: the transition, James said, meant that the religion's "day of inwardness was over: the spring is dry."

Unarius was a group of the healthy-minded type. James was more interested in the sick souls, but he had treated the healthy-minded first. He would have approved of Unarius simply because the religion worked and its members were happy and "the happiness which a religious belief affords [is] a proof of its truth." He warned the rest of us not to judge too harshly the fruits of an ordinary religion, as "A small man's salvation will always be a great salvation and the greatest of all facts *for him*." Unarius was on the right side of religion's account.

I went to my motel to rest before the special class. I channeled on the bed for a time, putting together the pieces of the dilemma the Unariuns were reluctant to address. September 11 had given some Unariuns the excuse they needed to explain the failure of the prophecy. The attacks had been followed by the uneventful turn of the new year, and then the channeling session in which Jack and David had contacted the Space Brothers to ask why the landing had not occurred. The transmission had not gone smoothly. Because Jack and David were not experienced channelers, the text they had produced required editing on the level of grammar and punctuation to make it comprehensible. This raised doubts. How filtered had the Space Brothers' message been? How could one edit the Brothers?

Since then there had been low-frequency mumbling within Unarius. As the storm of the failed prophecy continued to gather strength, it wasn't clear which of them would take charge, which of them would emerge with the order to batten down the hatches.

I walked back down the El Cajon strip, past the kung fu academy and 50,000 Books. Many of the Unariuns were already gathered in the Star Center's small theater, chatting and laughing.

"Hi," Nanette called when she saw me. "Come join the funny farm!"

A woman was telling a story of witnessing, just that day, one hundred white doves in a local park. They fired like lights up toward the mountains. Another woman claimed to have seen one of the Space Brothers' ships while on her way to work. She'd pulled to the side of the road to watch for a time, grateful they were still hanging around. Dottie Millen teetered into the room and situated herself in the front row, near the stage. She got her amplifier device going so she could listen in on conversations behind her. When she recognized a voice, she interrupted to call out a greeting without turning around.

"Is that Celeste back there? Hi, Celeste!"

It seemed to me that Kevin was the Unariuns' best chance for a new leader to emerge from within their ranks. He had a kind, self-effacing charisma. But it was just chance that Kevin had been the leader of the open house yesterday and would also facilitate the class today. Celeste, in fact, dismissed the thought that the Unariuns would ever need a leader. Uriel had offered warnings about centralized leadership before crossing over, and hadn't the Unariuns been doing just fine for a decade, taking book orders and belatedly going digital?

Kevin brought the room to order and asked all of us to relax and lift ourselves to our higher consciousnesses. The class session began with a recording of Uriel:

> *And the sun everlasting which shall bring forth the fruit in full measure . . . and as ye have planted well thy seed and the ground has been well tilled, and fertile is the soil, thus shall ye see the ripening fruit. . . . Watch, be careful, dear ones, for the thorns and the thistles shall, from time to time, appear upon thy path . . . The ways of the seeker are not easy, but are strewn with the errors of the past . . . lost is he that knoweth not this grain of truth, but that ye shall, dear brethren, carry well and high this banner of Unarius, this the banner of infinite truth, unto all whom you shall meet . . .*

The selection from Uriel's library of channelings was chosen at random, and most everyone sat through the reading with their eyes closed, some lolling to soothing background chords. After twenty minutes, Franklin lowered the volume on the prophet and Kevin pulled a rolling blackboard in front of the group. He wrote "Budda" in large letters and took it in stride when Lonnie corrected his spelling. He explained that "Buddha" meant "awakened." He compared this to Uriel, who, he recalled, would sometimes come down from her home to prod her students toward enlightenment.

"You gotta wake up!" the prophet had barked when she wasn't in her godmother character. "You're all a buncha robots!"

Kevin smiled at the memory and argued that we needed new myths. He said old myths—like Christianity—had been fine for a preindustrial world. He stopped short of saying that Unarius provided the new myths he prescribed. Instead, he scooted back to the blackboard and wrote "The Landing, 2001." The Unariuns shifted uneasily in their chairs. Kevin said that for seventeen years he'd believed the Space Brothers were going to land. He took a breath. Then he asked, "Okay, how many of you think the Space

Brothers are still coming?" The hands went up. Then Kevin asked how many thought that just maybe they were coming, and then how many had given up. He put the survey on the blackboard.

They Are	Maybe	Not
12	6	4

What was important about the failure of the landing, Kevin said, was what it said about our past lives, the errors of history. The failed prophecy was not a failure at all. Rather, it was a psychodrama set in motion by Uriel to allow us to work out past-life conflicts. It was a blessing in disguise! He made reference to Jack and David's controversial channeling session, hesitating on this point, and gently eased into a diagnosis of the jealousy and doubt that had begun to emerge within the group and was threatening to pry apart their fragile civilization.

"What we are getting at after all this is that each of us has to become our own teacher. We have to appreciate the expression of another soul. We have to love that information. And if that information is not, quote unquote, of the highest, that doesn't mean we have to cut it down."

He opened the floor to speakers, and Lonnie raised her hand to say that she had heard the rumblings, too. She admitted that as Jack and David's transmission came through she'd wondered about it.

"I relate to what people are saying," Nanette agreed. She was the one who had transcribed the transmission from the audiotapes. "Because I had problems putting the sentences together, where the periods should go. And I had the thought that maybe it hadn't come from the Brothers."

Jack and David had been sitting quietly, but now David spoke up in their defense. "It doesn't matter who's up there," he said. "It's how we feel for that person. I think we should send them our positive thoughts."

"Exactly!" Kevin said, arms wide. "We're human beings! There's none of us who's just going to go up there—and be God!"

The room stiffened. The reference to God was a slip because Unarius was a science and not a religion. The error triggered a moment in which we all considered the changing shape of the dilemma. The Unariuns were trying to learn from history, and they truly did behave, as a group, more civilly than most who gathered around secondhand mysticism. They were solving the problem of their failed prophecy by criticizing their need for it to be fulfilled. They were fighting to remain on the right side of religion's account.

The talk came to William, who so far had sat with arms folded as if to hold in his Carolina drawl. His charisma was the natural competitor to Kevin's, and when he took a heavy breath to speak we all fell quiet. "I went through a lot of things with this," he said. "It all started when the Trade Center went down. For me. From there it went into the Conclave. Then— well shoot, there was so much stuff going on I can't even hardly figure where to start. When the transmission came after New Year's, I was excited. So when Jack got up there and started receiving information, I immediately felt a reaction. I recognized as I was sitting here—I was trying to *choose* the information. Now, I knew I needed to get rid of that. I needed to push that out of the way. Jack and I talked the next day, and after I talked to a few more people I started thinking something's wrong here. I am reliving something. The bottom line is this—I didn't really want the landing to happen. I said, well now it's what lands in my consciousness that's important. I was different at the beginning of the year. But well, when the Trade Center got hit, I realized there's no way. This world's going to have to be on its knees before the Brothers come."

"That is absolutely it," Kevin said. "Why would they not land? Why? Because if they did, they'd be doing more harm than good. They would not be using Unariun principles! They would be adding to the negation on our planet. Did you ever talk to an alcoholic? Because before they get help, they have to get to a point where they almost die. They pass out a few times, or don't remember where they've been. They finally say, 'I give up!' It's the same on our planet. That's what the teachings are about. It's about becoming your own teacher. Isn't that right, Dottie?"

Dottie flinched. She was surprised at being singled out, and adjusted her amplifier. "That's right! Each of us is different. We've come a long way from different situations. What I know is within myself. Doesn't matter what you say, or anybody! I know what I believe. I know!" She laughed at the simplicity and beauty of her science. "Everything happens for a reason. If the Brothers don't show up at two-oh-oh-one, there's a big reason. I can go along with that. I can believe that. If they can't come in two-oh-oh-one, then they can come another time. A better time. I have things to learn. I have things to do."

Dottie's amplifier squawked once, quietly. Kevin waited to see if anyone else was going to chime in, but the meeting had worn itself out.

"We can't objectify our pasts," Kevin said in summation. "Obviously, there are layers, but the goal is to pull out the tremendous knots of negation in our psyche. And if we can shine the light of intelligent reason and logic, then, with the help of the Unariun Brothers, these things can be turned around, and our lives can be made whole."

I drove back to the landing site late that night. My rental took the curves better than the Space Cad, and the turns in my directions came quickly. I pulled up to the locked gate, killed the lights, left on the overhead dome as a beacon, then climbed out and approached the fence. I crimped my fingers through the chain link to trespass for the second time in three days.

I hit the landing site hard. The stars lit the path well enough, but the odd California shrubs took on spooky bulk in the shadows. I climbed up and down a hill as the desert's cold conscience crept in, the sky fogged over with the glaze of the Milky Way.

As I would find once I dug into his biographies, pinning William James down on what he thought on any given matter was never a simple thing. His chroniclers were often exasperated by what they read as inconsistency. But this was exactly what I would come to like about him. James was willing to think in print, to entertain in print. His work was his participation. For most of his life, he was more concerned with shaping the discussion than winning the argument. James had decried the notion that need explained belief, but it wasn't quite right to say that for James belief had nothing to do with what a person had been through. It was certainly true of him. And when James treated the idea of conversion in *Varieties,* he might as well have been summarizing the troubled histories of the Unariuns and Kevin's argument as to why their prophecy had failed:

> *There are only two ways in which it is possible to get rid of anger, worry, fear, despair, or other undesirable affections. One is that an opposite affection should overpoweringly break over us, and the other is by getting so exhausted with the struggle that we have to stop,—so we drop down, give up, and* don't care *any longer. Our emotional brain-centres strike work and we lapse into a temporary apathy. Now there is documentary proof that this state of temporary exhaustion not infrequently forms a part of the conversion crisis. So long as the egoistic worry of the sick soul guards the door, the expansive confidence of the soul of faith gains no presence. But let the former faint away, even but for a moment, and the latter can profit by the opportunity, and, having once acquired possession, may retain it.*

The healthy-minded Unariuns had dodged their way back to faith, retained their profit.

After James had boiled religion down to parts, he acknowledged that his sick-soul and healthy-minded categories were only tools. Reality was a more nuanced affair. James's own story would reveal that he had suffered the exhaustion he described. And what he learned from it was that variety itself—a species of inconsistency—was the key to his own salvation.

Another kind of inconsistency would be my salvation. The religious scholar Mircea Eliade once wrote that the Greek divine forms, the gods, came about as a result of a grand process, a combination of "confrontation, symbiosis, coalescence, and synthesis." This in turn would become my process, in lieu of a spiritual journey, for creating James, for understanding his work, his life, his letters, and the fragments of his thinking that could be traced through the religious movements that had emerged in his wake. I would follow his trail, and he would be my genius in the Roman sense, my conscience, my god with eyes.

I made it back to the glass gazebo and the WELCOME SPACE BROTHERS 2001 sign. There was nothing else there. There were no magic fists descending from the skies. There was no nausea in my inner ear to indicate whatever a parallax was. It was just a dark world hibernating through a tepid winter. It was an awful and silent place. The stars above remained fixed, twinkling disappointingly. They did not merge and flit away in some memorable flash.

Then one of them moved. I blinked and it moved while I watched it. But it was only a jet, a man in a machine, vaulting toward some sparkling city in an unsteady world.

1842–1864

At barely two years of age, William James was already a brother and a world traveler. In 1844 his father, Henry Sr., a budding religious scholar and philosopher, took the young family abroad on a trek to pursue European thinkers in London. But British philosophical society proved dispiriting, and the little clan retreated to rural Windsor. Here, Henry Sr. experienced something that changed the entire course of his life. One night after a family dinner an inexplicable fear came over him. He later wrote of it:

> To all appearance it was a perfectly sane and abject terror, without ostensible cause, and only to be accounted for, to my perplexed imagination, by some damnèd shape squatting invisible to me within the precincts of the room, and raying out from his fetid personality influences fatal to life. The thing had not lasted ten seconds before I felt myself a wreck; that is, reduced from a state of firm, vigorous, joyful manhood to one of almost helpless infancy.

It wasn't until Henry Sr. spent time recovering at a spa that he found an explanation for the odd mood. A fellow patient suggested that the episode was what Swedish mystic Emanuel Swedenborg called a "vastation." A religion had sprouted up around Swedenborg's writings, and for Swedenborgians vastations were positive cathartic experiences. Henry Sr. located Swedenborg's books, absorbed them, and considered himself a Swedenborgian mystic for the rest of his life. Years later, in *Varieties,* William James cited his father's episode as an example that proved that even a sick soul's conversion could come swiftly.

Henry James, Sr., had not had a particularly remarkable career to that point. His own father, William's grandfather, had been one of the richest men in the United States. He was considered a rigid Calvinist, and had fourteen children. All of them rejected their upbringing. Henry's rebellion took the form of a wild collegiate lifestyle that resulted in significant bills to his father, who threatened to cut him off. Henry ran to Boston, worked in journalism for a while, then followed one of his brothers to the Princeton Theological Seminary in 1835. His father died, and a family lawsuit erupted over a will that distributed the estate's funds unevenly. In 1837, Henry wound up with an annual income ten times what his father had intended. He never worked again.

Like William much later, Henry Sr. bristled at standard academic thinking on religion and rejected the study of institutionalized religion in favor of personal revelation. He left Princeton without graduating and moved to New York, where he took his first steps toward a personal religion and cultivated literary ambitions. He set about a family life. A Princeton friend, Hugh Walsh, was a member of a prominent New York family with two eligible daughters. When Henry married one of the sisters, Mary Walsh, the mayor of New York performed the ceremony. The other sister, Catharine, became a fixture in the James household as well. William James was born a year and a half later, on January 11, 1842. Henry James, Jr., arrived not long after.

Henry Sr.'s introduction to Swedenborg came in 1844. To me, Swedenborg's vastations sounded a lot like the rock-bottom moments common to the Unariuns, and, as it happened, Swedenborg has been cited by sociologists as source material for UFO religions. In 1758, Swedenborg wrote *Concerning the Earths in Our Solar System,* which told of the mystic's journeys to the "earths" of Jupiter, Mars, Mercury, and so on, as well as to a half dozen other planets in the "starry heavens." Each was inhabited by civilized people, human beings, making for a loose confederation of worlds linked by belief in a familiar Christian God. As in Unarius, our Earth had a "comparatively *low* Place in the Scale of finite Intelligences."

The Swedenborgians themselves, who still exist today and have a cathedral outside of Philadelphia, never considered Henry James, Sr., a formal member of their church. The philosophy Henry Sr. went on to craft for himself has been described as less a Swedenborgian system than a precise reversal of his father's version of Calvinism. Henry Sr. repented for all his youthful shenanigans. He went on to write thirteen books and lectured frequently, though his philosophy appeared to move no one but himself. William, who may have achieved all the success his father once hoped for, called Swedenborg his father's "bundle of truth." This retained just a hint of an intellectual conflict between father and son that began early and was never really resolved.

If Henry Sr.'s personal religion was his father's Calvinism reversed, then his policy toward raising his family was the opposite of his father's domestic vision as well. His goal for his children was to surround them with an "atmosphere of freedom" while working to prolong their innocence of the sins for which he himself still paid dues. After Windsor, the family returned to the United States and added two more sons, Wilky and Bob, in Albany, New York. Alice James, the lone daughter, came along in 1848 in New York City.

Henry Sr. might have had difficulty converting anyone to his philosophy, but he had no trouble amassing a collection of friends and thinkers. The James children were sheltered by wealth and their father's careful manner, but the visitors to the household proved to be a near perfect listing of mid–nineteenth-century influential thought. The children were free within the constraint of a unique private education. They split early on into three groups: William and Henry were the most favored for tutoring; Wilky and Bob got less of it and were permitted to enlist in the army for the Civil War; and Alice was her own private group, tied emotionally to William but lost intellectually in the family mix. The stories of the James household appear idyllic from one perspective: the children called their parents by their Christian names, and once they began their own literary magazine. They put on theatrical productions, directed by William and often starring him as well. Henry Sr. encouraged discussion at the dinner table, the children heatedly taking up questions of morals or taste or literature. A common story claimed that one debate had resulted in knives brandished over supper. At the beginning of *Varieties*, William James revealed that the initial endowment of the Gifford lecture series he was delivering had been announced by his father one night at dinner.

In "Is Life Worth Living," William wrote of the skepticism that came of "too much grubbing in the abstract roots of things":

> *This is, indeed, one of the regular fruits of the over-studious career. Too much questioning and too little active responsibility lead . . . to the edge of the slope, at the bottom of which lie pessimism and the nightmare or suicidal view of life.*

If James was thinking of his family at this moment, he didn't betray it but it accurately described the flip-side opinion of the James household experience. The Jameses were a brilliantly dysfunctional unit. Henry Sr. would prove susceptible to "divine rages," and the children would speak of home as depressing. All of them eventually suffered from either nervous ailments or addictions of one kind or another. Prodigious letter writers, they displayed an inordinate amount of interest in their failure of bodily function. The James household was an exercise in metaphysical quandary turned to hypochondriacal whining turned again to actual hysterical ailment. The whole family cast a black spell on itself. Yet a century later William, Henry, and Alice each have intellectual societies dedicated to them.

As a boy, William James was described as outgoing and quick to make friends, and he bragged that he was rougher than the more reticent Henry, with whom he shared a bedroom. Together the two boys explored the neighborhoods of New York above Washington Square Park, visiting carnivals and attending local theaters. It was clear the boys had temperamental differences, but their bond would last their lifetimes. The collected correspondence of William and Henry James is as complete a record to be found of letters between men so influential. Mostly they complained of back or bowel or money problems. (William to Henry: "Boils are surely the most evolving things in nature—Christian doctrine is nothing to them.") In a late memoir, Henry wrote of the two young boys stumbling across old corpses in catacombs in Switzerland, and William once described the two young men walking together through the ruins of the Colosseum. Their imaginations were linked, but William admitted that "Harry's orbit and mine coincide but part way." Early on, William doubted that much would come of Henry's attempts at writing. William would later sing his brother's praises, but he often found Henry's style too ambiguous and opaque. Henry regretted that William could not access the heart of his work, but for his own part he enjoyed William's productions. In short, William struggled with Henry's fiction because he read it as philosophy, and Henry enjoyed William's philosophy because he read it as a novel.

William's interests as a boy were like the early dabblings of a mad scientist. He had the basics of a chemistry lab, including Bunsen burners and test tubes, and he fiddled with experiments into adulthood. He forced Henry to pose for photographs that he developed in an improvised darkroom. Most significantly, he began to show an interest in drawing at around age eleven, though it wasn't until the family went to Europe that he would consider pursuing art as a career. This would prove to be the battlefield on which William would first confront his father's will.

Bouncing between the United States and Europe was a policy that William James eventually adopted for his own family, though his reasons were different from his father's. Both clans ping-ponged across the Atlantic. Henry Sr. claimed that he wanted to escape an America descending into decadence, but the destinations he chose tended to correspond with his literary ambitions. He was happy to offer his children a sense of worldliness and was pleased when they soaked up languages; William in particular showed a talent, and would later correspond in French and German. The time abroad saw the children exposed to a range of tutors. The concern for William's education trumped that for his siblings. He knew this and regretted it. When he first visited the Louvre in 1855 he began to think of art as more than a boy's amusement.

For Henry Sr. there was considerable difference between "Artist" and "artist." The Artist was the ideal condition of man, a spirit set free to exemplify the potential of the human soul. A simple artist of the type William hoped to become was not "the perfect man, the man of destiny, the man of God." Henry James, Sr., was an overbearing father in precisely the opposite way we think of overbearing fathers today: he was liable to stand in his children's way if they moved toward taking up any kind of career from which they might actually make a living. He argued vehemently against their going to college at all. The result for William was preoccupation with occupation and a strong desire to study in an institution. Early on this took the form of interest in painting, and his father's odd stance on the matter kicked off a debate recorded in their letters. At eighteen, William wrote his father:

> *Why should not a given susceptibility of religious development be found bound up in a mind whose predominant tendencies are artistic as well as in one largely intellectual . . . I am sure that far from feeling myself degraded by my intercourse with art, I continually receive from it spiritual impressions. . . . There remain other considerations which might induce me to hesitate [but] these however I think ought to be weighed down by my strong inclination towards art, & by the fact that my life would be embittered if I were kept from it.*

The argument continued as William studied art in Paris, as the family returned home for a time, and as they bounced back to Europe again in 1859. In Geneva, William took a number of practical courses in anatomy, attending dissections. He sketched the cadavers. In 1860, he told his father he had decided on an artistic career. Henry Sr. finally relented, and the family returned to the United States so William could study with William Morris Hunt in Newport, Rhode Island. "We went home to learn to paint," Henry Jr. later wrote.

William James's early life is not perfectly recorded. The family established a house in Newport in October 1860, but William gave up painting by the following summer. The precise reason for this is gone. Biographers have suggested that Hunt was less than encouraging, that William had begun experiencing problems with his eyes, that he simply lost interest, that the outbreak of the Civil War changed his priorities, and that he had suffered from his first bout of crippling hysterical ailments. Of this last, some have suggested abandoning art was itself the thing that sent William spiraling. Regardless, within a year art disappeared from his thinking, and vocationally he didn't know which way to turn.

When the Civil War began William volunteered for a ninety-day service in an artillery company, but Henry Sr. intervened so that neither he nor Henry Jr. could fully enlist. A compromise was struck that allowed the two men to move to Boston, William to study chemistry at the Lawrence Scientific School, Henry to enter Harvard Law School. Over the next two years, Wilky and Bob both enlisted in the Union Army, serving as officers of regiments of black soldiers. Both William and Henry were deeply affected by not participating in the war. William dropped out of school once, and helped care for Wilky when he returned home badly injured. Henry left law school. The accomplishments of the younger brothers, who both reenlisted, heightened the sting of William's directionlessness. He returned to Boston to resume his studies and began to accumulate the friendships that would last his lifetime: Oliver Wendell Holmes, Jr., Charles Sanders Peirce, Thomas Wren Ward. William moved from the Lawrence Scientific School to the Harvard School of Medicine. The family again followed him to Boston, moving into a new residence in May 1864.

The narrative arc that biography imposes on a life fails William James more than most. In 1864 he was too frail and weak to fight in the war, though possibly it had been not enlisting that weakened him in the first place. Henry Sr. wrote of the "vituperation" he received from his older sons for refusing to allow them to head to battle. The extent of James's education gets lost in the tangle of travel and tutors and argument. His first unsigned reviews appeared in the *North American Review* in this era. More important, he had begun absorbing the world's thinking. One biographer claimed that by the age of twenty-two he had taken in as much philosophy "as many professors of the subject possess at their retirement."

Just as easy to forget was James's boyishness. When he was twenty, he began a new journal with an inscription that included a quote from Emerson. On the next page he took a precaution in case he ever misplaced the book:

> To any one into whose hands
> this book may fall—
>
> If I am alive,   do not read it
> If I am dead,   burn it
>
> &oblige,
> Wm. James

Old Ones

Our lives are . . . like trees in the forest . . . [which] commingle their roots in the darkness underground. . . . Just so there is a continuum of cosmic consciousness, against which our individuality builds but accidental fences, and into which our several minds plunge as into a mother-sea or reservoir.

—William James

Fergus. The whole day have I followed in the rocks,
   And you have changed and flowed from shape to shape,
   First as a raven on whose ancient wings
   Scarcely a feather lingered, then you seemed
   A weasel moving on from stone to stone,
   And now at last you wear a human shape,
   A thin grey man half lost in gathering night.

—William Butler Yeats
   "Fergus and the Druid"

1. RHIANNON AND ARIADNE

A little more than a year after I visited Unarius, I had a lot of William James in my pocket. My bank account had reversed its fortune, and I was back on the road in California. I had learned that if Southern California drew UFO groups, Northern California drew Paganism.

On Highway 99 north of Sacramento it was best to keep your headlights on all the time. Local groceries and dead motels had been named for the road, and curly strips of truck tire littered the asphalt, describing old panics. For a while I headed straight toward the lonely outcropping of the Butte Mountains; then the road veered west toward Chico. My directions led me into the hills above town, up a gently winding ascent alongside a canyon that was a millennium's work of a stream since gone dry. Cows leaned into the green slopes, and the various strata showed through the grass, the land's accidental archaeology. Overhead stood great pine trees, their cones as large as pineapples, paired like testicles. Most often in tree worship one sees the veneration of the oak, or switches of rowan or hazel or apple, but even the tree of knowledge cited sexuality, and it all spoke of fertility in one way or another. I was on my way to see a Druid healer.

"I might have to do something about this weather," Rhiannon Ysgawen told me on the phone when she saw the forecast for Beltane, the Druid New Year and the celebration I would attend. But whatever she'd done, it still looked like rain. The original Druids were said to have used a golden sickle to harvest mistletoe for rituals, and on satellite photography a sickle-shaped storm front was moving across Northern California. It would rain for my entire stay.

Above the canyon, I entered Cohasset, a green hill town whose only store was a gas station. I stopped and called Rhiannon and she told me to keep climbing; she would meet me at a crossroads. I found her idling in a rickety station wagon. She was groggy from a night of partaking of the sacred herb by the campfire. A small round woman with delicate glasses that sat halfway down her nose and wild reddish hair that framed her face like a cowl, she wore baggy clothes to hide a matronly bulk and a moon pin that had belonged to a mother dead of cancer. Tattoos peeked out from under her sleeves.

"Follow me in," she said. "I have to go get Jimmy—my son. I'll be gone a few hours. Ariadne will keep you company."

We coasted down into the remote hollows. The road twisted so often around large trees, managing extreme grades, that it was impossible to sustain an imagined map of the place. Even sunlight seemed to have a hard time straining down this far. Homes sat back among the glens, squiggles of smoke rising from rudimentary chimneys. In almost every yard stood dismembered pickups and neglected motorcycles, and invisible wind made the trees speak in orthopedic moans. Rhiannon's house sat at the end of a long, muddy drive, a wood-paneled shack crammed with stuff. A harp stood near the center of the living room, rugs hung on the walls, a woodburning stove provided heat for the place, and an oscillating fan was set up as a perpetual bellows. I had woken them from their pot crash: Rhiannon, her partner, Jay, the drummer of the Celtic band they played in, and Ariadne, the twenty-two-year-old seeker who had come to Rhiannon for her first initiation, at tomorrow's ritual.

"Built it," Rhiannon said, when I asked her where the harp had come from. Then there was a flurry of activity and I was left alone with Ariadne.

Ariadne was an actress from Los Angeles. She could have been fourteen or thirty-four. She had been at the house only fifteen hours longer than I had, but she had already gotten high by the campfire, slept, ate, and woken up shiny and tired. William James loved camping and campfires, and some of his most profound meditations came from the experience of a mild evening and trees mingling overhead. He camped with philosophical companions, and colleagues in psychical research. The trips offered relaxation and the occasional lampooning, as in "The Great Cigar," a poem by one of James's friends that sent up his use of consciousness-expanding substances:

> *It was full eight inches long,*
> *But not* pro rata *strong,*
> *And this was what the wily Willie thunk:*
> *"I will nicotine my soul,*
> *And survey the godhead whole,*
> *And snatch celestial secrets by a drunk."*

> *And first of all he bit it,*
> *And next of all he lit it,*
> *Then sate him down to get the Giant view*
> *With the first puff he did breathe, "Oh*
> *My," he said, "Oh me, though,*
> *I fear I've bitten more than I can chew."*

Ariadne had the straight blond hair of a fairy, eyes just as light and smart. When she turned her back for a moment I glimpsed the cartoon snake stained into the small of her back. We sat at the kitchen table and she told me her story.

Ariadne was her given name. She had grown up as a well-off outsider near a military base in Colorado. Her mother owned a remote mountain bed-and-breakfast and rescued injured animals, she said, and her father had been an attorney, one of the finest public defenders of his generation. It was her father who had made her a seeker. He'd been a demanding man, haunted by alcoholism and private demons, and Ariadne's family had not been the first family he'd raised. A daughter born earlier had committed suicide before Ariadne was born. As her father aged, his ego turned on him and he came to believe that his new family would be better off without him. He left the house with an innocuous remark one day, used a credit card at a supermarket, and several days later his car was found parked near an abandoned mill. They never found his body—the family still left plaintive pleas for information on websites—and Ariadne sometimes suspected that he had gone off into the mountains to live as a hermit.

Ariadne was pleasant and fresh and gorgeous. What she liked most about Rhiannon's home, she said, was the absence of overt male attention, a thing she could not avoid in Los Angeles. As she spoke, Ariadne accented her words by twiddling the fingers of one hand before her as though to engineer convulsions in a puppet tied onto her knuckles. She had excelled as a child equestrian, she said, and she had achieved a black sash in kung fu. Sexual awakening had come early, as had mononucleosis, which, combined with her father's disappearance, served as the cocoon that marked her passage into adulthood. She had acted locally by then, and when she recovered from the illness she left high school and moved, at age fourteen, to Miami to pursue a career. She studied with acting and voice coaches, and wound up landing the lead in an independent film about the early life of Bette Davis, a project with a budget of $2 million from the production company of a prominent actor. She had begun accumulating animals and exploring Druidry at about the same time. It turned out that Ariadne and I had investigated many of the same Druid factions over the Internet. Six months before, Ariadne had headed to Los Angeles with a menagerie of creatures stuffed into her convertible: a neurotic pit bull, a python, a pregnant tarantula, a bold iguana, and a wide-eyed sugar glider in an oversized birdcage.

"Would you like to see the stone circle?" Ariadne said.

"Yes."

Outside, the sharp blade of the storm had begun to trickle down on the hollows, wetting the leaves and needles overhead. Ariadne pointed out a pair of trees on Rhiannon's property that had twined together as they had grown into the sky, an image that spoke to Druids of romance. Ariadne tried to spell out the tree cosmology for me, but stumbled because she was still a student. The stone circle stood just down behind the house, a scraped-out arena shaped by a dozen huge oblong stones half-buried in the earth. Some of the stones had names, and Rhiannon had calculated their weights. In addition to James, I'd studied Druidry a good bit in preparation for the trip, and I knew there was an irony to the whole stone-circle business. The catch was that Stonehenge, the original megalithic structure, predated the historical Druids by several thousand years. Recent theories have suggested that Stonehenge—always a magnet for bizarre research—might have been an import from Switzerland (based on bone analysis of an ancient grave discovered near the site), and that the actual design was not a calendar at all but a representation of female genitalia (the altar was the clitoris). Neo-Paganism exploits whatever links to the past it can to nurture the sense of a surviving tradition, but modern Druidry was perhaps alone in the Pagan family in defying the historical accounts of their actual predecessors. Still, today's Druids have been relatively successful: in 1962, a sign attached to the fence enclosing Stonehenge read: PRESS PASSES AND DRUIDS ONLY PERMITTED.

"It's not what you expected, is it?" Ariadne said as we looked over the circle and the yard where Rhiannon's private water tower stood. But what did one expect of Druids? White robes and beards? Tree huggers and wicker men? The question might have been rhetorical, reflecting Ariadne's own doubts. She was beautiful, but she had admitted in the house that she had trouble believing in herself. As well, she occasionally heard voices, she said, and feared what they meant. I asked what had drawn her specifically to Druidry.

"It just kind of clicked. That's not really a good way of putting it," she added, but felt no need to find a better way. "I don't talk about it much. If it's not something that you're interested in, it just seems kind of weird if you start talking about crystal balls and seeing the future."

James would have agreed. In *Varieties,* he argued that feeling offered the ineffable hint that the intellect realized with belief:

> Feeling is private and dumb, and unable to give an account of itself. It allows that its results are mysteries and enigmas, declines to justify them rationally, and on occasion is willing that they should even pass for paradoxical and absurd.

On the way back to the house, I asked Ariadne about her chronology: the dates she'd given and her age didn't quite jibe.

"Okay," she admitted. "Really, I'm nineteen."

2. TREE MEDITATION

More often than not, Druidry is used to fill in historical gaps spanning the transition from naturism and totemism to polytheism, from prophet to wiseman and scientist. The best accounts of Druids come from classical writers, most notably Julius Caesar's memoir of waging war in Gaul for a decade. The earliest reliable suggestions of Druids go back only a few hundred years more, to an anonymous Greek writer. Nothing is known for certain in the history of Druidry. The tradition, borrowing from Pythagoras, it's said, believed knowledge was power and advised against writing anything down. There are no original sources.

What's fairly certain is that when the Romans invaded Gaul they found a valued caste of persons that they called Druids—it's not clear whether the Druids called themselves Druids—and that a network of some kind linked the caste together. The etymology of the word *Druid* has branches like a tree itself; sometimes it seems like a title, sometimes like an adjective. Most often the word is associated with an Indo-European word for oak, *dru,* and there's plenty of good evidence explaining why a tree-worshipping culture would emerge: oak was a food-yielding tree, and acorns were a source of food even after civilization turned more traditionally agricultural. Medieval accounts tell of Lithuanians and Estonians making sacrifices to oak trees for good crops, and trees were often identified as transformed ancestors. A problem is that while some Celts may have worshipped a prime deity in the form of an oak, it's not clear that Druids originated with the Celts, or that the Druids originated with a culture that knew the oak tree at all. Other explanations claim that *Druid* is closer to *wizard* or *magus,* or that it speaks to the opening and closing of ways, or that it combines *superior* and *priest.* There are nagging suggestions of wood and doors in other languages: Sanskrit's *drus,* meaning tree, Lithuanian's *durys,* meaning door, and Gaelic's *druidim,* meaning "I shut." And there's always the possibility that the Greeks made a quick association between oaks and wisemen and imposed the label.

Regardless, the Druids were known across Europe and Asia Minor, and a similarity of beliefs suggests contact between Indo-European and Near Eastern civilizations. A Druid-Brahmin parallel is easy enough to discern. Eventually, as Christianity crept into Britain, the Druids were targeted for conversion, suggesting that at least the missionaries perceived them as a prototype clergy. The classical writers hadn't been so clear on the priest comparison, however, and the Druids were credited with having served many roles—doctors, lawyers, teachers, psychologists, historians, prophets, astronomers, philosophers, political advisers—making them a distinct learned class identifiable by their clothing, initiation rituals, and tonsure haircuts.

Even before the Romans pushed the Celts north, Britain and Ireland had become a home for Druid colleges, to which students would retreat to study. Novitiates passed through protracted courses, achieving intermediary degrees such as Bard or Ovate; the entire education, spanning poetry, anatomy, botany, and history, was said to take twenty years. What had probably started as a primitive religion had evolved into an intellectual class seen as an intermediary with supernatural forces. Druids were said to be able to divine the future from fire, clouds, sneezes, and birdsong. They were pacifist (though certain later Druids were also military leaders) and exempt from tax. Evidence of scientific knowledge among the Druids (mathematics, calendars, and primitive surgical techniques) made them, for the historian, a convenient bridge from prehistory to history.

For an invader, Caesar spoke fondly of the Druids. He listed the Greek gods they worshipped—later accounts would claim he imposed alternate identities on figures of Hindu origin—and he claimed that Druids "preside over sacred things, have the charge of public and private sacrifices, and explain their religion." After Caesar, however, classical writers turned on the Druids, slandering them for their primitive ways. Researchers suspect an early propaganda campaign, as the peaceful Druids had begun to assist with resistance to the invasion, possibly instigating pockets of rebellion. Where once Druids had been known to erect "Druid fences," magical walls between rivals to prevent battles, they now encouraged revolt and took part in conflicts, with intimidating cries and gestures. Accounts tell of Druids playing a prominent role in rituals of human sacrifice and reading the future from the spilled entrails of captured Romans. Tales spread of giant wooden effigies stuffed with live persons and set afire, of Druidic fogs and an ability to inflict madness and forgetfulness, of secret observances in remote groves. Even today Druid groups are called groves, though it has been pointed out that this last observation came from an invading force from whom the Druids, reasonably, would be trying to hide. The propaganda campaign worked, and the Roman appreciation of the Druids quickly turned to contempt of a religion characterized as inhuman. Augustus forbade it in an otherwise tolerant empire, and Tiberius set out to destroy it, a policy that would hold through the reigns of Claudius and Nero. Druidry gave focus to Celtic nationalism—Druids regained their authority briefly in the third century—and was cited as a reason for Rome to march on Britain. The Druids retreated but the Isles were never fully conquered, and ultimately Christianity had to complete the job of their annihilation.

Irish Druidry remained distinct in a number of ways—these Druids were said to be shape-shifters. On one occasion they claimed to be the creators of the heavens and the Earth. Irish tradition claimed that Druids had arrived there in 270 B.C. Celtic deities at the time numbered, by varying accounts, as many as 374 or as few as twenty. A precise figure was tricky to calculate because many of the gods were worshipped in triplicate, an Indo-European practice that may also have inspired Christianity's troublesome Trinity. Druid researchers leaned toward the compromise of thirty-three Druidic deities, as the number figured prominently in other aspects of Celtic culture and completed the link to both Hindu and Persian cultures, whose gods also numbered thirty-three, according to the Vedas.

Initially, Christianity and Druidry coexisted in Britain, and Christians were said to emulate Druidry in the establishment of a powerful clergy and monastic lifestyles. Saint Brigid had begun her study as a Druid, only to be rejected and sent off to the Christians, one story said; another claimed that a group of white-robed Druids had tried to poison Saint Patrick at a feast. Although wiped out completely in Gaul, the Druids may have lingered in

Ireland. One account claimed they survived in small pockets until as late as A.D. 1500. The Druidic gods fell into retreat as well, moving into the hills and becoming source material for accounts of little people, *sidhe, zíne,* leprechauns, fairies, and the like.

When a Druid revival began at the end of the Middle Ages—triggered by a book later shown to be a forgery—it was a chance to fill in a lot of unexplained history. The birth of the modern era and growing urbanization triggered nostalgia for rural ways, and Druidry reemerged to a frenzy to take credit for Europe's Christian-free past. The French felt it symbolized a Gaulish history, there was great pride in Welsh communities, and even Germany tried to claim ownership. Germany had never had Druids, but it did have Yggdrasil, a cosmic tree that was the center of the universe. Early scholarship suggested that Druidry was connected to Jewish blood-cleansing rites, to Indian festivals, to Pythagorean metempsychosis, to the practices of Egyptian priests, and to the fire-lighting ceremonies of Cherokee Indians. With no real data available, researchers assumed that everything pre-Christian was linked, and among the first crazy theories of Stonehenge was the belief that it was the site of one of those Druidic colleges. The figure of the Druid was heavily romanticized when the eighteenth century rolled around. The revival of this era is better described as invention, but that didn't prevent the likes of William Blake from signing on to the belief that Druids were descended directly from Noah and the patriarch, or Wordsworth from identifying himself as a Druid in early poems. The late eighteenth century saw the creation of Druidic rituals, and early in the nineteenth century men donned false beards to make themselves more Druidish for ceremonies. Various popular novels eventually came to celebrate Paganism, and formal Druid organizations cropped up, operating essentially as a form of freemasonry.

The oldest continuing Druid organization in the United States is the Reformed Druids of North America (RDNA), begun in response to the religion requirement at Minnesota's Carleton College in 1963. Several students conducted a mock ceremony using liquor as sacred waters, on the argument that the word *whiskey* originated from Druid services. To everyone's surprise, the movement grew into something more than a protest. As with other Druid groups until that time, the RDNA was supplemental to other faiths—their first archdruid would also become an Episcopal priest—but that would change when a splinter group, Ar nDraiocht Fein (ADF), borrowed the loose platform meant to celebrate nature and transformed it into a for-mal faith rooted in modern magic. For a time the ADF called itself the largest neo-Pagan organization in America.

In her search for a Druid grove, Ariadne had focused on the ADF, and I had contacted the RDNA, interviewing one of its founders. We had both investigated others as well, only to reject them all in favor of Rhian-non, who was the cordemanon of Nemeton Awenyddion, a college of the American Gwyddonic Order. Rhiannon's Druid college was mainly on-line, but she claimed that the order's American history stretched back even further than the RDNA, to 1791. "We originally come from Wales," she wrote in response to a query letter I posted on an RDNA website, "and we are traditional in the old ways."

Rhiannon's house, I came to think, was nature slightly ordered. Guitars stood upright on stands alongside fiddles and thunderdrums and a man-dolin. Celtic designs and the Druid awen symbol—a circle with two verti-cal lines passing through it—filled walls sometimes made of corrugated tin. Quartz crystal necklaces for divining ley lines dangled all over—Rhiannon made them—alongside rattles, dream catchers, bits of precious stone, and dragon figurines. A rotted-out tree trunk served as a doorstop, and branches that had grown in suggestive shapes were on display like art. Tins of tobacco, coffee cans, oil lamps, switches of herbs, a Reiki certificate, fractal art, candle wax lumped sad over ornate wooden holders—the place had a kind of Pagan clutter to it.

Rhiannon returned with both of her children: Fiona, a six-year-old girl with wide-spaced teeth and the wild, woolly hair of a wolf-child, and Jimmy, a lanky adolescent who was a first-level Druid initiate and had an altar set up on his bedroom dresser. For a while there was chaos as the chil-dren thrilled at company. Fiona showed Ariadne a small plastic sheriff's badge pinned to her shirt, and Jimmy gave me a lesson in a language he was inventing in a spiral notebook—a simple code shuffled letters around. We joked that it looked like Welsh.

Rhiannon kicked them out so she could tell the story of how she'd be-come a healer to my tape recorder. We gathered around the kitchen table with tea. Her first contact with the Pagan world came through a psychic grandmother, who gave her books. Rhiannon's parents were strict Catholics and her grandmother's literature was always burned when it was discovered. By the time Rhiannon was thirteen an RDNA grove had sprouted up in Orinda, California, and Rhiannon was spending a weekend with a member family when she had a vision of their cat, run over by a car. A week later, the vision came to pass. The family approached her with a letter about their grove's seer program, but the letter, too, was burned.

Like Ariadne, Rhiannon left home at fourteen. She moved to Redding to live with an uncle, and soon after she herself was struck by a car, a truck that threw her thirty-five feet into the air and put her into a coma. She stayed in intensive care for three months after coming out of it, but wasn't herself for some time. "Another entity came through," she said. She had Jimmy not long after she recovered, and began the healer's path, going through massage school at eighteen. She studied various nontraditional medicines—acupressure, shiatsu, deep-tissue massage, Reiki—and, echoing redactor historians who had linked Druidry to just about everything, she believed that many of these healing practices had their origins in Druid orders.

A chance meeting altered her path next: a Scottish Druid waiting for a bus spied the awen necklace she had made for herself. The Druid was headed to Mount Shasta to deliver a lecture on crystal healing. The man offered to guide Rhiannon's study when he came back down from the mountain. They had worked together for two weeks; then he disappeared into New Mexico and she never saw him again.

She began to study the mythology. She took up dowsing and kinesiology, and became a licensed minister. She discovered that the basic philosophy of Druidry could be found in other cultures, tree cosmologies appearing in Mayan, Hindu, Egyptian, and Chinese traditions. Mainstream research agreed with this much: "cosmic trees" like Yggdrasil were a part of cosmologies all over Asia, "tree spirits" had played a prominent role in soteriological rites in India and Crete, and the mythological structures of various cultures included the belief that people either were descended from trees or had been created from the wood of the cosmic tree. Even Christianity borrowed the tree symbol, but used it differently. It was turned into a gallows, Christ's cross cut from the tree of knowledge of good and evil.

Ariadne interrupted to point out that she had failed to describe the tree cosmology to me, and Rhiannon produced a diagram to help explain it, a faint outline of a big oak tree overlaid with an intricate pattern of lines indicating interactions between leaf, trunk, and root. "The roots are our past," Rhiannon said, "our ancestors, the cauldron of rebirth. The middle world is the trunk. It is the here and now, where we honor the nature spirits. The branches reach out to the spirit of otherworldly guidance, the shining ones, the gods and goddesses."

I steered us back to chronology. Once well on her path, Rhiannon contacted the RDNA again only to discover that her learning had taken her past them. They published articles that she began to write because she couldn't find a genuinely good book on Druidry by anyone else. She began organizing rituals in 1995. She offered her first classes on mythology and tree meditation, and the Druidic college she formed became part of a larger affiliation of Druids stretching from California to Pennsylvania to Kentucky, a group presided over by eighty-one core members. She moved to Cohasset when she heard a band called Beltane play at the community center, and sat in with them on harp. The new house had good energy, Rhiannon said, and the ley lines she'd dowsed to figure out where to put the stone circle passed right through the house, right over the table where we were sitting. This thought made us all pause. Ariadne suddenly placed her palms flat on the table, as though to measure its vibration.

"Someone is listening," she said.

"What?" Rhiannon said.

"You feel that?"

"He's got a tape deck recording."

"Oh, okay. *That's* what's listening!"

The construction of the new stone circle helped Rhiannon confront the death of her mother. The energy helped with her estranged father, too, who grew interested in Druidry after becoming a widower. "Miracles happen," Rhiannon said. Now she conducted online classes at various levels, starting students out with tree meditation and the cosmology, but moving them on before long to dowsing with L-rods, geomancy, and what she'd discovered of the lore. She charged nothing for the classes even though she worked part-time as an acupuncturist's assistant and used food stamps. She had merged not long ago with another Druid group, and working together they hoped to find some land and build a real college someday. As well, she had made contact with a group of genuine Welsh Druids in Wales, who would communicate only with those who spoke genuine Welsh and showed the memory. Rhiannon hoped to visit Wales in a year or so to continue her education. In the meantime the classes would continue, Rhiannon teaching groups that began at twenty or more and whittled themselves down as the simply curious fell away. And more seekers like Ariadne would make their way to the warm shack of Rhiannon's house to participate in rituals during solstices and equinoxes, and attend the healing rites held on the sixth night after each full moon.

We rode down into Chico for lunch and groceries. At the supermarket the energy of the other shoppers was so strange it made the top of Rhiannon's head tingle. She and Ariadne teased each other about having thirteenth moons. The two were hitting it off, comparing tattoos and histories—not quite mother and daughter, and not quite teacher and student either. At lunch Ariadne told us that she used almost no electricity in her apartment in Los Angeles, and that neighbors sometimes complained of the smell from her place—she had been known to start small fires inside. She said she hoped Druidry would confirm that she wasn't crazy, that she was actually just seeing a lot of things the general public didn't see.

I'd read a lot of William James by then, but at moments like this my secular hackles went up anyway. I wasn't like James in this regard, not yet. It was one thing to hear Pagans talk about invoking gods and goddesses, another to hear the Unariuns debate the validity of channeled documents, and still another to hear tell of what sounded like garden-variety hallucination. It wasn't just that a voice might be a symptom of mild schizophrenia; it was the fear of what others might suspect of me if I entertained it without appropriate scrutiny. This was precisely what had happened to James. He had become interested in the occult as a very young man—his early book reviews were of Spiritualist texts—and his involvement in the study of unusual phenomena, psychical research, waxed and waned over his life but never disappeared. For some, James's interest in the occult was cause to question his social judgment. For others it cast a shadow across the rest of his work. Some biographers excised psychical research from his story almost completely, while others simply failed to mention that he had done a significant amount of work in his final few years summing up what psychical research had found, or failed to find. The fragmentation in academic study that James lamented imposed itself on later understandings of his life. If straight biography is difficult to begin with, then it might be impossible for William James.

But James would not have blinked at a hallucination. He had begun *Varieties* with the admission that if one were "bent as we are on studying religion's existential conditions, we cannot possibly ignore [the] pathological aspects of the subject." He could have been even more frank than this: *Varieties* itself had emerged from an interest in abnormal states, to which James had turned in the mid-1890s. Religious leaders, he argued, were clearly what we were accustomed to labeling as disturbed. But James refused to reject them for serious consideration for this reason. Insanity was often linked to genius, he said, and genius offered up its fruits readily. In fact, the fruits of genius were rejected *only* when they were of a spiritual order. The arts and sciences were rife with marginal prodigies producing fruits from the blossoms of their psychoses, but

> *in the natural sciences and industrial arts it never occurs to any one to*
> *try to refute opinions by showing up their author's neurotic constitution.*
> *Opinions here are invariably tested by logic and by experiment, no mat-*
> *ter what may be their author's neurological type. It should be no different*
> *with religious opinions.*

He didn't stop there. Too much sanity, he said, was just as dangerous a thing as too little of it. "Few of us are not in some way infirm, or even diseased; and our very infirmities help us unexpectedly." Here was one of those moments when James was likely to give the impression of inconsistency, as he later admitted that belief—his own belief—helped keep him more "sane and true." Almost all of *Varieties* could be boiled down to the argument that regardless of whether religious beliefs had anything to do with the world of facts, regardless of whether they emerged from experience we would label healthy or sick, they clearly offered us the fruit of a life more interesting and better balanced.

At lunch, Rhiannon and Ariadne explained that the tools of Druidry, the signs, the divination, the crystals, were only symbols to allow a person to access something already inside them. This was the surprise of modern Paganism, really. Modern magic wasn't magic the way non-Pagans thought of it. There was no such thing as *super*natural. There was only the natural, and there would always be a natural beyond that which the experimental method could access. "It is certain that the whole system of thought which leads to magic, fetishism and the lower superstitions," James wrote, "may just as well be called primitive science as called primitive religion." The collective unconscious, the placebo effect, hypnotism, the unconscious brain, trance states, psychosomatic symptoms, consciousness itself ("tho't transference being only a name for the unknown," James once wrote to a friend)—we had names for the phenomena that science couldn't really grip, and magic, for many, was the attempt to manipulate those things through symbol and belief. Or at least this was the definition of *magic* I'd come up with. It was a word every bit as oily and slippery as religion or God, and it seemed that the answer to life's riddle, at least in part, was made up of the attempt to put a finger to certain ambiguities, to palpate or divine the pulse of a world that was green and ruthless and alive, to fashion or adopt a cosmology that looked like a tree, or whatever else you needed, so that at least it all made sense and kept the madness at bay.

Back in Cohasset we put away the groceries and pretended we were all a family for a while. Fiona climbed into my lap for a story, and Jimmy, smitten, kept challenging Ariadne to chess. Ariadne entertained everyone with a medley of impromptu soliloquies (she was an actress, after all), jumping from a harsh British cockney accent to that of a lewd French princess, then on to fearsome Klingons and petite Hobbits, and back to a buxom German countess. Rhiannon lit a few candles, put on some Celtic music, and began dancing around the tight furniture. The house started to feel like a remote frontier shack, when the work has been done for the day and the cold and the Indians are both far away, and at worst it was life as one of William James's camping trips. At best—as when Rhiannon took up her double-stringed mandolin and struck a minstrel pose to strum an ancient chord—the room came to feel blessed and special. Jimmy knew how to accompany her on a synthesizer, and Ariadne wedged herself in next to me on the sofa to whisper of Rhiannon's talent, "And she's self-taught, too." Rhiannon was self-taught in many things. Like the old multitasking Druids, she knew the body's twenty-eight pressure points; she had studied Lakota tradition, not to mention Celtic and Welsh; she was a tattoo artist; she could lead government-recognized ceremonies; she had refinished her own fiddle; and she could perform acupuncture on family and friends as long as she didn't charge for it. Eventually, she and Ariadne began work on a song together—Ariadne had the voice of an angel—but generally what they came up with was a bit unbalanced; there were too many words for the melody, or not enough, so they simply scrunched them or stretched them accordingly. Come evening, Rhiannon admitted that a lot of her source material for Druidry was modern fantasy novels, her faith entrusted to the research of creative writers or, more likely, ghostwriters. The old Druid lore had never been written down, and the new Druid lore no one would take credit for. There was no such thing as Druidry. Modern Druids like Rhiannon simply tried to erase a century of scientific specialization to return to a time when they could be wise in all things, knowledgeable enough to be a teacher or maybe run a college.

Rhiannon sent the children to bed and set about explaining tree meditation to Ariadne. It started with thinking of yourself as a tree. "First," Rhiannon said, "imagine the roots coming out the bottom of your spine. Leave time for the roots to push through the stone. Push through the dirt, then push through the stone." She explained that even with a small oak tree, taproots could run deep to find groundwater. "When you hit water, this is the underworld. Bring that into the roots, into your legs. Then grow up from the shoulders, into the otherworld. You branch out."

"Does it go out your head?" Ariadne asked.

"Sure, out your head," Rhiannon said.

Ariadne asked what her dreams meant. Rhiannon compared them to dream journeys, an exercise in which a dream was constructed with significant blanks to trigger rhetoric. The talk made us sleepy and ended the night. I stayed in Jimmy's room, a nook off the living room. The log stove burned beside me, and a century's worth of spiders had been at work in the corners, making pillowy foams of web that rose and fell in the wind of the perpetual bellows. The bed itself was a massage table. I lay down thinking that what the history of Druidry demonstrated was that invention eventually *was* history. If Druids had spanned the gap between the known and the abyss, then their method of remembering constituted the twine bundling myth, lore, story, and history. The rain fell all night, pattering the half-tin roof. Rhiannon couldn't really control the weather. She knew that. But she liked to believe that she could, that it was possible. Either way the effect was clear: the house was warm, the children polite and friendly, the place constructed as Druidry had been constructed, from a loose clutch of tradition and habit.

3. Godfeast

First and foremost, Rhiannon was a healer.

Just at the end of the Civil War, William James dropped out of medical school so he could go along on a research expedition to South America. His one and only contact with a primitive culture coincided with his first effort at self-healing, and helped steer him toward pluralism. It's perhaps an exaggeration to say that William James invented psychology in an attempt to cure himself of his complex of insecurities and frailties, but it's an observation that his biographers have at least hinted at. One account claimed that "William's illness—whatever its cause or exact nature—was propelling him into the very field in which he would someday make his own great contribution."

James was halfway through a stifling tour of medical school when he learned of an Amazonian collecting expedition that was being headed up by Professor Louis Agassiz. Agassiz was traveling to the jungle for samples of Brazilian wildlife and to root out evidence of a South American ice age. A museum at Harvard was named for the professor, but James had mixed feelings about Agassiz's invocation of God as the explanation for nature. Still, James was charmed by the naturalist, and thought of him much in the same way he would later think of religious adherents: their work might be irrelevant or unreadable, but their certitude was infectious and inspiring. The expedition sailed for South America just as the Union was firing the final shots of the war.

James's adventurousness was quickly checked by his constitutional frailty, and his effort at self-healing would result from seasickness he experienced during the three-week journey. "No one has a right to write about the 'nature of Evil,'" he said in a letter home, "or to have any opinion about evil, who has not been at sea." Seasickness would appear often in James's writings, and in *Varieties* he would claim that "prolonged seasickness will in most persons produce a temporary condition of anhedonia." Anhedonia is defined sometimes as the inability to feel pleasure, sometimes as faithlessness. It was a diagnosis commonly used—along with melancholia, hysteria, and neurasthenia—to describe mysterious emotional ailments, species we would now lump under the genus of depression. Members of the James family seemed particularly susceptible to whatever they were. William was so profoundly struck by seasickness that years after his Brazil trip, when he had access to a laboratory, he helped perform experiments on more than five hundred deaf-mutes, ostensibly to confirm a theory linking the semicircular canals of the ear to dizziness. But from this he hypothesized a cure for seasickness: "the application of small blisters behind the ears as a possible counter-irritant to the excitement of the organs beneath, in which the most intolerable of all complaints may take its rise."

Once the voyage ended, James's health problems were compounded by an ailment beyond his ability to cure: he contracted smallpox and promptly decided that he was more suited to a speculative life, pronouncing himself "the very lightest of featherweights." The disease would pass in a month but almost blinded him, and his eyes bothered him for the rest of his life. When he recovered, he caught up with the expedition team to begin collecting trips, documenting hundreds of new species of fish. At first, James was impressed by the many tattooed Africans in the country. He described the local Indians as "mentally barren" but "exclusively practical." He befriended a spider monkey and swooned over a Brazilian girl to his family: "Ah Jesuina, Jesuina, my forest queen, my tropic flower, why could I not make myself intelligible to thee?"

Assigned to another collecting trip, James sought out a friend on the expedition to accompany him. When James found the man, he caught him photographing three local women who allowed "utmost liberties" for the camera.

The scene was disillusionment. The next morning James left alone on his expedition, in a canoe, accompanied by his chief guide, Urbano, and five other Indians. Urbano was old and distant, but once they headed into the wilderness the mood of the group relaxed. James began to feel more comfortable than he had at any other time in the journey. "There is not a bit of our damned Anglo-Saxon brutality and vulgarity in either masters or servants," James wrote of Urbano's village. Urbano was fit to be the friend of any man, he thought, and when any of the natives spoke, it was "in an easy, slow tone, as if all eternity were before them." After the visit, James continued collection trips for Agassiz, but usually went alone. He returned home just after Christmas 1865.

James completed medical school, but, as with the historical Druids, he wouldn't go on to be strictly a doctor or a priest or a scientist. Rather, he would be all these things—part healer, part scientist, part activist. In the mid-1880s, James attached himself to the British Society for Psychical Research, following his interest in Spiritualism. He helped to found, and almost single-handedly sustained, an American branch of the group. James was interested in the occult not because he believed in the supernatural, but because he believed that belief itself might offer potentially curative effects. The Society for Psychical Research was an initial sortie flown into the territory of the subconscious mind. Before James helped turn psychology into a science, doctors, mind-curists, and psychic researchers were all more or less on par with one another, and James would note that the results of the mind-curists and Christian Scientists were not so different from those of accepted medicine. Much later James argued publicly that "mental therapeutics should *not* be stamped out, but studied, and its laws ascertained." Soon after, he anticipated that he would be "banded with the spiritists, faith-curers [and] magnetic healers."

If Druids were a bridge leading from primitive to civilized, then James considered himself a similar bridge headed in the opposite direction. In an essay wrapping up his findings in psychical research, James claimed that science had shot a rift into the world, a chasm in understanding. In *Varieties,* he suggested that we might one day look back on science as a "temporarily useful eccentricity." This was what the Society for Psychical Research was all about. James wanted to explore the very thing that modern Pagans now call magic, and just as they longed for a union with the old, James argued that the Society, by exploring that which science had chosen to ignore, restored continuity to history: "It has bridged the chasm, healed the hideous rift that science, taken in a certain narrow way, has shot into the human world."

Near the end of his life, James attended a congress where Sigmund Freud was speaking. One of Freud's colleagues reported James as saying, "The future of psychology belongs to your work." This was less compliment than prophecy—one biographer has noted that James said substantially the same thing to a Buddhist meditation teacher—and, anyway, James had expressed doubts about the symbolism in Freud's technique, his "obsess[ion] with fixed ideas." James had reviewed the very first of Freud's papers to appear, linking Freud and Breuer to earlier studies and occult practices. But by the time of the congress the extent of Freud's influence was clear. For Freud's part, a newspaper report of the same congress quoted him as condemning "American religious therapy." It was dangerous and unscientific. "Bah!" James wrote to a friend, as his health began to fail. His reputation began to fail as well, and even Josiah Royce, a close friend whom James had recommended to precede him at the Gifford lectures, circulated a rhyme—more barb this time than lampoon—after James published his findings about a medium named Eusapia Palladino:

> *Eeeny, meenie, miney mo,*
> *Catch Eusapia by the toe,*
> *If she hollers, then you know*
> *James's theory is not so.*

Now James is the *Huckleberry Finn* of psychology—discussed, but not emulated. "If anything," one biographer wrote, "James is embraced as a great son of Harvard and as a hero of the older intellectual community at large, while most young psychology students barely know his name." Like a Druid, he is receding to a kind of fiction, and any biographer who hopes to do him justice needs to acknowledge that any history, known or unknown, firsthand or handed down by conquerors, is as much memory as imagination and probably serves just as well as a portrait of the historian.

In the morning Ariadne revealed that, okay, she was really only seventeen. And she would have been more than happy to dance the maypole in the rain, but Pagans weren't masochists and only two other couples made it out for Rhiannon's Beltane celebration: Richard and Hel, and Karen and Pyramid. A giant woman with long gray hair, Hel shamelessly contorted her body and peeled back sections of clothing to reveal tattoos on great bulbs of flesh. Karen wore a Pagan style hat, thick and rough-hewn, and a quilt skirt, and Pyramid was dressed in a lumberjack's plaid, and the two of them spent a lot of time staring into each other's eyes. For a while we tried to get a fire going in the rain, but eventually Rhiannon decided to hold the ritual inside.

Fiona was sent to her room to watch a movie. The rest of us rearranged the furniture and formed a circle in the living room around a votive candle perched on the head of a wooden idol. The ritual would begin with a tree meditation, continue with the invocation of a god and goddess, and conclude with a fire prayer. Rhiannon ran through the tree meditation again: the taproots, the otherworld, the underworld, sky energy running down, underworld energy running up, all of it merging at our core centers. We sang a unity song, and then Rhiannon explained Beltane, called Calon Mai in Welsh: "It's a festival of initiation, rebirth, and fertility. It's the earth warming up—the body is the dragon, the fire is the burning in the cauldron, and life springing from that. It's about initiation and change." This last was a reference to Ariadne, who was to be initiated during the ritual; she tensed a little beside Jimmy and cleared her throat. Beside her, Karen and Pyramid held hands. Richard sat in a chair. I stood between Hel and Jimmy, who already had his thunderdrum waiting. At the end of ritual, we would have a potluck Godfeast.

Fiona interrupted to complain that someone had shut her bedroom door and it scared her. Rhiannon let her keep it open, and continued with the meditation. We closed our eyes. Outside the wind blew droplets from the trees and we could hear the heavy spatter on the forest's mulch. Ariadne sighed heavily and clutched air with her hands. Only Hel kept her eyes open, irises dead as dimes. Rhiannon talked us through our growth as trees, the water-energy coming into our roots. That energy became the leaves that sprouted up and took us to the otherworld. She paused occasionally to let silence infiltrate the room, and our collective mood turned calm and solemn. "Let us open our eyes and look around at the grove of trees," she said.

Now we were Druids.

We headed into another awkward song, the simple primitive melodies and lyrics jammed in like jigsaw pieces (*Let peace fill your soul, let peace make you whole . . .*), but by the third time through it started to become ritual just through the repetition of it. I set down my notebook to really sing, jostling my head with the others on certain words to show I really meant them. Rhiannon then set about the lighting of herbs for the invocation, going at a bunch of sage with a handheld butane torch and worrying aloud that the smoke would make us high. "Manawyddion! We call to thee! To cross over to your homeland," Rhiannon suddenly bellowed out, and it took the rest of us a moment to realize that it was another song.

Next came the communal sharing—we passed a cup of wine, placed a palm on one another's shoulders, and proclaimed, "In mind, body, and spirit, we welcome the ancestors." When Karen passed the cup to Pyramid she looked long into his eyes and spoke the words as though they were a vow.

"I want to do this part," Fiona said, out from her room again and creeping into the circle.

"You want to be blessed by the ancestors?" Rhiannon said.

She nodded and executed the rite. "I like that part!" she said.

Hel began the invocation. "Spirits of the otherworld, spirits of the shining ones, we call to you now." We went around the room again, waving smoke over one another's backs. Rhiannon introduced the goddess we were calling to join us, Bleudywedd, she of growth, new life and flowers, the spirit of the owl and the spirit of wisdom, and the god, Llew, who was born into our world too early. When the god and goddess had been properly welcomed, Rhiannon intoned a poem:

> *Fire of the heart, fire of the mind . . .*
> *Burn with us by well and fire and sacred tree. . . .*
> *Thus is the sacred grove claimed and hallowed.*

She passed around a bowl so that each of us could grab a small bit of sage to toss onto the candle. We sang two more songs (*Hail to the force of the awen, we are reborn with the land . . .*) and Fiona began the burning. Jimmy went next, but the kid had grabbed an extra-large handful, and for a moment it looked as though he had snuffed the sacred flame.

"Oh, Jimmy," Rhiannon said.

But Jimmy spotted something in the votive candle: the sage was burning hot, and in a moment the wax split in two and separate flames sprouted up. "Hey, Mom!" He pointed excitedly. "It's lighting everything else up. There's two flames!"

"That's gotta be a sign," Richard said.

"That's unity," Rhiannon said, "and watch, it's going to grow together." The flames obeyed until there was a single hot orange wedge of fire. "All right. This is contemplation time. We look into the fire, and if you see anything that resembles a pattern or a symbol, please, speak what you see."

We were all quiet for a moment.

"I see a blade," Pyramid said.

"I see this design," Fiona said. "A *Y* with a zigzag around it."

Rhiannon stepped around the stand. "I like to look at it from all angles. It's dancing."

"I see a master and his dog," Ariadne said, "playing together."

"You're seeing the messenger from the underworld. Where's the hound?" Rhiannon looked at Jimmy, who usually played the hound in initiation rituals. The hound helped initiates through the gate, which was really just crawling between someone's legs. Jimmy was still staring at the candle. "I saw an eye," Rhiannon said. "Right in the middle, just a second ago."

"Someone is screaming," Ariadne said. "A rabbit."

"I see a cobra," Pyramid said.

"I see a cobra," Jimmy said, "*and* a rabbit."

"A cobra and a rabbit together," Ariadne said.

"I see a lion," Fiona said.

"I told you about the symbolism of the hare," Rhiannon said. "It's the seeker path. It learns to listen and watch."

"I see a lion," Fiona repeated.

Ariadne said, "There's someone looking out. There's someone in a cave."

"It's the new initiate!" Rhiannon said. "She's being called forward to take her oath."

"Oh, dear!"

"I call forward the new seeker," Rhiannon said.

Ariadne stepped forward, and Rhiannon put her through an oath that would hold her to the clan. She asked Ariadne for her magical name, but no one could think of a name better than Ariadne.

Ariadne was asked to recite the four truths. "Self-respect . . ." she began, but then she was stuck, and self-respect wasn't one of the truths anyway. Rhiannon walked her through them and Ariadne received a clan candle and a torc, a heavy Druid necklace.

"This is the time of the return of the energy," Rhiannon said. "Remember our place of being merged with the boundless. Let us look for patterns in our lives that keep us from being in harmony and truth with self-honesty and self-responsibility. When you find the location in your physical body, open up that place. As the boundless moves through you, it pushes that energy out to the fire. Allow it to pour out of your body. Allow the boundless to heal you."

After the Godfeast, after we'd cleaned up the house and moved the furniture back in place, Ariadne and I went for a walk in the wet woods. "I think that's one of my biggest goals. To become a better storyteller," she said. We strolled down past the maypole into Rhiannon's stone circle and passed the small stone altar as the forest dripped and swayed. Ariadne pointed out a section in the canopy where the trees had all taken an odd turn in their growth—this, Rhiannon had taught her, was the effect of ley lines. I didn't have the heart to tell her that the study of ley lines only went back as far as the 1920s and was more of that peculiar scholarship on British megalithic structures.

"Would you like to see where the fairies gather?" Ariadne said.

"Yes."

Versions of fairies have appeared in a number of cultures, many of them untouched by Celtic mythology. Ariadne admitted that she had resisted believing in them at first. Then one day, growing up in Colorado, she had seen a series of lights moving across a ridge inside what was supposed to be a vacant military firing range. Colorado was known for Tommy-knockers, the spirits of dead miners. The Tommy-knockers were two feet tall, with long beards and wrinkled skin. In ancient cosmologies, a variety of black-smith gods emphasized the importance of metals to the emergence of civi-lization. Further back, the smelting of ores featured prominently in a range of creation stories, and mythologies of mines were commonly associated with the same mountains that were linked to fairies. Specifically, the Tommy-knockers traced their origin to the knockers of northern England, the *coblynau* of Wales.

In Rhiannon's backyard the fairies gathered in a rotted-out tree trunk that we found after stumbling through the property for a while. Ariadne said that when she made it as an actress and bought a house for all her ani-mals she would find a large stump and have it converted into a commode for her bathroom.

Back in the house, Rhiannon had Celtic music going again, and she was restringing her harp. The song playing just then was about Lindow Man, a first-century corpse that had been preserved in a bog and was believed by some to be a Druid sacrifice because mistletoe had been found in his stom-ach. Rhiannon got the harp restrung and played for a bit. The children were in bed, and the house was back to that cozy shack, that comfortable clutter. I was with people I didn't know, and who didn't know me, but the moment achieved the intimacy of clan.

"Tell me the story about the keyhole symbol," Ariadne said. Like the awen, the Druidic keyhole symbol had some kind of significance. It looked like a fat bolt lock, with three dots over it.

Rhiannon set the harp back in place and joined her on the sofa. "I al-ready told you about that."

"Yes. But I want you to tell me again. I want to know about the drops."

Rhiannon rolled her eyes, but it was just a show. She paused for a mo-ment to collect her thoughts. "Okay," she said. "You need to know this." And she began her story.

1866–1878

Just before he left Brazil, William James wrote to his family:

> *The idea of people swarming about as they do at home, killing them-*
> *selves with thinking about things that have no connection to their*
> *merely external circumstances, studying themselves into fevers, going*
> *mad about religion, philosophy, love and sich, breathing perpetual*
> *heated gas and excitement, turning night into day, seems almost*
> *incredible and imaginary—and yet I only left it eight months ago.*

He arrived back in Boston in early 1866, too late to reenter medical school for the summer. A pair of cousins—Kitty and Minny Temple—were staying with the family for a time, and the house was lively. Of James's siblings, only Henry and Alice were at home, and William commented that they both seemed better off than when he had left. Wilky and Bob had set off for Florida after the war to run a plantation, paying ex-slaves a fair wage. The business would fail, but for the time being it served as a reminder to William that he had still not made any clear steps toward a career. The Temple sisters—Minny in particular, immortalized in family lore for her vivacity—eased the anxiety by employing William as an escort to a variety of social functions.

But the Temples did not stay, and the happiness of home did not last. The fall of 1866 marked the beginning of a major emotional crisis for James and, in fact, for the whole family. Alice had been suffering severe hysterical attacks since she was fourteen. She was prone to fainting if conversation became too heated, and her hair began to gray at eighteen. Emotional and physical illness infected everyone. William called the house loathsome. By spring Alice would be taken to a special facility in New York for women with nervous dispositions.

William resumed medical school in the fall. His friendship with Oliver

Wendell Holmes, Jr., intensified as the two men met frequently to compare ideas. James predicted extravagantly that Holmes would make the U.S. Supreme Court. For a time they both vied for the same girl. James lost, and Holmes married the woman. The lack of significant romance in James's life was becoming as troubling an issue for him as not having a clear professional future. He worried that he would never marry. One letter from the period suggests that he felt spurned when Kitty Temple married without notifying him ("I must say that considering the relation we have been in to each other for so many years past I little thought it would come to this as soon as my back were turned."), and the story of an awful date can be read into the invoice that James sent Theodora Sedgwick (a lifelong friend, nevertheless) for compensation for orchestra tickets, carriage fares, a soda water, and a plate of lost soup. James requested a balance of ninety cents, and also asked for the return of "whatever letters of mine you may still have in your possession, and the diamonds, silks &c which you have at different times been glad to receive from me." Eventually James wandered onto more extravagant avenues to explore his physical desire—he later confided to a friend of an incident whose possible result made him "shiver," though he felt he "had 'come of age' through the experience." Biographers have suggested everything from masturbation to prostitutes to explain the episode. Two recent novelizations of James's life suggest that he fathered illegitimate children.

But whatever it was didn't cure him, either. His symptoms at this stage of life have received a host of description. He suffered from either "partial incapacity" or "trembling weakness." He had back pain, insomnia, eyestrain, and digestive problems. He himself would call it "dorsal insanity." He confessed to his father and to Thomas Wren Ward that he had thoughts of suicide, and biographers have gravitated to a line in his correspondence in which he divulged that his mind drifted to images of the pistol, the dagger. Early in 1867, James made private plans to leave for Europe, ostensibly to seek a cure at German baths, but perhaps simply to escape the residue of romantic jilting. The journey surprised Holmes. The two men would pick up their friendship when James returned, but by then their philosophies had begun to diverge, and they soon faded from each other's social circles.

James sailed for Paris in April 1867, and his journey over the next year took him to Dresden, Teplitz, Berlin, Heidelberg, and Geneva. He stayed in boardinghouses, and took cures of mineral water and thermal baths. He tried blistering therapies and electric shock. He met Herman Grimm and had a chance encounter with General George McClellan. He wrote book reviews, which he sent home with instructions that the family make whatever changes they liked and publish them if they could. They did. James longed for romance, and from one of his boardinghouse rooms he regularly spied a troupe of German girls through a telescope and thrilled that they knew he was watching. Another woman he admired from afar he described as "the consolation of [my] life," but he could not bring himself to approach her. That James was a prude is a common perception of his early life, but later in the trip he befriended an American pianist, Catherine Havens, only to beg off a relationship with her on the claim that he was not psychologically prepared. The same excuse would nearly ruin the courting of his wife a few years later.

James looked back on his German trip as wasted time, yet the seeds of much of his thinking were planted there. His exchanges with his father in the period reveal a growing willingness to challenge both his father's thinking and his written work. James was immersed in reading throughout the trip, and when he was not seeking cures he attended physiology lectures that helped shape his thought on the relationship between mind and body. He wrote to Ward that perhaps it was finally time for psychology to become a science. But this was no consolation, and he felt himself slipping further into despair. His mother begged him to return so she could care for him. "I am coming home to get well," he told Ward, and was back in Cambridge by November 1868.

Coming home didn't help either, but James returned to medical school anyway and continued writing reviews. He produced a thesis on the effects of cold on the body and secured his graduation with a cursory oral exam in June 1869. James was a doctor, but he was already skeptical of the philosophy of medical science, what in *Varieties* he called "medical materialism." Decades later he lobbied against a law that licensed only trained doctors to practice medicine, arguing that therapeutics was in "too undeveloped a state for us to be able to afford to stamp out the contributions of all fanatics & one-sided geniuses." The rigor of Harvard Medical School increased dramatically just after James finished.

The years between James's return from Germany and the beginning of his teaching career are not well recorded. Almost all of 1869 was razored out of his private journal. He resumed his friendship with Minny Temple for a time, and Minny's doubts about Christianity may have helped James with his own movement away from his father and orthodoxy. She had described "Paganism" and "Natural Religion" as the viable alternative to Henry Sr.'s philosophy. Minny's independence and vigor made it that much more of a shock when she died of tuberculosis early in 1870. The death struck Henry Jr. and William hard. Henry Jr. later described Minny's passing as the end of their childhood.

Biographers have hinted that James may have checked himself into the McLean Hospital in this era, when it still stood close to the James house and before it took in the likes of Robert Lowell and Sylvia Plath. Actually, he may have checked himself in several times. But it's true, too, that he visited asylums for research, and what records there are don't always make it clear what his business there was. Regardless, he spiraled through the period, and Minny's death was an added blow. After medical school James established a rigorous reading course for himself, building the foundation for the philosophy he would develop through the rest of his life. "I can't bring myself," he wrote to his brother, forecasting a criticism of the healthy-minded type, "as so many men seem able to, to blink the evil out of sight, and gloss it over. It's as real as the good, and if it is denied, good must be denied too." His dilemma climaxed on Walpurgisnacht 1870, the day before Beltane, when the writings of Charles Renouvier, whose work he had first discovered in Germany, took on a new role for him. James simply decided that his mood would improve. Renouvier had argued that will was the sustaining of a thought by choice, when other thoughts might also be possible. "My first act of free will shall be to believe in free will," James translated into his journal. It was an intellectual break more than a physical or emotional one, but he would later note that without Renouvier he might never have broken free of the "monistic superstitions" he had grown up with.

He needed a more active life. He vacationed alone in Maine that summer, but it wasn't until Harvard offered a new lecture series the following year that he caught the break that would give him a trajectory. He enrolled in a course on the structure of the human eye. The class initiated a string of good luck. He renewed an old friendship that gave him access to a laboratory at the medical school, and began some personal experimentation. More important, he resumed a relationship with the new president of Harvard, a man who had once been his teacher. Now James had a means for contact with the outside world, the bustle and motion beyond the fermentation of his mind. At thirty years of age he was offered his first teaching position, for a course called Comparative Anatomy and Physiology.

The rest of the James siblings found trajectories as well, though not all were as profitable. Wilky and Bob's farm in Florida finally failed and both men headed west for other ventures and marriages; Wilky would die young of heart and kidney trouble, and Bob would become an alcoholic. In 1872, Henry and Alice left for their own tour of Europe, and Henry, for the most part, would not return. He settled in England. For a time William was left alone in Cambridge with his mother and father.

He threw himself into teaching in January 1873. He found the work exhilarating but consuming. He wrote to others that he imagined he would make a fair teacher over time. James as instructor would prove to be as inscrutable a version of him as any: for all the later accounts that described him as lively and energetic in the classroom, others disparaged him as rambling and disorganized. Like most academics, James tended to underestimate teaching's social value, simply for himself. Late in life he complained about teaching and threatened to quit even as it helped sustain him emotionally. Gertrude Stein, Teddy Roosevelt, Learned Hand, George Santayana, W.E.B. Du Bois, Mary Calkins, G. Stanley Hall, Ralph Barton Perry, and a number of other prominent personalities were all James's students and acknowledged his influence in one way or another. After James's first course, he was offered the bulk of the courses in the Anatomy Department. By the fall of 1874 he had taken charge of the school's Museum of Comparative Anatomy as well.

There would never be a vacation in James's life that wasn't characterized as a retreat or recovery: after his first two semesters, he set off for Italy to live with Henry for a time and regroup. Before he left, William called Henry "[my] twin bro," and once they were living together in Florence, William wrote home, "At present Harry is my spouse." The brothers were beginning to come into their own, but Henry was a bit ahead. His writing was attracting attention the breadth of which sometimes surprised William. William began to offer criticism of Henry's work, though he always balanced it with praise. Henry dismissed the repeated appeals for clarity: the imprecision that William disliked in philosophy was a tool Henry used to convey the ambiguity of reality. William tried to explain reality; he couldn't appreciate it. The criticisms that Henry, in turn, offered about his brother tended to sound more like compliments: he once claimed that William spoke a different language from the rest of mankind, but that he was a personality who would "lend life and charm to a tread-mill." Still, the brothers were beginning to grow apart. Both had grown up cosmopolitan, but just as William was becoming comfortable with an American personality, Henry was settling into European values and manners. Henry begrudged William his disregard of social conventions; William wanted Henry to marry and become a man. Nevertheless the two men took pains to spend time together throughout their lives, and when William died Henry described it as a mutilation of himself.

James returned from Italy in 1874 to resume teaching. When graduate-level courses were first offered at Harvard, he took the opportunity to give an advanced course on the relationship between physiology and psychology. This class is sometimes thought to represent the formal introduction of modern psychology in America. Students, however, understood the work as more philosophical in nature. James would have agreed. He was already considering ways to have himself moved to the Philosophy Department.

Outside of teaching, he began to write essays to which he was now willing to sign his name. The solution to his emotional crisis led to pieces tackling the battle between free will and determinism, and through the mid-1870s he published a number of articles in *The Atlantic Monthly* and *The Nation*. His main social outlet through the seventies was various clubs of intellectuals. He affiliated himself with a number of groups over the years, including the Scratch Eight and the Aristotelian Society, joining and falling away as ideologies drifted. Early on, James helped found what is perhaps the most celebrated of these groups, the Metaphysical Club, which included the likes of Oliver Wendell Holmes, Jr., Charles Sanders Peirce, and Chauncey Wright. The group always remained informal, stressing the intellectual diversity of its members. Discussions sometimes became heated. James accidentally characterized the meetings in a letter that tried to smooth over an evening that had resulted in a "clash": "my only wonder is that we have not long ago been all of us led by the apparent impotence of argument upon the hardness of each other's hearts first to vituperation, & then to bodily violence."

Henry Sr., too, became interested in attending club meetings, and he was invited to lecture at a gathering of the Radical Club, a loosely Unitarian group. Henry Sr. became a regular visitor. One night early in 1876, he set off to a meeting, and came home excited with the peculiar news that he had met the woman who would become William's wife.

William promptly attended the next meeting of the Radical Club. Alice Howe Gibbens was a teacher, along with her sister, at a girls' school in Boston. Like William, Alice's father had studied at Harvard Medical School but never practiced. From there his life had taken a queer turn: he got himself caught up in illegal dealings and apparently slit his own throat when Alice was in her late teens. Alice and her mother and sister used the estate to live in Europe for a time, but now they had returned home so the girls could find work. Alice attended meetings of the Radical Club to explore religious questions and to find an outlet for her own personal radical streak, which dated to fervent abolitionist feelings she had held as a girl.

The relationship began with exchanges of books and long walks. James swooned. Biographers understand Alice as James's second great stroke of luck after the teaching job. The two wrote passionate letters to each other whenever they were apart. Yet the portrait of Alice that has filtered down is incomplete by her own design: years later, compiling James's correspondence after he died, Alice burned many letters, including many of her own. An entire alternate biography of James went up in flames.

Still, a personal side of James emerges in his letters to Alice that survived. He was kind of hammy. He felt the two of them were one, and found a thousand ways to say it. By September, he was ready to make a claim on her, and did so through a letter: "To state abruptly the whole matter: I am in love, *und zvar* (—forgive me—) with Yourself." The courtship continued but was marred by a number of breakups, particularly when James claimed, as he had in Germany, that his emotional condition made him a poor candidate for a husband. Alice eventually came to agree, and they split for a time when she went on an extended visit to Canada. The departure sent James roiling, and when she returned he did not hesitate to pursue her again.

James would always decry his own ability as a prose stylist, but perhaps this was because he was saving his best material for private communications with his wife, notes detailing his surroundings and his doings, sent over a lifetime:

> *Over the right-hand near mountain the milky way rose, sloping slightly towards the left, with big stars burning in it and the smaller ones scattered all about, and with my first glance at it I actually wept aloud, for I thought it was you, so like was it unto the expression of your face—your starry eyes and the soft shading of your mouth.*

> *The weather has been glorious, and in the sort of Sabbath stillness and loneliness of the valley the mountains have sunk into my soul with their*

beauty as at no previous time this summer. And with them all our past together here, dearest; I have felt you again as a young girl when you lived in your shy and sacred independence, & confided in me and gave yourself to me. . . . Darling, at bottom, our relation is exactly what it was in those days, as rare, as metaphysical, as tragic—and we will live up to it forevermore.

Oh darling! I pine for my exile to come to an end, & for that of the swarthy sorceress who now rules over you to begin. There is no fun in living apart from thee for more than 2 days.

William James married Alice Howe Gibbens in July 1878, and their first son, named for James's father and brother, was born ten months later.

King

Jacob was left alone. And a man wrestled with him until the break of dawn. When he saw that he had not prevailed against him, he wrenched Jacob's hip at its socket, so that the socket of his hip was strained as he wrestled with him. Then he said, "Let me go, for dawn is breaking." But he answered, "I will not let go, unless you bless me." Said the other, "What is your name?" He replied, "Jacob." Said he, "Your name shall no longer be Jacob, but Israel, for you have striven with God and men and have prevailed."

—Genesis 32:24–28

Men who see each other's bodies sharing the same space, treading the same earth, splashing the same water, making the same air resonate, and pursuing the same game and eating out of the same dish, will never practically believe in a pluralism of solipsistic worlds.

—William James

1. Jesus Freak

"All right," Rob Vaughn said, "everybody that brought a Bible, open up to Ephesians 6. Chris, would you open us up with a word of prayer?"

In the serious literature that has been produced in analysis of the world of professional wrestling—and surprisingly there's a good bit of it—the wrestling ring is often called the "squared circle," which is a way of pointing out that it echoes the sanctity of altars, magic circles, or whatever sacred space you chose. This was in Lititz, Pennsylvania, a little town older than the United States, and I'd road-tripped here from Texas with the Christian Wrestling Federation, which was the brainchild of native Texan Rob Vaughn, a.k.a. Jesus Freak, who sat just to my left. In a little while the men who sat around us were going to stage a series of Christian-themed wrestling matches designed to shepherd an unlikely congregation into a local church. We'd spent the last hour or so putting the wrestling ring together, and now we were all seated inside it, its shape decidedly square but our prayer gathering decidedly round. Next to Jesus Freak and going around from him were Wildman Wes Word, High IQ Quentin Lee, Tim Storm, Shaun Osborne, Mace, Ace of the Blackbird Posse, A. J. Styles, the New York Nightmare, the Ticking Time Bomb Scotty Wrenn, and Chris Idol, who wasn't really the preacher of the group—though a few of them were ministers—but he was sort of a spokesman (even though he was a heel). Thinking along this vein, I'd already spent a good bit of time trying to figure out whether the Christian Wrestling Federation, the CWF, was more show, business, ministry, or new religion. You could make a good argument for any of them.

"Let's pray," Chris Idol said. "Precious Father God, I just thank you so much for bringing us here, God, through the distance and the time changes and the lack of rest, Lord. Father, it's an amazing thing to know that you are going to work, God, and that all you've asked of us is to be willing.

Father God, begin right now to shape this weekend, Lord, and speak to us through scripture. In your name I pray. Amen."

"Amen," said me and the wrestlers.

It's probably best to start with an admission: you really can't re-create the speeches of Christian wrestlers from Texas. On the one hand, you might get caught up in the language of wrestling, the euphemisms that softened its blows: bad guys were "heels," good guys were "babyfaces" or just a "face," and the thunderous, explosive cracks of a wrestler hitting a mat— painful-looking slams whose report threatened the eardrum even at a distance—were called, simply, "bumps." And on the other hand, Christian wrestlers tended to engage in the hyperhumility of conservative Christian rhetoric, which meant they took every opportunity to denigrate themselves and elevate the Precious Lord Father God, and peppered their speeches with all variety of God synonyms, which both flattered him and gave the speeches a hitch step that enabled the speaker to speak in complete sentences. All of which meant that these boys could *talk.*

Rob got the Bible study going after we raised our heads. "Talking with everybody these last few weeks, and doing the show down in Rockwall last week, seems like everybody's personal lives have been under attack here lately. Something that keeps coming back to me over and over is Ephesians 6. Verse 10.* We've talked before about putting on the armor of God. It's kind of comparable to playing a football game. You never went out and played in a game without a helmet and shoulder pads. And in a war you wouldn't go out there without a gun, without being trained. You wouldn't do that without putting on your daily armor. So why, as Christians, do we do that? Why do we get up every day and let Satan kick us between the teeth? It's a daily battle, so therefore put on the full armor of God, so that when that day of evil comes you may be able to stand your own ground."

For James, the Ephesians quote would have fallen into the category of equanimity, a fruit of religion he listed in *Varieties* under the heading of "Saintliness." It was a characteristic that seemed to him as admirable as it was ineffable:

---

*"Henceforth you must grow strong through union with the Lord and through his mighty strength. You must put on God's armor so as to be able to stand up against the devil's stratagems" (Ephesians 6:10–11).

Whoever not only says, but feels, "God's will be done," is mailed against every weakness. . . . There is something pathetic and fatalistic about this, but the power of such a tone as a protection against outward shocks is manifest.

To just the same extent James seemed confused by this, the Ticking Time Bomb Scotty Wrenn—who chose his name because he looked a little insane and a potential to explode was the sum total of his gimmick— was perfectly comfortable with it. He nodded to Rob and compared the Bible's metaphor to putting new tires on a car. You wouldn't want to drive from Dallas to Pennsylvania with bad tires, would you? Of course not, Rob agreed, and he went on with a more complete description of the armor of God, according to Ephesians: sword of spirit, breastplate of righteousness, shield of faith, helmet of salvation, and so on. A. J. Styles, a small but quite famous wrestler on one of the mainstream professional circuits, reminded us that since we were all Christians we were different from people who were strictly of the material world. All the more reason for that armor. Rob returned to his football metaphor, which was admittedly easy for him be- cause before he had become the leader of this bizarre ministry he had been a star quarterback in high school and then a football coach. He now ex- tended the metaphor: we were all the quarterback and Satan was some God-awful linebacker blitzing us on every play: "That's where Satan is going to attack. He's going to attack that quarterback. 'Cause you're the one making things go." Then Wildman Wes Word, whose name really was Wes Word, a young white-blond man who came from perhaps the deepest recess of Texas, pointed out that there was nothing in Ephesians that pro- tected one's back. For Wes, this was a sign to never surrender, but for the others it meant that we needed to watch each other's backs against the at- tacks of Satan in the world. After some beating around the bush, a number of the wrestlers admitted that the thing they were most vulnerable to was lust and women. This was how Satan kicked you in the teeth. The Ticking Time Bomb told a story about a woman who was "totally frigging hot" who had propositioned him at a tanning salon recently. For a moment the thought that had gone through his mind wasn't *Help me, Jesus* but *Man, she ain't bad.* "I talked to A.J. about it all the way up here," he said, playing off the watch-each-other's-backs motif. "Man. The Devil's going to find your strongest weakness and that's where he's going to hit you every time."

Rob steered us to conclusion as it was getting late and we needed to book the show. A couple of the members of the troupe were new to the CWF, so there were some introductions to be done. "This is probably totally brand-new to some of you guys, you never done this," he said. "Tonight before your matches, guys will be praying with you before you go out. But we don't want you to think that we're a bunch of weirdos. We just truly believe that God can use anything, whether it's music or wrestling or whatever, for his glory. It's not really about the wrestling. It's about the people who will come tonight and walk away with their lives changed."

He gave the floor to Chris Idol, who was the "booker," the writer of tonight's show. Before Chris revealed the plot he'd devised for the evening, he layered onto Rob's introduction. Last Sunday in church, he said, he'd heard the story of when Jesus was twelve years old and vanished for a time to worship in private. Didn't you know, Jesus asked when his parents found him, that I'd be about my father's business? "I been reading a lot of wrestling books lately," Chris said, "and you hear that phrase come up a lot. Doing big business. I hear Hulk Hogan saying it. And that's what our business is right here. Our business is the Father's business."

To be honest that night's show fell a little flat. A wrestling show is essentially theater, a play written, revised, and performed with a combination of script and improvisation, all in the span of a couple of hours. Among scholars who have taken up the subject, it's not uncommon to compare wrestling shows to morality plays or Japanese Noh theater (the wrestlers compare them to soap operas), the event's mood of flamboyance seeming to lend itself to exaggeration in analysis. "Wrestling is not a sport, it is a spectacle," wrote Roland Barthes, "and it is no more ignoble to attend a wrestled performance of Suffering than a performance of the sorrows of Arnolphe or Andromaque." Chris Idol's book for the night was a bit less ambitious. There would be two shows in Lititz on consecutive evenings, and he worked his narrative backward from a culminating match that would come tomorrow, a bout between A. J. Styles and the Ticking Time Bomb for some kind of title. The basic plot revolved around Chris himself. It was the CWF's second year in Lititz, so Chris Idol already had a reputation here as a heel. As luck had it, the CWF was short one referee; Chris exploited this. He would come out tonight in the ref's outfit and announce to the crowd that he had repented for all his old sins. He would ask for a chance to prove himself as a fair-minded umpire. The Christian spirit would prevail, and the night would proceed with a few matchups headed toward a confrontation between the clean-cut beauty of A. J. Styles and the Triad

(Tim Storm, the New York Nightmare, and the Ticking Time Bomb), an alliance of heels that the people of Lititz would remember from last year. Chris Idol would ref the matches fairly until the Time Bomb wrestled Ace—then Chris would strip off the black-and-white jersey, and, showing how easy it was to backslide from one's Christian walk into sin, he would join the Triad and they would all put the boots to Ace until A.J. came out to rescue him. This would set up the second night and the match that would prove that redemption was never easy but the righteous always prevailed.

But that first night ran a little rough. The narrative for the evening ended with Chris Idol breaking his promise, backsliding to heeldom. The heels won. The effect of this wasn't apparent until the time came to appeal to the crowd for decisions. At the end of each show, one of the wrestlers of the CWF—often Chris Idol, but sometimes Rob or someone else—would climb back into the squared circle and speak for a while and eventually encourage the crowd to pray an initial prayer to Christ. If this was the first time you had prayed this prayer, and you were willing to attest to it by raising your hand, this was a "decision" and the beginning of your Christian walk. Several of the wrestlers had the dates of their own Christian departures tattooed on their bodies. In the two years the CWF had been up and running they had amassed thirty-two hundred decisions. Tonight it was Rob's job to make the appeal. Jesus Freak stepped into the ring and talked for a while about Ephesians and the armor of God, and then he asked us all to bow our heads and keep them that way so that people could raise their hands without shame. But when the time came—maybe it was the wrestling, or maybe it was the way we'd written the book—nobody in the crowd of more than a hundred Pennsylvanians raised their hand.

2. THE ROCK GYM

A week earlier, I had arrived in Dallas on a day when a factory explosion sent a mushroom cloud blooming over the Metroplex, an image captured by newscopters and repeated on local broadcasts as though to remind Texans that even though conservative Christianity popped up everywhere here, the dead land and the dry heat still echoed an industrial-furnace vision of Hell. The CWF was headquartered at the Rock Gym in Rockwall, a Dallas suburb, and the drive from the airport took me through the heart of the hot city. Vast cinema multiplexes loomed up at cloverleaf exits, but not until I was close could I see that they were not theaters but monstrous megachurch temples. A chunky downtown skyscraper wore the logo of Trinity Industries, and I spotted a brand name on fat metal trash bins: Trinity Waste Services.

Rockwall had been its own town once, but it had long since been gobbled up by the sprawl of Dallas. My map of the place showed that cartographers couldn't keep up with the advance of drywall mansions all clambering for a view of a man-made lake. Rockwall's town square had suffered the fate of town squares all across the country—one of its sides had become a speedy thoroughfare, and the business district had been reduced to consignment shops, used-appliance stores, Chinese takeout, and a single family diner holding on by nostalgia alone. I drove past the Rock Gym out on Industrial Boulevard, a row of tin hangars housing a variety of enterprises; nearby was Checkmate Embroidery and a bottle-recycling facility.

I met Rob and his wife, Anissa, for lunch. Rob was a large, puffed-up sausage of a man with a spriggy collection of hair like a campfire perched on his head and two thick earrings in each ear. He and Anissa had identical tans from the booth at the Rock Gym. Anissa was attractive even as she had begun a bloat that foreshadowed middle age, and she wore a layer of careful Texas makeup. They had been sweethearts since junior high. Together, they were eager to attribute everything good about their lives to God. At the restaurant, Rob began by quoting from the Bible about sacrificing one's body to the Lord, but after that he was content to let his eyes wander, a sweet brute with delicate glasses that gave him an air of fashion and intelligence. For the most part, Anissa spoke for them.

Their history was a gumbo of fairy tale and biblical epic. Rob grew up in a humble home about fifteen minutes from Rockwall, but never had much religion at first. He met Anissa at twelve years of age—her father was a high school football coach—and just a short while later he attended a Bible retreat and made his Christian decision. "Right that there," he said, "I prayed the sinner's prayer and invited Christ into my life and heart." The exact date was on his arm.

Rob's star-quarterback status earned him a scholarship to a small college. The couple didn't like to talk about the breakup that resulted when they ventured into secular academia, except to say that it was the result of temptation. On his own, Rob got a degree in kinesiology and went into coaching, his movement from assignment to assignment through the dust bowl like a period of desert wandering: first he was an assistant coach at a Baptist academy, then a defensive coordinator at McPherson College in Kansas, then a receivers' coach in northwest Oklahoma. Some recruiting calls back to Texas put him in touch with Anissa's father, and Rob couldn't resist the impulse to ask after his old love. One talk reignited the romance, and marriage loomed quickly.

Then began the shift toward show business. Rob took a coaching job in Minnesota in the Arena Football League, a venture that combined the spectacle of professional wrestling with actual athletics. But the league had a noxious mood of indulgence, and the couple was soon back in Texas. Rob worked as a personal trainer until he met a member of the Power Team, a band of circus strongmen that used feats of strength as a vehicle for a Christian message. Rob joined for a time, but found the Power Team just as disappointing as arena football. A month after leaving, he ran into an old friend who was now a professional wrestler. By then, Rob had bulked up from his quarterback physique to more than 280 pounds; the friend suggested wrestling school. The idea held a strange attraction for Rob. "Jesus Freak" was born. In August 1999, Rob and Anissa were relating the experience to some friends when someone wondered aloud whether a ministry could be made of it. Rob admitted that at first glance the world of wrestling, with its half-naked women used as props and its multitude of foul-mouthed heels, was an unlikely source for the Christian message. But he'd had a feeling about it.

The reading I'd done to prepare for my time with the CWF made that feeling seem not only possible, but inevitable:

> *Seeking but not always finding, impatient for results, anxious for authenticity, ever sensitive to hypocrisy, the religious life of the American people may not yet have experienced the turbulence of professional sports. . . . But it does seem to be heading in that direction. (Alan Wolfe,* The Transformation of American Religion: How We Actually Live Our Faith*)*

> *The action at the heart of the event is simple and predictable, as ritualized as Sunday Mass, as temporal and celebratory as Mardi Gras, and as much a rite of passage as a Bar Mitzvah. (Sharon Mazer,* Professional Wrestling: Sport and Spectacle*)*

> *It is a duration, a display, it takes up the ancient myths of public Suffering and Humiliation: the cross and the pillory. It is as if the wrestler is crucified in broad daylight and in the sight of all. I have heard it said of*

a wrestler stretched on the ground: "He is dead, little Jesus, there, on the cross." (Roland Barthes, "The World of Wrestling")

Rob and Anissa prayed for three weeks for guidance and decided to take the chance. They approached it as a business, setting up as a nonprofit organization and generating a website. They started mailings before they had a wrestler, even before they had a ring. Rob had never believed in miracles before the CWF, but Providence seemed to provide at opportune moments: he stumbled across Chris Idol and a few others running their own backyard wrestling club at a Baptist college in Benton. Suddenly, Rob had a troupe. And once the CWF was up and running, they received a donation of $32,000 for a trailer from a man in Florida they had never met, and who never came to a show.

The first show was put on in May 2000, and *The Dallas Morning News* reported the story on the front page of the metro section. A deluge followed: Rob did more than a hundred radio interviews the first week. The publicity drew bookings from small churches all over the country, each looking for novel ways to grow their congregations. More wrestlers appeared as well, like-minded Christians. Soon the CWF was crisscrossing the nation, averaging a show a week—not turning a profit or even breaking even but tallying up decisions on Rob's website.

The second half of 2001 saw a Job-like test of resolve. Just before a trip, Rob's blood pressure shot up, his systolic reading climbing over 180, making him a candidate for stroke at thirty years of age. "That was the day I gave up wrestling," he said. Jesus Freak retired to the front office. Publicity dried up, and for a while it looked like the CWF had been just a fad: some of the core wrestlers moved on or started families, and it wasn't clear the organization would survive. "Faithfulness, resilience," Rob said, when I asked what triggered the resurgence. Part of it was acknowledging that he couldn't do it all himself—Rob delegated some of his authority. As well, the CWF needed a permanent home base. So he gathered together a board of directors made up of local business owners and created the Rock Gym, which helped the CWF become stable, independent, and profitable.

"We think of the CWF as a doorway," Anissa said. She had worked in the computer industry and was versed in the art of corporate presentation. "Not a literal doorway, but a figurative one. And standing right before that doorway is Satan. If you don't come to the doorway wearing the armor of God and ready to do battle, you're not going to make it."

"I mean," Rob said—he spoke more in rough draft—"who did Jesus hang out with? The tax collectors, the prostitutes, the lepers. These were the people who needed him. I think of what we're doing like that."

That night's show was attended by a group of teenagers from a part of Dallas that had the highest child-mortality rate in the whole Metroplex, I was told. As well, a young man named Danny arrived from Toronto. Danny was born-again and wanted to be a wrestler. His wrestling school back home had folded. He'd heard about the CWF two days ago and had immediately set out on a pilgrimage via Greyhound. Fifty hours later he'd arrived in Dallas, his first time away from home. He'd hitchhiked to Rockwall.

A few fans made their way to the Rock Gym early, kids reserving parking spaces for the wrestlers. As they arrived, the wrestlers gathered in a common area of the gym's office to change clothes and pray. The lineup tonight included Reckless Ricky Jackson, Shiloh, and the Great Rayu, who was actually a Hispanic man named Carlos who immediately sat and began applying makeup, a black-and-white samurai pattern.

"Mike and Wes'll start and call me out for kicking Mike in the face last week," Chris Idol said, writing the book once the room came to order. "I'll say, 'You beat me last week but I got something for both y'all.' I'll help Ricky beat Mace, and we'll put the boots to him until Rayu appears and makes the save . . ."

Only Rob wrote any of it down—the others listened and nodded and laced their boots. Watching them write the book was a little like watching a rock band who can't read sheet music compose as a group. Men offered up bits of dialogue they planned to deliver or plot twists that made for a better moral.

"Let's do Bible study real quick," Rob said, looking at his watch. We stood in a circle and held hands and Rob quoted John 3:30, about God growing greater and man growing less. "I have to make myself more aware of this," he said. "Me becoming less, God becoming more. I mean, for months before we opened this gym I prayed God would make this an incredible place where people's lives would change. You guys who aren't coming to Pennsylvania with us, keep us in your prayers. Last year, we had eighty-one people get saved. God just moved up there. The last night, Chris spoke, and it was like the Holy Spirit talking. It was like gettin' chill bumps, watching people get saved."

It was Chris's turn to speak tonight as well.

The front of the Rock Gym had been remodeled and filled with donated weight equipment, but the shows were held back in what had once been a warehouse for a photocopier-repair service—the cement floor was still marked with ink stains. Metal folding chairs surrounded a huge ring beneath a brilliant lamp. The space felt like a venue for cockfights or illicit boxing matches. But the crowd was different: Anissa and Rob had expected mostly teenagers when they'd started the CWF, but they were surprised when their audience skewed both younger and older, kids left at the event as a kind of day care, and adults who were sometimes versed in wrestling history and lore. I took a chair in a corner. A young wife with her son squeezed in to my left, and we all made room for a severely disabled man in a wheelchair to my right. The youths from that tough Metroplex neighborhood were on the next leg of the ring, and included one boy in a T-shirt that said VICIOUS, another with a limp and no arms in a shirt that said FEEL THE RAGE, and a rowdy kid wearing elbow pads and an upside-down visor as a fashion statement who sometimes stood up and did backflips for no reason.

The night started out with the bit of plot that Chris had devised and a match between Mace and Reckless Ricky Jackson. In my experience with the CWF so far I had decided that professional wrestling had about as much in common with a demolition derby as with a morality play. You knew no one was going to get hurt, but the fascination was in watching men come close to it. Beyond the back bumps that sounded through the warehouse like gunshot, the technical language of wrestling undermined its violence—there were holds, moves, high-flying stunts. In studies on professional wrestling much has been made of the fact that the fans are aware that it's not real. "In what we consider the epitome of suspended disbelief," one treatment claimed, the fans "are people who want their emotions ignited." It's true that a move or a hold sometimes failed, and it was hard then to suspend disbelief: the wrestlers looked kind of corny. But it was also true that when a move was executed well, when it was as fluid as a dance and the injured wrestler sold the injury perfectly, you could not help but react as though it were real. In that moment, when it was revealed that empathy was instinct, the suspension of disbelief emerged as the natural state of the mind—deep down, one could not help but believe even when one knew to the contrary. Suspended disbelief *is* belief. Professional wrestling was close enough to a re-creation of violence to amount to ritual. You could choose to doubt, or you could choose to engage in a species of extreme faith that lasted only as long as the instant it made you forget the illusion. As an outsider who would never have attended a wrestling match otherwise, I found myself engaged in a battle—a discourse—that amounted to finding it all a little preposterous, yet at the same time flinching when Shiloh or Wildman Wes Word really seemed to be taking a licking. So I sort of understood when the man next to me began to jerk around in his wheelchair—he'd been a wrestling fan for years, he told me—and talk to the wrestlers: "Come on, Wildman! Get up! Get up! Watch it! Hey, hey, hey! Foul! Ref! Watch Chris Idol over in the corner! Oh, that was a nice rollover—nice move, Rayu!"

But I was far from a convert. I chuckled between matches when Rob got up and asked for some quiet time so he could remind us that while the Devil may win a round or two, he would never win the fight because Jesus would be there to make the save. But I was alone in this—even the Metroplex teenagers adopted Rob's solemn countenance—and William James was there to warn me again not to discard the effects of belief just because they were temporary: "Some of you, I feel sure, knowing that numerous backslidings and relapses take place . . . dismiss it all with a pitying smile as so much 'hysterics.'" But this was a shallow response, James said. He himself doubted the long-term value of the religious revival as a tool for true conversion, and he believed that the "violent accompaniments" of revivals were attributable to "a large subliminal region, involving nervous instability." But no matter—did we dismiss love simply because it might not last forever? "So with the conversion experience: that it should for even a short time show a human being what the high-water mark of his spiritual capacity is, this is what constitutes its importance."

The matches continued when Rob was done. The room was soon full of temporary believers, primed for an appeal. When it was all over, Chris Idol climbed into the ring and apologized to the crowd for the heel character he had played. Chris was a powerful speaker, but it wasn't anything he said that made him so—it was the passion of his belief, or it was the Holy Spirit. "I just want to take a second and stop being who I was before," he said. "Everything we done in here the last hour, all that fighting and stuff—it all leads up to this point right here. This is why there's a CWF, what I'm fixin' to tell y'all right now." He gave his talk, and as the evening began to break up, the wrestlers coming out to sign autographs, all those Metroplex teenagers formed a circle in the warehouse and began an impromptu revival, some of them sobbing at the evening's mood of community and message.

3. This Is Not a Show

In *Varieties,* before splitting people into sick souls and healthy-minded types, James introduced an even more basic bifurcation: religious institution and religious experience. He dismissed the former. Religious institution he defined as "the art of winning the favor of the gods," and he noted that it tended toward corporate exploitation and watered-down feelings at best. James was famously opposed to large organizations of any kind. "I am against bigness & greatness in all their forms," he wrote to a friend. "The bigger the unit you deal with, the hollower, the more brutal, the more mendacious is the life displayed. So I am against all big organizations as such, national ones first and foremost." Yet *Varieties* also acknowledged that "for [some], on the contrary, superabundance, over-pressure, stimulation, lots of superficial relations, are indispensable."

"I like big churches," Rob told me on Sunday. "Just for the community and the contacts."

The CWF wasn't officially associated with Lake Pointe Church in Rockwall, a Baptist megachurch linked to the premier megachurch movement in the country. But Rob and Anissa and basically everyone in Rockwall had been going to Lake Pointe for years, and the CWF had performed in their gymnasium. "Association" meant money, and though Lake Pointe supported ministries in Russia and Africa, there was no formal association between Lake Pointe and the CWF.

Rob and Anissa picked me up half an hour before services. The Lake Pointe complex was as expansive as a mall or a small airport. It had a bookstore, a coffee shop, a hospitality center, a prayer garden, a nursery, a discovery center, and a computer lab, all surrounding a central sanctuary that had been designed by a Broadway producer. The sanctuary could seat several thousand.

Texas droves arrived by bus and dispersed to the outer classrooms for Sunday school. Sunday school was what Rob and Anissa called age-segregated Bible fellowship (it was divided into Serving Years, Strengthening Years, Shepherding Years, and so on). The sanctuary was actually called the "Worship Center," and the service amounted to more Christian exaggeration from speakers ("You're absolutely perfect in every way, Lord. You're pure, you never make mistakes, you are perfect, perfect, perfect . . .") and a series of songs ("All About You," "You Are the Famous One") performed by a standard rock band and a troupe of singers whose images were displayed on twenty-foot-high television screens flanking the stage. We applauded each number. Then came a sermon from Pastor Steve Stroope, who had begun the church years ago as a righteous twenty-seven-year-old. Pastor Steve blended homily and stand-up comedy—he joked about how some things were simply beyond human control, like the Texas Rangers: only God could help them. He offered a smattering of Bible quotes and a message of cooperation: if one took responsibility for one's spiritual growth, God would provide the rain and the light to ensure that harvest. Then he disappeared for a bit and reappeared on a giant television screen above the stage, half-submerged in some remote water tank. A number of people waded into the mise-en-scène to be dunked and sanctified.

It was several days still before the CWF was headed to Pennsylvania. I tried to figure out why Lake Pointe wasn't funding the CWF when it would have been easy for them. Rob was as confused as I was. I was thinking like this now: wrestling made violence into entertainment in the same way Texas megachurches turned religion into entertainment. Wrestling had acknowledged itself as a show, but megachurches still denied it.

I caught up with Pastor Steve on Monday in Lake Pointe's upstairs office complex. He was just headed out the door to a conference in Chicago. "I'm running late," he said, "so we'll have to keep moving."

We hurried toward Lake Pointe's parking lot and I spelled it out for him: the CWF and Lake Pointe both employed devices of entertainment to convey their message, so why wasn't the association between them more formal?

"We are not a show," Pastor Steve said. He agreed that there was a relationship between storytelling, humor, and the message, but he called the CWF a "parachurch." They were to Lake Pointe what the bridesmaid was to the bride, and ultimately the CWF would prove unable to bring in the Kingdom. "We're not putting on a show here—if someone came and was just entertained, well, then they didn't get it."

"Strange as it may seem," writes a contemporary religious scholar, "the idea of 'God,' like the other great religious insights of the period, developed in a market economy in a spirit of aggressive capitalism." Another claims that "if we were forced to say in one word who God is and in another what the Bible is about, the answer would have to be: God is a *warrior*, and the Bible is about *victory*."

Wrestling imagery appears pretty regularly in the history of God. Stories of epic battles between ancient gods either serve as explanation for creation or describe how one god displaced another, ushering in a new era. In Babylonian mythology a long, arduous battle between Marduk (the sun god) and Tiamat (the sea) amounts to a creation story as Marduk, the victor, splits Tiamat open to make the earth and the sky. A number of other matchups answer varieties of cosmological question: Zeus-Typhon (the Hittites), Yam-Baal (the Canaanites), Re-Apophis (Egypt), Ninurta-Asag (Sumeria), and Thraētona-Azhi Dahâka (Iran). These battles—in which one god might be "killed" only to return the following year to ensure good planting seasons—were then reenacted with ritual combats among groups of celebrants, a practice that is still in place in India and Iran.

In the Bible, Yahweh begins as a war deity, one among many, whom people turn to when necessary, and in Kings he is invoked to perform feats to outshine the silence of pagan gods. It's been pointed out that in Psalm 82 Yahweh cannot transcend the older deities peacefully, and some sources suggest he taunted the lesser gods for their impotence and uselessness. In this reading, the Bible amounts to the story of God winning jurisdiction over the world and eventually acquiring compassion—in wrestling terms, he made a transition from heel to babyface and in a daring cross-circuit matchup proved himself stronger than the gods of the Canaanites. When I traveled with the CWF it was easy to imagine myself as tagging along with a pantheon of gods who retold all those battle stories on a regular basis. As Barthes put it, "no one can doubt that wrestling holds that power of transmutation which is common to the Spectacle and to Religious Worship. In the ring, and even in the depths of their ignominy, wrestlers remain gods because they are, for a few moments, the key which opens Nature, the pure gesture which separates Good from Evil."

The origin of wrestling is gone, but its earliest associations are often with religion. The oldest known record of wrestling is a bronze statue discovered near Baghdad at a religious site, and the word *Israel,* based on the story of Jacob in Genesis, has been translated as "Wrestled with God." Wrestling was originally a part of rites associated with funerals, harvest festivals, and mating rituals. Sumo wrestlers clap their hands to awaken gods and stomp their feet to extinguish evil. The Roman games began as legitimate sport but ended with throwing Christians to the lions, so perhaps it's not a surprise that wrestling was shunned as a pagan activity when Christianity came of age. Through the Middle Ages, wrestling survived in rural communities and sneaked away to taverns in cities. Modern wrestling owes a great deal to Irish immigrants who settled in Vermont, and the style of wrestling that developed there and spread through the United States after the Civil War helped create modern collegiate wrestling. As an athletic amusement, "scientific" wrestling had only a fledgling baseball league to compete with through the later half of the nineteenth century. Success sent wrestling on its way to spectacle. Greedy promoters realized that stories and rivalries were often more interesting than the protracted matches. Troupes of wrestlers appeared as early as the 1880s, associated with circuses and eventually vaudeville, and gaudy outfits and outrageous behavior were soon a part of the game. Wrestling proved unfit for broadcast via radio and struggled through the Depression, but was perfect for television. Only then did the last traces of genuine sport disappear, which made professional wrestling a narrative-driven re-creation of violence. "The lust for blood is not simply ghoulish," wrote one eager scholar of wrestling's forgiving audience, "but a desire to witness the stigmata."

The plots of wrestling were most successful when they exploited or incorporated modern fears or desires. An effete heel like Gorgeous George—who was educated as a psychologist—permitted the audience who hated him an expression of conservative sexuality through inverse proxy. The wrestling match, it's generally argued, allowed a venting of emotions that came about as a result of crisis. Some of the most famous wrestling gimmicks reflect contemporary political turmoil—German and Japanese gimmicks after World War II, Russian caricatures during the Cold War, the "Iron Sheik" in the wake of the Iranian hostage crisis.

Another religious scholar claims that

> in every aspect of the religious life, American faith has met American culture—and American culture has triumphed. . . . Religion in the United States is being transformed to the point of nonrecognition. . . . The most exotic religion in the United States is also the most familiar. . . . It is time for Americans to stop discussing a religion that no longer exists and to concentrate their attention on the one that flourishes all around them.

Professional wrestling has roots in Britain and France, but researchers have long held it forth as an expression of American outrageousness, the output of a wildly free frontier culture. It might have been only this that professional wrestling had in common with William James. Like Ben Franklin and Mark Twain, James eventually shouldered the reputation of an unruly American, with a coarse manner and a repugnance for things old. "The weight of the past world here is fatal—" he once wrote to his sister, from Rome. "This worship, this dependence on other men is abnormal. The ancients did things by doing the business of their own day, not by gaping at their grandfathers' tombs." His embrace of unusual religions and psychical research, and the radical definition of truth that eventually came from Pragmatism, brought him a combination of prestige and dismissal. According to one biographer, James was characterized as "'typically American,'—a sort of homespun product of the backwoods" and "a mind and a doctrine to be expected from a nation of hucksters." James's defenders argued that this was unjust: Americans had been pragmatic long before Pragmatism ever appeared, and the motion of James's thinking reflected that of the world at large. Europeans rushed to hear him, and even *Varieties* smacked of an American sensibility. Once the book appeared, Josiah Royce described it as having "the spirit of the frontiersman, of the gold seeker, or the homebuilder. . . . [It is] full of the spirit that, in our country, has long been effective in the formation of new religious sects."

"James the psychologist," one biographer complains, "and James the philosopher often slip into James the artist, leaving his critic to follow a chameleonic trail." Yes. It's as though James's Pragmatic method must be applied even to how he is remembered. In some reports James is lively and robust, in others depressed and practically an invalid. Biographers seem unsure whether to align him finally with the faithful or the skeptics. His reaction to America was just as varied. In letters, he described a "naked, vacuous america" and said that Americans were "too greedy for *results*." Writing to H. G. Wells, he claimed that "callousness to abstract justice is *the* sinister feature . . . of our U.S. civilization. . . . [It is] understandable in onlooking citizens only as a symptom of the moral flabbiness of the exclusive worship of the bitch-Goddess **SUCCESS**." At the same time, James considered America a central feature of himself, particularly when he was away from it. "God bless the American climate with its transparent passionate impulsive variety," he wrote from Germany, and, when he was once two years in Europe, he admitted to longing for "American vegetation with an American tree over my head and an American squirrel chittering at me."

His criticism of average Americans would always be tempered by a corresponding fondness, as expressed to Henry James, Jr., during the planning of the trip that produced *The American Scene:* "Drop your english ideas & take America and Americans as they take themselves, and you will certainly experience a rejuvenation."

What James perhaps liked most about America was its resistance to large organizations. Forced to choose between a megachurch and the Christian Wrestling Federation, James would undoubtedly have preferred the bridesmaid to the bride. And if the CWF was on the brink of becoming its own pararealigion, then it teetered on the edge of a cliff from which Pragmatism had already plummeted. Early in life, James wrote a long letter to Oliver Wendell Holmes in which he lamented that religious geniuses were no longer possible. He called for some mode of popular thinking in which "every individual [could be] a real God to his race, greater or lesser in proportion to his gifts and the way he uses them." It's tempting to backtrack further and tick off the wise men who frequented the James home when William was a boy: Thoreau, Alcott, Tennyson, Mill, and Emerson, whom James would later describe as a "literal divine presence" in the home. Biographers note that James's philosophy was never a mere theory but a set of beliefs. They tend to shy away from the grander claim: James attempted to cure himself with science and psychology, but when these proved ineffective he turned to philosophy to craft a system that would allow him the kind of comfort he had borne witness to in others but was incapable of experiencing.

James was tickled by the popular reaction to *Varieties.* A clergyman wrote him a letter claiming that James had put himself in the company of Isaiah and Saint Paul. James replied, "Why drag in Saint Paul and Isaiah?" In 1903, the first college-level course completely devoted to James's work was offered at the Academy of Neuchâtel, and in the same year a group of Italian thinkers began a magazine entitled *Leonardo,* devoted to exploring Pragmatism. One critic argued that James's version of Pragmatism came from his inability to understand that of Charles Peirce, but Peirce himself wrote to James, "You are of all my friends the one who illustrates *pragmatism* in its most needful forms."

James summarized Pragmatism with two main points, then spent books explaining them. The first was the Pragmatic method. This was simply a way to approach questions or paradoxes. In determining the difference between ideas, especially ideas that seemed opposed to one another or mutually exclusive, the Pragmatic method advised estimating the *effect* of an idea, as opposed to objectively assessing its nature or origin. The second main point of Pragmatism was a definition of truth. An idea was "true," James would argue, well after *Varieties,* if it bore us practical fruits for life, if it helped us reap gains. More on that later.

The *Leonardo* group, who took Pragmatism as their anthem, was, according to one biographer, "a band of devotees already engaged in the practice and propagation of a new gospel." One of them, Giovanni Papini, wrote to James, "I am still quite young, dear master . . . but I am eager to go on working in your path."★ James did not discourage the *Leonardo* group, and he wrote of their "determination to make of pragmatism a new militant form of religious or quasi-religious philosophy."

A few years before *Leonardo,* James had discovered and embraced the work of the eventual Nobel winner Henri Bergson. The two men's theories overlapped, and when James's *Pragmatism* appeared Bergson wrote to him, "You speak . . . of those 'saving experiences' which some souls have been privileged to enjoy. . . . Your book, combined with *Varieties of Religious Experience,* will generalize experiences of this sort. . . . That is where the religion of tomorrow is to be found." And three weeks before James died, he wrote to F.C.S. Schiller, a fellow Pragmatist,"I leave the 'Cause' in your hands. . . . Good-Bye & God bless you!"

4. THE MAIN EVENT

Somewhere between Texas and Pennsylvania, I bought the Christian wrestlers a groggy breakfast. All I remember from the meal is Rob describing one of the wrestlers I would meet in Lititz. "Oh, you're going to love the New York Nightmare," he said. "Him and his wife, greatest people you ever met."

There were eight of us in the van: a few wrestlers, a couple of roadies, and Danny, the Toronto pilgrim. Rob was a veteran traveler, but a number of them were new and hadn't been out of Texas much. I slept through northern Arkansas and woke to a vision: a giant black pyramid outside Memphis, ominous and biblical in the night. It was neither church nor

★Papini would eventually have ambitions of starting a religion of his own in America. James responded: "To think of that little Dago putting himself ahead of everyone of us . . . at a single stride. And what a writer!"

tomb—it was a sports facility. "If you see something like that again," Danny said when he emerged from a nap, "wake me up."

Rob let Wildman Wes Word drive for a while and snored for the whole flat length of Tennessee. The sun rose over Knoxville, and then we shot north through Virginia and into the lobe of western Maryland. We passed every major cavern complex in North America. "I've castrated bulls and shorn sheep, but I ain't a cowboy," Wildman Wes Word said, staring out across the green land. "I like this. I can see the wind blowin'. And no dirt."

In Lititz, we united with the rest of the troupe. We set up the ring on the night of that first flat performance, tuning the thick ropes like the strings of a guitar.

In the morning I walked through a graveyard called God's Acre. Lititz had been named for a Bohemian village where Moravians had found refuge after their leader was martyred in the fifteenth century. Now it was a Christian enclave. Lancaster County, I'd read, was home to perhaps as many as one thousand Christian churches, as well as two Christian radio stations, a dozen Christian bookstores, a Christian theater, Christian support groups, the Christian Bowhunters of America, and a Christian motorcycle club. In today's newspaper there was a story about an African American pastor in Louisiana—a man once accused of spouting racism from the pulpit—who was now offering cash to Caucasians who came to his services. "This is not a good idea," he said. "It's a God idea."

The shows were held in the gymnasium of the Lititz Community Center, and the troupe gathered there again for Bible study a couple of hours before the final show. Chris Idol began our talk with the thought that we each have to use the gifts we're given to glorify God, be it the speech of Jeremiah or the thrill of wrestling. Tim Storm reminded us that God used many things to speak his word—a burning bush, a still small voice. "God can do anything," he said. "God can use professional wrestling." Overhead, a ventilation fan turned slowly in a breeze, squeaking on each revolution like the wheel of a wagon in which we made lazy progress. As postmodern as it all seemed, travel with the Christian Wrestling Federation occasionally lent itself to ancient moods. A. J. Styles got reflective: "I been praying these people would get excited about what they're going to see tonight, about how they look up at us 'cause we're on a pedestal, like superstars. And I thought about how exciting it is that two thousand years ago a man died on the cross for us, and how we're like that up here."

We were pressed for time to write the book again. We worked backward from the finale of A.J.'s signature move on the Ticking Time Bomb as a finisher. Chris spelled out the matches, and we filled in the gaps. Somewhere in there A.J. would make a save to establish himself as a face, and then he would be forced to choose a member of the Triad to wrestle so as to earn the right to fight the Time Bomb for the title. He'd pick Chris Idol, who had joined the Triad the night before when he'd strayed from redemption. Then someone had an idea: what if one of the wrestlers interfered during the title match and Rob—Jesus Freak—had to break away from his role as ring announcer to intervene? The faint aura of orderliness normally associated with wrestling would be replaced with anarchy. Good versus evil would be complicated by the deeper question of order versus chaos. Rob grinned. It would mean coming out of retirement, but there was the glory to consider. They agreed on the plan. Finally, there was speculation that last night had not gone smoothly because we had forgotten to pray over the seats, as the CWF sometimes did on the road. The wrestlers spread out to cover the room. The New York Nightmare stood in one spot, spread his arms, and wagged slowly back and forth. Wildman Wes Word walked past all of the chairs, consecrating them. Chris Idol walked around with his hands clasped over his nose as though he were about to sneeze, and Tim Storm squatted on a chair and squinted, as though attempting to orchestrate the peristalsis of his bowels.

The variety of prayer recalled James. Just as the question of James's belief or lack of it had been difficult to pin down, so, among those who were convinced that he did believe, was it hard to determine what kind of god he finally ascribed to. Early in life he had seemed more inclined to doubt, later he described a finite god not necessarily a creator deity, and eventually Pragmatism's notion of truth seemed to accept a kind of pluralism in which a diversity of gods was possible. Even though James had indicted both his brother and a good many philosophers for ambiguity, he had remained stylistically aloof in describing his personal belief. When a fellow philosopher once begged James to clarify his position and steer himself clear of an anthropomorphized deity, James replied:

Why should you not be tolerantly interested in the spectacle of my be-lief? What harm does the little residuum or germ of actuality that I leave in God do? If ideal . . . may he not have got himself at least partly real

by this time? . . . When you shall have read my whole set of lectures
[Pragmatism] . . . I doubt whether you will find any great harm in the
God I patronize—the poor thing is so largely an ideal possibility.

In *Varieties,* James sounded a more tragic note on this count. Wondering
whether the "science of religions" he prescribed could itself become a religion, he worried, perhaps for himself, that "the best man at this science
might be the man who found it hardest to be personally devout."

James was so elusive on the question of God that when biographers
looked to cite a concrete statement from him, they turned not to any of his
writings, but to a questionnaire he responded to in 1904. It's not clear
whether those conducting the study knew the respondent was the preemi-
nent American philosopher of the day. Here are a few of his responses:

What do you mean by God? A combination of Ideality and
(final) efficacity.
Is He a person—if so, what do you mean by his being a person? He
must be cognizant and responsive in some way.
Or is He only a force? He must *do.*
Why do you believe in God? Is it from some argument? Emphati-
cally, no.
Or do you not so much believe *in God as want to* use *him?* I can't
use him very definitely, yet I believe.
Do you feel that you have experienced His presence? Never.
Do you pray, and if so, why? I can't possibly pray—I feel foolish
and artificial.

After praying over the seats, the wrestlers spent a while slow-motioning
through the specific details of their matches, fine-tuning the finale, which
came to include a flying body slam from the top rope. I took a chair near
the landing spot, and the wrestlers retreated to the dressing room to gather
themselves and pray some more. One of the roadies put on the music of a
Christian rap artist to welcome the audience.

The night started with a match between High IQ Quentin Lee and
Shaun Osborne. The scheduled interference occurred, and A.J. made the
save. The final match was set. Ace and Tim Storm took a battle into the
chairs at the far end of the room, and a matchup between Mace and Wild-

man Wes Word proved that sharing one's testimony could make all the difference in a life.

Then came the main event. A.J. and the Time Bomb were more experienced wrestlers than the rest, and their moves were high-flying acrobatics made up of front flips and intimate embraces, twisting rolling maneuvers as evocative of swing dancing as of violence. Up to that point, the crowd, as I'd seen in previous shows, had bought only halfway into the plot of the night—kids sometimes rooted for heels for the safe rebellion of it, and adults exercised a generalized skepticism. But A.J.'s acrobatics soon captured all of us—nothing looked like it hurt, really, yet the narrative and the battle and its outcome suddenly came to matter to everyone. Disbelief gave way to belief as a function of narrative, pageantry, and conflict. Late in life William James wrote an essay called "The Moral Equivalent of War," a plea for the active arousal of quality feelings in man. For James, trauma always triggered a corresponding goodness, and it was in the midst of calamity, he said, be it natural disaster or nations in conflict, that the goodness of man came to the fore, his ability to generate compassion and offer assistance. Professional wrestling, I decided, was just this—a pantomime of war, only its equivalent, ritualized and repeated, and here packaged to make persuasive an appeal that would come later. Now the moment of crisis arrived: one of the Triad ran out from the dressing room, clotheslined the ref, and someone took that dive from the top rope, the descent to the concrete floor signaling our descent into complete disorder. By then, we, the audience, were completely susceptible to the possibility that an actual fight had broken out, that the script we knew had existed had accidentally been abandoned, and that what we witnessed now would truly tell us whether the order of the world was something worthy of our faith, whether, as James once wrote to a friend, there really was anything doing in the universe. It was near pandemonium. Just in time Jesus Freak appeared, smashed the interloper's head into a metal post, and A.J., stunned but still going, strengthened by Christ, climbed back into the ring to execute his finisher on the Time Bomb. But it was not the Time Bomb who exploded when Rob banged out the three count—it was the rest us, a room of the wildly ecstatic, shrieking and enraptured, a thrill unavoidable and enabled by god warriors and the book we'd all written together, about victory.

It took a while for the ecstasy to evaporate. When it did, Chris Idol appeared again in the ring, transformed once more from heel to preacher. He called all the wrestlers out, motioned for silence, and asked everyone to re-member Romans 10. "I don't think you brought your Bibles, but if you did, then we're in church. The word of God is near you. So listen up. Listen to what I have to say. Because if you confess with your lips that Jesus is Lord, and believe in your heart that God rose from the dead, you will be saved. Because this book? This is not a book of suggestions or maybes. This is a book of promises. Like this show, everything we did, like a lot of the garbage I gave everybody last night and came out here a totally different person—in the end, look who prevailed: the one who had Christ in his corner. There's a promise in this book that says that if you have Christ in your life, you will prevail."

He segued into a talk he'd used before, a description of the sufferings Christ endured on the cross. The cat-o'-nine-tails Christ was whipped with was studded with glass and bits of metal. The cross itself was rough and splintery. The spikes driven through his hands felt like someone taking a pair of pliers and crushing the bones in your elbows. "You think these wrestlers here are tough?" Chris said. "Jesus Christ was the toughest human being that ever walked the planet. But he died so he could laugh death in the face, and rise again. So that one of you might have eternal life. *One* of you. He rose again on that last day. Last night, A.J. got kicked, guys got beat down tonight, but they got back up. Jesus Christ is alive. Alive in the hearts and spirit of every one of these wrestlers.

"Now, I'm going to give you an opportunity to pray right now. If you're ready to pray that prayer, pray with everything you have inside you. You don't have to say it out loud. I'm gonna let you pray it silent. Bow with me. Dear God, I believe that you sent Jesus. I believe Jesus Christ died on the cross for me. I believe that three days later he rose from the dead. I believe that through him I can have forgiveness of my sins, that I can turn away from the sinful lifestyle, that the Holy Spirit can come live inside of me, that I can be a part of the family of God. Thank you for Jesus's death on the cross. Amen. Now keep your heads bowed."

He asked for those who had prayed that prayer for the first time to raise their hands. I didn't look, but I heard A.J. and Rob and the others moving about, distributing literature to those who identified themselves. Eventu-ally, Chris told us to open our eyes and raise our heads.

"Now, let me tell you one more thing. What's going on here, since that last bell rang—this is why we do what we do. If you never been to church before tonight, well, now you been to church, 'cause we just had church in here. We didn't have regular church, where you start with a prayer and everybody sings—but this was church, y'all. Thank y'all for coming. Bring people back, but when you do, I challenge you, don't tell them about the wrestling, tell them about the ministry, tell them about what God is doing."

Early the next morning, I caught a ride to the airport with some of the wrestlers. I was headed to New York, Rob was driving back south to another show in Tennessee, and some of the wrestlers were just flying home.

On the drive, the wrestlers played an alphabet game, going around in a circle in the van and naming professional wrestlers whose gimmick began with letters in sequence. They ran through the alphabet three times before anyone repeated. "Moment of silence," someone said when the wrestler named was someone who had died. Or, more simply but just as reverently, "Ten count."

1878–1890

In 1878, Henry Holt and Company had been publishing books for a little more than a decade. Holt himself began a search for an author to write a psychology textbook that he wanted to publish the following year as part of a series on science in America. He found William James through a contact in the Metaphysical Club. James accepted but begged for an extra year for the project, and signed a contract just months after he was married. The book took him twelve years to complete. Four years after he had begun, he admitted to a friend that he had written only six pages so far.

The period in which James was writing *The Principles of Psychology* saw him finally leave his parents' house and build more than one home for himself. In the span of a year he lost a large chunk of his immediate family, and within a decade he went from being one of five siblings to a father of five children. He wrote not only the three thousand manuscript pages of *Principles* but also many of the essays that would be included in *The Will to Believe*. He taught at Harvard consistently through the 1880s. James thought himself lazy his entire life.

James and his new wife, Alice, rented a set of furnished rooms in Cambridge. Just as he took on *The Principles of Psychology,* he taught his first formal class in philosophy, in 1879. James had never received instruction in either philosophy or psychology, and once quipped that the first lecture he ever attended in psychology was one he gave. Psychology was a lonely field in the 1880s. James had few real peers. When he began *Principles* he still had confidence in laboratory study and longed for Germany, where experimental psychology would come to thrive. In the summer of 1880, he traveled to Europe again. The trip was validation for an uncertain man with a book contract: the quality of the thinkers he found reassured him that he deserved to be counted among their ranks, and he came to realize that French and German philosophers and psychologists had been ignoring one another. French work on the subconscious and German laboratory science would eventually embody a basic schism in psychology—James spoke both languages and came to know all the important men.

The James family reunited a final time at Christmas 1881. James's mother died a month later, and his second son, William, was born shortly thereafter. Henry Sr. slowly failed through 1882. James's biographers have been quick to make an archetype of James's relationship with his father; the rages of both men and the fragments of heated feuds in their correspondence fuel a vision of the relationship as the father of all father-son battles. Henry Sr. was less a father than a mentor that James rejected. Yet what characterized the relationship best was not the battles, but the intimacy that persisted even as both men acknowledged a gulf of opinion neither was inclined to bridge. "I want you to feel," James had written to Henry Sr. when he was twenty-five and in Berlin and just beginning to break away intellectually,

> *how thorough is my personal sympathy with you, and how great is my delight in much that I do understand of what you think, and my admiration of it. You live in such mental isolation that I cannot help feeling bitterly at the thought that you must see in even your own children strangers to what you consider the best part of yourself.*

James and his father repelled each other precisely because they projected the same force of will into the world. Neither was content to follow in others' footsteps. They were similarly dependent on their wives, and prone to fierce fits of anger. Both men moved their families freely to and from Europe. Alice James, William's anhedonia-prone sister (all of James's biographers have struggled to find strategies to contend with the fact that both James's wife and his sister were named Alice), described in the diary that brought her posthumous fame the strange transition from living in a household ruled by William and Henry Sr. to living with the nurse who became her main contact with people. In 1889, she wrote of William,

> *he is just like a blob of mercury, you can't put a mental finger upon him. H[enry] and I were laughing over him and recalling Father and William's resemblance in these ways to him. . . . It seems to come from such a different nature in the two, in Wm., an entire inability or indifference "to stick to a thing for the sake of sticking," . . . whilst Father, the delicious infant! couldn't submit even to the thraldom of his own whim.*

Henry Sr. was usually described as more robust than William, and of a more inebriated temperament when it came to religion. Despite having dabbled in drug-altered consciousnesses, William preferred emotional sobriety when it came time to theorize. Henry Sr. announced that he had no need for skepticism; William believed skepticism was necessary if a system of thought would ever prove valuable for anyone but himself. Their varying philosophies made for a tumultuousness that biographers have been quick to mythologize. Tenderness won out in the end.

In the fall of 1882, William was again in Europe visiting his brother when word came that their father was fading quickly. Henry made for home; William stayed in London at the family's request—they worried what effect the scene might have on his "exaggerated sympathy for suffering." Henry Sr. was starving himself to death. He claimed that he had already embarked on the spiritual life and no longer had a taste for the material world. He had dictated the eulogy he wanted read at his funeral: "Here lies a man, who has thought all his life that the ceremonies attending birth, marriage, and death were all damned nonsense." William finally decided to head home himself. He wrote his father a letter in case he was too late. Neither he nor the letter arrived in time:

> *Darling old father. . . . We have been so long accustomed to the hypothesis of your being taken away from us, especially during the past ten months, that the thought that this may be your last illness conveys no very sudden shock. You are old enough, you've given your message to the world in many ways and will not be forgotten; you are here left alone, and on the other side, let us hope and pray, dear, dear old Mother is waiting for you to join her. If you go, it will not be an inharmonious thing. Only, if you are still in possession of your normal consciousness, I should like to see you once again before we part. I stayed here only in obedience to the last telegram, and am waiting now for Harry—who knows the exact state of my mind, and who will know yours—to telegraph again what I should do. Meanwhile, my blessed old Father, I scribble this line (which may reach you though I should come too late), just to tell you how full of the tenderest memories and feelings about you my heart has for the last few days been filled. In that mysterious gulf of the past into which the present will fall and go back and back, yours is still for me the central figure. All of my intellectual life I derive from you; and though we have often seemed at odds in the expression thereof, I'm*

sure there's a harmony somewhere, and that our strivings will combine. What my debt to you is goes beyond all my power of estimating,—so early, so penetrating and so constant has been the influence. . . . As for us; we shall live on each in his way,—feeling somewhat unprotected, old as we are, for the absence of the paternal bosoms as a refuge, but holding fast together in that common sacred memory. We will stand by each other and by Alice, try to transmit the torch in our offspring as you did in us, and when the time comes for being gathered in, I pray we may, if not all, some at least, be as ripe as you. As for myself, I know what trouble I've given you at various times through my peculiarities; and as my own boys grow up, I shall learn more and more of the kind of trial you had to go through in superintending the development of a creature different from yourself, for whom you felt responsible. I say this merely to show how my sympathy with you is likely to grow much livelier, rather than to fade— and not for the sake of regrets.—As for the other side, and Mother, and our all possibly meeting, I can't say anything. More than ever at this moment do I feel that if it were true, all would be solved and justified. And it comes strangely over me in bidding you good-bye how a life is but a day and expresses mainly but a single note. It is so much like the act of bidding an ordinary good-night. Good-night, my sacred old Father! If I don't see you again—Farewell! a blessed farewell! Your/ William

Henry Sr. died before even Henry Jr. made it across the Atlantic. Near the end he became delusional, calling for his dead wife. His last words reportedly were "Oh, I have such good boys—*such* good boys." William read of the death in a London newspaper, and later said the feeling struck him much more than he had expected. The family buried Henry Sr. but did not obey his wishes for a trite eulogy. Henry Jr. read William's letter over the grave.

In addition to the rest of the work he completed in the 1880s, James sifted again through all his father's books, culling the passages that best represented him. James wrote a one-hundred-page introduction for the volume that resulted, and *The Literary Remains of Henry James* was published in the fall of 1884, a few months after William's third son, Herman, was born. After six months only a few copies of the book had been purchased. If James was discouraged by this, it didn't show in his productivity. Henry Sr.'s death fixed at least a portion of William's future. Anticipating *Varieties,* he wrote to his brother: "Father's cry was the single one that religion is real.

The thing is so to 'voice' it that other ears shall hear,—no easy task, but a worthy one, which in some shape I shall attempt."

Herman James died as an infant in 1885. He had probably contracted an illness from his mother, who had suffered from whooping cough just before he became sick. James was stoic in letters he wrote of the death, but Alice's grief taught him something of the power of the maternal bond; the image would repeat in his work. Alice's interest in psychical research increased dramatically after Herman died.

When in 1882 the British Society for Psychical Research sent a group of emissaries to the United States, James had been enthusiastic. The group offered the argument that chemistry had emerged from alchemy, astronomy from astrology. They hoped publicity and added membership would bring them more data and inaugurate a science of psychical research. The American Society for Psychical Research was organized in 1884. James joined and served as its president and chief investigator for several years, concentrating on trance mediums. He was sometimes flip in his descriptions of its activities ("We are founding here a 'Society for Psychical Research' under which innocent sounding name, ghosts, second sight, spiritualism, & all sorts of hobgoblins are going to be 'investigated' by the most high toned & 'cultured' members of the community"), yet he devoted many hours to the SPR. He required students in his psychology courses to participate in experiments. Gertrude Stein's prose style is said to have been influenced by the study on automatic writing she produced while working in James's laboratory.

Beyond its exploration of the unconscious mind, James hoped psychical research might offer valid therapies, for himself and others, and he relished the opportunity to cast doubt on an increasingly sectarian scientific world. In an article that first appeared in *Scribner's Magazine* in 1890, James defended five years of psychical research:

> *If I may employ the language of the professional logic-shop, a universal proposition can be made untrue by a particular instance. If you wish to upset the law that all crows are black, you must not seek to show that no crows are; it is enough if you prove one single crow to be white. My own white crow is Mrs. Piper.*

Leonora Piper was an unusual medium, an otherwise unassuming woman who became a sensation for a time. James was the first to admit that the vast majority of SPR cases were mistakes or hoaxes, but Piper had convinced him. She was exceptional. She did not crave publicity as other mediums did, she was not particularly suggestible herself, and eventually she resented the criticism she received and retired to a life without fanfare.

James took Alice to see her shortly after Herman died. Piper came close to divining Alice's maiden name, and offered details about her family and the circumstances of Herman's funeral. Alice had nursed James's father until he died, and now she had lost a son. She believed in Piper at once, and eventually James toyed with the idea that Alice herself might have powers of some kind.

In 1874, James had described to a friend the two potential discoveries that could come of psychical investigation. What would be revealed, he said, was either

> *a force of some sort not dreamed of in our philosophy, (whether it be spirits or not)*—or, *that human testimony, voluminous in quantity, and from the most respectable sources, is but a revelation of universal human imbecility.*

And as late as 1909, he acknowledged that his work had turned up nothing definitive:

> *I confess that at times I have been tempted to believe that the Creator has eternally intended this departure of nature to remain* baffling . . . *so that, although ghosts and clairvoyances, and raps and messages from spirits, are always seeming to exist and can never be fully explained away, they also can never be susceptible of full corroboration.*

Psychical research interested James, but he was not entirely consumed by it. By the summer of 1886, he had begun to grow bored and suspected he was spending too much time on it. *Principles* loomed. The 1880s saw James fully immersed in his interest in psychology, but the work in psychical research would prove to be the better bellwether for his next shift, toward abnormal states and mystical religious experience.

For now, he needed to write his book. He spent more and more time away from his family to work. Alice bore two more children, Peggy and Aleck, and they all moved into a new home in Cambridge. In 1889, James returned to Europe to attend the International Congress of Physiological

Psychology in Paris, acting as the American representative. On the way home he stopped in London to see Henry and visit his sister for the first time in five years.

For William James, the emotional shocks of the 1880s were offset by professional and marital success; Alice James, wedged even tighter into a moral chasm than her brother, had no buffer at all. As well, she had lost William himself, to a woman with her own name. William's early letters to Alice (with greetings like "Beloved Sisterkin," "Sweetlington," and "Beloved Beaulet") are indeed of a more intimate nature than his letters to her after he married, but when biographers have implied impropriety or insensitivity on this point they exaggerate the case. (William's greetings to Henry: "My Dearest Harry," "Beloved Brother," "Dearest Heinrich.") Still, Alice found herself in an asylum just around the time William married, and again after her parents died. Her savior of the period was Katharine Loring, a close friend whose success in confronting Alice's condition offered lurid possibilities: either she was Alice's lover or she was more aggressive with medication (opium). In 1884, Alice's mental health improved and she headed to London with Loring, living off and on with Henry. Her condition would vary; often she was barely more than an invalid. When William made his visit, the brothers didn't tell her he was coming until he had arrived. Henry took Alice to an outdoor café, and William watched from afar for a signal from Henry that it was safe to approach. The brothers didn't know it then, but Alice had already begun work on her diary, a record of the last few years of her life that, by itself, would be powerful enough to trigger, generations later, the Alice James Society, Alice James Books (a poetry imprint), and a Susan Sontag play, *Alice in Bed*. Alice James is the patron saint of overlooked women.

James returned to Cambridge after the visit and worked on getting *Principles* in shape for publication. At the end of 1889, he received a letter from Holt, who asked some chatty questions and then wrote:

> *All these things call up a vague, though possibly mistaken, impression that you once had some idea of sending me the manuscript of a Psychology to publish. If you remember anything of the kind, please let me know how the matter stands.*

James was always a little put off by Holt's wryness. When the book was ready he became frustrated that Holt would not begin typesetting the pages until the final manuscript was in. He wrote to complain that seventeen hundred pages were complete and Holt should start. "Publishers are demons," James wrote,

> *there's no doubt about it. How silly it is to fly in the face of the accumu-*
> *lated wisdom of mankind, and think just because one of them appears*
> *genial socially that the great natural law is broken and that he is also a*
> *human being in his professional capacity. Fie upon such weakness!*

Holt wrote back:

> Of course *you "don't know why I need the whole of the manuscript be-*
> *fore printing begins." It's not in your line to know. If you were gradually*
> *being converted to a demon, however, by the disappointments occasioned*
> *by authors, you would know all about it.*

James published *The Principles of Psychology* when he was forty-eight years old. He wrote to his wife that the completion of the project "proclaims me really an efficient man—and last not least 'the 2nd Messiah' about to be!" *Principles* quickly became the most widely used textbook in America. It was eventually translated into German, French, Italian, and Russian. A year or so later, Holt asked James to produce a pared-down version of the book. The longer edition became known as "James," and *Psychology: Briefer Course* took the nickname "Jimmy." When *Briefer Course* also performed well, James compared his success to Mark Twain's.

Some James biographers ignore *Principles;* others call it his magnum opus or compare it to *Moby-Dick*. James's elation was short-lived, and his ultimate feeling about the book was ambivalence. He had once likened the state of psychology to that of physics before Galileo, and he had worried about launching psychology as a science without offering a basic theory of consciousness. The books predating such a theory needed to be written, he said, but they would all (his own included) quickly prove obsolete. Looking back on it after some years, he thought *Principles* was a good psychology, but he also described it as unreadable. When he delivered the book to Holt he claimed it was

> *a loathsome, distended, tumefied, bloated, dropsical mass, testifying to*
> *nothing but two facts: 1st, that there is no such thing as a* science *of*

psychology, and 2nd, that W.J. is an incapable.
Yours provided you hurry things up,
Wm. James.

In the mid-1890s, James turned more definitively to abnormal psychology and religious experience, precisely because no quarter of psychological
investigation had been able to produce even a single fundamental law of
thinking. Consciousness was every bit as elusive as psychical research.
Rather than a theory of consciousness, James had offered in *Principles* a
metaphor for it: the "stream" of consciousness. The image, he wrote his
wife, had come to him at a meeting of the Scratch Eight, and he first published the idea in 1880.

The stream of consciousness—a stream of "thought and feeling"—
helped edge out metaphysical explanations for thinking, and from there the
science of psychology began its lurch toward Freudian psychoanalysis on
the one hand and Wundt-Skinner behaviorism on the other. James blazed
the trail to that fork in the road but took neither route himself. He set off
again into the brush, to philosophy, to look for a God that could apply to
our "real world of sweat and dirt." The old myths were no good for James,
either. The God of Christianity was majestic but too remote to make a difference. God needed to be *more;* he needed to get dirty. "The prince of
darkness may be a gentleman, as we are told he is," James wrote, "but whatever the God of earth and heaven is, he can surely be no gentleman."

Satan

---

Passive happiness is slack and insipid, and soon grows mawkish and intolerable. Some austerity and wintry negativity, some roughness, danger, stringency, and effort, some "no! no!" must be mixed in to produce the sense of an existence with character and texture and power.

—**William James**

When women bear children, they produce either devils or sons with gods in them.

—**D. H. Lawrence**

And if we have to declare that the idea of God is a symbol signifying an actual presence in the world of facts, should we not expect that the idea of the Devil also represents a reality?

—**Paul Carus**

1. The Devil Is a Gentleman

When Anton Szandor LaVey founded the Church of Satan in 1966, its main processing center, called Central, was located at the Black House in San Francisco, an old Victorian that LaVey had coated with black submarine paint because he couldn't find black house paint. The Black House stood as a prominent San Francisco landmark until LaVey died in 1997 and an effort to recognize the house as a historical landmark failed. It was replaced with condominiums. Leadership of the church passed to High Priestess Blanche Barton, LaVey's third and final significant other, but Barton, caring for LaVey's young son, Satan Xerxes Carnacki LaVey, could hardly manage church administration by herself. So in 2001, Barton passed leadership to High Priest Peter Gilmore, a longtime member of the Council of Nine, and his wife, High Priestess Peggy Nadramia. Peter and Peggy lived in Manhattan; Central now operated out of a post office box at Radio City Music Hall.

When I first contacted Central, Gilmore wouldn't tell me where the church offices were, or even if there were offices, and when we scheduled a lunch in Manhattan he told me just to go to midtown, west side, and call him. I went to Fiftieth Street and Ninth Avenue and ate a piece of pie at a place called the Renaissance Cafe. Then I went outside and dialed.

"Okay," Gilmore said. "Just behind you should be a diner called the Renaissance Cafe. I'll meet you there."

My heart cinched. It was my first private Satanic scare. Periodically during my time with the Satanists, I slipped into infarctions, sudden frights, a kind of response conditioned in all persons reared in Judeo-Christian cultures. History has seen a number of Satanic scares. The Inquisition, arguably, was one big one, and another had occurred in the United States in the 1980s. Both had more to do with Christian politics than Satan, but knowing that didn't prevent the response. I was scared, and it turned out that's exactly what the Satanists wanted me to be.

I went back inside to wait and see what a Satanist looked like. I had a pet theory about Satanism that I had been forming while reading James: it wasn't really all that evil in the end. James had returned often to the idea of evil, and even the Devil, in his thinking. He believed that man and the universe were basically good, but, true to his sick soul nature, he refused to ignore the presence of evil in the world. In fact, he suggested that goodness, in order to be fully felt, needed to be occasionally lost, or at least "menaced":

> *The devil,* quoad existentiam, *may be good. That is, although he be a* principle *of evil, yet the universe, with such a principle in it, may practically be a better universe than it could have been without. On every hand, in a small way, we find a certain amount of evil is a condition by which a higher form of good is bought.*

Anton LaVey had never cited William James as a source in any of his writings, but James had basically spelled out the basic doctrine of the Church of Satan. I hadn't yet worked all this out when I met with Gilmore, and I would spend a good bit of time in Satanism putting it together, wrestling with Satanic philosophy, homing in on what Satanists meant exactly by words like *Satanic,* and *diabolical,* and *evil.* The definitions all seemed to flip when Western civilization's good-bad duality was turned on its head, and not even James was a help on that count.

There would be no mistaking Gilmore. He appeared in the street dressed in a thick black winter suit and a hat with a small red feather stuffed into its brim band. He gave the hat an anachronistic tap when he saw me, and smiled deviously. Gilmore had a goatee, demonically sculpted, but he still had a head of hair. Some Satanists, following LaVey's lead, eventually shaved their heads as a rite of passage, and if Saint Peter was responsible for our vision of Hell, if a horned devil with a pitchfork and hooves was really Pan in disguise, if Milton's *Paradise Lost* was the emergence of Satan as a sympathetic character, then LaVey's devilish legacy, beyond borrowing from James, was a fashion statement and a code of conduct for surviving a world that was itself becoming Satanic.

During our talk, Gilmore insisted that the Church of Satan was atheist and even humanist. But he also said, "We're a very carnal group of people." This was delivered matter-of-factly, as though members simply preferred their meat rare, which was how he ordered his hamburger. Gilmore characterized the church as a cabal with active members all over the world, folks whose prominent professional positions might well be compromised if he even hinted at their identities. Satanism was not a social organization—indeed, one of their basic tenets was that Satanists need not like one another—but Gilmore was a decidedly nice guy. He was hugely polite and well-spoken. He had groomed his eyebrows some, exploiting their bushiness so that they curled up to sharp points. And he used them well. I realized that I had never met a man who used his eyebrows so well. They jumped and skittered like little animals, little imp-demons, and from time to time he performed a double-clutch with them to indicate that something was particularly devious. He wasn't direct, but neither was he evasive.

The lunch was a mutual vetting. I told him I wanted to meet LaVey's son, Satan Xerxes, now ten years old, but Gilmore leaned away from it initially. He suggested that I participate in a ritual with an informal grotto of Satanists in Canada, led by a couple who had outfitted their home with various themed rooms and a secret ritual chamber. Blanche Barton had called it the Black House of the North. Gilmore agreed to contact them, and then we just chatted for a while. At first, I was hesitant to speak the name Satan aloud in public—even Gilmore whispered it once—but by the end of our talk it seemed the most natural thing in the world.

2. THE BLACK HOUSE OF THE NORTH

In addition to everything else William James accomplished in the 1880s, he purchased and renovated a farmhouse in northern New Hampshire near where he had honeymooned. In 1886, he had gone north for a week's vacation to relieve nervous tension, and on a hike he had found the farmhouse for sale. James bought the ninety-acre plot plus an adjacent meadowland and began the work to turn it into a retreat. He moved the barn, graded the land around the house so that it appeared raised, and reported to a friend on his progress that "the mother earth is in my finger-nails and my back is aching and my skin sweating with the ache and sweat of Father Adam." The three-story home with a gambrel roof and three chimneys—called Chocorua for the lake on which it sat—served as an idyllic summer home for the entire James family.

James was of two minds on artificial utopias. If Western duality had helped create the Devil that balanced and enabled God, then James, writing on perfect societies, could just as easily swing that other way, and in a manner that would please Satanists. In the mid-1890s, when James was traveling the country and lecturing to help pay for indulgences like Chocorua, he described, in a talk on what makes living significant, a week he had once spent in an idyllic community in upstate New York. He first painted the town of ten thousand in splendid color. The land was gorgeous, the industry of the inhabitants ambitious and successful, they had music and sports, and there was a complete lack of crime and poverty. The community offered a variety of religious services, including meeting places for minority sects. There was economy, culture, equality, "the best fruits of what mankind has fought and bled and striven for under the name of civilization for centuries." So James was surprised that he felt relief on leaving the town. What was missing was the primordial and the savage; the tameness of the place made its culture second-rate, he said. He lashed out at "This human drama without a villain or a pang; this community so refined that ice-cream soda water is the utmost offering it can make to the brute animal in man." In a letter he was less opaque in prescribing for the community "the flash of a pistol, a dagger, or a devilish eye, anything to break the unlovely level of 10,000 good people."

I flew to the Black House of the North. I couldn't tell the customs people where I was staying because I hadn't been given an address. Not only were Satanists not evangelistic; they understood that whatever made Satanism successful was a function of their being small enough, and mysterious enough, to remain hidden while still posing a tangible threat.

I met the Reverend Robert Lang and Priestess Diana DeMagis in a hotel lobby in Toronto. Robert was a stonemason, and Di asked that I describe her only as a health-care professional.

Years after LaVey died, fashion was still an important facet of the Church of Satan. Robert wore a tight black suit, like Gilmore's; Di's hair was teased into gentle curls, and the way she had of pursing her lips and looking out from between the swirls served as a pretty good definition of Satanic sexiness. They each wore a Baphomet, an inverted pentagram with an elongated goat's head inside it; it was the official symbol of the Church of Satan and dated from the Knights Templar. As well, they had matching rings that testified to their membership in some kind of vampire organization. We grabbed lunch and headed for the Black House.

The study of new religious movements comes with its own variation on Heisenberg's claim that observation changes the thing observed. James said it this way: "The trail of the human serpent is thus over everything." My study of new religious groups had become a study of James's impact on religion, but now my own observation was becoming part of the equation. The Satanic ritual I would observe was being staged for me. The same group, not long before, had conducted another ritual for a photojournalist. The Christian wrestlers had ritualized entertainment for an audience; Satanists did the same thing for the performers.

Robert drove as though he was performing, too. Anton LaVey's weird calliope music played on the stereo and an Egyptian idol bobbed on the dash as Robert gunned the engine, steering us half an hour outside of Toronto. The Black House of the North sat on a small highway between towns, on a plot carved out of the northern forest, the blacktop drive flanked by sculpted shrubs. A giant crucifix planted on a neighbor's land had grown several feet after the neighbor had paid a brief visit to the Black House some time ago. But other than a Ouija board and a few gargoyles on the porch to scare away Jehovah's Witnesses, the place was actually modest from the outside, a rural acreage visited by moose, wolves, and feral cats. Inside, however, the house was an armory. Satanists had a thing for swords.

"Satan" for the Church of Satan was really shorthand for "other," a recognition that moral and religious systems based on good-bad dualities—all of monotheism—were as dependent on personified evil as they were on benevolent gods. "Other" could mean Satan, or it could mean any of the dozens of devils and demons who had played the bad guy in most of the world's religions. Church of Satan members could resonate to the imagery of whatever Devil they preferred, and rituals might recognize any number of evil incarnations.

Robert and Di leaned toward the Egyptian, at least in dashboard decoration and home decor. The family room of the Black House was called the Library of Antiquity. A pyramid fountain trickled near the front door; Egyptian shawls swathed their computer's power tower. A blunderbuss hung above the bar, and a big jackal-headed Egyptian god stood on the stone hearth that filled the back wall. A full-sized sarcophagus bookcase took up a corner and held Robert and Di's collection of H. P. Lovecraft. All about were random dragons, ram's-head lamps, anything with hieroglyphics on it, and across the floor was spread a rug with a shiny portrait of Tutankhamen.

Then there were the swords. I wasn't sure it was in keeping with the Egyptian theme, but sharp metal knives and daggers hung everywhere in the Library of Antiquity. And not only there but basically everywhere in the house—you were never more than a step away from something meant to cut flesh. Almost at once, Robert showed me his collection of canes, each of them actually a sword cane, all of them gathered together in a stand near the front door, just in case. The sword cane was probably the best possible metaphor for Satanism. If religion was a crutch, then the Satanic crutch—the Devil was often portrayed with a limp—was actually a weapon on the inside.

Or at least that's how the Satanists might have thought of it. The Church of Satan considered itself an applied psychology. A blend of psychology and religion was something else the Satanists had borrowed from James. Back in New York, Peter Gilmore had even cited "Satanic pragmatism" as the logical alternative to misguided idealism. *Varieties* had done much more than just describe religion; like Heisenberg, its observations had interfered with it. Throughout his life, James had insisted that religious or philosophical systems prove themselves useful, that they make a difference not just for the geniuses or the philosophers who conceived of them. He had wanted a thing that would cure not only himself, but everyone else, too, who was incapable of mysticism or healthy-minded prayer. After treating the healthy-minded type fully, he moved on to the sick souls. "Here," he wrote,

> is the real core of the religious problem: Help! help! No prophet can claim to bring a final message unless he says things that will have a sound of reality in the ears of victims such as these. But the deliverance must come in as strong a form as the complaint, if it is to take effect; and that seems a reason why the coarser religions, revivalistic, orgiastic, with blood and miracles and supernatural operations, may possibly never be displaced. Some constitutions need them too much.

The Church of Satan gave James's screw another turn when it adopted his quest as its own. Anton LaVey had recognized a need for a specific brand of person and invented Satanism as the device to address it. The Church of Satan combined fervent disbelief with elaborate ritual making. Periodic Satanic scares aside—all thoroughly debunked—the Church of Satan had claimed to be the first public organization in Western civilization to openly revere the Satanic ideal. Derivative groups had since cropped up (First Satanic Church, First Church of Satan, the Temple of Set), but for Robert and Di the literalness of those groups actually made them less Satanic.

"These people think Set is real," Di said, as the tour of the Black House continued. "As in, they talk to Set the way a priest would talk to God."

I was beginning to acclimate to the Egyptian vibe, so actually it didn't sound so strange to hear one Satanist lash out at another Satanist's weirdness. In the backyard, Di nearly came to tears as she showed me the trapezoidal monument they had erected to commemorate a pet cat, Lynx. The trapezoid was an important Satanic symbol. The shape was supposed to represent economic hierarchy somehow, a social chart with a few winners on the top and many losers below. The chopped-off pyramid on the back of the U.S. one-dollar bill was a good example of it. Satanists liked things like that. They liked pointing out that the world was quite Satanic already, and becoming more so with revenge in the judicial system, sex on television, gluttony in our Big Gulps, violence basically everywhere. Meanwhile, Satanists themselves had a keen reverence for life, for animals and children in particular. Not only did they condemn live sacrifice—it was a waste of energy, LaVey had written—but both animals and children were believed to be closely in touch with their brute natures. In other words, they were Satanic.

The tour continued inside, downstairs. It turned out that Robert and Di had played it low-key in the Library of Antiquity, deferring to relatives who perhaps didn't know they were Satanists. We filed down a tight staircase. The basement complex was a red-walled dungeon, a twisting Satanic museum of skulls and diabolical knickknacks and spooky art of squidlike Leviathans squirming over the walls. This art was sometimes Robert's. He had been an animator before turning to stonemasonry, and the images were born of his admiration for Lovecraft and his carnal imagination. It was all maze down there. The corridors had a humid, womby feel; I constantly turned the wrong way. One bedroom—where I would sleep—was called the Funhouse, and was decorated entirely in black and white, with harsh angled patterns on the walls, a lion on the rug, a hypnotic spiral on the ceiling fan. Another was themed autumn with life-sized pine-barren wallpaper, a real tree trunk, and a stuffed vulture in a corner. A bathroom was entirely pink, a photo shrine to two dead blondes LaVey supposedly had been romantically involved with: Marilyn Monroe and Jayne Mansfield. The first was probably an invented story, but Mansfield had in fact been a priestess in the Church of Satan. The ritual chamber was somewhere close by, hidden; Robert and Di left it for tomorrow's surprise.

Back up in the Library of Antiquity, we popped a few Mooseheads and

Robert and Di told me how they'd met and become Satanists. The stories of induction into the Church of Satan were uniform for almost all the Satanists I spoke with: an early sense of alienation led to fascination with occult imagery, which led to forays into occult bookstores, which inevitably led to the discovery of LaVey's *The Satanic Bible,* penned in the late sixties. *The Satanic Bible* was less a Bible than a collection of scattered thoughts outlining a philosophy celebrating indulgence. It argued that the Seven Deadly Sins were a fabrication of organized Christianity, an attempt to keep man in an irresolvable state of guilt from which only the Church could provide refuge. The book made just enough sense to have gone through thirty printings. Robert had first found *The Satanic Bible* in early adolescence and had called himself a Satanist all through high school, even though his parents snatched away his *Bible* when they found it under his bed. He officially joined the Church of Satan after reading *The Satanic Witch,* a later LaVey work.

He met Di one night at a bar. A friend of Di's was interested in Robert at first, but Di was the prettiest one there, he said. Robert began, "I was a bit conceited, I suppose, so . . ."

". . . he asked me to dance, and I did," Di finished.

She picked up the story there. They dated for a month before Di discovered that Robert was a Satanist. She wasn't scared. It turned out that her collection of H. P. Lovecraft was larger than Robert's. He steered her to *The Satanic Bible,* but it was *The Satanic Witch* that hooked her. *The Satanic Bible* was the theory; *The Satanic Witch* was the application. Here, LaVey claimed that Satanists were people unafraid to acknowledge the world as it actually was. The trick to happiness was in learning how to make an imperfect world work for you, whoever you were. If people believed in witchcraft, or believed you were a witch, you could use it to fool them. Satanic magic was all sleight of hand. The model witch in *The Satanic Witch* was the character from the 1960s television show *Bewitched.* That this was a stereotype meant only that the idea had deep cultural penetration and potential. Between the lines of *The Satanic Witch* was the quiet acknowledgment that Western duality applied to more than just good and evil, and that society's trapezoid shape meant that someone was always on the bottom. LaVey's books offered realism over activism and amounted to manuals that appealed to the excluded. Which didn't mean, necessarily, that Robert and Di came off as intellectually derailed (though they did have an entire room decorated with horror-film action figures), but it was apparent, in how they had come to interact, in finishing each other's sentences or playing the foil for each other's offbeat proclivities, that Satanism helped them stay on track. It made them, I wanted to say, good.

"I absolutely loved that book," Di said, of *The Satanic Witch*. "Anton's sense of humor really comes through in that."

Robert and Di were of the first generation of Satanists who had not had the opportunity to meet Anton LaVey personally. They both spoke of him with reverence, calling him either "Anton" or "Dr. LaVey." They became active members of the church as a function of being a couple. They befriended another Canadian Satanist couple, an older pair that included a member of LaVey's inner circle, and Robert and Di eventually inherited the Satanist magazine the other couple had founded. It was through this work that they had come to know High Priest Gilmore and Magister Michael Rose, a man who was traveling from Alabama to lead tomorrow's ritual. Robert and Di were Satanist up-and-comers.

From LaVey's books I could follow the whole idea of using others' beliefs against them, but how did it really apply to what Satanists did alone in ritual? I'd see it soon enough, but I asked anyway as we listened to music and held a kind of vampire court in the Library of Antiquity.

"Ritual is a way of reinforcing my values as I see the world," Robert said. "It helps me focus my understanding to a fine point. It's almost like a meditation, but instead of just meditating you're actually taking a concentrated force of will and trying to achieve something."

"Ritual allows us to use childlike imaginations," Di said. "It's important, as an adult, not to lose that. A certain childlike innocence makes you a better person. In the ritual chamber you suspend disbelief, you're actually using imagination. In there, the imagination is reality, it is the truth. You leave the real world outside."

"What are your definitions of good and evil?" I asked.

"Good is what I like," Robert said. "Evil is what I don't like."

"So Satanism is still about being good."

"To me, it's good." He paused. "There is no good and evil. Is a tornado evil when it destroys your home? No, it just is. It's a force of nature. I have no problem being nasty if someone's nasty to me. Most people would call that evil."

"But it's not," Di said. "It's *lex talionis*. The law of fang and claw."

This was the kind of conversation that could easily kindle talk of capital punishment, and it did. Robert and Di lamented the fact that Canada did not execute violent offenders. They cited a particularly horrifying case in which a man and woman had been convicted of abducting people and using them as sex slaves before murdering them. In any other context the case might have suggested Satanic underworlds. But Robert and Di's Satanism only made them wish the punishments had been more severe—the wife in the case had received three years of jail time and had achieved a law degree while incarcerated.

"In Canada, prison is college," Robert said, viciously.

When we turned in for the night, I went down to the Funhouse alone. I shut the door and turned to the dizzy black-and-white room. Then I noticed the baby carriage in the corner. I hadn't seen it before because it was black, like the wall behind it. An upside-down crucifix hung from its handle, positioned so that the shadow from the lamp in the hypnotic spiral ceiling fan fell across the face of the doll taking the place of Satan's child. The baby carriage was an image from the end of *Rosemary's Baby,* the Roman Polanski film that owed all of its imagery to the Church of Satan. Anton LaVey had worked as a consultant on the film and had actually played the Devil in the movie, appearing in an almost unrecognizable cameo to rape the heroine and father Satan's spawn into the world. Just a few weeks after the film was completed, Polanski's girlfriend was murdered by the Manson family. At one time, one of the killers had participated in Church of Satan rituals.

I'd gotten pretty comfortable with Robert and Di upstairs, but now I hit my second Satanic scare. I climbed into bed. I was somewhere in Canada, but I didn't really know where, and I had no car. I was in the basement of a house with wild red walls, enough swords for Rome or Troy, and a Satanic ritual chamber just a few feet away. The ceiling fan was trying to hypnotize me, a glass ball on a shelf was puttering away its silly Frankenstein energy, and Rosemary's baby was staring at me. The Black House was quiet. I checked under the bed, left the freaky light on. It was okay, I told myself. The real Rosemary's baby, LaVey's son, was three thousand miles away.

3. Satan Xerxes

James was a little out of step with the general thinking on the outright origin of God:

The ancient saying that the first maker of the Gods was fear receives vo-
luminous corroboration from every age of religious history; but none the
less does religious history show the part which joy has evermore tended
to play. . . . This latter state of things, being the more complex, is also
the more complete.

The argument he was trying to refute was also the argument that most believed led to the Devil. Devil worship, this line of thinking went, preceded
the worship of a benign deity because worship was fear-based and it was
easier to fear a perceived evil. In some lines of inquiry, demonolatry was
the first stage of religion and stretched back five thousand years. At first,
demons were supernatural entities with limited personality and tended to
be associated with negative phenomena, such as violent storms and natural
disasters. In the East, these demons were incorporated into larger monisms
conceptualized with entire pantheons of deities. The demons were bad but
necessary to the whole, and groups who worshipped either god or devil
figures alone were each counted as heretical. Hinduism and Buddhism each
had their demon figureheads—Kali and Mara—but it wasn't until Zoroaster,
in Persia, that a demon, Ahriman, began to exhibit a distinct personality.
The basic good-evil duality of Western thought is attributed to Zoroaster,
who demonized and personalized the otherwise neutral nature gods. Persian
culture came to thrive on the notion that a kind of moral warfare was a
fundamental aspect of nature, Ahura-Mazdā's struggle with Ahriman.

Ironically, one scholar concluded, it was precisely the same awe of a
fearful power that ultimately planted the seeds of Set in Egypt and that of
Yahweh in what became Israel. A demon had morphed into God, and now
it was God who was feared. (In the Middle Ages, the Cathars would insist
that Yahweh was Satan.) But Judaism still needed a demon. *Satan* is a He-
brew word—scholars offer many translations, but "adversary" is the most
common. Satan isn't truly personalized in the Old Testament. Most often,
he appears as a type or brand of angel, referred to as "a satan," and has been
described as God's covert field agent, dispatched to the world to do God's
dirty deeds. Satan comes to life most clearly in the Book of Job, in which
God and Satan formulate a bet on what would happen to Job's faith if God
allowed Satan to strip him of the rewards of a loyal life. This Satan, incar-
nating evil, splitting off from Yahweh and promoting the profane, completed the dualism Zoroaster started. The invention of the Devil makes as
good a marker as any for the beginning of Western civilization.

The anthropomorphized Satan began to play a significant role in peoples' thinking around the time of Christ. For Christ himself Satan was a symbol of moral wickedness or evil; he once addressed one of his disciples as Satan. Christ's temptation by the Devil echoes Buddha's temptation by Mara.

Human sacrifice is considered characteristic of Devil worship but actually traces its roots back to prehistoric, predualistic religious superstition. Eventually an animal was substituted for a person, often a goat—thus, some conclude, "scapegoat" and the goat in the Baphomet. Some interpretations of the Passion describe it as a metaphorical representation of the last human sacrifice, with the Passion itself as a battle between Satan and Christ. Christ's death is either a ruse to trick the Devil or a way of paying him off. As Christianity developed, the religion quickly came to mean deliverance from a pervasive evil. Satan's ascent begins there, his autonomy growing through the Gospels. The Gnostics crafted visions of Doomsday and Hell with borrowings from Egyptian, Persian, and Indian mythology. Satan first took the form of foreign gods—a serpent or a dragon or a prince among many demons. His influence was immediately effective propaganda, and even Christ was once accused of being demon-possessed. One group of Gnostics, the Ophites, worshipped the serpent of the Old Testament's creation story precisely because he granted knowledge and offered the possibility of progress. The Yazidis of Persia, from whom LaVey would borrow the fashion tip of a shaved scalp, worshipped Ahriman because they were an oppressed people and they identified with Ahriman's otherness.

Early Christians were not an educated lot and didn't realize they were borrowing from pagan ceremonies for just about every ritual they created. When the similarity was discovered it was attributed to Satan's wiles. Early on, Satan was associated with authority. Many early Christians—including Saint Paul, who called Satan "the god of this world"—believed the Second Coming was close at hand and understood Rome as the single world government of the Book of Revelation. The leader of Rome was Satan or the Antichrist, and "Caesar Nero," in Kabbalistic code, with some numerological fiddling, added up 666. (So do variations on "Prince Charles," "Henry Kissinger," and "Santa Clause.") But when Rome debauched itself, undermining its claim to divine authority, its people looked elsewhere for religious satisfaction. Christianity barely beat out the cult of Mithras to become the official religion of Rome. Hell continued to take shape with the input of Orphism and Saint Peter. Eventually the underworld borrowed imagery from northern mythology: Hel was the name of a Norse god. Dante recorded Christianity's spread to the north with descriptions of Hell's icy sublayers.

When Rome fell Christian, Satan fell, too, from his status as ruler of the world to that of a rebel attempting to undermine a kingdom now ruled by a Trinity described with civil metaphor. Around the eighth century, as the Devil's prominence and autonomy began to grow, the manner in which he manifested leaned more toward the obscure. Satan was again coupled with destructive phases of nature, diseases and ills. He was that aspect of the world that man must overcome with faith and guile. On the other hand, understanding nature too deeply was itself a prideful act, and Satan was associated with the attempt to understand nature through science. Eventually, both Bruno and Galileo would be labeled children of Satan. Depictions of Faust (William James once said that Goethe's *Faust* was worth learning the German language for) often portray him as a representative of science and knowledge.

Satan's image was vulgarized steadily through the Middle Ages, even as his prominence came to rival God's. The Inquisition (what James called "the most striking practical application to life of the doctrine of objective certitude") was ultimately more about Satan than witches, as witches were defined as those who wanted or had tried to copulate with Satan. The forty-five articles of the Council of Toulouse, in 1229, made heretic burning a Church-sanctioned industry. Satan's greatest trick was not convincing the world that he didn't exist, but persuading it that he did: when the Church legitimized belief in witchcraft, Satan became the greatest of all self-fulfilling prophecies. Rural healers came to believe that they were practicing a Devil cult, and began to conform to the model attributed to them. Actual Satan worshippers began to appear, making genuine attempts to contact a Satanic force they were now compelled to believe in. Reports of Black Masses followed by promiscuous sexual activity appeared as early as the thirteenth century, a period now considered the pinnacle of Satan's influence. Deranged individuals used the Inquisition as an explanation for the demons in their minds—they confessed to intercourse with the Devil and were executed. Soldiers hoped to find protection in battle through contact with the Devil, and all manner of attempts to divine the future came about. Satan was never so powerful as when the Church insisted on his existence and monstrous visage.

The Reformation did not change Satan's image immediately, though his usefulness as a label was apparent: Luther regarded the pope as an incarnation of Satan, and the Roman Church as the Kingdom of the Devil. The practice of witch burning ended slowly—it may have been one of the few things about which all Christians actually agreed—with Protestants, ironically, lending a flavor of religious ritual to late executions. Eventually, the practice was squashed with the help of crusaders who argued against the existence of the Devil. Satan was absorbed into a God whose omnipotence must logically have accounted for him all along. The Devil became a trickster, a figure of tragedy. Which was about where James, for all his talk of the good of evil, would have wanted to keep him:

> *the world is all the richer for having a devil in it,* so long as we keep our foot upon his neck. *In the religious consciousness, that is just the position in which the fiend, the negative or tragic principle, is found; and for that very reason the religious consciousness is so rich from the emotional point of view.*

Though the Devil is often considered a liar in the popular imagination, there is no story in which the Devil is known to lie or be deceitful. Throughout the Bible he remains God's loyal servant. Indeed, it is the followers of God who deceive the Devil, fooling him at every turn, and it was for this reason, in literature, that Satan came to demand a signed legal document for all his contracts with men. Outside of literature the idea of Satan continued to backfire, as a number of popes were accused of signing pacts with the Devil.

Belief in Satan was eventually discarded as a necessity for Christian life. The Devil died long before God did, though he remained prominent in the imagery of those sliding down the Protestant side of the Reformation's pitched roof. It was Milton's Satan in *Paradise Lost* that finished the Devil's new look, a gentlemanly manner of dress and a sophisticated mien as consolation for his tragic coda. The Devil lost his influence but became a sympathetic character, a legitimate protagonist. In contrast to God's inscrutability, Satan's presence in the world and his contracts made him easy to understand. Wasn't Lucifer's fall from grace an echo of man's own fall? Hadn't he, like man, expressed free will and chosen his own destiny? It was easy to read Satan as a projection of flawed humanity. Satan was a flexible god. "As God's image is little with the little and great with the great, so it is with the Devil's," wrote one religious scholar.

Once we understood this, it becomes clear that the conversion to Evil can be as great an act as the conversion to saintliness and the Good. . . . Restoring Evil's original and independent greatness also enhances the glory of the saintly and the Good, and thereby confers greater dignity upon the world of men.

Satan Xerxes Carnacki LaVey was a homeschooled kid. He lived in California, which meant that he had to have his own registered school. Xerxes' school—they called him Xerxes—had exactly one registered student, and one administrator-teacher. Blanche Barton.

On the day I first met Blanche Barton—six months after the ritual in Toronto—a major-league baseball team televised a public ritual to destroy a baseball that people believed represented a legendary curse on the team. Experts plugged the ball with explosives, and after an extended televised countdown the condemned ball jumped once from the electrical charge and exploded from the inside out. The curse, it was supposed, was lifted.

I mentioned the display to Blanche when we met for dinner. For her, it was further evidence that the world was more Satanic than it was willing to admit, the old pagan instincts poking through the two millennia of Christian indoctrination.

"You're getting it," she said, meaning the whole idea of Satanism.

I was disappointed that she hadn't brought Xerxes, but I was prepared to wait. Going to Toronto had been kind of a ruse so I could earn the Satanists' trust, slip in, and get to meet the kid. I had decided that if Satanism was all about sleight of hand and cold reading and manipulation, then the Satanists would at least appreciate it if I did it to them. Blanche had dyed her hair blond for the thirteen years she'd been with LaVey in San Francisco, but now she was back to her natural brown in Southern California. She wore an elaborate occult pendant, but only a small Baphomet on a lapel. Blanche had entered Satanism as a teenager through the usual channels, first *The Devil's Avenger* and then *The Satanic Bible*. She'd had a secular upbringing, and believed that hers was a mind hardwired for bucking the system. Every child hits a stage where they question the culture that was given to them, she said. Her parents took a look at *The Satanic Bible* and wrote the check themselves for her Church of Satan identification badge. Blanche ritualized privately through high school. She graduated valedictorian and was elected Phi Beta Kappa at the end of college, on LaVey's birthday. She wrote him a letter, a magical hello, she said, and he wrote back to tell her to look him up. She did, even though she was three decades younger than he was.

"I met him," she said, "and he was this handsome, dynamic, understated, scintillating man, and I knew I could not leave him."

It was already the twilight of LaVey's career, but Blanche signed on as coworker, confidante, lover, caregiver, and biographer, producing books on LaVey himself and on the history of the church. They conceived Xerxes in 1993, and when LaVey's heart infarcted one evening a few years later, Blanche breathed life into him until an ambulance arrived. "I was yelling at him," she said. "It was like calling down a dark cavern. I said, 'Don't die, don't you dare die. Your son needs you. I need you. Stay with us.'" LaVey came back on the third shock from the defibrillator, and later they all joked that it had been a miracle the ambulance was so close.

LaVey had once claimed that Satanists were fleshly people and that cremation was inappropriate for them, but as his own time grew near he feared that his celebrity would invite grave desecration and he opted for hellfire. When he died two years later, Blanche complied. "It was a ceremony, it was a thank-you," she said of the small ritual they performed for him. The legal battles over his will began shortly after the press conference to announce his passing. The Black House was already gone by then, but its contents were up for grabs, Blanche and Xerxes pitted against two estranged daughters that LaVey had fathered long before. LaVey was said to have owned Rasputin's sled chair, the confession chair from Britain's Hell-Fire Club, a Byzantine phallus, an Aztec sacrificial knife, and an exhaustive collection of occult films. Blanche made concessions on the material goods to maintain control of the church.

"I felt I had two legacies to fulfill," she said. "One was to protect and educate his son. *Our* son. And the other was to preserve the church."

Blanche still did radio interviews occasionally, but she spent most of her time as teacher-administrator of Xerxes' private school. I asked her if she had had any romances since LaVey. She shook her head, but it put her into a reflective mood.

"I was in love with the man from when I was twelve years old. I spent thirteen years with him, twenty-four hours a day. When he leaves, it's like, what the hell do I do? Would be nice to hold someone's hand, talk to someone, have someone to watch movies with."

She seemed to consider the possibility of another love in her life, a pact with a man to rival the contract she'd signed with LaVey. But it was no good.

"He's a tough act to follow," she said.

4. BEES MAKING HONEY

The Church of Satan was not a social organization, but it was turning out to have more than its share of simple love stories. Even before I met Blanche, there had been Robert and Di, and Magister Michael Rose, our ritual leader in Toronto, would soon be moving to Canada for a woman named Jen, a new Satanist but an old friend of Robert and Di's. Their wedding was scheduled for November 1, the Day of the Dead.

"You know those notes hold no sway," Di said, as I scribbled away in the Library of Antiquity. We were killing the morning before Rose and the others would arrive. "You're not allowed to interview Satanists before noon. Robert! Is your cup the double dragon?"

There was some confusion with the coffee cups. "No, I think I'm the wizard," Robert called from the kitchen.

He joined us in the library and began a lecture on the imminent downfall of Christianity, comparing its recent expansion to the bubble effect of a star just before it explodes. Robert roiled his hands as he spoke, as though molding his thoughts. "Christianity's cloisters are growing," he said. "The worst thing you can do is be intolerant."

I told them my theory about Satanism. It was risky because I still had to meet Satan Xerxes, and telling a Satanist they weren't really evil might have been just as problematic as telling a Christian that Satanism was about being a good person. Satanism, I said, wasn't about figuring out what evil meant— it was a way of figuring out what good really was. Robert and Di liked it. You didn't necessarily need to indulge, Di said, when you knew that you *could* indulge. She went on for a time about the joys of monogamy, and then, by way of contrast, she told a story of a prominent Satanist who had had prosthetic horns implanted into his skull.

Magister Rose and Jen arrived later in the afternoon with dishes for our preritual feast. Robert and Di had scheduled time for me to interview everyone as they arrived. Rose was a giant, approaching seven feet tall, his socks strangling his ankles, his shoulders hiked up behind his neck, his head shaved like LaVey's. But Satanism made him more hulk than fat. His voice ground into my chest. He described the ritual we would be performing later on, derived from combinations of texts designed to offer protection against the keepers of mainstream society, politicians and such, he said, whose goal it was to disguise the nature of things, to veil reality.

"Satanism is our tribe," Rose said. "Most of us, when we were young, were something of an outsider. We stood apart from our peers. I know in my case I couldn't understand what people thought—I couldn't become one of them." When he found *The Satanic Bible* he experienced a sense of almost knowing what would be on the next page as he took it in. Rose had met LaVey once. He had published his own magazine for a time, and Central had eventually granted him permission to use the Baphomet seal, making his work official Church of Satan material.

"Once a philosophy becomes a coherent thing, it almost becomes an organism," Rose said. "It wants to survive. We help to perpetuate the philosophy, but that's not what we set out to do. It's like bees making honey. They're not *trying* to make honey. What works is what's true. What is is much more important than what should be."

"What is evil?" I said.

Rose shrugged. "Evil is the other guy."

Jen had conducted private research on the Church of Satan on the Internet. When she decided to join, Di had provided her with half a dozen books. Now she sat primly beside her giant magister, one hand patting the boulder of his knee.

"I asked him if he wanted to become part of my witch collection," she said, summarizing their courtship.

Rose smiled like a man desired. "She came to one of our get-togethers. We talked a bit, then stayed in touch through e-mail—"

"Oh!" Di said. "You're leaving out the most important part!"

"Well, I left a letter for Jen, to be delivered after I had gone home."

"An old-school gentlemanly thing to do," Robert said, nodding.

Di preened. "And Jen has carried that letter around in her purse ever since."

The rest of the Toronto grotto, Greg and Ian, arrived a short while later in a fanfare of fashion and embraces, both of them dressed in the requisite black suits, Baphomets dangling over their hearts. In a world without Satanism, Ian might have seemed bookish and slight and quiet, and Greg would have come off as mouthy and hyperactive.

"I am not going to tell you, exactly," Ian said, when I asked what he did for a living. "I work in the public sector. I'm a policy analyst."

"I'm in a similar position," Greg said. "A lot of what I do involves working with law enforcement. On the side I'm a martial arts instructor."

Ian and Greg both had non-Satanist girlfriends. The two had met by chance at a bus stop, recognizing each other by their clothes and Baphomets, and now they, like Robert and Di, sometimes finished each other's sentences when they talked about Satanism.

"Satanism requires self-mastery," Ian said. "You have to be hard on yourself, honest with yourself. Many people just can't cut it."

"Being a Satanist doesn't make me who I am," Greg said. "Being who I am makes me a Satanist."

"What's the point of the aesthetic? The fashion?"

"It's fun," said Ian, "and in some cases it's useful."

Greg compared it to the villain tropes of popular film, where style always reflected a worldview. "A lot of bad guys are radical individuals—they're strong, they're powerful, their motives are not dictated by the will of the mob. The mob becomes jealous, hence they become the bad guy."

"Society has a certain idea of what bad people are," Ian said. "For us it's fun to manipulate that. To a certain extent you reject that which is in yourself by dressing up as the Devil—becoming the opposite of the things you find contemptible in society."

"Satanism is nine parts respectability, one part outrage," Greg said. "Being able to dress like this"—he flicked the fingers of both hands over his suit—"confidently, proudly, is the noble right of a Satanist."

"But it's not just dressing in black," Ian said. "We're here, we're putting forth an image of being confident Satanists. But when I go to work I dress in a way that will have an effect on the people I interact with, and I come across as a person who's competent in what they're doing. Satanism is being in control of your environment through every tool at your disposal."

"It's who you are all the time," Greg said, excited now, moving forward in his chair. "Ian, Robert, Di, all the other Satanists I've been privileged enough to meet, they are the most *religious* people I've ever met. Religion is the most important thing in your life—by its very definition, it is your life. It's not going into a building or saying something when you wake up in the morning. It's who you are every minute of the day."

"What we do is more legitimate than mainstream religion," Ian said. "Because for the most part people aren't religious. They pay lip service to gods, pray whenever they feel like it. What we do permeates everything."

"And you don't have to make it do that, either," Greg said. "It's who you are and what you are. I don't have to consciously apply Satanic principles. I don't have to because I've been doing it my whole life. Satanism was just finding out that there was a name for what we already were."

LaVey was not only a tough act to follow. He was a tough act to describe. And to verify.

The Church of Satan story went like this: LaVey was born in Chicago in 1930 with an extra vertebra on the end of his spine. He had a father with mob connections and a grandmother with a Transylvanian heritage. He was precocious and quick with musical instruments, dabbled with occult texts even as a boy. His vision of the world crystallized around film noir imagery—he was attracted to the Luciferian antiheroes—and he bragged of early Peeping Tom experiences. A romantic jilting sent him off to the circus, where he became a roustabout. Life with carnies convinced him of the carnality of human nature and taught him the sleight-of-hand tricks that eventually took the place of magic in his system. An affinity for the big cats landed him a trainer's job, and eventually LaVey kept lions in the Black House, until a city law was written specifically for him and he had to donate his last cat to the San Francisco Zoo.

He met Marilyn Monroe while he was working as the musical accompaniment to strippers along Santa Monica's Ocean Park Pier—Monroe danced for a time before hitting it big—and their mutual disdain for religion helped trigger a brief tryst. In 1949 LaVey went to college to avoid the draft and studied criminology. He found employment as a police photographer, and the carnage he saw on the job convinced him once and for all that there was no God. "There is nobody up there who gives a shit," he told a biographer. "Man is the only god." He turned more toward the black arts, and once visited the Church of Thelema, a pseudo-Satanist group founded by proto-Pagan Aleister Crowley.

In *Varieties,* James noted that Walt Whitman was "often spoken of as a 'pagan.'" Whitman was seen as "the restorer of the eternal natural religion." Societies, James noted, "are actually formed for his cult . . . he is even explicitly compared with the founder of the Christian religion, not altogether to the advantage of the latter." Modern Paganism more readily draws its lineage through Freemasonry, late-nineteenth-century organizations like the Hermetic Order of the Golden Dawn, and the Spiritualism that James investigated through the Society for Psychical Research. Proto-Pagan personalities like Madame Blavatsky, a Russian traveler who claimed psychic

ability, combined traces of Christianity with the beginnings of Pagan philosophy, meshing the concepts of a unified world soul and reincarnation.
One of Blavatsky's displays in Europe was debunked by the SPR. It was "a
stroke from which her reputation will not recover," James wrote in his 1890
report.

Aleister Crowley was another prominent proto-Pagan. He left the Golden
Dawn after losing a power struggle with William Butler Yeats and founded
a separate organization, Ordo Templi Orientis. The scattershot nature of
Paganism at this stage was evident in Crowley himself, who, while considered a Satanist—his veiled references to sacrificing children were actually
accounts of masturbation—also wrote hymns to the Virgin Mary. Crowley
was an early Pagan poster child; he appeared as a character in books by
Somerset Maugham and Dennis Wheatley. Virtually all Pagan groups acknowledge a debt to him, though none claim him as a direct progenitor.

Crowley's organization warped into the Church of Thelema, and it was
this group that LaVey claimed to have visited in Los Angeles. It was a disappointing pilgrimage: Crowley was already dead, and the group wasn't very
Satanic anyway. LaVey went back to his photography job. He found himself
drawn to "nut calls," reports of unexplained phenomena, and he became
more psychic researcher than psychic, a one-man version of the SPR, investigating sightings of ghosts and UFOs. He quit the police department to
concentrate on the research, eventually conducting experiments on how
sounds and shapes affect mood.

He met his first wife at a haunted house and had his first daughter in
1952, while working as a ghostbuster and as San Francisco's official organist.
A circle of San Francisco characters—some of them prominent artists or
professionals—began to form around LaVey once he bought the Black
House, with its hidden panels and trapdoors and off-limits basement. In
1960, when he was thirty, he got divorced and married a fifteen-year-old
girl. By then he was a known authority on all things alternative and hedo-
nistic, and the meetings at the Black House became so popular—once, it
was said, a slab of meat from a cadaver was served to accompany a lecture
on cannibalism—that he began charging an admittance fee. It was a San
Francisco police detective who suggested that LaVey might be able to start
his own religion. Shortly after his second daughter was born, LaVey shaved
his head like the Yazidi devil worshippers and announced Year One of the
Age of Satanism.

An age of publicity resulted. Dressed in a devil outfit as campy as a Halloween costume, LaVey said a weekly tongue-in-cheek Black Mass over a naked girl used as an altar. He conducted a Satanic wedding, a Satanic baptism (of the new daughter), and a Satanic funeral. Press coverage was international, LaVey was called the Black Pope and the Saint Paul of Satanism, and he soon claimed a membership of ten thousand. Jayne Mansfield asked to meet him and was made an honorary priestess; LaVey later maintained that the car accident in which she died was the result of a curse he placed on her abusive boyfriend, who also perished in the crash. LaVey appeared in documentaries, in magazines, as a wax statue, and consulted on a number of films. His first biographer, a freelance journalist, became a high priest of the church.

In the initial years, the Church of Satan recalled the Hell-Fire Club, another nineteenth-century proto-Pagan group, which endorsed Epicureanism and claimed to appeal to society's upper strata. But a sociologist who studied LaVey's organization for more than two years came away thinking that, as a religion, the Church of Satan was most effective for those with a simpler need.

> *The Satanist is training himself to be assertive and powerful* as an individual. *Although he draws a sense of security from his association with powerful forces, he is finding inner sources of strength. He is casting off the need for powerful gods to protect and care for him, insisting that he is strong enough to care for himself. He commands the gods and does not beseech them. He is turning from an ethereal and other-worldly orientation to a somewhat more realistic assessment and concern with the mundane and real world.*
>
> *Perhaps it is for this reason that marginal religions such as the Church of [Satan] should be encouraged. They appear in many cases to be revitalizations that spring, in response to a changing world, more directly from the needs of the individuals who comprise their membership.*

But this wasn't what LaVey had in mind when the Church of Satan began a reorganization sometime around 1970. Satire was always an important component of Satanic rituals, but LaVey wanted the church to be more than a gang of pranksters. He drew a distinction between social misfits and productive members of society who nevertheless felt alienated, and he turned the church into a loose cabal that would take it beyond the structures of organized religion. There would be no churches, only private altars in homes. It would be a religion beyond the reach of consumerism. In 1975, a schism occurred within the church over how priesthoods were obtained and the literalness of the Devil. A significant number of officers defected and formed the Church of Satan's main rival, the Temple of Set.

LaVey set about a more reclusive existence, concentrating on writing and his odd collections. Though no one was quite sure what it had to do with Satanism, LaVey announced plans to build artificial humans, mannequins that could be used as sex substitutes. He remained a Satanic pied piper—he appeared to have a knack for encountering those who would eventually become serial killers—but he lay low during the Satanic scare of the eighties, a recovered-memory debacle stemming from reports of child abuse at day-care centers. LaVey fell out with his second wife and fell in with Blanche. Just before Xerxes came along, a *Rolling Stone* journalist asked LaVey if he'd ever tried to have sex with one of his dolls. He had, he said, but an earthquake had begun almost immediately, so he'd stopped because he'd figured God was trying to tell him something. "God" was only a figure of speech, he said, but the journalist pressed a little further to get at what he really believed. LaVey described "a balance of nature. A natural order. That's God. And that's Satan. Satan is God."

The journalist dug into LaVey's history as well. An orchestra LaVey claimed to have played with had not existed when he said it had. The circus acts in which he'd performed were actually part of an entirely different circus than the one he'd cited. The Marilyn Monroe story was denied by the owner of the club where she was supposed to have danced. The San Francisco Police Department had no record of LaVey's employment, and the City of San Francisco had never had a city organist. Worst of all, the birth record the journalist dredged up in Chicago listed a "Howard Stanton Levey" born on LaVey's same birth date. Confronted with the discrepancies, LaVey threatened the journalist's family and then asked that his myth not be dispelled.

Which maybe wasn't so far off the point. William James—in the same lectures in which he described the hollow culture of a world without evil—argued that belief in will could translate into action, and that the way to generate an emotion was to act as though it already existed. "Action seems to follow feeling, but really action and feeling go together," James wrote. This was an elaboration on an idea he had first described in *The Principles of Psychology*, what later became known as the James-Lange theory of emotion. Feeling, particularly in the "coarser" emotions, actually followed action. We ran from the bear, and then felt fear. We sobbed, and then felt sorrow. Once one recognized this, it became apparent that the process could be reversed: it was possible to manipulate feeling by willing action. Smiling *made* one happy. To feel brave, act *as if* you were brave. In *Varieties,* this idea was ratcheted up to God—borrowing a bit from both Kant and John Stuart Mill—and the "as if" was adopted not to curtail loss as in a wager, but as a creative energizing strategy:

> *We can act* as if *there were a God; feel* as if *we were free; consider Nature* as if *she were full of special designs; lay plans* as if *we were to be immortal; and we find then that these words do make a genuine difference in our moral life.*

Satanists became interesting and potent people precisely because they acted as though they were interesting and potent, and because Christian fear and Western duality enabled it all. LaVey's story proved that myth and belief helped generate fact. The Church of Satan existed: it had created Xerxes, and though the Black House was gone another had appeared in its place. To believe that ritual mattered without belief in the object of worship was to acknowledge that one of the parties fooled in the process was oneself. The applied psychology of Satanism was self-application, reverse psychology, Jamesian.

5. EVIL FRANKLY ACCEPTED

We gathered in the Library of Antiquity after our feast, the preritual jitters tensing up an intimate cocktail gathering serenaded first by the Mediaeval Baebes on the stereo, then a recording of the Red Army Choir. I flipped through a stack of Satanist magazines from Central, reading one of the personalized inscriptions to Robert and Di: "Enjoy the transcendent ooze— Hail Satan!" Over in a corner, Di gossiped to Ian about a new breed of Satanist that had come about in the late nineties. "I don't take any shit from those little gothlings," she said. Robert challenged me to a chess game on an ornate set, but he didn't like my fifth move. "You're mean," he said. "Damn you."

Then he laughed, thank God.

The grotto gathered around us as we played. Greg, for some reason, announced that he had done a master's thesis on Fascist Germany. At first this seemed the logical extension of Greg's high-strung temperament, a mood that Satanism hadn't quite been able to defuse and that the others sometimes noted with sly smiles. Satanists didn't have to like one another, after all. But, like a secret accidentally slipped, Hitler and Fascism now seemed to keep popping up as a subject as Robert and I moved back and forth on the board. The Nazi connection was all part of the LaVey myth. The führer's fascination with the occult, a rumored Nazi organization called the Black Order of Satanists, and Nazi imagery later employed in Church of Satan rituals had all helped to form Satanism's foundation of authority and power. Nazism was just as effective as Satan in generating fear in others, and LaVey had not hesitated to use it. And now our gathering began to feel less like a cocktail party and more like a Nazi ball. Di claimed that Canada's largest bookseller had just been bought by a Jewish-owned company. All the *Mein Kampf*s had disappeared. It was too bad, she said, because the book had just been reprinted with a nice orange cover. Look, here was a copy, in fact; Di passed it around.

I looked at the book but hid my reaction. Long before the Church of Satan had borrowed from Fascism, Fascism had borrowed from James's Pragmatism. Mussolini had once listed James as one of his inspirations, claiming that Fascism owed a great deal to Pragmatism. "James taught me that an action should be judged by its results rather than by its doctrinary basis," the dictator had said.

When the chess game was over, Rose announced that it was time for ritual. He and Jen went downstairs to prepare. Robert found me a hooded robe, black with purple trim; it weighed on me like chain mail. Di handed out slips of special paper on which we would inscribe desires that we would sacrifice to an open flame. "Heavy book sales," she suggested for my wish. Then she leered through her curls. "Or perhaps you were hoping for something more immediate."

I smiled shyly. I was left alone for a moment as the others got dressed or conferred with Rose on the details of their roles in the ritual. The stereo ran through to more of LaVey's haunting organ music. Now I was in my third Satanic scare. The fountain pyramid dripped beside me, I was dressed in a Benedictine's robe meant ironically, I was buzzed on some elaborate wine, and I had a Satanic wish in my pocket. I thought about getting out of there. Here was my plan: I could grab one of the sword canes, sneak out past the gargoyles, and run apostate through the Canadian black to the neighbor with his giant cross. I was scared not for myself this time, but perhaps for the thought that James, by advocating pluralism and, rhetorically, on a number of occasions, anarchy (to a friend: "All the evil in the world comes from the law and the priests and the sooner these two things are abolished the better"), had accidentally given momentum to movements based in hate.

Only, it wasn't so. It had been demonstrated that though Mussolini had flirted with philosophy he had invoked James, an American, only for propaganda. The dictator couldn't even be shown to have read *Pragmatism*. Still, James had staked out freedom for religious movements, and, like that old Heisenbergian rule, he had enabled them to some extent. He was the serpent that lay across Satanism. LaVey had claimed that Charles Manson, Hitler, and LaVey himself were the twentieth century's keepers of evil, and if belief could generate good, I thought, then certainly it could generate bad as well. My Satanic scare was that I had misjudged the Satanists, that in trying to trick them into letting me meet Xerxes I had been tricked into thinking they weren't really evil, that there was no such thing. I had adopted James too deeply, too uncritically, and like him I was too willing to be duped. My scare was that Baudelaire had been right, after all: I had been fooled into thinking the Devil didn't exist.

Before I could make my break, Greg reappeared in a skull T-shirt, his own robe thrown over his arm. He was excited. I followed him downstairs to the action-figure room to wait with Ian. Greg warned me that the ritual might make us all feel a little drunk.

Di called us down the hallway.

The ritual chamber sat behind an innocuous black bookcase set into the wall at the end of a dead passage. The bookcase swung out on magic hinges. We took turns stepping through into the Black House's deepest socket, a hot, dark, candle-lit cell of a room with paneled black walls and a faux-stone floor. At the head of the room stood two pink-satin-lined coffins, upright but cockeyed alongside an altar strewn over with ritual paraphernalia, skulls and daggers, a couple of pitchforks, candles melting lewdly, and a few items borrowed from Buddhism or Christianity for the heresy value. A golden meter-wide Baphomet stared down at it all. Opposite was a false fireplace flanked by more swords and a large red trapezoid marked with a pitchfork symbol and *Caesar Nero* written in code. The room had a gong and a collection of battle-axes and a poster of LaVey with a hapless boa constrictor shawled over his shoulders. There was a sound system somewhere, and some kind of ritual sound track was playing, a deep-throated groan of music and drumbeats. Jen was standing in one of the coffins. She was wearing a long red wig, and had stripped down to a piece of lingerie that looked so uncomfortable it might have doubled as torture equipment.

The ritual began with Rose, the only one of us without a hood, turning quarter circles to tones Greg sounded on the gong. Rose lit a few candles on the altar and began in Latin: *"In nomine dei nostri Satanas Luciferi excelsi."* He gave a brief introduction, commanding the powers of darkness to come forth and join those of us who had rejected the false gods, we rare creatures treading the sinister path. Rose's writing was a little loose for my taste, but for him it was all in the delivery anyway, even innocuous phrases recited in a tone of dread and scorn. This room was a portal to the abyss, he said. Here we stood amidst the coils of Leviathan. It was the sigil of Baphomet that served as a gate to the undefiled wisdom that was to be read by the dark light of the black flame of Satan. Rose swiveled around to face his tiny congregation, his scalp already shiny with damp and light, lips curled back over a jagged maw of teeth, and his voice tickling us all in that place where LaVey was said to have had an extra vertebra.

"Oh, hear the names," Rose bellowed. "Baphomet! Abaddon! Mephistopheles! Astaroth! Typhon! Beelzebub! Bast! Diabolus! Lilith! Asmodeus! Melek T'aus!"

We chanted the names behind him and then we parodied communion, drinking from a chalice of ecstasy, an unholy grail, sipping at the infernal nectar of sin to rejoice in the damnation of the righteous prophecy. It was all a bit over the top, and if I was going to be feeling drunk at the end of it, it was because I'd already been tipsy before and because the chalice was filled with absinthe, I think. Apart from a smirk I got from Di, the ritual played out straight, its satire as deeply buried as a joke without a punch line, more mockery than fun. Rose and Robert began a tandem reading. Rose delivered explanations of the nine keys to Satanic wisdom, and Robert recited sections of the poetry of Sir Francis Dashwood, a founder of the Hell-Fire Club. Di periodically lit candles over the fireplace, and Greg sounded in on the gong. The drums on the sound system began to accelerate. Ian reached up to smear away the moisture gathered on his brow.

I wondered what James would have made of this religion so thick with bells and smells but steadfast in its skepticism. Ultimately, his own thinking took a turn the Satanists would have despised. In "The Moral Philosopher and Moral Life," written in 1891, James set out a view of the good that was sufficiently diabolical. The "good" was what *felt* good. For James, the mind and body were intimately connected, emotion and sensation flip sides of a coin forever spinning. In a world where there was just a single person, he wrote, there would be no reason to even consider a variety of good beyond that which was viscerally pleasing. "Surely, there is no *status* for good and evil to exist in, in a purely insentient world. . . . In its mere capacity, a thing can be no more good or bad than it can be pleasant or painful." In the world of the solitary thinker, "so far as he feels anything to be good, he *makes* it good. It *is* good, for him." This thinker became a kind of divinity, steeped in moral solitude. But the introduction of a second thinker to that universe created a complexity of moral systems, dueling preferences and goods, a "moral dualism." And it was this kind of duality, in which one's desires and indulgences might run contrary to another's, that proved to James that ethics were distinct from God. No good, no desire, ought to be denied, and the best possible universe was the one in which the most possible desires could be indulged. This was the *goodest* universe, and "the best simply imaginary world would be the one in which *every* demand was gratified as soon as made."

But James's Satanic streak began to veer away from there. For what kind of ethical system could apply to a pluralism "in which individual minds are the measures of all things, and in which no one 'objective' truth, but only a multitude of 'subjective' opinions, can be found?" A system of complete indulgence was impractical and "the actually possible in the world is vastly narrower than all that is demanded." James saw only two choices. One, the choice of most philosophical systems, was to try to create a system that enacted a singular set of rules for all to follow. James likened this to trying to hold back an ocean with a broom. Or, he wrote, one could believe that the best possible world was the one in which the *most* goods were possible, the *most* demands met. "There is but one unconditional commandment, which is that we should seek incessantly, with fear and trembling, so to vote and to act as to bring about the very largest total universe of good which we can see."

From there James turned decidedly away from Satanism, because ultimately the argument turned to God. The desire for the greatest good could manifest in two kinds of moods, he wrote. Like the healthy-minded and the sick souls, it was another Jamesian bifurcation. The *easy-going* mood sought as its good only to avoid present ills, but the *strenuous* mood, which could accept present sacrifice in exchange for a greater good over time, was the preferable choice. And it was God—even as an indulgence—that triggered the strenuous mood:

> *The capacity of the strenuous mood lies so deep down among our natural human possibilities that even if there were no metaphysical or traditional grounds for believing in a God, men would postulate one simply as a pretext for living hard, and getting out of the game of existence its keenest possibilities of zest. Our attitude towards concrete evils is entirely different in a world where we believe there are none but finite demanders, from what it is in one where we joyously face tragedy for an infinite demander's sake. Every sort of energy and endurance, of courage and capacity for handling life's evils, is set free in those who have religious faith. For this reason the strenuous type of character will on the battle-field of human history always outwear the easy-going type, and religion will drive irreligion to the wall.*

Jen was beginning to get uncomfortable in the coffin, shifting back and forth on her feet. I felt sorry for her, but it would be a lie to say that I didn't look at her from time to time, that her nakedness did not add energy to the chamber. Which maybe proved that Satanism had a point to make too. It's not God that's compelling in a ritual—it's reverence, for God, for anything. The strenuous mood is interactive, from one person to the next; you see it in another, you want it in yourself. God was the one indulgence that Satanism would not allow. But for a certain brand of person, Satanism must exist *because* Satan did not, and these people, hooded and smirking, playing with evil and Fascism, climbing society's trapezoid with the help of a crazy inverted belief—they were more poignant than potent. They posed no real threat. They were not the easy-going type, and they had found a home. And even if they were evil, maybe the world needed them, too, for the flavor they added to it.

When it came time to offer our requests, we took turns moving forward to stab our slips of paper onto the point of a heavy knife and hold them over a candle, where they exploded softly. Di approached the altar, kissed the skull, and said, "Oh, my beautiful and dreaded Leviathan, hear my request tonight." Ian recited something in Latin. Greg stepped forward and sliced his hand on the knife; later he would make sure that we all knew he had actually bled. Then it was my turn. I took the knife from Greg and pushed my slip of paper onto the blade. I stepped up to the flame and thought about the word I had written. James had once said, "An evil frankly accepted loses half its sting and all its terror." I was no longer afraid of the Satanists. I burned my wish.

"Shemhamforash," I said.

"Shemhamforash!" the grotto called behind me.

"Hail Satan."

"Hail Satan! Hail Satan! Hail Satan!"

6. Birthmark

Six months later, back in California, I met Satan Xerxes at a coffeehouse a few days after my dinner with Blanche. Waiting inside, I spotted the two of them walking outside on the street, just as I had with Peter Gilmore in New York, their film-noiry outfits dissonant with the pale ache of the California winter sun. Xerxes wore a felt hat and a blazer, a little red tie, and wrinkled khakis like a prep school kid. His hair was as messy as Tom Sawyer's, and he had one mole between his eyes and another on his lower lip, and you just had to think twice about birthmarks on a boy named Satan.

I shook Xerxes' hand when they came inside. I was speechless. Satanism didn't seem to help us at all with the awkward moment that comes about when one party has been waiting for another. Besides, I need now to admit, I was distracted by thoughts of an old child-of-Satan movie, not *Rosemary's Baby,* but another where the demon child actually grows into preadolescence before his telltale marks are uncovered, and the hero, once he makes the horrid discovery, hesitates too long before sacrificing the boy—just long enough so that Satan comes to thrive again in the world. I was paralyzed in the face of Satan Xerxes. I was the first journalist to get to meet him, Blanche had told me, and I was thinking now that it was probably a good idea that they were keeping him, for the most part, under the media radar.

Historically, there are perhaps as many Satan-spawns-a-child stories as contract-with-the-Devil stories, but it's only of late that they have become cautionary tales in which Satan's child survives and the return of the Devil's influence appears imminent. Medieval literature teems with children of demons remarkable for precociousness or rapid growth. In 1275, a historical account told of a sixty-five-year-old woman burned at the stake after she bore a child with a wolf's head and a serpent's tail. A whole class of stories uses the Satan's child motif to reiterate the persuasiveness of the Christian message: Satan tries reproduction in a final power grab as his influence wanes. In one of these tales the child becomes the Merlin legend: the Devil rapes a noble girl who forgot to genuflect before going to bed, and she bears a boy, Merlin, whose demonic heritage is apparent from his hairy appearance. The Duchess of Normandy, in a similar story eventually turned into an opera, resorts to Satan when God won't provide for her barrenness, producing Robert the Devil, a roguish tyke. Both Merlin and Robert exhibited the magic and power of their heritage, but these stories and others proved to be variations on a theme in which the Devil's tricks were plentiful but insufficient—the children turned to God in the end and ascended to Heaven.

Xerxes seemed to be living a pretty normal life for a homeschooled kid. He was an attentive boy, sedate in the way of children who have spent more time around adults than other children, and once we sat down with our coffees he said that he might want to be a psychiatrist someday because he was both a good talker and a good listener. The exploding-baseball ritual came up again. "I don't know baseball," Xerxes said. "I'm a geek!" He considered his video-game box his best friend, he said, and he admitted that he had once hugged it when he came home from a camping trip.

"Do you remember your father?" I said.

"I do. Sometimes it's almost like I dream about him. It sounds weird but it's true."

"He went through an initiation ritual when he was six," Blanche said. "He chose it."

"I chose it," Xerxes reiterated, and then he told us a theory he had about the brain: that our bodies were just shells for its independent organism. I was beginning to like Xerxes. He was smart, precocious without conceit, presumptuous but not particularly righteous.

"I started as a Christian," he said. "Then I was Jewish. I was even a Hindu, maybe. Then I was an Atheist. Now I'm this. All kids follow the religion of their parents."

It was easy to suspect that Xerxes had been subjected to indoctrination, and surely his talk smacked of a script trying to prove that this wasn't the case. But indoctrination is as stigmatized a concept as cult, or magic, or Satan. Cults are religions of which one does not approve, *magic* is another word for *miracle,* Satan is the other guy's god, and all those misdefinitions are proof of fear's tendency to label. Xerxes was right: children did tend to follow the religion of their parents. And when we approved of it, it was evidence of values. Except for Satanism. Satanism appealed to those who felt compelled to reject the religion of their parents, and those children who had grown up as Satanists—LaVey's daughters—had ultimately turned against him. Even Blanche had said that all children question the values of their parents, the values with which they are raised. Xerxes was beginning to rebel if only because he had not yet fulfilled his mother's prophecy.

I asked Xerxes what he thought the definition of religion was.

He ran it through the organism of his brain. "Religion doesn't mean anything. But without religion, the world would be a bland place. Religion makes people feel good. It helps the world go around."

It was James in a boy's nutshell. His mother beamed.

1890–1898

"How well one has to be, to be ill!" Alice James, the sister, wrote in her secret diary. Alice's health problems received a variety of diagnoses over the years—nervous hyperesthesia, spinal neurosis, rheumatic gout—all of which helped her not at all as she began to fail. In 1891, she wrote of her brothers, beginning with Henry:

> *Within the last year he has published* The Tragic Muse, *brought out* The American, *and written a play,* Mrs. Vibert . . . *combined with William's* Psychology, *not a bad show for one family! especially if I get myself dead, the hardest job of all.*

Alice had suffered for so long that it came as a relief as much as a shock to everyone when she found a lump in her breast in May 1891. "To him who waits, all things come!" she wrote on the thirty-first. William suggested hypnotism and consulted the medium Leonora Piper about Alice, and finally advised her to take as much morphine as she desired—that was what opium was for, he said. "I know you've never cared for life," he wrote to her, and he tried consoling her with the argument that the mind could not simply go "out" when so much of its functioning remained hidden for most of our lives. Alice dismissed this and told William that he was just now, at age fifty, coming to the wisdom she had known at fifteen. Alice's biographer compared the agony of her deathbed to that of Ivan Ilyich. On March 5, 1892, she sent William a telegram that read, "Tenderest love to all farewell Am going soon." She died the next day.

Katharine Loring arranged to have Alice's diary typewritten. Four copies were printed. Loring waited until 1894 to send one each to William and Henry. Henry was scandalized that his sister had kept a diary under his nose, and that she had included in it so many familiar names. William thought it was a significant literary effort and ought to be published. He shared his copy with a friend, prefacing it with a description that still holds true:

> *Some parts of it will say nothing to you for lack of a key to the persons etc.; some will bore you but there are some beautiful things well said, and beside the dramatic pathos as it nears the end—she with her cancer—it seems to me a very vivid expression of one of the most vivid and able characters I ever knew.*

The diary wasn't published in its entirety until 1964.

The 1890s saw James complete a transformation from experimental psychologist to religious scholar and philosopher. He maintained his full teaching load, but now began to offer courses focusing exclusively on abnormal psychology. Abnormal psychology was the gremlin in the works of psychology. James had written *Principles* without a theory of consciousness because most theories of consciousness that existed were easy enough to dispel with a quick glance into abnormal behavior. Depressed in 1893, James attended eighteen sittings with a Christian Science practitioner and reported better sleep. He wondered how the practitioner would do with patients in a lunatic asylum. In the mid-1890s, he turned his attention to abnormal states with the hope of finding cures, or at least ways to alleviate symptoms—sometimes his own.

The posts to which James was now appointed reflect the academic world's ongoing descent into fragmentation: in 1893, he was elected president of both the American Association of Psychologists and the British Society for Psychical Research. He would have preferred the latter. Much later, James wrote to a friend that he regretted it when studies of his work focused exclusively on what he called his "psychological phase, which I care little for, now, and never cared much." By the spring of 1892, he was working to recruit Hugo Münsterberg, then a promising young German psychologist, to come to Harvard to take over the experimental laboratory James had founded. James had never enjoyed lab work, and the hire would free him for philosophy. The relationship with Münsterberg stands as evidence of James's departure from psychology. The two men exchanged friendly letters for years (James once assured Münsterberg that Harvard was not a school one needed to be ashamed of), but Münsterberg and others would eventually attempt to discredit James's view of psychology and turn the whole of it toward the German laboratory model. Long before then, the relationship suffered a strain when James convinced his more cynical friend to attend a séance and Münsterberg caught the medium moving a table with her foot. The men's dealings remained cordial, but James would later take offense when it appeared that Münsterberg, given temporary reign over their academic department at Harvard, would displace him completely.

James was on sabbatical for 1892–93, and the family traveled across Europe for the period. To this point in his life, James had done a fair job of insulating himself from the real work of child rearing, and travel with a full family without the work of a book to shield him tested his patience and his marriage. A row with Alice on the trip was their eldest son's first revelation "of the fact that two people who love each other can hurt each other so cruelly." In midlife, the James marriage assumed a pattern of William delivering outbursts, followed in short order by emphatic apologies to Alice.

The usual belief among biographers is that when the family returned home, psychology was out of James's system completely, and his thinking turned more toward philosophy. The truth is that his philosophy would always be shot through with a psychology outside the mainstream. And arguably, for James, philosophy was just as flawed. "Plato, Locke, Spinoza, Mill, Caird, Hegel," he wrote in *Pragmatism,* "these names are little more than reminders of as many curious personal ways of falling short." And later: "Philosophy has often been defined as the quest or the vision of the world's unity. . . . But how about the *variety* in things?" In late 1896 he gave a series of lectures on abnormal states that served almost as a prototype for *The Varieties of Religious Experience,* with talks entitled "Genius," "Witchcraft," "Dreams and Hypnotism," and "Demoniacal Possession." All were equal subjects of inquiry, phenomena that must be incorporated, he thought, into any description of consciousness that aspired to universal law.

By then James was a well-traveled lecturer. Psychology may have receded into his imagination—he had at least self-exorcised adherence to the strict laboratory approach—but for the time being it was still the family's bread and butter. Their two houses both required servants, and an attendant was needed for the horses at Chocorua. *Principles* offered James added income if he dumbed it down and took it to the public. After he returned from sabbatical he took the lecture show on the road, delivering the series to gatherings of schoolteachers in Boston, Norwich, Colorado Springs, Chicago, and Buffalo. By his own admission, the lectures were *Principles* without the "analytical technicality," focusing exclusively on practical application. The result was "popular in the extreme."

By all accounts James was an engaging speaker, entertaining in manner and in the vivid descriptions that characterized all his work. His talks were dotted with self-effacement, comic efforts at anticipating the objections of his audience, and clever introspection on everyday experience that shed psychological insight. His audiences in the mid-nineties were made up mostly of young women. James complained of the dimness of these listeners, of how long it took them to move from one idea to another, and he once wrote to Henry that lectures "have an awful side (when not academic) . . . it is a sort of prostitution of one's person." James often threatened to abandon the lecture circuit, but, as with teaching, it energized him more than he was willing to admit. Too, the fact that he was now surrounded by young women certainly wasn't unwelcome—once, a woman admitted to James that she kept a portrait of him in her bedroom.

We tend now to think of a penchant for flirtation as a "weakness," but James would not have described it that way. Through the 1890s he made a habit of courting intellectually flirtatious relationships with much younger women, high achievers who satisfied a splinter of himself that his wife could not touch. A fight with Alice had erupted when William admitted that one of these relationships had evolved into a single kiss. "I often have a desire to kiss people," he wrote to her later,

> *(which I regret to say I have never yielded to except in the one instance you know)—but to repress which seems to me churlish and inhuman. It has nothing to do with any deeper confidence, and doesn't seem to me to conflict with any preexistent relation of the* heart; *it is merely a natural expression of passing tenderness and cordiality.*

James's correspondence is loosely spattered with friendly rendezvous that Alice may or may not have been aware of, but if there was ever any evidence of extramarital relationships it was excised as Alice edited the letters. In 1897, James revealed to his wife his feelings on the odd balance they achieved in middle age:

> *You write of the "peace" that you now have, I being gone. How sad it is that two people who live but for each other should find so much "peace" when parted. Yesterday afternoon I was haunted by the tho't of your pale*

*face, transparent and beautiful in bed, after each of those childbirths, still
turning to me and anxious to do something for me. Darling, I do not
forget!*

James waited several years to collect the efforts of his road trips. *Talks to
Teachers* appeared in 1899. He published the lectures with the hope that he
would "remove [him]self from the temptation ever to give them again."
The negotiations for *Talks* coincided with those for *The Will to Believe,* published in 1897.

The Will to Believe was the first of James's books that attempted to syn-
thesize the true pluralism of his thought. *Principles* had been, at least in part,
an elaborate assignment from Holt. The new volume included essays from
as far back as 1880, and staked out a multifaceted but consistent vision. In
the preface he introduced radical empiricism, a personal doctrine delineat-
ing which aspects of experience could or should be weighed in describing
reality. One must remain empirical, he argued, because all facts were hypotheses; and one must remain radical because some facts remained beyond
our ability to easily catalog them. Radical empiricism confronted both reality and how we perceived it, and argued for the value of the subjective,
particularly in a world dividing itself into materialistic sects. In other
words, he was preparing to present the idea that pluralism outperformed
monism, and that variety itself could help shape the foundation of a belief.

The Will to Believe contained ten essays. In "The Sentiment of Rationality," James announced that what he wanted to do was soften the confession
that no real account of experience can be given, and "reconcile us with
our impotence." In "Reflex Action and Theism," he argued that while
God was the natural belief of the mind, the living truth of the proposition
was another matter. "Great Men and Their Environments" and "The Importance of Individuals" defended free will on the argument that individual minds had in fact managed to change the course of history, and in "On
Some Hegelisms," James attacked the bugbear of the neo-Hegelian Absolute, which he considered a philosophical monistic God-substitute just as
irrational as the thing it wanted to displace.

The title essay was the most famous of the book, though James came to
regret his word choice in the matter. "The Will to Believe" presented the
argument that for "non-momentous occasions," issues over which "objective nature" could offer no concrete answer, one should have the *right* to
believe whatever worked best for oneself. That is, if logic and reason could

give us nothing firm on, say, the idea of God, then we should each be free to choose whichever idea worked best for us, whichever had the most "cash-value." "We ought," James wrote, "delicately and profoundly to re-spect one another's mental freedom—then only shall we bring about the intellectual republic."

This was already well down the road toward Pragmatism, but before tackling it head-on, James first, as he wrote to a friend, needed to defend "'experience' against 'philosophy' as being the real backbone of the world's religious life." *Varieties* was in his sights. He had an old score to settle, with his father, and a pact with his wife besides. "You must not leave me," he had written to Alice in 1883,

> *till I understand a little more of the value and meaning of religion in Father's sense, in the mental life and destiny of man. It is not the* one *thing needful, as he said. But it is needful with the rest. My friends leave it altogether out. I as his son (if for no other reason) must help it to its rights in their eyes. And for that reason I must learn to interpret it aright as I have never done, and you must help me.*

𝕬𝖚𝖙𝖍𝖔𝖗

Every now and then, however, some one is born with the right to be original, and his revolutionary thought or action may bear prosperous fruit. He may replace old "laws of nature" by better ones; he may, by breaking old moral rules in a certain place, bring in a total condition of things more ideal than would have followed had the rules been kept.

—William James

It is not certain that our time has lacked gods. Many have been promised, usually stupid or cowardly ones. Our time does, on the other hand, seem to lack a dictionary.

—Albert Camus

1. The Tiny Bridge

When Julian Jaynes published an explanation of the birth of God in *The Origin of Consciousness in the Breakdown of the Bicameral Mind* in the late 1970s, the initial reaction was that he had produced a work on the order of Freud or Darwin. One reviewer claimed the book rendered whole library shelves obsolete. Jaynes's background was as varied as William James's: he taught psychology at Princeton for more than two decades; he served as a visiting lecturer at other universities in English, philosophy, and archaeology departments; he contributed to courses in medical schools and helped to edit scholarly journals dedicated to the study of behavior and brain chemistry. *The Origin of Consciousness in the Breakdown of the Bicameral Mind* was his only book.

Theories of demons predating divinities aside, most modern thinking on the origin of God tends to stick to the evidence of cave paintings and early burial rituals. These had generated a pantheon of vague hypotheses of creation myths and divine forms, but no one was really sure which had come first, gods, souls, or the afterlife. The basic belief was that religion had assumed a complex form including all these elements by the fifth or sixth millennium B.C.

Jaynes disagreed with all of that, and, really, *Origin* set out to explain more than just the birth of God. His main proposition came as a shock. Early man, he argued, exhibited a kind of split-mindedness, the hemispheres of the brain unevolved and operating independently. In short, everyone before roughly 3000 B.C. was operationally schizophrenic, effectively unconscious, ruled over by hallucinatory inner voices. This was the bicameral mind.

That men could be "unconscious" but still productive was the tough part to swallow. Consciousness was not required for thought, Jaynes claimed. He offered laboratory evidence suggesting that all the important facets of thinking could work without it, and claimed that whole towns and small civilizations had emerged without individual subjective awareness. This put Jaynes firmly into the behaviorist school of psychology. Consciousness was an unnecessary sidecar, he said, "the shadow that loyally walks step for step beside the pedestrian, but is quite unable to influence his journey."★

Just as in the religious movements I was visiting, William James seemed to pop up a lot in Jaynes's thinking. First, Jaynes cited a chapter of *The Principles of Psychology* as containing the clearest refutation of Huxley's "conscious automata" theory of man. But then Jaynes attacked the alternative. Our best conception of consciousness, William James's stream of it (no citation this time), wasn't a theory at all. At best, it was an inexact metaphor for how subjective consciousness perceived itself. Metaphors and narratization, Jaynes wrote, were features of consciousness but not its origin or nature. William James would have agreed. Consciousness was, and is, psychology's big unanswered question. Behaviorism had essentially banished it, and psychoanalysis had worked it into a simplistic system.

It's an exaggeration to say that Jaynes likened his bicameral mind strictly to schizophrenia. Rather, he described an earlier physiology of the brain that was more susceptible to the kind of auditory hallucinations known to occur in healthy people exposed to stresses. Never far from James, Jaynes used data from the Society for Psychical Research to claim that 7.8 percent of normal men and 12 percent of normal women had experienced some kind of hallucination. He either ignored or was unaware that William James had conducted surveys on this same question. James's results were more balanced between the genders. In 1892, he found that 13.5 percent of the normal population reported hallucinations. The number went up slightly four years later.

And hallucinations were where Jaynes's god came into the picture. Split into distinct sections, the bicameral mind, in moments of stress or need, essentially consulted itself, perceiving hallucinations that took the form of self-commands. Men understood this as gods. The mind was split between an executive-god portion and a lower, more common portion that was just the man. Even this echoed James, who had suggested in *Varieties* that the mind was split between an "official self" and a "subliminal self." For James, our basic ignorance of consciousness was directly related to our ignorance

---

★Jaynes cribbed from James. *The Principles of Psychology:* "So the melody floats from the harp-string, but neither checks nor quickens its vibrations; so the shadow runs alongside the pedestrian, but in no way influences his steps" (p. 137).

of anatomy. He once wrote to Oliver Wendell Holmes that "psychology is not *à l'ordre du jour* until some as yet unforeseen steps are made in the physiology of the nervous system." Julian Jaynes seemed to have concluded that those steps had been made: brain cartography had discovered physiological linkages between that part of the brain responsible for language and that part tied to hallucinations. "Here then," Jaynes wrote, "is the tiny bridge across which came the directions which built our civilizations and founded the world's religions."

Jaynes turned literary critic to show that the bicameral mind had been possible five thousand years ago. The theory made easy work of the characters of the *Iliad* and the Gilgamesh legend. The old epics' action-packed plots were just what one would expect from a bicameral people. The texts lacked words for conscious thought, and characters openly consulted gods. Gods, then, were man's volition. Deaths triggered hallucinations; the dead were often called gods. Jaynes's first god was a dead king whose voice echoed in those who remembered him. This explained the primitive practice of burying the dead with food and provisions—dead kings particularly so.

The breakdown of the bicameral mind—the emergence of consciousness—took a thousand years and had multiple causes. First, the success of bicameral systems engineered their own failure. Communities grew larger but were unprepared for the stress of encountering other bicameral communities, as became inevitable. Next, written language helped. The ancient words from which we get *hieroglyphics* and *hieratic* meant, literally, "writing of the gods," and early reading was closely associated with "hearing" written texts. As written language filtered through a society, the authority of the gods was challenged. Finally, the millennium beginning in 2000 B.C. saw a series of catastrophic geologic changes to the planet that forced bicameral populations to flee their homes. The gods, their selves, didn't know what to do. In the Gilgamesh legend the gods flee to Heaven out of fear of a great flood.

A 1230 B.C. Assyrian carving depicting a living king kneeling before an empty throne was the first evidence of the departure of the gods. "The mighty themes of the religions of the world are here sounded for the first time," Jaynes wrote. The gods receded into the sky, and prayer and worship emerged as men tried to communicate with a force that seemed to have forsaken them. Consciousness evolved to contend with growth that felt like abandonment. The character and plot of the *Odyssey*—strikingly different from the *Iliad*—revealed the subterfuges available to minds bursting into conscious awareness. "The whole long song is an odyssey toward subjective identity," Jaynes wrote. By the time he turned to the Bible, he had established the bicameral mind not only as an origin of consciousness and the birth of God, but as a literary theory explaining all of ancient literature: the fall of man was the breakdown of the bicameral mind, and the bicameral period was our lost Eden.

Man was reluctant to let the bicameral mind go. Jaynes cited an age of prophets of questionable mental status and civilizations that for a thousand years left their most important decisions to oracles who spoke the will of gods. For a time, Jaynes wrote, man could will a return to the bicameral mind just as modern man now wills a belief in free will. He failed again to cite William James on this point, and when he described modern consciousness as a "buzzing cloud of whys and wherefores," he seemed to be hearing the oft-quoted "great blooming buzzing confusion" that James had used to describe the consciousness of a child.

After the initial hype of Jaynes's work faded, critical voices began to appear. Reviewers homed in on the theory's arrogance. A prominent William James scholar claimed that the main problem with Jaynes was that he did not seem to have understood what James meant by stream of consciousness. A scholarly treatment of Jaynes linked him with a whole field of theories relying on unfalsifiability: "They are products not of the scientific world view but of an altogether different world view, one that can best be characterized as poetic or religious in nature." Jaynes acknowledged as much himself, but tied the bicameral hypothesis to science for that very reason: "In this period of transition from its religious basis, science often shares with the celestial maps of astrology, or a hundred other irrationalisms, the same nostalgia for the Final Answer, the One Truth, the Single Cause. . . . And this essay is no exception."

2. AUTHORS OF THE UNIVERSE

Again like William James, Julian Jaynes had a literary flair that probably cost him adherents in a stylistically bereft academic community. But even without style it's easy to see why the bicameral mind appealed to writers. "The first poets were gods," Jaynes wrote.

John Updike and Joyce Carol Oates are the godparents of turn-of-the-millennium American literature. The two have edited collections of the best American short stories and essays of the twentieth century, respectively, each of them including themselves and the other in their volumes. Both responded to Jaynes's theory.

Jaynes had emphasized the importance of metaphor and the grandeur of language to subjective identity. Consciousness narrated a world sensibly incomplete. Writing itself triggered consciousness, and the creative side of the brain was the seat of God. Updike* wrote, "When Julian Jaynes speculates that until later in the second millennium B.C. men had no consciousness but were automatically obeying the voices of gods dictating, usually in metre, from the right halves of their brains to the left halves, we are astounded but compelled to follow . . . through all the corroborative evidence." Oates responded more opaquely, exploring a split-mind hypothesis in several pseudonymous novels, their passages sometimes seeming divined from Jaynes, who was her colleague at Princeton. That she had written under a pseudonym, from a mystical alter identity, suggested a kind of bicameral residue.

That a pair of authors gravitated toward a theory celebrating narration would not have surprised William James at all. "If we follow any one of them," he wrote, meaning either theologies or philosophies,

> *we do so in the exercise of our individual freedom, and build out our religion in the way most congruous with our personal susceptibilities. Among those susceptibilities intellectual ones play a decisive part.*

Varieties: "The saints are authors, *auctores,* increasers, of goodness."

The founder of Scientology, L. Ron Hubbard, was one of a small band of authors who helped sketch out the mechanism of modern science fiction in the 1930s. Scientology didn't have a God. And it had only one prayer, written in verse. It began with the hope that the "author of the universe" would help men come to understand their spiritual nature.

Scientology owned a lot of Hollywood. First there was the expansive campus and mother church off Sunset Boulevard, once a hospital. The cross street was L. Ron Hubbard Boulevard. Not far down the road was the L. Ron Hubbard Life Exhibition, a personal museum, and a bit farther west was Celebrity Centre International, a vast mansion that was one of half a

---

*Updike's short story about the 9/11 terrorist attacks was called "Varieties of Religious Experience."

dozen or so such facilities around the world, offering specialized courses to assist artists in their creativity. It was cordoned off by hedges and set on land spotted with ponds and gazebos. At the end of Hollywood's Walk of Stars stood Author Services, Inc., which referenced not Scientology's prayer but L. Ron Hubbard again—it was a five-story building with a full-time staff of twenty-four devoted entirely to handling Hubbard's written work. It was a literary agency for one man. Back up the Walk there was a large Scientology testing center, a contact point for bringing people into the church.

I got a motel room not far from the Celebrity Centre and staked out the testing center before I approached. Los Angeles cooked like an asphalt pancake, hot and ridiculous on the cracking griddle of California. I could feel the smog in my hair. It was about a week before L. Ron Hubbard's birthday celebration—one of two main Scientology holidays, along with the publication date of their central text, *Dianetics: The Modern Science of Mental Health*. For the birthday, six thousand Scientologists would cram into the Shrine Auditorium downtown for a videotaped presentation of a celebration held across the country the night before. Scientology owned Hollywood, but Los Angeles wasn't actually its headquarters. The church was made up of dozens of separate organizations (orgs), each claiming financial autonomy, all of them loosely overseen by a controversial group called the Sea Organization. The Sea Org was in Florida.

But I didn't know about that yet when I first went to Hollywood to research the church. By 2004, fifty years after formally becoming a religion, Scientology, arguably the most successful new religious movement of the twentieth century, appeared to have erased itself from the culture's data bank. I knew of rumors of litigations, I knew of prominent actors who were members, and I vaguely recalled television ads from the seventies about exploding volcanoes. But I didn't really know anything specific; and no one I knew knew anything. I went to them cold, the only group I visited without first announcing myself.

The testing center was settled in among all the familiar landmarks: Frederick's of Hollywood, the wax museum, Grauman's Chinese Theatre. It was staffed with two or three young people dressed in prep school fashions, and a slightly older and higher-ranking individual who remained hidden until important decisions needed to be made. One of the younger workers sometimes stood out in the street to proposition passersby, offering an E-Meter, a device used in Scientology therapy, for free demonstrations. I watched for a while from the other side of the street, then crossed and approached the young man positioned there. I'd read about it, I said. I was interested, I said. And that was all I had to say.

The basic decoration motif throughout all Scientology buildings blended corporate stereotype and lost adventurers' clubs. The bookcases and heavy desks were all dark-stained stuff, the couches were all hard, tight-stretched leather, and color schemes vied for the dreamy lulls of dusk and dawn. Scientology substituted *technology* for *word* in its religion—most everything was about spreading the "tech"—but this was the most futuristic thing about it; the rest of the time its talk and its fashions indulged in nostalgia for L. Ron Hubbard's youth, a kind of lost and necessary hopefulness. The front of the testing center strained to recall a one-room schoolhouse, with a couple of rows of small wooden desks all facing deeper into the room. I took three tests, a personality inventory, an IQ test, and some kind of association analysis. The first ran two hundred questions. Many were about depression, about whether I preferred to lead or follow, and some seemed designed to gauge whether I was answering questions the way people normally did. I'd spent so much time reading William James by then that it was actually more natural for me to guess at how he would have answered. So that's what I did. Then they gave me the IQ test, eighty questions in fifteen minutes. I was up to question four before I realized that part of the test was noticing that the numbering on the answer sheet ran right to left. I lost a minute erasing.

I finished with just a few seconds left. My test administrator seemed pleased. I was pleased that he was pleased. The association test took only five minutes, and when I was done I was led back to a hard couch to watch a video while my scores were tallied. It was then that I noticed what was perhaps the strangest thing about the testing center, a thing that would hold true for all the Scientology buildings I would enter. The walls were all bookcases, deep heavy expensive shelves, and they were all filled with books. The strange part was that it was all the same book, *Dianetics: The Modern Science of Mental Health,* the gleamy copies fanned decoratively, or the bright hardcover spines lined up with titles bold on the vertical. Scientology was a library of one author.

A young man I'll call Eric appeared with my test scores on a graph. He would read them like an electrocardiogram. He introduced himself, asked me who I was. I gave him William James's history instead of my own, starting circa 1870, when James was about to have his breakdown. I fudged the dates a little, killing his parents off a few years early: my father had been a mystic, I said, he had died recently, we'd disagreed about God even as we were very close, I was left a fair income, but now I was unsure what direction I wanted my life to take, I had read a great deal of philosophy and studied medicine but I had doubts about that, I knew I couldn't follow my father's religion, I had yet to find a meaningful relationship though sometimes I longed for women, and I sympathized a little with the occult because intuitively I knew that science did not have all the answers and that truth needed elasticity to be true.

"I see your pain," Eric said, indicating a crash on my graph lines. He circled the fixed point of my sadness in red ink for emphasis. "There's a good bit of philosophy in Scientology, you know. You can see a lot of it in Plato and Herbert Spencer."

"Really."

"Yes." Then Eric said, "Have you ever thought about being a writer?"

I stayed in James. In 1905, between writing *Varieties* and *Pragmatism,* James had described himself, in consecutive letters, as a "graphophobe" and a "graphomaniac."

"I have a brother who's a writer," I said. "He's a little vague for me."

"It seems like something you'd be good at."

"You think?"

"Well, you scored very high on the IQ test." Eric circled another dot. "Extraordinary, really . . . for someone walking in off the street."

I shrugged. "So is there a course or something I should enroll in?"

"Well, yes." Eric was used to a harder sell. "But are you sure you want to approach it so"—he jiggled his hands in the air as though juggling the words he might use—"journalistically?"

I told him I didn't think of it like that. I had read an article about Scientology written by someone outside the church, I said, and it had interested me. This much was true—that morning I'd read an article claiming that Scientology's rootedness in science fiction was precisely what made it a good example of the American occult. The article had been written by a doctoral student and was based on field research in Los Angeles, just the type I was doing, sort of. And the writer had provided a list of people and texts that Hubbard had claimed to be familiar with: Taoism, Descartes, Durant, Korzybski, Vedic hymns . . . and William James. But the article dated from the early seventies, before Scientology erased itself from history. I was seeking, I told Eric. I was in pain, I reminded him. And I had made the pilgrimage to Los Angeles to follow my interest.

"Okay," he said, and then he hedged into a roundabout pitch that concluded with a blunt query into how I would be paying for services.

"Cash."

He disappeared to consult with his higher-up, a woman in a corporate suit who eyed me once over before giving me the okay to head over to the mother church. Eric came along as an escort. I liked him, basically. I believed he believed he was helping me.

The mother church and campus was home to a variety of orgs, each in a separate building off L. Ron Hubbard Boulevard, some of them dedicated to the very highest levels of Scientology study. I would be encouraged to visit only the glass-fronted Dianetics Center off Sunset. Out near the street, a dated electronic marquee transmitted pixilated, grammatically incomplete rhetoric: DO YOU WANT BETTER RELATIONSHIPS? DO YOU WANT TO IMPROVE COMMUNICATION? Eric and I parked. The lobby inside churned with people intent on urgent matters. To the left was a pastry kiosk and several living rooms' worth of couches, ahead was a concierge desk, and to the right was another of Hubbard's private libraries, the selection now expanded to include the hundreds of books and pamphlets he'd written while he was alive. He died in 1986.

I met several workers (whose names I've changed): Oscar, a kind of Scientological gopher; Geraldo, a handsome Hispanic man; and Aaron, a slight, bespectacled man who would be the coordinator of the class I would take, the Hubbard Dianetics Seminar. Oscar gave me a ticket to the birthday celebration coming up and Eric helped me with some paperwork, doing a good bit of it for me, actually. But it was Geraldo who guided me through the church disclaimer, a lengthy legal document called the Religious Services Enrollment Application, Agreement and General Release (hereinafter "Release"). The title was printed in the swoopy font of a wedding invitation.

"Initial all these spots, then sign here at the back," Geraldo said. Then he caught himself. "Read it! Then sign."

The Release established L. Ron Hubbard (hereinafter "LRH") as an American author and philosopher, and described the etymologies of Scientology ("the study of knowing") and Dianetics ("through soul"). I initialed subsections that established that Scientology would not have any particular effect on me, and that I was not entering Scientology with the belief that it would cure me in any way. I agreed that the E-Meter was "not intended or effective for the diagnosis, treatment or prevention of any disease" and that "all mental problems are spiritual in nature." I also claimed that I had "no record of [having been] committed in an institution for mental or emotional disorders." I relinquished all rights to ever sue the church for anything, and no one I knew or would ever know in the future could sue on my behalf, either. I was in full agreement with the "religious belief" that psychiatric labels were a kind of cruddy way of talking about mental competency, and in the event that anyone ever tried to lock me up for so-called lack of competence, I fully expected Scientologists to intercede.

On the level of paperwork, the Release was less a contract with the Devil than a thirty-year variable-rate mortgage of my soul. Geraldo chatted me up as my hand cramped from the dozens of initialings. I repeated the James story, and Geraldo said he was sorry that my father had passed. He explained that the church could serve as a complement to membership in other religions and that there was nothing in Scientology one had to "believe" in. But then he looked at me with his dark salesman's eyes, poised to take mental note of my reaction, and tried out one of Scientology's basic postulates.

"But maybe he's not 'dead.' Maybe he's still out there. Maybe he's just waiting to enter another body."

"Maybe," I said. "Can I get a copy of this?"

"Sure."

But Geraldo forgot to get me a copy of the Release. He passed me back to Oscar so I could get a private viewing of the church's official orientation video. I already had a temporary ID card, but I would not formally be a member of the church until I saw the movie. Oscar took me to a small theater in the middle of the building, twenty or thirty empty seats that faded to black when he closed the door behind me. I sat and hugged my satchel. If a public-address system had suddenly begun a countdown that ended with the whole building blasting off from its foundation, I would not have been particularly surprised. But instead a movie screen lit up—it *was* Hollywood—and we, the audience, me anyway, we were suddenly flying through space, either in a ship or maybe just looking for a body, and we cruised through an asteroid belt, headed for Earth, and when we found it we zipped by some satellites and came in range of a transmission of synthesized organ chords calibrated to glory. We pierced the atmosphere and swished down to the surface for flybys of prominent Scientology buildings, the mother church in Los Angeles, the vast mansion that Hubbard had occupied in England for a while, and a cruise ship that served Scientology as a kind of floating monastery for high-level research.

The camera settled into a subjective point of view in Los Angeles. We encountered a young narrator who would guide us on a formal tour of the church. The man seemed like a zombie not because he was a Scientologist, I thought, but because he was a bad actor. Scientology teemed with bad actors. The movie rushed us through the L. Ron Hubbard Life Exhibition for a quick biography, and then it teleported us to one of the LRH libraries for some book recommendations. Here we visited with an official whose title was "LRH communicator," a woman who overread her lines but reminded us that the word *founder* also meant *author*. Next we stopped in with a director of processing, a balding man cast from the stereotype of Watergate intelligence officials. In a few short minutes he managed to lay out the battle Scientology waged against psychology and to demonstrate the gains that were possible through Scientology therapy.

From there the film eased into a montage of testimonials from actors and professionals. For the finale the narrator reappeared in a Scientology hallway, at the threshold of a chapel before services. The narrator began a tortured speech, overplaying his hand gestures, and when he finished he turned his back and walked through the doors and was consumed with rising light. As with all Scientology films, the text had been written by L. Ron Hubbard:

> *I hope that I've helped to answer some of your questions. . . . Something happened in the world that was a bright piece of hope for man. Such a thing occurs every few hundred, or a thousand, years. Some genius rises, and man takes a new step toward a better life. . . . Clouds loom over this culture and planet. In this short interval, in this one place, we have our freedom before us. We can arise above the decay, the final flash that will inevitably extinguish this planet. . . . Right this instant, you are at the threshold of your next trillion years. You will live it in shivering agonized darkness, or you will live it triumphantly in the light. . . . We are not making any claims for Dianetics and Scientology. It is you who, when you've experienced what can be, are the one that will make the claim. What is true, is true for you. . . . If you leave this room after seeing this film, and walk out and never mention Scientology*

again, you are perfectly free to do so. It would be stupid, but you can do it. You can also dive off a bridge, or blow your brains out, that is your choice. But . . . if you continue with Scientology, we will be very happy with you, and you will be very happy with you. . . . We here in this org are really just doormen to the great highway found and built by Ron into a better future. . . . You can have it, or you can deprive yourself of it. The choice is yours.

3. Admiral (Biography I)

Maybe ancient lore of war between angels and fallen angels is a depiction of the battle that erupts between a religion's adherents and its apostates. A sociologist told me that religious biographies were almost always fiction, and that apostates always lied. Among new religious movements in the United States, this conflict is best embodied in the ongoing campaign between Scientology's formidable Religious Technology Center and a small band of ex-Scientologists working as debunkers. The battleground is the biography of L. Ron Hubbard.

The Scientology version is shorter and happier.

Lafayette Ronald Hubbard was born on March 13, 1911, in Tilden, Nebraska, the son of a navy man. The family soon moved to Montana, where Ron displayed a tough western precociousness founded in good schooling. He learned to ride horses at three and a half. He read early, and began processing Greek philosophy and Shakespeare before the home fire. He befriended a local medicine man, "Old Tom," and was initiated into the Indian's Blackfeet tribe at six.

Ron's father received a posting in Seattle when the boy was twelve. Here, Ron entered the Boy Scouts and became the youngest Eagle Scout in the organization's history. A journey to Washington introduced him to the first U.S. Navy officer sent to study with Freud. Ron was interested in Freud, but psychoanalysis left too much unanswered. At sixteen, he began a series of voyages to Asia, travels that initiated a lifelong fascination with ethnology. He studied the practices of pygmies in the Philippines, Kayan shamans, the Chamorros of Guam. He traveled with nomadic bandits, gained access to Buddhist lamaseries, and uncovered ancient burial grounds on remote Polynesian islands. He became consumed with the question of why there was so much suffering in the world.

Back in the United States, Ron's father encouraged him to study engineering at George Washington University. Ron took the first class in nuclear physics offered in America. In time away from his course work, he conducted private experiments with the Koenig photometer, a device that convinced him that thought was measurable. He took his results to psychologists at George Washington, but they weren't interested. The West, he decided, was as bereft of answers as the East. He left college depressed.

Ron began a career as a pulp-fiction author in the thirties, and his substantial profits funded much of his eventual research into the human mind. He contributed thrilling adventure tales to more than thirty magazines. In the same period, he directed several shipborne expeditions, conducting surveys of Puerto Rico and charting maps of British Columbia and Alaska. Ron earned a license to sail any vessel on any ocean and was elected to membership in the exclusive Explorers Club in New York City. Eventually one of his adventure stories attracted the attention of Hollywood. He was called to Los Angeles to help with the screenplay for *Secret of Treasure Island,* which was based on his work.

Early in 1938, Ron made a major discovery while working through a philosophical treatise. The basic common denominator of all life was "survival." Everything that was alive was driven by this single impulse. The truth was idiotically simple—that was why no one had seen it until now. Editors begged to publish the work at this stage, but Ron was reluctant to release an articulation of the world's greatest riddle without also being able to offer its solution. Then came the war. Ron was commissioned as a lieutenant in the U.S. Navy and served as a corvette commander, a sub hunter. Combat left him nearly blind, and he suffered trauma to his neck and back; when peace was restored he found himself in a California hospital among armed forces personnel liberated from POW camps. Here he began to test theories on therapy that had been fermenting inside him for years. Using techniques that eventually made up the core of Dianetics, Ron achieved miraculous results.

From there he began to work with people all over the country—actors in Hollywood, the mentally ill in Savannah, Georgia, others in New York, New Jersey, and Seattle. He cured himself as well. His recovery was so remarkable that the navy had a hard time confirming his identity when he appeared before a retirement board.

He compiled the results of sixteen years of investigation. An early draft of this work was called "The Original Thesis." Word of a revolutionary breakthrough began to spread. The first article on Dianetics appeared in *The Explorers Journal* and kicked off a massive letter-writing campaign for more information. Ron again offered his findings to the medical establishment, but it refused to even examine his results.

He decided to go public with a handbook. Columnist Walter Winchell claimed the book would prove as important as the discovery of fire. *Dianetics: The Modern Science of Mental Health* (hereinafter *DMSMH*) was published on May 9, 1950. The response was enormous. Ron hit the lecture circuit. *DMSMH* detailed the earliest version of "auditing," Scientology's religious therapy. In it, one explored personal history for moments of blockage and unrest. Recalling what has truly happened in one's life made one more confident, more clear. This improved eyesight, elevated intelligence, and cured a host of psychosomatic ailments. Even as *DMSMH* was published, informal groups of "auditors" began to appear, laypeople applying Dianetics techniques to one another. Within six months, 750 such groups had formed across the country.

Ron lectured and continued his research through 1951, a year in which he wrote an additional six books exploring the depths of the void in human knowledge. Within a year and a half he had isolated the real answer: man was neither body nor mind but a spiritual being. To this being he gave the name "thetan." Ron gave a series of groundbreaking lectures in Philadelphia in 1952, and various headquarters popped up in Kansas and Arizona, where Scientology was officially introduced. Ron then headed to London, where he offered auditor-training courses.

Students in Los Angeles were the first to recognize the movement as something more than a philosophy. Here, Scientology first established itself as a church in 1954; organizations all over the world followed suit. Through the late fifties, Ron rode a frenzied wave of spiritual breakthroughs. In 1956, Scientology was granted tax-exempt status by the IRS, only to have it revoked two years later when the IRS, Scientology claimed, redefined the word *church* specifically to attack it. By then, the forces of the medical establishment had aligned against the new religion, and Scientology began a campaign to protect itself. The battle raged for decades.

In 1959, Ron purchased Saint Hill Manor in England, a mansion that served as the headquarters for Scientology worldwide. Ron's research continued with the development of the E-Meter, which helped auditors locate moments of blockage ("charge") by measuring current put off by thought.

This made auditing faster and more accurate. More important, Ron completed the Bridge to Total Freedom, the specific set of steps and instructions by which one could achieve the status of "Clear." The precise method was spelled out on the new Classification and Gradation Chart. Clear was the end point of auditing.

The early sixties saw tremendous expansion and growth. The segmented structure of the church's many orgs was the result of Ron codifying the technology that led to effective administration. An organization called the Guardian's Office was initiated to protect the church from the harassment it experienced from the IRS, Interpol, and the Food and Drug Administration. Ron also codified the church's study technology, which allowed for faster learning. He promoted literacy in a visit to Rhodesia in 1960.

In 1966, Ron resigned from the directorship of Scientology to pursue research into levels beyond Clear. These were called the "Operating Thetan" (OT) levels. Here one learned the true origin of man. Scientology had begun purchasing ships by then, and Ron spent the next seven years at sea. The Sea Org was established in 1967, and in 1968 the world's one thousandth Clear appeared. The first Celebrity Centre opened in 1969. Now Ron discovered the inner workings of both the criminal and addictive minds, and how to cure them. In the seventies, organizations devoted to each, Criminon and Narconon, offered tech even to those outside the Scientological world. In 1975, the Sea Org established a land headquarters in Florida. This was called Flag Land Base.

In the late seventies, Ron moved to California to produce films and a lecture series that made attaining Clear and the OT levels more efficient. He took time out to return to his science-fiction roots, writing *Battlefield Earth* and a ten-volume satirical science-fiction epic. All were bestsellers.

In the early eighties, a threat to Scientology emerged: the Sea Organization discovered that the Guardian's Office had become too autonomous, and it was learned that the group was trying to take control of the church. Investigation revealed that corruption had hindered Scientology's expansion. In 1982, the Guardian's Office was replaced with the Religious Technology Center, to which Ron donated all Scientology and Dianetics trademarks. Author Services, Inc., appeared at around the same time with the specific mandate of ensuring that Ron's work always appeared in the form he intended.

In 1986, Scientologists gathered in auditoriums all over the world for a special meeting. Until that point most Scientologists had known Ron as the commodore of the Sea Org. Now they were told that he had been promoted to admiral. He was conducting research beyond his body. Some locations reported twenty minutes of standing ovation. *DMSMH* surged to the number one spot on the *New York Times* bestseller list for a second time, the only title ever to have done so. A few years later, Scientology finally won its long-standing battle with the IRS and received full tax exemption as a recognized religion. Since then, Scientology has continued to grow, counting millions of members in hundreds of missions on every continent of the planet. Ron's work has been translated into dozens of languages, including Sotho, Zhosa, and Zulu.

4. The Preclear

I showed up early for the first day of the Hubbard Dianetics Seminar, surprising thirty impeccably dressed Scientologists on the living room side of the lobby of the Dianetics Center, all of them clumped for a photo commemorating a meeting they'd just concluded. I wondered if they were all Clears. I was a preclear. I knew that now. Everyone who wasn't yet Clear was a preclear. Eric rushed out from the crowd when he spotted me, as though I was a troubled man escaped from the appropriate ward. He walked me upstairs to deposit me in Aaron's classroom. Aaron wasn't there yet, so Oscar set me up in a private viewing station with the orientation video. I told him I'd already seen it.

"No problem," he said. "The more you watch it, the more you get it."

Beyond the bright lobby, the Dianetics Center felt basically like an elementary school, and Aaron's room was something like a fourth-grade classroom, with a full wall of dictionaries and bowls of blocks set out on long tables. The dictionaries and blocks were Ron's study technology. What Hubbard had discovered was that people had trouble learning because they either misunderstood words or failed to generate substantial images from whatever they read. The blocks, Ron said, helped generate the intellectual mass of ideas.

In most Scientology buildings, the walls were decorated with photos or paintings of Ron, stations of his biography's wild ride, or fantasy art from the jackets of his science-fiction books. Most often, Ron appeared as a robust and benign redhead, around fifty, thick through the middle, fat with knowledge and wisdom. He wasn't remarkable in any way apart from the fact that his image was inescapable. In Aaron's classroom, Ron's picture hung on an otherwise blank wall, a cropped image of Ron in a sailor's cap, pointing emphatically up with one hand. Whatever he might have been saying at that moment paled beside the timeless gesture.

A few other students arrived, took seats, and opened their books, laying a dictionary beside what they were reading. An older Hispanic woman, a man with dreadlocks, two kids. Aaron arrived and brought me a dictionary of my own. He instructed me to begin on page one of a simple workbook. Aaron wasn't really there as a teacher—Scientology used "Course Supervisors" to monitor progress and provide materials—but precisely at one o'clock he announced, "Okay, let's take roll!" He read off our names and used a dramatic flourish with a pen to indicate our presence on a roll sheet. "Very good! You may begin," he finished, and we all went back to what we'd been doing before roll.

Hubbard had devised a split-mind theory not so different from Julian Jaynes's bicameral mind. The workbook spelled it out. There were the analytical mind and the reactive mind. The analytical mind was a perfect computing machine, filing everything away on the "time track," which was a record of "mental image pictures" that made up our pasts. It was only in periods of unconsciousness, from painful emotions or physical pain, that the analytical mind was interrupted. Here, the reactive mind took over. The reactive mind was stupid. In it, even unrelated things were perceived as equivalents. The time track continued receiving mental image pictures even when one was unconscious, and this allowed the dim-witted reactive mind to make false associations that could affect our lives and health. These were called "engrams": images stored in the time track during periods of painful unconsciousness. Engrams recurred later in life when similar stimuli appeared, making for unhappiness and disease. A classic example: a man has a car accident on a stormy night. He is injured and placed in an ambulance. On the way to the hospital, though he is unconscious, he hears and records one paramedic telling another that it's high time he broke off a romantic relationship. Years later, the injured man finds himself riding in a car with his girlfriend on another stormy night. The engram reappears and "keys in." The man suddenly decides to break up with his girlfriend. He doesn't know why.

Auditing was the process by which engrams were removed. Reliving events that generated engrams erased them. The auditor helped locate engrams by using an E-Meter to find charge. The reactive mind itself could be got rid of through auditing. A Clear was defined as a person without his or her reactive mind.

The Hubbard Dianetics Seminar would conclude with an auditing session, but that was a ways off yet and I was still struggling with some of the ideas. Aaron seemed disappointed with my progress after a couple of hours. Not because I was too slow, but because I was too fast. He criticized the little narrative I produced in my workbook to demonstrate that I understood the time track. Aaron was patient with his scolding.

"When does the time track begin?" he asked me.

"Birth."

"Okay. And when does it end?"

"Death?"

"No," he said. *"Now."*

He noticed that I had not yet used the dictionary he'd brought me, and insisted that there must have been words I had encountered whose definitions I didn't know. No, I said. Smooth sailing so far. He quizzed me on a few uncommon words.

Then Aaron said, "What is loss?"

"Now, that's a good question," I said. "One can lose one's orientation. You can lose your mind—"

"That's not what I mean. There are two kinds of loss." He lifted two blocks from a nearby bowl and set them on the table before us. One was a cube, the other more rectangular. One kind of loss was emotional, Aaron said, as when a loved one died, and the other was physical, as when we were injured. The common denominator was pain, and both made us vulnerable to engrams.

I nodded.

Aaron looked at the blocks and smiled. To humor him, I looked up the word *aberrate* to see if it could be used as a verb, as Hubbard sometimes did for people who departed from rational thought. It couldn't. I complained, and Aaron explained that Scientology sometimes used fresh nomenclature to move beyond old ways of thinking.

Eventually I realized that what I was being taught at this stage was a few basics of storytelling that would be useful when I retold episodes of my life in auditing sessions. In auditing, old episodes were replayed again and again to layer in detail, and eventually there was an effort to make connections between events in one's life, to make thematic sense of the time track's

narrative. The time track was life's text, and we could interpret it even when
its film seemed to have snapped. And this was the correct way to think of
the time track. It was likened to a movie of one's life, but of course that was
a metaphor, and if it had really been a movie it would have been a movie
with more than fifty dimensions.

The film language reminded me of what James had said about people
being drawn to religions in line with "personal susceptibilities." The bicameral mind had appealed to authors, and Scientology was hugely popular
with actors. I was beginning to see why. It flattered their skills. An "aber-
ree" was defined as someone who dramatized their engramic content in
life, and *DMSMH* claimed that an aberrated individual was "like an actor
playing his dictated part and going through a whole series of irrational actions." Higher levels of auditing allowed shifting between "valences," or
personalities, in a given engram. Individuality was a role one played. Breaking dramatization, like breaking character, made one ill. Free will meant es-
caping the engram's script. As it turned out, engrams could come from
watching movies just as easily as they came from life. Writing in 1950,
Hubbard claimed that most engrams found in adults came from the first
quarter of the twentieth century, and he listed the movies and actors he
thought primarily responsible: *Curse You, Jack Dalton,* Rudolph Valentino,
and Theda Bara.

The contempt Scientology had for psychology and psychiatry began to
clear up now as well. In Scientology, recognizable philosophy ended with
Herbert Spencer, and while Freud had been on the right track in psychology, he had been waylaid by the villainous German physiologist Wilhelm
Wundt. Psychologists were clear targets of attack in Scientology videos.
They appeared as vicious caricatures, demonically goateed, outfitted with
all the weapons of cult deprogrammers, and they screamed at innocent
patients or beguiled them with hypnosis. The videos seemed so intent on
making the point that Scientology was not inspired by psychology or hypnotism that the question of whether it was a synthesis of the two came
about quite naturally. The Scientology strategy was to borrow psychology's
diagnostic tests and therapies, then attack the sources. A common Scientology text claimed, "Psychiatry is seeking to create a world where man is reduced to a robotized or drugged, vegetable-like state so that he can be
controlled." It wasn't Scientologists who were brainwashed, they thought.
It was everyone else.

I have to admit that I had not gotten far into my study of James and religions before it occurred to me that either everyone is brainwashed in their own way or no one is. The Scientologists seemed perfectly happy with their split-brain theory and their fresh nomenclature and their bustling society as spiritually remote as the Amish. They didn't go out of their way to celebrate individuality—Hubbard argued that people were happier with a set of rules to follow—but did any system really? Did capitalism, as it slipped from pluralistic ambition into a spiritual homogeneity of Wal-Churches and cathedral malls? Did communism, as it killed God and offered the theology of the State in its place? Religious movements are founded on cynicism of the systems that precede them. The new set of rules could be writ on slabs carved on a mountain and presented as the doodling of God, or they could be Hubbard's twenty-one Moral Precepts, which included "Do Not Murder," "Be Industrious," and "Respect the Religious Beliefs of Others." When it came to consciousness, the mind, ethics, and morals, irrationalisms were all we had. Hubbard was more theory than theology. But Jaynes's bicameral mind, Freud's unconscious, the world's current thinking on brain chemistry based on incomplete data—these were all equivalent theory-gods. William James would have offered an even more sweeping list—Schopenhauer's Will-substance, Hartmann's Unconscious, Clifford's conscious automata, Kant's Transcendental Ego of Apperception—*and* he would have gone more directly at the heart of the establishment:

> *The principle of causality, for example—what is it but a postulate, an empty name covering simply a demand that the sequence of events shall some day manifest a deeper kind of belonging of one thing with another than the mere arbitrary juxtaposition which now phenomenally appears? It is as much an altar to an unknown god as the one that Saint Peter found at Athens. All our scientific and philosophic ideals are altars to unknown gods.*

By light refracted by my Jamesian variety of experience, I could now look in at the world of Scientologists, with their bizarre technology and lunatic structures, look in and see that criticizing them, diagnosing them as dazed and tricked and floating along through an illusion, condescending to them in that way was a fair approximation of what they thought when they looked back at you. A culture washes brains as surely as a cult does, and the fact that culture is mainstream means only that it's done a better job of it. To believe anything outside its narrow platform was to take on the role of rebel and revolutionary in a war of ideas, and perhaps this explained why Scientology imagined itself in a protracted conflict with the culture in which it was embedded.

But then there was Hubbard. The effort to deify Ron was so blatant that it smacked wrong long before I ever turned to the debunked version of his biography. I went to the L. Ron Hubbard Life Exhibition one day before heading to class at the Dianetics Center. It was a two-story rat's maze erected inside the gutted hollow of a historic structure. It was morning, midweek; I was the only person there for a tour. A tall, beautiful woman greeted me in the lobby. She made me wait five minutes to see if others would show up, then decided to direct a personal tour. We entered the maze.

The path followed Hubbard's life chronologically. Here were some of the merit badges he had won in the Boy Scouts, here was paraphernalia from Old Tom's Blackfeet tribe. Ron had been an accomplished aviator, and his goggles sat in a glass case. The museum had hundreds of the magazines to which Ron had contributed, and a small automated display told the story of one of his best-loved science-fiction adventures. All together, the museum counted almost thirty fields in which Ron had become professional. His literary output had exceeded twenty-five million words. Ron was a prodigious typist, my guide told me. He composed prose at ninety-five words per minute.

My guide was also the museum's curator. She was only thirty or so, but she had been a Scientologist most of her life. Her parents had also been Scientologists. This was typical. In the eighties, the move from the Guardian's Office to the Religious Technology Center had also signaled a transition of power from Hubbard's original band of followers to the first generation of Scientologist children, just then approaching adulthood. These children had once been members of the Commodore's Messenger Org, a personal service troupe for Hubbard while he was at sea. The children had become his most trusted resource. The current leader of the church, David Miscavige, was barely in his twenties when he emerged as a force in Scientology in 1981. Since then, second-generation Scientologists have controlled most of the church's activities. They have kept its fragmented organizational structure intact, though recently the church hired a public relations firm to help work on its image. They made new videos, sponsored the Goodwill Games, and celebrated a version of Ron's biography—I was inside of it—so unlikely that I found myself wondering what it was not revealing.

We came to a demonstration display for the E-Meter. I hadn't seen one close up. The E-Meter was a simple device, a metal housing with a Geiger counter–style display to measure electricity sent through the body via "cans," conductors held loosely in the hand. The E-Meter used the same basic technology as lie-detection equipment.

My guide handed me the cans. They fit easily in my palms.

"Now I'm going to give you a little pinch. Watch the dial."

She pinched my arm much harder than she really needed to, and the needle on the E-Meter jumped and settled back into place.

"Okay, now *remember* the pinch."

I recalled the pinch and the needle moved again, not quite as strongly.

"See?" she said, a lifetime's belief reinforced. When she wasn't looking I gave one of the cans a squeeze. The needle jumped insanely.

My guide had been through the museum hundreds of times, but she sat diligently by my side as we entered more tiny movie theaters to watch short films about Narconon and Criminon. Scientology knew who the seekers were, and they knew the most persuasive medium with which to address them. I broke from my James biography for a moment to deny that I'd ever taken recreational drugs, but my guide seemed skeptical and we watched the drug film anyway. Then we made for the exit, passing a complete set of LRH's written works and the Moral Precepts printed on an inner wall of the maze. Finally, there was a wall of awards Ron had received. Plaques from officials in large American cities, small foreign countries. When we got close we tripped some kind of motion-detection equipment; lights came on and a recording kicked in. It was Ron. He was delivering one of the thousands of lectures Scientology had recorded and preserved. Hubbard's voice was soft and dreamy, soothing, the vocal equivalent of a tenor saxophone licking out a ballad. He was a storyteller, a poet-prophet, and really it might have been just his sultry, sleepy solos that accounted for all of Scientology. I approached the wall of awards. They climbed floor to ceiling, some of them far too high to read. The voice continued, surging along on a spiritual crescendo, and then at an orchestrated moment the wall itself began to rumble with the gears and workings of an automation not yet complete. I heard a click, like slack taken up between railroad cars, and then the wall of awards began to move. There was a seam in the middle. The walls parted there, a bit jerky but magical enough, and gave through not to a passage or another movie but to another wall of awards, more ribbons and mounted gold leaves, the recognition the church had earned the globe

over. The walls parted again, and then again. Hundreds of citations. Some
music began to accompany LRH now, competing with his mood, and as
the speech ended the walls parted a final time to reveal a head shot of Ron
as large as a man, a thoughtful Ron with his chin cupped in his palm and an
expression that might have been sheer wisdom, wisdom cleared and perfected, a photo not of Ron's face at all, really, but a portrait of his thetan,
shining bright through the imperfection of his flesh, and when that stood
before me, an iconic God face, the music surged orgiastic, and the notes it
chose pricked me deep and sexed my skin.

Then the music stopped and the museum was as quiet as a warehouse.

"Well," said my guide, smiling. "That's it."

5. THE SOLE SOURCE (BIOGRAPHY II)

Only a few books about the inner workings of Scientology have ever been
published. A number of them have been met with suppression efforts on
the part of the church. One book, *The Scandal of Scientology,* published by
journalist Paulette Cooper in the early seventies, was met with a harassment campaign designed to land her in a mental institution.* Cooper was
just the first in a series of journalists who investigated the church only to
find themselves investigated and attacked in turn. But Scientology debunkers were just as often ex-Scientologists like Bent Corydon, whose
book *L. Ron Hubbard: Messiah or Madman?* fended off four lawsuits in the
late eighties. The most prominent and meticulous of the debunking works
is probably *A Piece of Blue Sky,* published in 1990 by Jon Atack, a British ex-
Scientologist who had advanced well into the OT levels. Five years after
publication, Atack told an audience at a German conference that he had
been made the subject of a harassment campaign and a legal deluge that
had bankrupted him and destroyed his marriage. An English libel suit
brought by a Scientologist eventually found one defamatory comment in *A
Piece of Blue Sky.* Atack told his conference audience, "My quest to understand and to help the many people damaged by Scientology has led me to
public humiliation and bankruptcy. . . . I have been a tiny David oppressed
by a Goliath of dreadful proportions."

---

*The action against Cooper was orchestrated by the church's Guardian's Office, which
was disbanded in 1981 and whose activities the church later disavowed.

The history of Scientology put forth by the debunkers was chock-full of shocking allegations.

Hubbard's early life is essentially lost, but the evidence debunkers offer suggests that the official biography is exaggeration by several orders of magnitude. Ron's Blackfeet tribe turned out to be many miles from where he lived in Montana, and what he knew of them came from someone else. The navy man who taught Ron psychoanalysis actually existed, but Hubbard's teenage diaries—which became public during a lawsuit—made no mention of the officer or of Ron beginning his work on the mind around that time. The same diaries contradicted his claims of having studied various cultures in Asia. The young Hubbard held the Chinese in contempt in entries detailing short visits to Beijing and Shanghai. By way of contrast, the journals were packed with early attempts at pulp fiction.

Ron settled for a prep school after failing an exam to enter the U.S. Naval Academy. He graduated high school a year late. At George Washington University, he did take a class called Molecular and Atomic Physics, but he failed it. He never graduated from college.

The evidence for his surveying expeditions came mostly from short newspaper articles he wrote himself. Expedition members later admitted that the trips had been a bust. One, the Alaska Radio Expedition, turned out to have been just Ron and his first wife. Their boat malfunctioned, and they got stuck in Ketchikan until Hubbard could write enough stories to get them home again.

He had first married at twenty, and fathered two children in the 1930s. He was living in New York at the time and eventually became part of the Golden Age of Science Fiction, his work appearing in *Astounding Science Fiction* alongside that of Isaac Asimov, Robert Heinlein, and A. E. Van Vogt. Up to that point, he had written adventure stories under a variety of pseudonyms including Morgan de Wolf, Legionnaire 14830, Joe Blitz, and Elron. He earned a penny a word and scraped by on a prodigious output. He resisted science fiction at first. The writers who knew Hubbard reported that his vivid imagination was just as easily applied to the events of his life as to his fiction.

By then Ron was already tinkering with mystical self-help. In the late thirties he wrote a book called *Excalibur,* full of knowledge that had come to him, he said, when his heart stopped during an operation. No one would publish it. He left New York dejected, returning only when he came to terms with science fiction.

Debunker Atack cited Hubbard's naval records as evidence that he had used bogus recommendations to get himself assigned as an intelligence officer in the Naval Reserve. He was first rejected for his eyesight but eventually received a commission when American commitments stretched the armed forces thin. Before the war broke out, he tinkered as a low-level intelligence officer, working in public relations. When hostilities began, he bragged that he received a command even though he'd slept through an anti–submarine warfare course. The account he later gave of a protracted battle his ship waged with a submarine was contradicted by other officers, and an assessment of Hubbard's competence at the time listed him as "lacking in the essential qualities of judgment, leadership and cooperation." Hubbard received four awards in the war (he claimed twenty-one), and none were for combat or wounds. He suffered from recurring conjunctivitis, and what he called his "machine-gun injuries" appear to have been dramatically exaggerated. A chronic complaint was a duodenal ulcer, which laid him up at the end of the war, though in private papers Hubbard admitted that he had used illness as a way of avoiding discipline. One debunker suggested that he hypnotized himself to simulate symptoms.

In 1945, Hubbard was in California. He began to dabble in the occult, meeting Jack Parsons, a prominent member of Aleister Crowley's Church of Thelema, the same group Anton LaVey would visit a few years later. Parsons worked on the rocket project at Caltech that eventually became the Jet Propulsion Laboratory. He would later die in an explosion in his home, and he has a crater named for him on the dark side of the moon. Parsons was impressed with Hubbard at first, and reported to Crowley that Ron was "the most Thelemic person I have ever met." According to a number of debunkers, Hubbard acted as the seer in sex rituals with Parsons, streaming mystical poetry while Parsons performed the necessary operations to conceive a kind of female messiah that Crowley had prophesied. For his part, Crowley was not impressed and wrote to a deputy in New York, "Apparently Parsons or Hubbard or somebody is producing a Moonchild. I get fairly frantic when I contemplate the idiocy of these goats."

Hubbard married Parson's sister-in-law before he divorced his first wife, and eventually he swindled Parsons on a deal involving the sale of a boat. Ron's new wife would figure prominently in the emergence of Dianetics. But eventually she left the movement and reported that Hubbard had been an abusive husband, and that he had once asked her to kill herself. He had performed sleep-deprivation experiments on her, she said, and she called him a "dangerous lunatic" and a paranoid schizophrenic. When she and Hubbard eventually split, she signed a statement calling him a "fine and brilliant man," and received two hundred dollars a month to support their child.

After breaking with Parsons, Hubbard continued to practice Crowley's "magick" and produced a document under self-hypnosis called the "Affirmations," sections of which were read into the record during the same lawsuit that released Hubbard's teenage diaries. A portion reads, "All men shall be my slaves! All women shall succumb to my charms! All mankind shall grovel at my feet and not know why!" For debunkers, the "Affirmations" was evidence that Hubbard had tranced himself into delusion, and they listed "magick" among the primary source material for Scientology.

By 1949, most of the writers who knew Ron had heard him say that he wanted to start his own religion because that's where the money was. There's disagreement as to whether *DMSMH* took Hubbard six weeks to write or was written over an eighteen-month period in Savannah. Regardless, it claimed to offer a cure for everything Hubbard himself suffered from: poor eyesight, various bodily ailments, psychosomatic illnesses. The founder of Gestalt therapy, a political science professor at Williams College, and several NASA scientists were among those who took Dianetics seriously at first. Auditing produced a light trance with possible therapeutic value. Hubbard did approach mainstream medicine with the therapy, but submissions to *The Journal of the American Medical Association* and *The American Journal of Psychiatry* were rejected. He turned to his fellow science-fiction writers when Dianetics groups began to pop up around the country. A. E. Van Vogt recalled receiving $5,000 in checks from people interested in courses even though he had refused to participate. Hubbard's editor at *Astounding Science Fiction* helped as the movement gained steam, and the Hubbard Research Foundation was incorporated to handle inquiries.

Atack claimed that Hubbard's output the following year was fueled by alcohol and phenobarbital. He experimented on preclears with Benzedrine. He became paranoid and claimed that the Russians had approached him and asked him for his work. Dianetics threatened to come apart almost as soon as it came together: two original supporters—in fact, the first publisher of *DMSMH* and the doctor who wrote the book's introduction—suddenly resigned and warned that Dianetics could be dangerous in untrained hands. In 1950, an event was held at the Shrine Auditorium to demonstrate the power of a Clear. Noted fringe-religion author Martin Gardner described

Hubbard introducing the packed house to "Sonya Bianca," who was said to have attained perfect recall. However, in the demonstration that followed Sonya proved unable to recall the color of Hubbard's tie when his back was turned. A large part of the audience got up and left. This seemed to indicate a larger trend. "By the end of 1950," Atack wrote, "Hubbard's world was collapsing." In April 1951, Hubbard resigned from the Hubbard Research Foundation.

Perhaps the most controversial part of *DMSMH* was its claim that engrams, rooted in the misinterpretation of words, could result even from events predating the acquisition of language. Many engrams were said to come from prenatal experiences, in fact. Every coital experience a woman had while pregnant transmitted to her child the worst of all possible engrams; *DMSMH* narrated a scene in which maternal orgasm created "unconsciousness" in an unborn child. Hubbard was willing to trace memory back to the level of the cell, but the independent Dianetics groups didn't stop there. Laypeople began to audit memories from previous lives. This created the movement's first major schism, separating the past-life believers from those who believed that talk of past lives ruined a potentially useful therapeutic technique. But even as the organization faltered, Hubbard found supporters. A Wichita man offered funding for a new organization, and Ron jumped at it. He continued producing the materials that would later be familiar to Scientologists, but it wasn't long before the Kansas organization fell apart as well. Ron was arrested during a public lecture for failing to return money he had borrowed from his own outfit. The complaint eventually resulted in Hubbard forfeiting all materials relating to Dianetics; for a time even the use of the terms *Dianetics* and *L. Ron Hubbard* was in dispute. He was left broke. Debunker Corydon wrote, "Hubbard was left with two choices: give up the 'save Mankind game' entirely, or start fresh, start another movement, write more books, and lecture like crazy."

Scientology was the new movement. Hubbard worked off a more religious model this time around. By then, he had married for the third and final time, and the new wife, Mary Sue Hubbard, helped name the new movement. The word *scientology* had been coined in 1907, but had first been used as a derisive label for pseudosciences. Auditing itself appeared to have been borrowed from the mind-cure movement, which William James had described in *Varieties* as including "passive relaxation, concentration, and meditation, and . . . something like hypnotic practice." Hubbard's E-Meter wasn't new either; the idea could be traced back fifty years, and he originally spoke of the device strictly in terms of its profit margin. Hubbard now embraced past lives wholeheartedly, and the Scientology cosmology began to take shape. The noted Philadelphia lectures described a civilization called Arslycus in which all mankind had been slaves for ten thousand lifetimes. Eventually the history would come to include the "OT III Incident," a catastrophic event linking evil "psychs" (read: psychologists) with priests that had occurred on this planet and seventy-five others that were all part of an intergalactic confederacy. The bulk of the OT levels were made up of the removal of something called "body thetans."

The basic legal strategies of Scientology began to evolve in the late fifties, when Hubbard turned his attention to derivative groups that sprang up and employed the original Dianetics techniques (the Process, Abilitism, Amprinistics, Eductivism, and so on). Hubbard recommended a whirlwind of legal action against the groups, slap suits intended to harass. He suggested as well a policy of hiring private detectives to investigate Scientology's critics. Ron regained the rights to Dianetics and fused it with Scientology. "We should be very alert to sue for slander at the slightest chance so as to discourage the public press from mentioning Scientology," he wrote. Soon the Hubbard Communication Office *Manual of Justice* appeared, which established an intelligence agency within Scientology, the submovement that eventually became the Guardian's Office and then the Religious Technology Center. The *Manual of Justice* laid out the strategy of "noisy investigation," whereby critics' personal lives were dredged up and made public to exert pressure on them. "Intelligence we get with a whisper. Investigation we do with a yell," Ron said. By 1961, this branch of the church was called the Department of Official Affairs and was described by Hubbard as "the equivalent of a Ministry of Propaganda and Security." Its goal was to bring the government and hostile philosophies into compliance with the goals of Scientology. A famous doctrine, Fair Game, said that anyone who posed a threat to Scientology could forgivably be "tricked, cheated, lied to, sued, or destroyed."

Fair Game most often applied to people outside Scientology, like journalists, but now Hubbard began to experiment with the E-Meter as a tool to root out "suppressives" within Scientology as well. The E-Meter would be used for routine security checks on Scientology administrators. In 1959, Ron's oldest son left the church. Hubbard claimed that Ron Jr. had been unable to "face an E-Meter." Ron Jr. became one of Scientology's most outspoken critics, but eventually he too recanted.

Shifting to a religious format failed to quell government interest in Scientology. The church had received tax-exempt status, but it was revoked in 1958 when the IRS realized that Hubbard was profiting from the movement. In 1963, the Food and Drug Administration raided a building in Washington, D.C., and confiscated a batch of E-Meters. After a flurry of legal activity, the E-Meters were returned with the stipulation that they could not be advertised as effective in the treatment of disease—the same caveat embedded in the enrollment release today. By then, Ron was tucked away in England. Scientology was so popular now that English airports had special counters set up to direct Scientology visitors to Saint Hill. Its annual income was growing exponentially. In 1965, Hubbard disavowed all his original research and declared himself the sole "Source" of all Scientology material.

In 1966, the "World's First Real Clear" appeared and was called the pope of Scientology. Ron's retreat to the Sea Org allowed him to escape an English government that now decided it had seen enough of him. Hubbard called England a police state and shoved off. The Sea Org initiated a military-style discipline. Its members wore navy-style uniforms, and eventually they signed a billion-year contract of loyalty. In Los Angeles there was talk of the "Space Org," and members fashioned the uniforms of the Galactic Patrol from seventy-five million years ago. Hubbard led the Sea Org on a cruise to survey his past lives. He was now believed to be the red-haired man the Buddha had claimed would appear in the West. Throughout, Hubbard produced a variety of new programs and OT levels, seeming to subsist entirely on hallucinogens. One ex-Scientologist reported that he had become obsessed with removing his own body thetans.

The Sea Org came to serve as a kind of boarding school for Scientology kids. The Commodore's Messenger Org appeared, employing preteens assigned to Hubbard's care. Messengers reportedly received little education, were separated from their parents for long periods of time, and did Ron's bidding. The *Los Angeles Times* reported in 1990 that "the youngsters, whose parents belonged to Hubbard's Church of Scientology, would lay out his clothes, run his shower and help him dress. He taught them how to sprinkle powder in his socks and gently slip them on so as not to pull the hairs on his legs." Before long, the Sea Org began to implement punishments ("heavy ethics") for those who failed to meet expected production levels. Scientology ethics is one of the most controversial aspects of its history. In 1986, *Forbes* described the church as "complete with finance dictators, 'gang-bang sec[urity] checks,' lie detectors, 'committees of evidence' and detention camps." While church officials claim that life in Scientology is akin to monasticism, Dr. Stephen A. Kent, a sociologist at the University of Alberta, has suggested as recently as 2003 that Scientology "remains a threat to the human rights of both its members and its opponents."

The first ship Hubbard bought had once been used as a transport for Winston Churchill but had served most recently as a cattle ferry. Debunkers characterized the experience on the boat as something closer to prison or a slave galley. The Sea Org had been formed so that Hubbard could keep his most loyal officers close to him, but his paranoia crept in even here: members' letters were censored, and Hubbard coordinated the group around a "shore story" they used as cover in port. The ships cruised the oceans, looking for a home. "We own quite a bit of property over the world," Hubbard said in 1971. "We will be acquiring more, as well as some countries." But Scientologists were kicked out of Greece, and their ship was stoned in Madeira by a Portuguese mob who thought they were CIA. The Rhodesian government refused to renew Ron's visa, and Scientology was banned in much of Australia from 1965 to 1973. In France, Hubbard was convicted in absentia of medical fraud; the decision was later overturned.

It's generally agreed that Dianetics began as an earnest attempt on Hubbard's part to cure himself. But by 1968 his self-therapy methods had failed terribly. He began to disintegrate at sea. He became vastly overweight, grew his hair below his shoulders, and sometimes wore a full beard as a disguise. A large growth appeared on his forehead. He was still a hypnotic personality and sometimes came off as gentle and nurturing, but just as often he was characterized by bizarre outbursts and screaming fits. He was a chain-smoker and wore glasses his entire adult life. He surprised those beneath him by demanding a supply of painkillers. He often felt close to death. In 1975, he secretly received medical treatment after suffering a heart attack. In better times Hubbard dressed fantastically in his commodore's uniform, polished shoes, a slick cap, and braided lanyards, and delivered impromptu lectures in the tight ship corridors. Ron had bedded female students of Scientology discreetly throughout the sixties, but he did so more brazenly once the Sea Org set sail. One harrowing account told of an impotent Hubbard failing to consummate a rape. The Messengers who worked most closely with Ron were teenage girls who wore uniforms of knee-high boots, miniskirts, and bikini halters.

The rest of the church grew increasingly bold. A steep auditing price increase was initiated in 1976. Low-level auditing had been affordable to that point, but soon Scientologists were going tens of thousands of dollars into debt to advance into the OT levels. Mary Sue Hubbard had been in charge of the Guardian's Office since it had appeared, and in the late seventies the G.O. became an aggressive information-gathering machine. Agents were trained in covert operations, and the church ran "ops" to infiltrate newspapers and government agencies. Agents who infiltrated the IRS made off with tens of thousands of pages of documents. Much of the Scientology world was awash in shady dealings; there were code names for Hubbard's home in Culver City and for the hacienda near Palm Springs used as a winter headquarters. The Sea Org gave up on its plan to take a country and began acquiring property in Clearwater, Florida. The G.O. profiled and harassed the local mayor.

Hubbard became convinced that the G.O. was riddled with suppressives. By then his contact with the church was limited to the Messengers, the only Scientologists he still trusted. Some were as young as ten years old. The Messengers' power increased accordingly. *The New York Times* reported that "Mr. Hubbard [had] retreated increasingly into seclusion and usually saw only members of the messenger corps, who were granted the right to discipline adult church members."

The G.O. infiltration scam finally fell apart in 1977. The FBI raided Scientology buildings in Los Angeles and Washington, and eleven G.O. officials, including Hubbard's wife, eventually served time for burglary and a number of other charges. Later Scientology literature would claim that the G.O. itself had been infiltrated by "individuals antithetical to Scientology," and that Sea Org executives overthrew and disbanded it. Indeed, the next few years amounted to a war within Scientology: the G.O., the Sea Org Messengers, and independent mission holders all angled for power. It was a battle between those who had been seduced by Scientology and those who had been raised in it. Hubbard's writings, for the first time, shifted from "scientific research" to "scripture." The G.O. was purged. Twenty-one-year-old David Miscavige began his power play within the church by leading the movement to cut Mary Sue Hubbard off completely. He would become the church's leader. "It's like the *Lord of the Flies,*" a former franchise holder told *The New York Times.* "The children have taken over." In 1983, 611 members were suddenly declared suppressive. Many went on to form derivative groups, and the newly formed Religious Technology Center was assigned the job of interfering with the competitors. Author Services, Inc., emerged to protect the scriptures. The church adopted an entirely new organizational structure in what debunker Atack called "a hasty attempt to divide the sinking ship of the Church of Scientology of California into watertight compartments."

The church lost half its membership in the new schism, but it didn't sink. Hubbard went into seclusion for the period now linked to the vast science-fiction novels he produced in later life. Some Scientologists believed he had already died or been murdered. In 1986, Ron suffered a stroke in a motor home in California. He left most of his money to "Author Trust Fund B" in a will written the day before he died. *DMSMH* hit the bestseller list again, but an investigation by *The San Diego Union* eventually revealed that sales figures had been manipulated by Scientologists ordering copies and returning them all across the country. Scientology continued to suffer from legal problems. Lawsuits cropped up over who owned the scriptures, and over church members who had died after refusing medical attention. Foreign governments moved against Scientology, most notably Germany, which stripped it of its religious status and tax exemption.

One of the Sea Org ships wound up as a restaurant and another was chopped into scrap metal. But in 1988, the church bought a new ship, and in 1990 it reported assets of $500 million. Later it revealed a $300 million annual income from auditing. Current estimates put church membership at roughly 100,000.

Debunkers insist that the covert operations continue: in 1991, *Time* reported that three prominent Scientologists had used the rare-coin business to launder money and that the church had plotted to plant operatives in the World Bank, the IMF, and the Export-Import Bank of the United States. In the late nineties, *60 Minutes* did a story about Scientology that focused on the church's treatment of an old foe, the Cult Awareness Network. The Scientology strategy had been to flood the organization with membership applications, sue it into oblivion when the applications were denied, and then buy the group when it went into bankruptcy. A few years before that, Scientology formed a national coalition of IRS whistle-blowers that eventually sparked an investigation into the IRS by Congress. By 1993, the church had more than two thousand lawsuits pending against the IRS and its officials and was busily conducting noisy investigations of those officials, exploring their personal financial dealings. One day David Miscavige walked unannounced into IRS headquarters and asked to see Commissioner Fred T.

Goldberg, Jr. No one knows what was said in the meeting that resulted, but a commission was formed and was granted greater access than had ever before been given a government agency investigating a religion. After the church paid $12.5 million as part of an agreement with the IRS, all Scientology organizations in the country were awarded tax-exempt status and all Scientology lawsuits against the IRS were dropped.

"The war is over," Miscavige told Scientology audiences.

As a direct result, the U.S. State Department has formally criticized the German government for discrimination against Scientologists.

6. The Win

When I completed my workbook, Aaron sat me down with *DMSMH* and just told me to read. The book was scripture but throughout Ron insisted it was "strictly test tube." It was a bad book; it was even poorly written. But that didn't matter: Ron was the author, and that alone made him the god of Scientology.

F.C.S. Schiller had once called William James a god of Pragmatism in a letter, and James had replied that the praise had made Alice feel as though she were a goddess. James had compared movements based on therapies (which he called "therapism" or "therapo-mania") to drug addiction, but it's likely that if he had been around when Scientology emerged he would have been among those who supported it at first, those who hoped auditing was a valid therapy. He probably would have been more flattered than disturbed that a good bit of Scientology appeared to be borrowed from nineteenth-century philosophy and his own work. James, too, had acknowledged earlier sources: *Pragmatism* was subtitled *A New Name for Some Old Ways of Thinking,* and in a letter to one of his sons, James joked that philosophy was "easy enuf, all but the writing. You just get it out of other books and write it down."

James was a contemporary of both of Scientology's polarizing philosophers, Spencer and Wundt. An experimental laboratory that James started at Harvard predated Wundt's German lab by four years, and James and Wundt have been called the two popes of nineteenth-century philosophy. But the practice of psychology in the laboratory bored James, and while he hoped physiology would shed light on the mind-body relationship, experimentation tended to lead to theories that eliminated the mind and consciousness completely. James ultimately questioned both Wundt's results and his own. Originally, James had sought out Wundt when he first went to Germany in 1867, but a decade later he described Wundt as "a rather ordinary man who has '*worked* up' certain things uncommonly well." Wundt's writing had "a strange mania for appearing *smooth*," which amounted to mental dishonesty. As for Spencer, James was baffled by his popularity and called him a charlatan. James's first signed publication was an attack on Spencer, and near the end of his life James described Spencer's system as "knocked together out of cracked hemlock boards." The best thing James would say about Spencer was that he was "occasionally more *amusing* than Wundt."

It's so easy to draw parallels between Hubbard's life and James's that the similarity starts to seem intentional. Hubbard suffered from James's same laundry list of ailments, including eyestrain, insomnia, backaches, and depressions, and both men started movements while searching for their own cures. James was described as a convincing speaker who, according to his wife, sometimes exhibited strange outbursts. Both men attacked the behaviorist branch of psychology. Hubbard's realization that "survival" was the basis of all life was borrowed whole hog from Spencer, but the idea of Clears seemed to trace back to prominent Pragmatists, for whom "clearness" was the desired goal for ideas. And the precise characteristics of Clears might have been lifted from James's acerbic anticipation of Spencer's conclusions:

> *We should then have, as the embodiment of the highest ideal of mental development, a creature of superb cognitive endowments, from whose piercing perceptions no fact was too minute or too remote to escape; whose all-embracing foresight no contingency could find unprepared; whose invincible flexibility of resource no array of outward onslaught could overpower; but in whom all these gifts were swayed by the single passion of love of life, of survival at any price. . . . There can be no doubt that, if such an incarnation of earthly prudence existed, a race of beings in whom this monotonously narrow passion for tribal self-preservation were aided by every cognitive gift, they would soon be kings of all the earth. All known human races would wither before their breath, and be as dust beneath their conquering feet.*

The similarities continued from there: James wrote of a "tone of health" and Hubbard employed a "tone scale" to describe the spectrum of human moods. James has been described as a Columbus of the inner life, and Hubbard wrote in *DMSMH* that the history of Dianetics was "a voyage of discovery, of an exploration into new and nearly uncharted realms, *terra incognita,* the human mind." As for engrams and breaks in the time track, James cited cases of hysteria as examples of the brain recording information without conscious awareness, and he had used a metaphor of the joints in bamboo wood to illustrate how a conscious stream of experience could be interrupted even as it remained continuous. Here he was probably invoking the work of Pierre Janet, a French psychologist whose "psychogenic hypothesis" suggested that traumatic memory could be converted through symbolic representation into dysfunctional symptoms. James would have noted that mental healers had been aware of the same thing for years. For the reactive mind, James might have gone to Janet again for another split-mind theory: something experienced unconsciously, as in hysteria, Janet said, was consciously registered by a second personality in the same body. (Multiple personalities in a single body was easy enough to defend with the observation of what is now called dissociative identity disorder.) As to thetans, James had described in *Principles* a trifold division of self culminating in "the Spiritual Me," which was "the very core and nucleus of our self, as we know it, the very sanctuary of our life. . . . This sense of activity is often held to be a direct revelation of the living substance of our Soul."

In designing the Bridge to Total Freedom, Hubbard appeared to have borrowed James's most common metaphor for Pragmatism's definition of truth, the alpine climber. The metaphor went like this: a mountaineer approached a gorge. His predicament required him to attempt a leap across it. If he jumped without a belief in powerful forces that mustered strength within him, he would fall. But if the same mountaineer was inspired by belief, James said, he would strengthen himself such that he would reach the other side and prove the truth of his belief through measurable result. Hubbard's version, the Bridge to Total Freedom, an echo of the "tiny bridge" Julian Jaynes had crossed to complete his theory of the bicameral mind, incorporated the boon of the industrial revolution into the scenario:

> One might here use an analogy of bridge engineering. Let us suppose
> that two plateaus exist, one higher than the other, with a canyon between
> them. An engineer sees that if the canyon could be crossed by traffic, the
> hitherto unused plateau, being much more fertile and pleasant, would be-

come the scene of a new culture. . . . The engineer, by . . . discovering
new significance in his materials, manages to throw a bridge across the
canyon. . . . Others cross over his bridge and examine the new terrain
with delight.

James would have been curious about Scientology, but ultimately he
would have argued that the subconscious was a potential source of strength
and not the cause of poor health. Scientology was another of those systems
pounded together out of scrap wood, but its growth and success would
have grabbed his attention. James might have argued that the main difference between himself and Hubbard was that Hubbard was a religious genius, while James was not. Hubbard had borrowed, too, James's line that
every once in a while a genius comes along with the potential to change
the world, but Hubbard had failed to continue with James's description of
the type in *Varieties:*

Such religious geniuses have often shown symptoms of nervous instabil-
ity. Even more perhaps than other kinds of geniuses, religious leaders
have been subject to abnormal psychical visitation. Invariably they have
been creatures of exalted emotional sensibility. Often they have led a dis-
cordant inner life, and had melancholy during a part of their career. They
have known no measure, been liable to obsessions and fixed ideas; and
frequently they have fallen into trances, heard voices, seen visions, and
presented all sorts of peculiarities which are ordinarily classed as patho-
logical.

Even though James labeled religious geniuses mad, he admired them for
the certainty their experiences afforded them and he longed to experience
such an event himself. James never had an experience that he would call
overtly mystical, but he did eventually have several experiences he couldn't
explain. His descriptions of them sound terribly like the prototype for Scientology auditing. The last followed a dream, but the first three occurred
while he was awake, during conversations he was having, although, he
wrote,

I doubt whether the interlocutor noticed my abstraction. What happened
each time was that I seemed all at once to be reminded of a past experi-
ence; and this reminiscence, ere I could conceive or name it distinctly,

developed into something further that belonged with it, this in turn into
something further still, and so on, until the process faded out, leaving me
amazed at the sudden vision of increasing ranges of distinct fact of which
I could give no articulate account. The mode of consciousness was percep-
tual, not conceptual—the field expanding so fast that there seemed no
time for conception or identification to get in its work. There was a
strongly exciting sense that my knowledge of past (or present?) reality
was enlarging pulse by pulse, but so rapidly that my intellectual processes
could not keep up the pace. The content *was thus entirely lost to retro-*
spection—it sank into the limbo into which dreams vanish as we gradu-
ally awake. The feeling—I won't call it belief—that I had had a sudden
opening, had seen through a window, as it were, distant realities that
incomprehensibly belonged with my own life, was so acute that I can not
shake it off to-day.

Eventually I got miffed with Aaron for quizzing me on the definitions of
words. I called him over and opened my book to the Bridge to Total Freedom
and asked him where *he* was on it. He didn't seem to think it was a rude
question. "Right here," he said, and pointed to a spot marked "Grade III."
I was scandalized. He was barely ahead of me! He wasn't even a Clear!
Aaron saw that I was annoyed. But he still had the wild card of auditing to
play, and now he began pairing people off.

Auditing was as precisely scripted as an audition. The preclear ran
through the memory, while the auditor gently prodded for details that
could be "contacted." When the preclear appeared to have run through the
chronology of the memory, the auditor prompted a return to the beginning. Eventually one can solo-audit with one hand on an E-Meter and the
other writing it all down. But early on the auditor was stuck to the original
statements Ron had written to standardize the process. Running a memory
might mean going through it a dozen or fifteen or twenty times, until
something in the memory revealed the etymology of your current mood
or until some relationship decoded your motivation or confusion. Such
progress was called a "win."

I was the auditor at first. Auditing can be dull, and Aaron told a group of
us that if we got bored or if we started to feel nauseous, it probably just
meant we were encountering charge. My first assignment was to listen to
a young man with dyed hair and black fingernails describe a breakfast in a
halfway house. He clearly belonged in Narconon. Next I was assigned to a

woman named Sarah. Sarah was in her late fifties but dressed like a teenager, and she told me a story about stopping for gas the other day and struggling to find a pump. If my boredom with Sarah meant that she had charge, then she was fully charged. I reminded myself of Rule 11 in the Auditor's Code about not getting angry but made a mental note to tell Aaron that the rule should really read "Don't Strangle the Preclear."

Finally, I was paired with a jazz musician named Lenny (Scientology is almost as popular with musicians as it is with actors) to run a memory of my own. Lenny and I sat across from each other. I closed my eyes. He told me to go back to an event in my life and tell him the story of it. I dropped James at this point in favor of a motorcycle accident I had been in when I was twenty, riding on the back of a friend's Honda 440 late at night in a Pittsburgh parking lot. The parking lot was on a river, and we first rode down by the water, then doubled back, splitting a pair of columns whose lighting made for an optical illusion that hid a low retaining wall blocking our path. We slid into it. My friend was injured somewhat less than I was, and he left me to find help. I had shaky memories of the time spent waiting, flashes of the ambulance and the hospital. There were all kinds of pain and unconsciousness to play with.

After the first few times I went through the memory, I did begin to recall details that I had forgotten, innocuous stuff mostly. The scene of the accident became a tangible space in my mind, a set that I could explore freely. It was almost like a movie that I could pause or rewind or run back at half speed, my memory, too, subject to horizons set in place by the technology I was familiar with. Lenny was gentle and stuck to the Auditor's Code. The light from the Los Angeles afternoon pushed through my eyelids, and the red that I saw was my own blood sifting through my skin. Then I saw something else, with another part of myself. I saw something in a corner of the parking lot: a black space, an emptiness, not at all a mass but a region of my memory that was entirely vacant. It appeared when I was alone and injured, at a moment when I found blood on the ground and realized it was my own. I didn't tell Lenny about the space right away; I ignored it a few times through the event. I began to feel a little queasy. Lenny kept asking me for details, smells and feelings. The questions weren't in Ron's voice, but they were his words, and now their inquisitiveness seemed the conspirator to my imagination.

"I see something," I said, while my old self shuffled around on the ground for the shoes that had been blasted off in the accident.

"What do you see?" Lenny said. "What do you hear?"

I peered into the corner of the parking lot. It's natural enough, I suppose, for a writer to feel the impulse to fill in space. It was my personal susceptibility, but I resisted it. The corner was dark; the space there had boundary and shape. It was a void, it was the incompleteness of my history, it was the riddle of my consciousness, it was the theme that my mind was concocting as it narrated its way to identity, it was my God-shaped hole. For whatever reason, even though it felt explicitly like a failing, I couldn't just fill it in. Lenny ran me through the memory a few more times, until I told him I had to pee. We stood.

"You were almost there, man," he said, shaking his head. "You almost had a win."

7. THE DEAD KING

The rest of my time in Scientology went by quickly. At the end of the week, I walked down Hollywood Boulevard to Author Services, Inc., where every Friday evening a group of actors gathered to perform a reading of one of Ron's old science-fiction stories. The crowd was all tanned, well-dressed folks who knew the air kiss and the head-shot smile. Five actors took the stage to read an old story that Ron had banged out at ninety-five words per minute. Still, the narrator was in tears by the end, and the audience leapt to a standing ovation. The actors bowed, and then they all gestured to a giant portrait of Hubbard beside the stage. The applause surged.

After the reading we were all led to the fourth floor of Author Services, Inc., for a reception. The fourth floor was a precise mock-up of an old adventurers' club, the rooms all sitting chambers decked out with gorgeous sofas and rugs and divans. The ceilings were all oak, the walls were all shelves, and the books were all Ron's. Heavy curtains blocked every window, and the whole complex might have been deep underground. Somebody's toy poodle, carved like a shrub, ran around yipping at people, and the Scientologists teethed little blocks of cheese from a buffet.

After a while a man named Hugh gathered those of us who were new and led us around a corner to a wooden staircase that spiraled impossibly up from the fourth floor. Above, ornate doors led off a catwalk. Hugh led us through one of them into a tight room with shiny metal walls, a vault. It was another museum, this time for the extensive process Scientology had invented for the preservation of Ron's books. Hugh walked us through the research. He told us that Scientology had advanced archival technology by studying mummification processes. The result was LRH Archival Record Paper, specially milled, and non-fading LRH Archival Inks. Books were bound in Irish linen cloth covers with gold labels. The eighteen-volume collection of Ron's tech bulletins and articles, the twelve-volume Organization and Executive Course set, a twenty-five-volume set of basic Scientology books, and the nine-volume Research and Discovery Series were preserved in this manner. And there was a special edition of *DMSMH,* the entire text acid-etched onto a full set of stainless steel plates.

Next Hugh showed us how the books were stored. Full sets of Hubbard's works were first wrapped in specially tested plastics and then locked into custom-designed boxes heatproof up to 1,600 degrees Fahrenheit. Oxygen was removed from the boxes and an inert gas was introduced. Duplicate sets of the boxes had been sent across the world and were buried underground in nineteen classified locations. The tour, and the evening, ended with a demonstration of the special hand-crank record player that Scientology had also invented to play Ron's lectures on stainless steel albums just in case the whole world lost power forever.

On Sunday I went to Scientology services at Celebrity Centre International. I walked the grounds before they began, weaving between ponds and gazebos, and I explored the lobby of the center itself, like a grand nineteenth-century hotel. I peered into Hubbard's office there: every Scientology building I entered had an effigy office ready for Ron, roped off like an iconostasis. Out near the main desk stood the door to the Religious Technology Center. Just beside it hung their ethical code, and I peered in to find that bit of the fine print that morally binds Scientologists to attack anyone they believe is attacking them. I tried the door, but it was locked.

Services were conducted out in a pavilion. A young man in a suit led us through Scientology's prayer—the author of the universe would help us come to know the author of the universe—and then he led us through a series of consciousness-raising exercises. We concentrated on obeying commands like "Wear a head," "Keep your right hand from going away," "Sit in your chair," and "Have two feet." The young man praised or thanked us after each order. After about an hour we dispersed.

A few days passed. Before the birthday celebration, I went back to the mother church campus and wandered into some of the buildings down L. Ron Hubbard Boulevard, where higher-level training was available. Inside, they were all adventure-corporate, with bulletin boards offering congratulations to people who had made OT levels. In one lobby a large day-care event was under way, sixty or seventy children all being watched over by Scientologists.

Down at the Shrine, Scientologists had been posted out in the streets to direct traffic for the birthday, and by the front doors stood great tents sheltering tables full of catering. One of the main features of Ron's birthday celebration was a tradition called the Birthday Game. It had begun years before when someone asked Hubbard what he wanted for his birthday and he blurted out, "Expansion!" The Birthday Game was a precise measure of which org within Scientology had managed the most gains over the previous year. Apparently, the Birthday Game had become politicized, and people were wearing pins in support of their favorite org.

Inside, the auditorium was vast and murmury with the voices of those who had made their way in before me, and no one seemed to remember that this was where the first demonstration of a Clear had gone so terribly awry. I sat across an aisle from an entire section of seats reserved with placards that read BEVERLY HILLS MISSION. This part of the audience filled in late, many of them coming in after the place was packed and hot and the lights had gone down. The show began with a booming announcer's voice welcoming us to the birthday celebration of mankind's truest friend, and then the curtains before the stage parted to reveal the screen on which would play the final movie I would watch during my time in Scientology.

The movie was tape of the celebration held at Flag Land Base the night before. Another announcer geared us up with talk of Ron's compassion. This compassion would allow us the joy of really being human, the voice said, and then of course there was Ron's gift of immortality itself. In the film, we could see the Flag Land Base audience rise to their feet for standing ovations, and we of the mother church followed suit. The announcer introduced David Miscavige.

Miscavige was slick onstage. He referenced the war the United States was waging then, and he spoke righteously of Scientology's staying on the proper path and being ready to clean up the aftermath of "their" mess. He cited statistics on how many people Scientology was reaching with Narconon and their literacy efforts, and then he moved into the theme for the evening.

"Tonight isn't our normal celebration," he said. "You can notch this one up on the calendar. For what takes place from here is about how we respond to the massive international demand for LRH answers at correct orders of magnitude." It was all about global freedom and planetary clearing and flipping the switch to an exponential level. "Tonight we're talking a new breed of organization exactly in line with what LRH describes."

Before he went into the details on this he handed the stage over to the church's official LRH biographer, who had more footage for us as a surprise. Now it was movies within movies. These were interviews with elderly people who had been close to Ron in the early days at Saint Hill. The gospel according to Ron's personal secretary. The gospel according to the Hell's Angel that Ron had befriended and set on a better path. The gospel according to the journalist Ron had hired on a whim.

When they were done, Miscavige reappeared. He began by putting Scientology in context, listing its growth and the many nations it had reached. The audience roared. Then he compared Scientology's numbers to those of mainstream religions. Scientology was the most successful new religious movement to come out of twentieth-century America, but even with optimistic data it was still relatively small. LRH, he said, had spoken of clearing the planet, and everyone knew that once that goal was achieved it was on to Target Two. All of which meant, basically, that they had a lot of work to do. This brought Miscavige back to the theme of organization. He stated it boldly: he wanted all Scientology orgs all over the world to be able to offer all the same services as Flag Land Base. This got a gasp from the mother church crowd. Miscavige slowed down. He began to quote from Hubbard. And even though Author Services, Inc., was on hand to make sure that Ron's work always appeared in the form he intended, Miscavige began to pick and choose, citing tidbits that showed that this new plan for reorganization was really what Ron had intended all along. This was the real birth of Scientology scripture, I thought. Scripture becomes scripture precisely at that moment when it loses all association with whatever it was before it was scripture. It stopped being history, it wasn't research, and it was no longer literature, either. Scripture was the antithesis of pluralism because by definition it could mean only one thing at a time, and, I thought, seated beside the Beverly Hills Mission, climbing to my feet with them to applaud another movie, it was ultimately this that would have revealed to William James the fatal flaw in Scientology. Scientology had tried to bottle enlightenment, but eventually the business had taken precedence over the experience it was trying to sell, and from there it was doomed to be ruled over by the symptoms it hoped to cure: paranoia, ennui, and a fear that science threatened free will. Ron's life had been co-opted in the effort, a glorified history mummified and entombed all over the world, and now he was the dead king who had become a god. He spoke to Scientologists still. It would be disingenuous if I never asked myself whether I wasn't using James in the same way, if by adopting his biography I played his voice mechanically in my mind. Or was it just me listening to myself? Biography could become scripture, too, and I found that as Miscavige demonstrated the transition between the two, I no longer wanted to listen to it. I was not curious about what Target Two was, and I didn't care if the great new org would allow someone to win the Birthday Game. The next time the audience rose to their feet, I slipped on my coat, picked up my bag, and left them all gathered in the Shrine as I snuck out the back into a chilly Los Angeles evening, with cool winds blowing down from the mountains.

1898–1902

In the mid-1890s, James had begun negotiations to deliver a series of lectures on religion at the University of Edinburgh. He accepted the Gifford appointment in 1898. The year before he refused the lectures because of his health, recommending his colleague Josiah Royce in his place. Eventually, when Royce was in Scotland, he reported back to James, "Everywhere they ask about you, and regard me as only the advance agent of the true American theory."

Edinburgh had quickly offered James the appointment again. James planned two sets of ten lectures, to be delivered in May of 1900 and 1901. For a time he believed a second book would stem from the end of the first. Long before then, however, he had difficulty getting *Varieties* moving at all. Poor health and a simple inability to produce the document nearly caused him to abandon the effort and resign his post at Harvard. He announced to a friend that what he hoped to do was defend even unusual religions by demonstrating that religious experience was humanity's most important function. He believed that he would fail at this, but claimed that "to attempt it is *my* religious act."

Just as biographies of religious geniuses are shaped into flattering narratives by zealous followers, James's biographers have tended to compress a pair of his experiences from 1898 that served as a turning point for both *Varieties* and his life. James's health has always been a point of biographical confusion—and one of the most fundamental contradictions of his life is that despite his various illnesses he was always an avid hiker. But now he was approaching sixty. One day in June, he climbed Mount Marcy, the top of the Adirondacks, and spent that evening with a group of campers from Bryn Mawr. The night around a campfire, immersed in nature, helped him sort it all out. He wrote to Alice that the perfect temperature of the night, a bright moon, and a clear sky made for a "state of spiritual alertness of the most vital description." He called it "a regular Walpurgis nacht." The gods of nature-mythologies seemed to meet inside him with the moral gods of his inner life, he said, and the thought that these gods had not much in common with one another helped cement the lectures for him. "It was one of the happiest lonesome nights of my existence," he wrote, "and I understand now what a poet is."

Several weeks later (some accounts insist it was the following day) James climbed Mount Marcy again, alone. He got lost on the way back, and what should have been a mild hike turned into a rugged descent without food. He fainted twice. When he finally stumbled back to safety, he had damaged his heart, and "aortic distress" badgered him for the rest of his life. Together, the two hikes up Mount Marcy were James's Mount Sinai, his revelation, and his wandering in the desert all wrapped into one. He emerged as a troubled prophet ready to pen his wisdom.

Or not so ready.

It went well at first, James feverishly collecting notes and materials. The whole family gave him the space and peace he needed to work without upsetting his heart. "But was ever man born of woman harder to take care of than William!" Alice complained to Henry James. Home eventually proved too distracting, and James decided to spend some sabbatical time and sail for Europe early. Before then, however, he took a trip to California to deliver a lecture entitled "Philosophical Conceptions and Practical Results." The talk was notable as it marked the formal public introduction of Pragmatism—which James attributed to Charles Peirce—but it revealed as well how *Varieties* was dominating his thoughts. James argued that what really kept the idea of religion alive was not the work of theologians, but individual religious experiences.

If you ask what these experiences are, they are conversations with the unseen, voices and visions, responses to prayer, changes of heart, deliverances from fear, inflowings of help, assurances of support, whenever certain persons set their own internal attitude in certain appropriate ways.

James's two oldest sons were already enrolled at Harvard by the time he and Alice were ready to leave for Europe. Aleck stayed with relatives; Peggy alone tagged along. Before they sailed, the work on *Varieties* took a turn for the worse. James's health deteriorated; he lowered himself into a sick chrysalis. After arriving in Europe, he spent the next several months seeking cures across the continent. He worked when he could, from bed, writing for two or three hours a day, making slow progress. When it appeared he could not make his deadline, James resigned the lectures again—they were simply delayed for another year—and asked Harvard for additional leave.

He stayed for a time at the baths at Nauheim, reading from the many testimonials and biographies he would quote in *Varieties* and agitatedly following the news of a sensational French trial. America's occupation of the Philippines grabbed his attention as well—he had vigorously objected to a growing sense of American righteousness, and had already lent his name to a burgeoning anti-imperialist movement. "It seems like a regular relapse into savagery," he wrote to a friend. "In the Philippine islands we are now simply pirates." James's former student Theodore Roosevelt, who would soon be the second name on the McKinley presidential ticket, represented the opposite side of the argument, publicly advocating aggressive militarism in a famous speech called "The Strenuous Life." James had dismissed the speech just before he left the country. "Although in middle life," he wrote, "[Roosevelt] is still mentally in the *Sturm und Drang* period of early adolescence." During the election cycle of 1900, James worried that the Democrats did not have a strong enough candidate, and he supported William Jennings Bryan only late: "The great thing is to get the republicans infernally *stopped;* and stopped quick!"

After Germany, the Jameses wandered to England and Switzerland and back again, trying different schools for Peggy and a range of cures for William. He experimented with baths and low-carb diets and he settled finally on injections that included extracts from the brains and testicles of goats, administered by Alice twice daily. They spent time with Henry and visited with a number of the philosophers and psychical researchers James had been corresponding with for years. They lived the variations he was synthesizing in *Varieties*.

James's health was shaky enough that he worried, exaggeratedly, that he might not survive the writing of the book. His mood infected Alice, who became depressed. Another epic battle between them forced its way into James's biographies, though tenderness returned soon enough. James reported that in his "pupal state" he was so weak Alice was required to hand-feed him.

They headed to Scotland in May 1901, a few days before the talks were to begin. Attendance for the initial lecture was four times what the Gifford series usually drew, and the crowd increased as the series proceeded. James reported that the delivery of the lectures taxed him and strained his heart. Between talks he spent most of his time in bed. In typical fashion, he would later claim to have been strengthened by the event as a whole.

The Varieties of Religious Experience: A Study in Human Nature is the story of how William James, a scientist whose curiosity and cynicism made for the polarities of an unlikely inner magnet, came to agree with the idea of God.

The lectures began with James's admission that he was exploring extreme examples of religious experience. He returned to this point several times, insisting that if the examples were approached with common sense and a "corrective of exaggeration," they would allow for conclusions about less extreme forms of spirituality as well. In the first lecture, he presented his argument that the fruits of religion should not be dismissed even if their source was questionable, and he stipulated that the talks would focus solely on personal experience. Religion for these purposes, he acknowledged, might just as easily be labeled "conscience" or "morality." He offered a definition of religion strictly for the lectures: "the feelings, acts, and experiences of individual men in their solitude, so far as they apprehend themselves to stand in relation to whatever they may consider the divine." He defended religion on the grounds that the world imposed its sacrifices and surrenders on all of us, regardless, so religion made "easy and felicitous what in any case [was] necessary."

In a later lecture he further characterized religion as "belief that there is an unseen order [in the universe], and that our supreme good lies in harmoniously adjusting ourselves thereto." Here for the first time James made the claim that the "unseen order" was not something that those who reported it had invested faith in—rather, it was something they directly sensed, or at least reported sensing. He insisted that the unconscious mind held sway over us on this point: if one had an experience of an unseen order, then no amount of intellectualization would void the experience. The "higher" process could not veto the "lower."

He continued on to the famous categories of the healthy-minded and the sick souls. Healthy-minded individuals, again, were those who tended to deny that evil existed, to look upon all things and see good. The sick

souls couldn't accept such a rosy picture. Each group had a distinct threshold for discomfort. The healthy-minded person was incapable of prolonged suffering; the sick soul seemed to choose it. It was no surprise,
James said, that the sick soul would require another solution, a different religion entirely.

The sick soul was James's own lot. He likened the inability of sick souls
to "believe" to an inability to fall in love. Falling in love involved none of
our intellectual faculties—one could not *decide* to fall in love. And one who
could not love was surely disadvantaged, just as the sick soul was "sick" precisely because he could not believe as readily as the healthy-minded man.

The sick soul was a pit, and once one had descended into it the climb
back out would necessarily be torturous. The sick soul was a cold womb.
And if one managed to return from its depth, the rejuvenation felt like a
second birth. Long before "born again" entered our lexicon alongside the
healthy-minded masses, James labeled the sick souls who managed to
scrape their way to happiness "the twice-born." James preferred this group,
as they did not blink out the world's harshest realities. The religion of the
sick soul, whatever it was, was the more complete system in the end.

Among sick souls the self-description of a split mind, a "divided self,"
was consistent across the range of cases James cited—Saint Augustine, Henry
Alline, and others. And chaos, he explained, characterized the process of
stitching closed the wound of our fractured selves. This, he acknowledged,
might well come from a movement away from religion, but it was the religious case that interested him. In this there were two routes of escape:
gradual and abrupt. Tolstoy was James's example of the gradual; it took the
writer two years to suture himself together from an emotional funk. He
demonstrated for James that if one had drunk "too deeply of the cup of
bitterness," the escape must necessarily be into "a universe two stories
deep."

Which initiated a discussion of conversion phenomena that perhaps revealed where James had mined the nugget that he had lobbed at Roosevelt.
James began the discussion by noting that conversion was a common oc-
currence among adolescents, and he quoted E. D. Starbuck, who argued
that adolescent conversions shortened "up [their] period of storm and
stress [*Sturm und Drang*]." But James was more interested in adult conversion, he said, which he believed to be truer to the "forms of [the original
religious] experience." For this he needed a fiat: within all of us was a cer-

tain core of identity, he wrote, a set of ideas to some extent learned—and so changeable—but central to our notion of ourselves. This "habitual centre of personal energy" was a "hot place," a group of concepts to which we devoted ourselves.

In adult conversions, one could see the process working: a buildup in the habitual center of one's personal energy followed by a self-surrender, a "throwing of our conscious selves upon the mercy of powers . . . which are more ideal than we are," and a bursting forth of an individual with a new center of energy. "Here if anywhere is the genuinely strenuous life," James wrote, calling out to Roosevelt. To this point, he clarified, psychology and religion continued to agree, since even psychology had to admit that a force outside one's conscious experience was clearly exerting influence over the conscious self.

Almost to the halfway point, James wrote a letter to a friend describing his feelings so far:

> *I have given 9 of my lectures and am to give the 10th to morrow. They have been a success, to judge by the numbers of the audience (300 odd) and their non-diminution towards the end. No previous "Giffords" have drawn near so many. It will please you to know that I am stronger & tougher than when I began, too; so great a load is off my mind. . . .*
> *Now at the end of this first course I feel my "matter" taking firmer shape, and it will please you less to hear me say that I believe myself to be (probably) permanently incapable of believing the Christian scheme of vicarious salvation. . . . In these lectures the ground I am taking is this: The mother sea and fountain head of all religions lie in the mystical experiences of the individual, taking the word mystical in a very wide sense.*

The next day, James finished off the first year with the argument that if a man could simply will a conversion within himself, alter his center of energy, this phenomenon was worthy of study regardless of whether the ideas that helped trigger it were based in fact. James wondered whether "will" was a conscious process. The unconscious mind, as James took it, was a discovery of only a couple decades before, and he considered the wall between it and consciousness a lacy boundary at best. Even casual observation revealed that consciousness was vulnerable to stealthy incursions from the unconscious mind. The exact permeability of this boundary was not the same for everyone, and the difference between the healthy-minded and the sick souls was explained by variety in the makeup of that spongy lattice.

James finished with a list of the fruits of religion as he saw them: a loss of worry, a perception of a truth unknown before, an objective change in the perception of the world, ecstasy of happiness. He warned his audience not to be too judgmental if the fruits of some religions proved dispiriting. Degree only separated the types. He ended with the first hint of what he would later call an "over-belief": if there *were* supernatural agents at work in the world, he said, they might well be acting upon us through our unconscious selves.

The Jameses stayed in Europe for a time after the first course of talks was complete. They had not been home in two years. Alice might have stayed on indefinitely—James described both her and Henry as "America-phobes"—but James longed "to steep myself in America again." They were back in Boston by the first week of September, and James immediately headed to New Hampshire to rest. While he was home, Leonora Piper retired in scandal; there was controversy over whether she was contacting spirits or simply reading her subjects' minds. That same month, Theodore Roosevelt became president when McKinley was assassinated, and despite their feud, James admitted that Roosevelt had some admirable qualities and might do well.

James turned exclusively to his second course of lectures. These went more smoothly. Over the winter, he rejected both philosophical appointments and the offer of an honorary degree from Oxford. He taught only one class, in the fall—replacing a professor who had suddenly died—and the course he offered fell directly in line with *Varieties*. By spring, the book was done.

The audience for the second set of lectures was even larger. James began by returning to the fruits of religion. ("By their fruits ye shall know them," he had insisted, biblically, the year before.) The first three lectures defined "Saintliness" as the name of a "composite photograph" of persons for whom spiritual emotions, the fruits, formed the centers of their personal energy. This composite included a feeling of life beyond selfish interest, a friendly continuity with an ideal power, elation and freedom, and a shift toward harmonious affections. These feelings tended to translate to a set of behaviors: asceticism, strength of soul, purity, and charity.

These characteristics were consistent across religions, though an even more fundamental feature of the spiritual life was the sense of a higher and friendly power. The scientist in James asserted itself here: one still did not have to believe that such a thing existed to recognize that the faith-state organically produced charitable feelings. It was important to note that these "inner shiftings" predated theology and were independent of any particular philosophy.

A survey of the testimonials of individuals who reported having undergone this inner shifting led James to an explanation for asceticism and self-sacrifice. When one became attuned to purity, he argued, the tolerance for an impure world was necessarily disrupted. The world became a more difficult place to inhabit. The healthy-minded might be able to say yes to everything, but the sick souls, converted, must find an outlet for the no that was their natural state. Various nos—self-denials—amounted to the ascetic impulse.

With the saintly characteristics in place, James asked whether these fruits could be used to defend the overall value of religion. He granted that the question might seem illogical: "How *can* you measure their worth without considering whether the God really exists who is supposed to inspire them?" James met this with the argument that it was the fruits of religion that generally convinced men to believe in the first place. An idea seemed true, and you believed it, because it "worked" for you in some way. This meant, hypothetically, that it was possible to reject a real god because its fruits were not what one required. And this led to James's plea for variety. The changing definition of God, from one of "cruel appetites" requiring bleeding sacrifices on down, charted the history of individual need. Some people required a religion of consolation, while others were more suited to religions of "terror and reproof," but they all had value. The fruits resulted regardless of the accuracy of their hypotheses.

With the fruits of religion in place, James returned to the larger canvas. He sketched again the process of a new religion: the mad prophet, the initial heresy, the transition to orthodoxy, and then to institutionalization. This cycle exonerated religious experience, James claimed, from the crimes laid at the feet of the institutional side of religion. For it was not religious experience that accounted for the "historic aberrations," the atrocious acts committed in God's name. Instead, the culprit was an exaggerated form of one of its expressions: convulsive devoutness, or fanaticism. Fanaticism was absurd, James said, particularly when one took a good look at the saints, whose extravagance often turned out to be a deficiency of intellect. Saints were our torchbearers of belief, "they show the way and are the forerun-ners," but it was a mistake to attribute too much to them. The many mirac-ulous acts attributed to Buddha, Muhammad, or any of a range of Christian saints were "a touching expression of man's misguided propensity to praise." This led James to dismiss the totalitarian Christian God, who lacked an "essential largeness."

Throughout the lectures James had referred to mystical experiences, but only late did he set about describing them. Mystical experiences were spontaneous personal interaction with a perceived divine. He suggested four characteristics: ineffability (more a state of feeling than intellect); noetic quality (insight into unplumbable depth); transiency (they came and went quickly); and passivity (a sense of being "held" by a higher power). Mystical states were worthy of examination because they seemed to offer wisdom and direction, and because all the major religions had cultivated them. Mystics might be crazy, James allowed, but that had nothing to do with the insight they offered.

Only a few things could be generalized from mystics' testimony: they tended toward optimistic monism; they were authoritative for the individ-ual but offered no conclusive proof of anything; and they undermined the notion that experience could be described with the senses alone. This last was the main point: "The counting in of that wider world of meaning might be indispensable in our approach to the final fullness of truth."

Moving toward conclusion, James asked whether philosophy could stamp "veracity upon the religious man's sense of the divine." It was "over-beliefs" that needed to be verified. James now defined an over-belief as the bit of intellectualization that men conducted to buttress feelings not other-wise explainable. But philosophy failed to verify anything. The problem was that it attempted to take the individual experience out of the equation; it wished to reclaim religion from mystery. But the God of philosophy, a "metaphysical monster," was an "absolutely worthless invention of the scholarly mind," and we were left with mystical experiences that offered practical fruits, but no system to understand them.

Now James approached prayer for the first time. Having dismissed the intellect's ability to create or refute belief, he returned to empiricism to argue that prayer (defined broadly) generated actual change. "In prayer, spiritual energy, which otherwise would slumber, does become active." This returned to the question of whether what was happening was "real" or was simply in the mind of the individual. And *this* returned to the subconscious mind. Just as the subconscious mind gave us our intuitions, hypotheses, fancies, persuasions, and convictions, so was it the fountainhead of our religion. And now James was ready to conclude with a final stab at God and to state the over-belief to which he himself was willing to attest.

He restated the question a final time: something real came to pass from religious belief, but how far should we go in saying the belief was therefore true? He was edging toward Pragmatism, as he had been edging all along, first pointing out that until recently truth had been defined only as that which had not yet been contradicted. Yet the study of religious experience yielded a difficult fact: the general view of reality was only a symbol, and when we "deal with . . . personal phenomena as such, we deal with realities in the completest sense of the term." Religion offered a solution, a *more*. But "is such a 'more' merely our own notion, or does it really exist?" The vast variety of religions all agreed that it did: some called it either God or gods, others a "stream of ideal tendency," and all argued that it *acted* as well. This variety of belief, James said, should be celebrated—"a 'god of battles' must be allowed to be the god for one kind of person, a god of peace and heaven and home, the god for another." One did not need to agree with God to recognize that through religious experience a person could achieve saving experiences that otherwise would not come. God, then, in whatever form, "was real since he produces real effects."

Beyond that, James offered his own over-belief, which he admitted was "of a pallid kind." Communication, he said, between some ideal state of things and man in the prayerful state actually happened, some link between the "more" and our subliminal selves. He did not claim to know what the communication was, but he recognized that by believing in it he had kept himself more "sane and true":

> *The whole drift of my education goes to persuade me that the world of our present consciousness is only one out of many worlds of consciousness that exist, and that those other worlds must contain experiences which have a meaning for life also; and that although in the main their experiences and those of this world keep discrete, yet the two become continuous at certain points, and higher energies filter in.*

At Alice's suggestion, James combined the final two lectures into a single day so they could make an earlier ship home. When he finished, the enthusiastic Gifford audience sang him "For He's a Jolly Good Fellow." James complained that whatever health he had managed to recover over the last two years had been eaten up by the book. When he and Alice landed back in Chocorua in June 1902, it was the first time the entire family had been together in four years.

Varieties was more widely read than anything else James produced. He had as much as predicted its popularity when he'd told a friend that it was "too biological for the religious, too religious for the biologists." He hoped he had done justice to "both God's friends and his enemies," he said, and the book proved to be a unifying force if only because religions of all sorts managed to find something in it supportive of their views. For Hugo Münsterberg, James's sometime antagonist, he advised not taking it up "till you're on your deathbed, when it will save your soul." Yet the book did not entirely satisfy. Just as James had once become a prominent psychologist without having written a book on psychology, so was he now a philosopher without having written a philosophy. *Varieties* was "all facts and no philosophy," he wrote to a colleague, and the system it prescribed still needed to be written.

"I actually dread to die," he told a friend a year later, "until I have settled the Universe's hash in one more book."

Godless

---◆---

The cultivator of this science [of religions] has to become acquainted with so many groveling and horrible superstitions that a presumption easily arises in his mind that any belief that is religious is probably false.

—William James

It is so easy for a Russian to become an atheist, easier than for anyone else in the world! And our people don't simply become atheists, they infallibly believe in atheism as though it was a new religion, without being aware that they are believing in nothingness.

—Fyodor Dostoyevsky, *The Idiot*

1. VANINI

Giulo Cesare Vanini was born in Taurisano, Italy, in 1585. He grew up wanting to study law, but when his father died he joined a Carmelite monastery and changed his name to Fra' Gabriele. He earned a degree in 1606, but when his studies took him to Padua he discovered the emerging skeptical thought of the day and reconsidered Catholicism. At first he longed to reunite all Christians. But this compromised his standing with the Carmelites, so he sneaked off to England to become an Anglican. In less than a year Vanini decided Anglicans were just as intolerant as Catholics, and he begged for forgiveness from Pope Paul V with a hundred crowns. When not distorting the biographies of religious geniuses, apostates may find themselves used as chits between religions, an economic battle waged with conversion as currency. Vanini's apology was to be accepted. But after an English archbishop caught wind of the plan, Vanini was imprisoned. In 1614, Catholic representatives helped him escape and flee England.

The battery of political persecution and exposure to philosophy led Vanini to unbelief. Religion was tainted by politics and power, he came to think, and skepticism was necessary for the development of reason. He campaigned now for Atheism, which promised social harmony and the renewal of man. He ridiculed the philosophical proofs of God's existence, attacked the history of religion. He published works undermining the metaphysics that supported the idea of God, borrowing huge tracts of text from other authors. By 1616, he was a wanted man on the run in France. He took a pseudonym, became a teacher, and practiced medicine, but he continued to proselytize and attracted a new following. In 1618, the town of Toulouse caught wind of his beliefs. He was imprisoned again and tried for Atheism, blasphemy, and profanity. He defended himself in court but was condemned to death. Vanini refused to beg God for forgiveness. He believed in the existence of neither God nor the Devil, he said. He asked that a doctor be on hand to witness that he died without fear. His executioner tore out his tongue, strangled him, and burned his body at the stake in a public square. Vanini was thirty-three years old.

2. THE PAINE ISSUE

James said that gross religious superstition could easily make one think that all religion was false. This pretty well described the effect Scientology had on me. But he suggested as well that the stitching up of the sickened soul could result from a movement toward irreligion.

The Atheist convention was held at a resort—in fact, it was the last resort. Once they had settled on a city to host the year's gathering, the American Atheist scout team set out to find a hotel with cheap group rates. The resort they chose was the last one they toured on a two-day trip. The site was loosely themed Native American, walls and decor dyed to a blanched color scheme, the whole place built on what some architect considered a novel idea: the hexagon. The rooms all had six sides. Corridors wrapped around adjacent cells like images in an M. C. Escher print, a geometric quilt of bleeding evolution. The Atheists would stay inside the maze for three full days.

Atheists held their national gatherings on Easter weekend, for the double entendre of irony and economy. The hotel was basically deserted. I checked into my hexagon and looked out windows that faced back into the interior of the structure, an indoor courtyard made up like a grotto. A piano played by itself, fake trees stood their eternal green, and a bar called the Cave was sunk halfway into the floor and domed over with caulked artificial rock. The Atheists had begun to gather.

I went downstairs to search for Arlene-Marie, the state director of American Atheists' Michigan chapter. Michigan was a big state for Atheists. I had arranged to attend the Godless March on Lansing that Arlene was planning for the following month. Arlene was a longtime unbeliever. She had been close with Madalyn Murray O'Hair, the tough, flamboyant grandmother figure who had founded the group. Several years before, O'Hair had suddenly disappeared with her family and $600,000 of American Atheists' money. O'Hair's success in removing prayer from schools in the United States had earned her the label "most hated woman in America," and for several years her disappearance remained a mystery, a range of media sources exploiting a lingering suggestion that she had been a con artist all along, Atheism her ruse. *Who's Who in Hell,* an encyclopedia of modern freethinkers, lashed out at those who refused to pillory O'Hair in print, and *Vanity Fair* reported a sighting of O'Hair in Auckland, New Zealand. But it was a ghost. Eventually, O'Hair's remains turned up with those of one of her sons and a granddaughter on a ranch in Texas. They had been kidnapped for a ransom and murdered.

All that was in the past now, however, and Atheism was trying to turn a new corner. The Atheists converged on the grotto's grid of hard sofas and coffee tables, and I found Arlene-Marie almost at once. Arlene battled her sixty years with bright red nails on her hands and feet, matching lipstick, and long hair pulled up into a teenager's twist. She looked me up and down. Her stare wandered behind lines of mascara, but it could suddenly smart on you too, I would find, like an accusation. When we had spoken on the phone, Arlene had decided that her goal would be to convince me that Atheists were capable of fun, that they weren't the unhappy drones of their stereotype. Arlene believed Atheists were the happiest people in the world.

She tried to introduce me around, but most of the Atheists were busy greeting old friends. As a rule, Atheists tend toward solitude, and the convention would prove as much reunion as intellectual exchange, an annual reminder that they weren't alone in their godless ways. The Atheists hugged, shook hands, shared stories. "As you can see," one man told me before rushing off to clap the back of a compatriot, "our hairdos quite cleverly conceal our horns." All weekend, the Atheists would impress upon me how relieved they were to be among people who thought as they did.

Arlene managed to herd a core group of national officers into the Cave to proceed with some serious drinking. Atheists have a reputation for belligerence and are notorious drinkers and cursers. "I'm putting grandmothers to shame, coast to coast," Arlene said, referring only in part to the perfect Manhattan, straight up with a twist, she carried around the bar with her. The Cave tried for a lewd, vaginal feel. Atheists don't believe in miracles, but I was beginning to as I watched Arlene squirt through the room without spilling her drink, precarious in a martini glass. I sat beside Eddie Tabbasch, a Beverly Hills lawyer famous for running for state legislature as an outed Atheist. He was a small, odd-shaped man whose clothes never quite fit him. "I didn't lose because I'm godless," he said, and smiled. "I lost because a large portion of my practice is representing prostitutes. I'm a hooker lawyer." Next to him sat Dick Hogan, a Texas contractor and the treasurer for American Atheists. Hogan was boyish and rich. "He's so rich he shaves his leather," Arlene told me, tipsy and weaving. Hogan had a drawly way of pronouncing the word *Texas* as though it had only one syllable. "I ain't rich," he shot back at Arlene. "But as long as I got a face, honey, you got a seat!" Then Hogan saw me taking notes. "Are you writing that down? He's writing that down. You write down the funniest things." He began telling a racist joke to the table at large until the others told him to knock it off—the usual saw was that Atheism lent itself to no particular politics, but in their plight Atheists did tend to identify with marginalized groups, minorities, homosexuals. "Sorry, sorry," Hogan explained. "I'm from Texas." Arlene changed the subject, recalling some similar night when a gang of Atheists appropriated a bar not so different from this one and spent the night concocting drunken slogans against a charge that riled them: that Atheism was a form of religion. The best of the slogans had been "If Atheism is a religion, then bald is a hair color." She laughed, and the rest of the Atheists sipped their drinks and nodded.

By then, James's words and my own thoughts were practically indistinguishable. "The more fervent opponents of Christian doctrine," he had once said, "have often enough shown a temper which, psychologically considered, is indistinguishable from religious zeal."

Ellen Johnson came into the bar then. Johnson was O'Hair's successor, the new president of American Atheists. Pretty, pert, and blond, she had the presence of a local news anchor. She'd had contacts in the Clinton White House, appeared routinely on talk shows, had lobbied for oppressed Atheists abroad. The previous November she had organized the nation's largest freethinking groups to a Godless March on Washington, an event that drew a crowd of three thousand to the National Mall. It was a good turnout for Atheists, and Arlene-Marie hoped to re-create its success with her advance on Lansing.

Johnson sat next to me, though she was leery of journalists. I couldn't blame her. She was one of those whom the press had punished for loyalty to O'Hair. While O'Hair had been a mannish woman but well-spoken and charismatic, Johnson was attractive to the point of distraction but not as buttery a speaker. When she gave speeches she leaned toward aphorism, watered-down versions of thought from famous freethinkers. I wanted to interview her. But she turned at once to Eddie Tabbasch and launched into a discussion on the difficulty of gathering unbelievers around a cause. Johnson was frustrated at the thirty million or so inactive godless she counted in America.

For their statistics, American Atheists put their faith in the American Religious Identification Survey (ARIS) from the City University of New York, first completed in 1990 and updated in 2001. The results showed Christianity on the decline, unbelief on the rise. Only a million Americans describe themselves as Atheists, but as much as 15 percent of the population, thirty million people, label themselves agnostic or secular or some other category that Johnson lumped under the godless umbrella. But even with all those numbers, American Atheists counted only a few thousand dues-paying members. O'Hair had once boasted of seventy thousand on her mailing list, but membership had lagged badly when she disappeared, and now the group was having trouble paying its bills. In interviews, Johnson claimed that organizing Atheists was like trying to herd cats—Atheists weren't sheep, it seemed, but they still needed a shepherd. Now she was exasperated. Americans were coming out as secularists right and left but were unconcerned with the threat organized religion posed to their civil rights.

"If they don't want to do anything, screw 'em," she told Eddie Tabbasch.

Tabbasch nodded. He complained about a new billion-dollar cathedral that had just opened up in downtown Los Angeles, then started in on some apocalyptic predictions of what would happen to the separation of church and state if Republicans were allowed to stack the Supreme Court. Two seats down, Arlene licked at her second Manhattan and threatened to swim naked in the resort's swimming pool. Atheism and nudism had significant correlation, apparently. Someone nudged my arm to ask my name, then followed up by asking whether I was the *real* J.C. This would become the refrain for the weekend. No, I said. I was named for two saints. Sorry. Arlene jumped up and moved from table to table, balancing her Manhattan like a plate on a stick, reciting decisions from appellate courts and correcting a statistic when she heard a man exaggerating the number of American godless. She came back around and threw an arm over my shoulders. "Honey, they got a home for me, and they want to put me there," she said. "I'm sorry we're so *boring*." Then she wandered off to chastise some other Atheists for failing to attend a protest two states from their home.

Outside the bar the Atheists had taken over the grotto completely. An Atheist pianist had set himself before the piano and was playing away, and a group of eight or nine state directors had gathered around a large table to trade horror stories—some had been fired from jobs for their lack of belief, some forced into retirement. Somehow the discussion turned to whether Thomas Paine had been a deist, then to what a deist was exactly, to what had caused the Dark Ages, to whether Pat Robertson really supported freedom of religion in a free Iraq. One man talked for a time about feeling very alone in his beliefs back home. The table fell silent at this. Atheists were almost invariably people who spent a lot of time arguing unpopular positions to family members and coworkers who were unlikely to be swayed. Now they bragged of making converts. "I got my parents, before they died," one man said, and a woman touched his shoulder in praise.

The Atheists were at home in the artificial grotto, but it wasn't long before the old habits kicked in and an argument ensued. Had Jefferson been enough of a prose stylist to pen the Declaration of Independence, or had Franklin and Madison pitched in and put Jefferson's name on it to exploit his popularity? Even as they argued, the Atheists seemed to realize that they shouldn't be arguing at all, that they should shelve their arsenals of horrific Bible quotations and call a cease-fire at least until Sunday's resurrection. The weekend was a chance to lower their guard. One man got up to turn in for the night and looked down at the woman he had been intimately chatting with. Evidently, he couldn't think of any last appeal to her except a continuation of their disagreement. "I'll have to set you straight on that Paine issue," he said, as though it were an invitation to inventive sexual behavior. "You'll disappoint me if you do," the woman said, flirting.

3. Buzz Aldrin Taking Communion in Space

Atheism has always been associated with persecution, and the old Italian Vanini was only one of many unbelievers that Atheists held up as martyrs for the cause. As with any saint, as with Anton LaVey or L. Ron Hubbard or William James, for that matter, prominent Atheist lives are shorn down to myth by zealous biographers. The distortion must seem only fair to Atheists, who argue that Atheism has been written out of history. "But it is also true," writes a recent scholar, "that the one group still looked upon with considerable suspicion by most Americans are those who profess to have no faith at all."

Freethinking scholars creatively cite religious and philosophical texts as evidence of the movement's historical dilemma: Jesus threatened unbelievers with hellfire; Plato said that Atheists were a danger to society and that death was the only remedy; Thomas Aquinas cited unbelief as "greater than any sin that occurs in the perversion of morals"; and John Locke, a pioneer of religious toleration, argued that toleration should not be extended to unbelievers. The exact definition of Atheism is difficult to pin down historically because its ancient adherents were suppressed and the definition of the word kept changing. It is known to have existed simply because of references in Euripides, the Upanishads, and other ancient texts. The literary efforts of those who were called Atheists weren't passed down—manuscript copyists of classical literature were all Christians.

Philosophically, Atheist scholarship traces its roots to the origin of rhetoric and doubt. It's generally agreed that before roughly the sixteenth century A.D., everyone held theistic views of one kind or another, and Atheism, which literally means the absence of theistic belief, meant in actual usage only that a given Atheist held a different belief from whoever was leveling the charge against them. Modern Atheists point to the Egyptian pharaoh Akh-en-Aton, from the fourteenth century B.C., for the first form of unbelief—Akh-en-Aton rejected polytheism to initiate a monotheism based around the god Aton. It was doubt of the prevailing mood. The pattern would repeat a millennium and a half later—early Jews and Christians were labeled Atheists for discarding pagan beliefs, as were Muslims, though Muslims themselves would use *Atheist* to describe someone who believed in God but was simply ungrateful.

Christians wrote the history of Atheism through the Middle Ages; Satan had invented it, and it went underground with paganism early in the first common millennium. Doubters were tortured and slaughtered as heretics through two waves of Inquisition. In the East, belief in God remained distant, mystical, and creative—impervious—but the literal interpretation of the Bible that emerged in Western Christianity made its inconsistencies vulnerable to thinkers who more and more became content to think for themselves, beginning around the sixteenth century. Fanaticism always triggers corresponding unbelief. Just as oracles and Druids slowly bled into wise men as prediction proved more reliable than prophecy, so did the emergence of scientific thinking and objective knowledge demonstrate that man need not rely on religion for answers. Atheists argued that secularism was inherently linked to progress, that unbelief was the natural outcome of the advance of civilization. Apart from eras of political strife, the history of the modern world from the sixteenth century on measures the gradual growth of the Atheist movement.

In the New World, religious toleration didn't catch on right away. Atheist scholars cite seventeenth-century laws in both Massachusetts and Connecticut that prescribed death for those who believed in the wrong god. But the presence in the colonies of many disfavored religions eventually encouraged pluralism and inspired the separation of church and state, the freedom of and from religion granted in the Constitution—emphasis on "from," Atheists note. That the United States is a Christian nation is a perverse revision of history, they argue. Most of the central founding fathers—Thomas Jefferson, George Washington, James Madison, Ben Franklin, John Adams—were deists who subscribed to an abstract creator that was certainly not the Christian God. And even deism, Atheists claim, was probably a veil for outright unbelief—*Atheist* was still a term of insult, and no one would have worn it voluntarily. The first appearance of the term "United States" came from one of the most commonly cited freethinkers, Thomas Paine again, who coined the term in letters addressed to troops during the Revolutionary War. And Paine *was* a deist, at least in name, though even he would label Christianity "a species of atheism" in noting links between it and paganism. Not even deism was particularly favored—Jefferson almost lost the election of 1800 when groups running against him labeled him an Atheist.

Atheism came to mean a complete absence of belief in God only in the seventeenth century, even later by some accounts. The thinking evolved: the first Atheistic philosophers argued for the elimination of God but perhaps not the infrastructure of religion; others argued that the complete abolishment of religion was a requirement for man's happiness. Then came Nietzsche's death of God, which had been professed before but never so dramatically—now the death was a murder by man and came with the subsequent promotion of man to god. The nineteenth century amounted to an Atheistic turn from a sterile negative outlook to one that attempted a positive, constructive, realistic view of humanity in the face of undeniable scientific progress. Atheism still couched itself in terms of smarts and courage—one had the guts to deny God—but it was these same arguments that would become entangled with the twentieth century's experiment with communism. Modern Atheism argues that religion is largely responsible for history's atrocities. By contrast, Atheism harms no one. But even without William James's insistence that institutional religion not be permitted to speak for religion's account, this argument accepts no association between Atheism and atrocities perpetrated by regimes of oppressive communism that took Atheistic inspiration—perhaps misguided or mistaken—from the works of men now considered the champions of freethinking.

Freethinking organizations enjoyed their greatest prosperity from 1860 to 1900, just as James was defending religion. These groups were often cults of personality formed around charismatic leaders known for irreverence, solipsism, and casual obscenity. Paine had been thought conceited by many—the press had described him as an "outrageous blasphemer" and a "loathsome reptile," and much later, Theodore Roosevelt called him a "filthy little atheist." Paine had shown a talent for getting himself in trouble. He was once scheduled for execution even as he was writing *The Age of Reason,* his attack on scripture. "As to the book called the bible," he wrote in a letter, "it is blasphemy to call it the Word of God. It is a book of lies and contradictions and a history of bad times and bad men." Paine's death in 1809 left a void in freethinking for a time, though the nineteenth century would come to see a proliferation of godless publications and organizations. A couple of generations later, Charles Bradlaugh formed the National Secular Society in England. Bradlaugh was another freethinker known for public outbursts of obscenity, and he often quarreled with those who became his lieutenants. Like Eddie Tabbasch, Bradlaugh ran for public office and eventually won a seat in Parliament, but he was imprisoned overnight in the clock tower when he refused to swear an oath on a Bible. He went on to win four consecutive elections.

As with Vanini, overt proclamations of Atheism in the face of death would become a theme in Atheist history, and Bradlaugh's daughter collected signed testimony that her father did not accept religion on his deathbed. As late as 1994, an effort was mounted to remove a statue of Bradlaugh from the town where he was elected.

In the United States, the main proponent of nineteenth-century freethinking was Robert G. Ingersoll, who spoke publicly on religion from 1875 to 1895. A Civil War colonel, Ingersoll began a political career as the attorney general of Illinois and was popular enough to have been governor if not for his outspoken agnosticism. As a public speaker—he advocated women's rights in addition to attacking religion—he was paid handsomely while crisscrossing the nation on the same lecture circuit that helped sustain James. To the alleged inspiration of the Bible, Ingersoll responded, "If it is true, it doesn't need to be inspired. Nothing needs inspiration except a falsehood or a mistake."

Modern Atheists acknowledge the irony that organized Atheism is most viable where religious pluralism is encouraged. The Atheist challenge has changed over time. The overt executions of the Middle Ages gave way to moral crimes perpetrated through legal loopholes. Early in the twentieth century, Atheists still could not testify in court. In a famous case, the law once allowed a rapist to go free when his eleven-year-old victim, in testifying, could not demonstrate her belief in the existence of a Supreme Being. Her testimony was excluded. A similar case in England denied justice to a four-year-old girl who fingered her murderer just as she expired—deathbed witness was admissible only for believers, and it could not be shown that the girl had understood the idea of an afterlife.

The first half of the twentieth century left organized freethinking in a shambles in the United States. American Atheists argue that Madalyn Murray O'Hair put Atheism on the map again. It's both true and untrue. Freethinking had been around for hundreds of years, but O'Hair was the first to publicly wear the name *Atheist* as a badge of honor. O'Hair's story has already receded to a prophet's mystery—the details are uncertain. Her crusade began when her son Bill Murray asked to be excused from saying the Lord's Prayer in public school. The case reached the Supreme Court. Mandatory prayer was banned at a cost: the O'Hair family was subjected to harassment from neighbors, and Bill was abused by his schoolmates. But O'Hair had found her mission. She created the group that would eventually take the name American Atheists and set out on a life that would read like a picaresque. She was another who relished profanity, and she would leave in her wake a long trail of ex-followers who testified to her greed and crankiness. O'Hair fled to Hawaii for a time after Bill, then grown, fell in love with a Jewish girl—a romance that eventually resulted in police involvement and a warrant for O'Hair's arrest. She got off on a technicality and went on to win battles on other legal fronts as well. She blocked Buzz Aldrin from taking Communion in space, she won a suit she filed after being jailed for refusing to take an oath for jury duty, and she won a case in Texas over a law requiring a person to hold a belief of some kind to sit in public office. O'Hair became a cult figure if not a cult leader—she was a pioneer guest on the talk-show circuit, and probably the most unlikely *Playboy* interviewee ever. "I need someone who can . . . slug it out, toe to toe, and I don't mean a physical battle," she said. "You think I've got wild ideas about sex? Think of those poor old dried up women lying there on their solitary pallets yearning for Christ to come to them in a vision." By then, O'Hair had a second son, Jon Garth, and Bill had had a daughter,

Robin. Both Jon Garth and Robin became prominent players in American Atheists, but Bill Murray's story would tack crazily. The Atheist take on him was that the Supreme Court case had left him susceptible to substance abuse and madness. He became an irascible teenager, a difficult adult. He wound up in a standoff with Texas police. He was arrested and went to jail broke. Then the story became bizarre, echoing the apostate battle that had ensnared Vanini. Bill was freed from jail, became associated with a Christian group, was born again, and, at least as Arlene told the story, suddenly had a wardrobe of pink suits and a fleet of pink Cadillacs at his disposal. He founded a ministry and wrote a book called *My Life Without God,* an attack on his mother. Although he didn't mention it in his own book, *Who's Who in Hell* said Bill claimed that Madalyn had once asked him to murder his grandfather.

O'Hair eventually retired from American Atheists, leaving it to Jon Garth and Robin, and it was only a short time later that they were all betrayed by an office worker. An ex-con named David Waters had earned their trust while plotting with an old cellmate, still in jail, to kidnap them all. When the cellmate was released, the O'Hairs disappeared. A bodyguard came to their house and found them gone, and the detail that told him that something was wrong—a detail that would later prove important for my own time with the Atheists—was a meal that was waiting for them on the table. They had been snatched before dinner. Shortly thereafter, $600,000 of American Atheist money was discovered missing. O'Hair was resurrected in that skeptical press, and there was the false sighting of her in New Zealand, others in Texas. Waters and his accomplice eventually confessed, and when the three bodies were finally recovered Bill Murray fought with Ellen Johnson over what would happen to them. "I have told Jon and Robin," O'Hair had said in an Atheist publication, "that when I die they should gather me up in a sheet, unwashed . . . and put me on a pyre in the back yard. . . . I don't want any damn Christer praying over the body. . . . I don't want some religious nut to shove a rosary up the ass of my body." Her remains were eventually interred in a small graveyard in Austin.

Part of Ellen Johnson's problem now was O'Hair's success. There were still anti-Atheist laws on the books—old statutes on testifying and holding public office—but Atheism's advances had made it unlikely that they would ever be enforced. At the same time, nobody was sure whether it was possible to claim conscientious-objector status to the draft as an unbeliever, and there was still a stigma attached to the Atheist label. Modern Atheists now waged their war on smaller fronts: they protested the word "God" on money, faith-based initiatives, tax breaks for religions when they are among the richest organizations in the world, and a hush-hush conspiracy to Christianize the globe. They were fervent defenders of the separation of church and state, but they lacked a specific transgression that could raise the ire of America's thirty million godless.

They now trade in rumors and offhand comments: when President George H. W. Bush once said that Atheists should not be considered Americans, Atheists jumped, spreading the comment far and wide. But they were vague on the circumstances of it. I asked Ellen Johnson about the comment that first night in the bar, when I managed to steal her attention for a moment. "Oh, *that,*" she said. "The problem with that was that we never had corroboration. The thing was, the White House never said it *didn't* happen." Two days later, I debated the quotation with an Atheist in a dirty T-shirt, the AA symbol strung around his neck. He looked at me as though I was a fool for not knowing that the entire conversation had been recorded by a man in Iowa.

4. THE SLEEPING UNBELIEVERS

The speakers began the following morning, after the Atheists rose and staggered through the resort's accidental meander to the larger hexagons of the conference rooms.

As a group, the Atheists were misfits. They had canes and walkers, they limped severely, they moved in wheelchairs. Even Pharaoh Akh-en-Aton had been a sickly king and had died young. The new Atheists were socially challenged or were confused on the level of fashion; they were missing fingers or they were dazed and lonely, or lonely and brave. They were a population of injury and reclamation. Some had wild, unshorn beards; some were young, neat professionals roused to action by the religious fervor awakened by worldwide terrorism. Most were there to socialize, and even though they weren't seekers there was the sense that they'd found something, a kind of contentedness that arose not just from a rejection of belief in God, but that rejection coupled with a community gathered around one like thing. Their comfort didn't come from an answer—it came from participation in the re-formation of the question. Here, they were not lonely.

Atheism was enough for an artificial world in hexagonal space. At breakfast, not one of them thought twice about the sausage, and no one cared that it was Good Friday.

"I have minor bouts of PTSD," said an Atheist at the table next to mine. A woman introduced herself to me and said, "I'm writing a book, too. I'm writing a book about courage." I chatted with the editor of the American Atheists newsletter, who argued that the best metaphor for organized unbelief was the health-care system, because religion was a disease. Out in the hallway, a man telling a story said, "I was the one sane person surrounded by stupid people."

I explored the book room before the speakers began. Six rafters converged to a black asterisk overhead, and the room was lit by a constellation of suspended light globes; it had a faint atmosphere of a sanctuary. Display tables stood flush against six walls and were layered over with the products of unbelief. For sale were bumper stickers that read, ONE NATION UNDER GOD—IRAN!; MERRY SOLSTICE; and ATHEISTS DO IT WITHOUT GUILT. Buttons: FIRST THEY BURN BOOKS, THEN THEY BURN PEOPLE and I THINK, THEREFORE I'M DANGEROUS. A joke body-detergent product called Repent promised fire-and-brimstone guilt-lifting action. Books included *Unzipped: The Pope Bares All* and *Pagan Origins of the Christ Myth,* inside of which were chapters titled "The Hidden Psychology of Nudity" and "Emily Dickinson and Paganism." A German publishing company was on hand to protest lingering blasphemy laws in the fatherland and to sell books—their logo, prominent on their banner, was the silhouette of the Persian devil Ahriman, a bullheaded man with a giant erect phallus standing up between his legs. In one obtuse corner a television played episodes of the talk show Ellen Johnson used as a vehicle for attack on religious groups, the Atheist answer to televangelism. As I passed, her recorded self said, "Our government is not talking about what religion is doing to people. We're the only ones, folks."

The real Ellen Johnson swished by me then in a pink dress, on her way to the speakers' room to kick off the weekend. The crowd was diverse, at least in terms of freethinking. O'Hair had given rise to modern Atheism, and her personality had created its schisms as well. Now there were a handful of godless groups in the country headed up by O'Hair's former disciples. The strategy in the wake of her disappearance seemed to be to use Johnson's beauty as a force of union around which the godless could gather. The success of their march on Washington suggested that the time was ripe to forgive old slights.

But a variety of Atheist groups also meant a variety of strategies for how to make freethinking viable. And once Johnson had dispensed with welcomes to the twenty-ninth annual National Convention of American Atheists, she congratulated a prominent godless lawyer from another group who had recently won a high-profile Pledge of Allegiance case.* Then she attacked him. Atheists had had their sights set on the Pledge of Allegiance ever since God was injected into it during a spike of spiritual fervor following World War II. The lawyer had won his case, Johnson said, but at what cost? He was now arguing that Atheism should acknowledge itself as a form of religion. This was in keeping with what James and most sociologists prescribed—freethinking groups are always included in lists of new religious movements—but to Johnson it was a form of failure. Pure Atheists were as upset by the label of religion as everyone else was by the label of Atheism. Watering down the movement would bring it to ruin, Johnson said. She would rather see Atheism shrivel. Her righteousness infected the crowd gathered quietly around the banquet tables. She wanted to be disliked, she said. She advocated civil disobedience as a form of expression. She attacked Tom Brokaw: the anchor had recently quipped in prime time that there were no Atheists in foxholes. Atheists claim that as many as 10 percent of servicemen list Atheism on their dog tags. Johnson reminded all of us that this year was the fortieth anniversary of the O'Hair case that had gotten the Atheist ball rolling again. Now they needed to focus on the silent godless hordes. American Atheists had filed papers to form a political action committee, but they would need several hundred thousand members before politicians would pay any attention to them. They needed to steal a page from religion, Johnson said, without becoming a religion themselves.

The crowd applauded and Arlene-Marie jumped to her feet when Johnson stepped away from the podium, but she was the only one. Out in the hallway during a break, Johnson blew by me when I tried to stop her to ask for an interview. Suddenly it seemed like a good idea that she wanted to be disliked.

*Like O'Hair, attorney Michael Newdow had filed the case on behalf of his child. The victory was eventually overturned and the Supreme Court refused to hear the case on the grounds that Newdow did not have proper custody of the child whose interests he claimed to represent.

Arlene was more congenial at lunch. Just to get her talking, I asked her what drew people to the Atheist community. "I think the answer to your question is easy," she said. "It's something inside you. It pulls you. Eventually, spending time with Atheists, it becomes an addiction. It ruins you. After you spend time with Atheists, you can't socialize with anyone else."

It seemed to be a common experience among Atheists that their unbelief stemmed from something deep inside them, something they couldn't quite put their finger on. It had the seduction of certainty and sounded a lot like James's conversions, I thought, the change in the center of personal energy. But they wouldn't have agreed with that.

Arlene-Marie was different, at least to the extent that she lacked the Atheist predilection to cantankerousness. She was never cranky. At the same time, her flamboyant manner and a fearless tongue had invited comparisons to O'Hair, a thought that triggered a devilish smile in her. Arlene's life didn't have O'Hair's tragedy, but it had been a wild ride nonetheless.

She had grown up religious, and believed that it was religion itself that had made her an Atheist. She was living proof of the freethinker's maxim that said Catholics make the best Atheists. Her mother had read to her from a set of encyclopedias when she was very young, so when the cosmological questions began she knew where to turn for a godless creation story. "I ran down the hallway and got the book—*A* for anatomy," she said. "I knew the colored pictures with arrows for your heart and all that. I asked my mom to show me where my soul was. Well, of course she was unable to do that. And from that moment on, I questioned authority, I didn't accept anything on faith. From that day on, I guess I was an Atheist."

She credited Atheism with giving her the confidence for a lifetime of adventure and authority. Her family had owned a small airplane, and Arlene could solo by the time she was seven. She usually kept the fact that she had been an active Girl Scout a secret, but she readily admitted that she had once aspired to the Roller Derby as a career. "I was a fast little skater. Yeah, that was what I wanted to be. Roller Derby skater!" When she was seventeen her parents divorced and suddenly she had to work; she found a job as a mortgage processor, which led eventually to real estate, still a source of income four decades later. She married, became an avid ballroom dancer, and joined the Nomads, a group of aviators who teamed up to purchase and jet-set in their own airliner. She adopted and raised a disabled infant,

Tina. "The only way I could have that child was if I had membership in a church and if I guaranteed the agency that she would have a religious up-bringing. That's the law." She took Tina to church through the full period of probation, five years and two months, then never went again.

She kept her unbelief quiet until the sixties, when it became acceptable. "Then, all of a sudden, there's a Madalyn Murray O'Hair. I was thrilled. I finally knew. Up until Madalyn, I don't know that I ever knew another Atheist. But now there was at least one other person in the world like me." Arlene joined at once and grew close to O'Hair's family. "I was awestruck," Arlene said. "Madalyn was my biggest hero. She was just the absolute biggest thing in my life. I would have done anything she asked me to. Which is scary. *Anything she asked me to do.* After that I had a real apprecia-tion for these cults where they could get somebody to rob banks. I mean, I never could imagine myself doing that, but I was so impressed with just being in her presence. And I don't think I was the only one—there were lots of us at that time, we were so isolated and lonely. And Madalyn was a treasure to us. And we just followed her. We were in awe of each other, in awe of her. Initially, when it started, it was like finding this incredible pearl you'd been looking for your whole life, and then all of a sudden there it was."

5. AUTOMATIC SWEETHEART

The conference speakers were chosen for the books they had produced, the work they had done, or the entertainment they could provide. A young woman had self-published a volume she had edited on the evil rise of the Christian right; a man had proved, using uncorrupted sections of the Bible, that there had been no historical Jesus of Nazareth; someone from the Ger-man publishing company detailed the two-year prison sentences that were still being meted out to blasphemers in Germany; and a young man showed up to the conference with his skin painted red and little horns protruding from his bald head—he was the complaints editor for a website called JesusDressUp.com. He smiled a lipsticky Satan smile, then admitted that he wasn't much of a public speaker and proceeded to stutter a lot.

Outside the hexagonal conference rooms was a central vestibule cut through with a broad opening for more hotel decor, a three-story artificial rock monolith. A waterfall started one floor up and fell to a pool one floor below. A thick plastic skylight filtered out ultraviolet rays from overhead, and silly paintings of primitive rock civilizations colored the walls. Underpaid maids tidied our beds as we listened to speakers go on about the horrors of Mormonism and the theory of intelligent design. Between presentations, the Atheists wandered into the vestibule to stand near the waterfall. Evaporation made for an invisible mist easy to mistake for a breeze. The Atheists pondered the monolith as though it were nature.

Intelligent design was a new name for the argument that sophisticated design in nature proved the existence of God. Characteristically, William James went both ways on it. "Assuredly," he wrote in the conclusion to *Varieties,* "the real world is of a different temperament,—more intricately built than physical science allows." But he had previously pointed out that a design once held to prove God's existence (such as the body's various reflex actions) could well flip over time and be used to disprove it. Even better was James's example of the woodpecker. The woodpecker's beak and skull seemed to argue for the existence of an intelligent creator—how else could the bird have developed such a perfectly shaped tool for extracting the worm from the tree? Perfect, James noted, until one considered the worm's point of view. Then the example made the opposite argument, the problem of evil, which asked how God could exist in a world where perfect terror was possible. In sum, design theory, for James, failed "to constitute a knockdown proof of [God's] existence. It will be convincing only to those who on other grounds believe in him already."

If religion was what had made Atheists of the likes of Vanini and Arlene-Marie, then James had had the exact opposite experience. He had grown up outside the church experience completely but nevertheless felt pulled toward the religious feeling. James used, in *Varieties,* his own emotional collapse in early adulthood as an example of physical trauma rooted in spiritual quandary. Recasting himself as an anonymous French "sufferer," James claimed "to translate freely" from his own old sadness: one day, philosophical pessimism and low spirits over his future had engineered a horrific vision of an epileptic patient from an asylum. The figure had green skin and black eyes and sat idiotic in its blank stare—like an Egyptian cat or a mummy. *"That shape am I,"* James wrote. The horror changed him forever. The fictional Frenchman expressed no doubt that "this experience of melancholia of mine had a religious bearing," and he would credit prayerlike mantras—"The eternal God is my refuge" and "I am the resurrection and the life"—for helping to preserve his sanity. James referenced his father's collapse—the one that led to Swedenborg—in a footnote to this passage and called it "another case of fear equally sudden."

James had needed faith of a kind, but his father's semimysticism required too much sacrifice of the individual into the idea of God. James consistently rejected tradition in favor of the present self. Yet as much as he longed for a system to believe in, he approached each that he encountered with a scientist's eye. At times, he almost sounded like an Atheist. He claimed to have only the slightest inkling of religious potential, but at the same time he distrusted science and believed that not all of mental life could be accounted for physiologically. Ultimately, he rejected agnosticism too because the evidence for or against it would never be complete.

I was troubled by the speakers at the Atheist convention, but I didn't really know why. Sometimes I wandered out of the room even as they talked. My journey through James and religion seemed to have hit a dead end. Irreligion, too, was supposed to be able to suture the sick soul, and after the roller coaster of Druids and Christian wrestlers and Satanists and Scientologists my soul was nauseous and like to vomit. But rather than a balm, irreligion seemed to offer more of the same. And the inconsistency that had annoyed James's biographers was beginning to get to me as well:

> *We must therefore, from the experiential point of view, call these godless or quasi godless creeds "religions"; and accordingly when in our definition of religion we speak of the individual's relation to "what he considers the divine," we must interpret the term "divine" very broadly as denoting any object that is godlike, whether it be a concrete deity or not.*

Wandering out in the vestibule, I found other Atheists. I met a man who thought it was appropriate to tuck the cuffs of his pants deep inside his cowboy boots and who wore around his neck a coin with a portrait of the last ruler of Rome before Christianity ran the table of Europe. I met another man who described himself as a factory grunt and carried around with him a sample of the little bits of plastic he spent most of his days molding. And one more man whose Atheism took the form of a personal crusade against circumcision—his organization was called NOCIRC, and he gave me a card with his name on it and a drawing of an extremely happy baby.

Were these shapes I? As I stood before the monolith waterfall, all of it moving but none of it alive, I thought of James's argument of the "automatic sweetheart." Here he had considered the possibility of a godless universe: it could be likened to an artificial maiden, he said, identical in all respects to a real woman but lacking a soul. Such a "sweetheart" would not be an equivalent because it would not inspire our complete sympathy. It did not work, Pragmatically, and a godless universe was just the same. For this reason alone, God was the *truer* hypothesis available to man. Of nonbelievers directly, James wrote as if they had lost their sight, or their hearing, or both:

> *Some persons, for instance, never are, and possibly never under any circumstances could be, converted. Religious ideas cannot become the centre of their personal energy. . . . Such inaptitude for religious faith may in some cases be intellectual in origin. Their religious faculties may be checked in their natural tendency to expand, by beliefs about the world that are inhibitive, the pessimistic and materialistic belief or the agnostic vetoes upon faith as something weak and shameful, under which so many of us to-day lie cowering, afraid to use our instincts.*

But to Atheists this was an old and boring argument. Of course they could enjoy nature. Of course they could experience wonder and beauty. God did not invent these things; indeed, it was the projection of wonder and beauty outside the human experience, to the divine, that threatened to reduce man to a loveless shell. Still, the Atheists acknowledged that religion had something they were missing. The speaker who was introduced as I returned to the conference chamber, a last-minute fill-in delivering a short presentation on freethinking in France, focused his talk on how Atheism lacked any kind of holy site to which to make pilgrimages. The convention wasn't a celebration, I realized. The world the Atheists imagined was as artificial as the hotel, which was the last resort but still a resource. It provided comfort for the misfits only when the schedule allowed for moments of casual social interaction. Otherwise their plate was full. Next up was a woman who was engaged in a legal battle to protect the museum she ran in a small midwestern town. It was a museum of religious oppression, and the woman was passionate because she was suffering oppression herself, from locals and court officials. "Get up! Fight!" she railed, causing the loudspeakers to shriek with feedback. "Don't let them put you down! If you lose your job, fight! Stand up! Say, I'm an Atheist!"

I looked back at Arlene, chatting with one or two others in the book room. Later, she would complain to me about Atheism's not having formal ceremonies. Atheism had godless versions of funerals and marriages, but what she meant was that she wanted more time to socialize. It was what the Atheists needed most. When Arlene listened to the speakers, she tried to make the speeches more an exchange than a lecture: she grunted approval, or talked back, or made vague suggestive moaning sounds. But it was inappropriate to the sober political course that had been laid out for the Atheists, a course that Eddie Tabbasch intended to describe as he ascended to the podium to explain how to run for political office and, more important, to tell us how to vote.

Tabbasch started off with a Jewish joke, and for almost his entire speech he would come off as a kind of bad stand-up comic, his expression anticipating laughs. He launched almost at once into the self-flattery that Atheists used to prop themselves up. "We are among the most intelligent and capable masters of reason," he told the crowd. "If you look at some of these dunderheads in office—boy, if they can handle the system, so can we. We are the keepers of the flame of intellectual depth when it comes to how the universe is put together."

He described the political campaign he had waged. He had knocked on fourteen thousand doors. He had lost, in the end, to a Hispanic woman, but he had soundly beaten the son of an incumbent. When he told the crowd he advocated the legalization of prostitution he got a big round of applause. He told the Atheists that the way for them to realize their potential was to vote for Atheist candidates regardless of issues. As he glided toward conclusion, Tabbasch's tone changed to the silky lull of a closing argument.

"All of us have come to Atheism because we have undergone a deep and finely honed analysis of how the universe is put together. We have a right to fool them and show them how competent we can be. We, as Atheists, have very organized minds—that's why we've been able to rise above the muck of superstition everyone else is still stuck in. Please help me to become the only Atheist to run for office in the early twenty-first century and not win."

6. CREW CUT

"I didn't want to be married anymore. I wanted to explore. I wanted sex. I wanted men. I wanted women. I wanted boys. So I did that. I was with

George. And we were making love. But I did that too. And now here we are, forty years later."

Atheism set Arlene free. She met her current partner, George, when she was helping organize a beauty contest associated with the Miss America Pageant. In addition to selling real estate, Arlene had made a living as an event organizer and creative social guru. She taught classes on confidence building to the newly rich. She gave instruction to men who wanted to be gigolos. "A couple of my students got really serious, kept their bodies in magnificent shape. I don't know what happened to them as time went on, but it's an interesting concept. It's a job." She won a variety of awards, including honors as outstanding woman of the community and the state, and for a while she wrote a newspaper column, a kind of anti–Miss Manners, "a form of etiquette with reason and logic instead of tradition." She and George began to sail—in addition to solo flight, Arlene had become the only woman in Michigan authorized to sail solo on a boat not more than twenty-seven feet in length—and now they spent several months a year on the Great Lakes, where they were free to practice nudism. " 'Cause that's what I am! A nudist! If I was off on my boat, I'd sail naked, I'd camp naked, I'd live at home naked." She had become the leader of the Michigan Atheists only of late, but she had all the right skills and beliefs. Her Godless March on Lansing had a specific target: the Michigan legislature had proposed a bill that would allow the Ten Commandments to be posted on public property. Of the state's 110 lawmakers, 63 had gathered to *introduce* the bill, she said, even though similar laws had already been struck down in other states.*

On the convention nights, the Atheists held dinners to distribute awards and show old video footage of Madalyn Murray O'Hair. The first night, a man was called to the front of the room to describe the group's financial straits. It was bleak, he said, and he pleaded with folks to forgo a house or car payment, if they could afford it. For some—for Arlene—the dinners weren't the social life they were looking for, and Arlene still wanted to prove to me that Atheists were capable of fun.

The second night, she arranged a junket to a nearby city's ritzy club district. Of course Dick Hogan would come, and a dozen or so others. The folks that gathered in the van were a pretty fair godless sampling: some outright Atheists, some secular humanists, some vague freethinkers, and all the

---

*American Atheists would play a prominent role a short time later when Alabama Supreme Court Justice Roy Moore attempted a similar move through judicial decree. American Atheists picketed early, and Moore was eventually removed from his post.

old distinctions and arguments, the extent to which Atheism could or should resemble a religion, were in the car. A debate ensued on the ride and almost turned nasty, Arlene going for a coarse image when she told one woman that her brain was an Atheist but her clitoris was just a humanist. The rest of us reeled. What did she mean? Arlene had upped the crudity ante to that of the legendary freethinkers, but we wondered to what extent her metaphor was even possible. Her argument was that godless people tended to waffle in their unbelief, and this helped no one. Arlene's eyes writhed in their painted sockets, either perfectly confused or perfectly tuned, and she saw that she needed to elaborate. She turned to me.

"So are you a turtleneck or a crew cut?" she said. It wasn't until she glanced at my lap that I guessed what she meant. "You're probably a crew cut. And the point is, you didn't choose it. You're one or the other, and it has everything to do with religion. I'm not interested in being a swinger, intellectually. Sexually, yes! Intellectually, no."

This ended the talk, in that no one could think of anything more shocking to say. The argument hadn't been organized particularly well, but Arlene had described the heart of the modern Atheist dilemma. Religion was everywhere. It was in the Buddha statue in the window of the hotel where the van dropped us in the city, it was in the blessings of the homeless as they begged alms while our group tried to find the club district. We wandered without direction through a spiritual obstacle course. No one knew the way. Maybe Arlene's clitoris metaphor had been unclear, but our journey's metaphor was more perfect. We wandered city streets in search of a club that would have us, and we were turned away when finally we found the right street but the hotshot doorman looked at how we were dressed and determined that we'd been overserved. We continued on—an exodus, free people looking for a promised land without a clear Moses—and it took us an hour to find a club that would have us. It was a crowded, oversized living room. Arlene and I squeezed together against a rail and shared a perfect Manhattan, straight up with a twist, passing it back and forth between us in a room full of uppity folks with crosses around their necks because it would be Easter in the morning.

The next day, the entire convention returned to the city for a short cruise on a Great Lake. Some of the Atheists plotted to pummel the guy who had dressed in an Easter Bunny outfit to entertain children, and two of our crowd threw their arms around each other to sing a retooled song in commemoration of the day: *"Raindrops keep falling on my head / But that doesn't mean Jesus Christ rose from the dead . . ."* We bounced around the lake for a bit, and I finally got to speak to Ellen Johnson as we were bused back to the hexagonal resort. She spent most of the interview dodging whatever she thought my questions were trying to suggest, but toward the end, when I asked her what her goals were, she accidentally echoed the Atheists' journey of the night before.

"I want Atheists to become organized enough so that politicians recognize us as a part of the United States population," she said. "We are marginalized and ignored. It is like we do not exist to anyone but ourselves. We are an afterthought. We want a seat at the table, and we have to work to be heard. We're not even in the building. We're still outside of the building, trying to get in."

7. THE GODLESS MARCH

About seventy-five people came to Arlene's Godless March on Lansing. The crowd of us strolled a quarter mile from a parking lot to the capitol building, but our permit required us to stay on the sidewalk. A wedding party at a nearby church heckled us as we passed.

Arlene had made a scroll listing all the religions measured in the American Religious Identification Survey—it hung from the lectern at the capitol, spilling down the concrete stairs. "No Religion" came just after "Catholic" and "Baptist," and was followed by a couple dozen others. The lineup of speakers hit all the familiar notes: a friendly man named Bob Brooks quoted Henry Clay's "All religions united with government are more or less inimical to liberty"; another man delivered an attack on intelligent design, with examples of inefficiency in nature (genetic instructions for tails in human beings, the legs of snakes at the embryonic stage, the flightless weevil with a pair of perfectly formed wings under a fused shell); there was a horrific quote attributed to Ralph Reed: "I do guerrilla warfare. I paint my face and travel at night. You don't know it until you're in a body bag. You don't know until election night"; and finally came Spike Tyson, who had been an Atheist in a foxhole, the man who had been Madalyn Murray O'Hair's bodyguard and who had won four Bronze Stars for service in Vietnam, which had left him using a walker. But because he was an Atheist, Spike could not be a member of the Veterans of Foreign Wars, the American Legion, or AmVets. "I am a living, breathing, in-your-face foxhole Atheist and damn proud of it!" he bellowed.

The crowd gave smattered applause as appropriate. They carried signs with the usual slogans (REASON IS NOT TREASON; NOTHING FAILS LIKE PRAYER; ATHEISM IS MYTH-UNDERSTOOD), and a kid wore a T-shirt that said GOD WAS MY CO-PILOT—BUT WE HIT A MOUNTAIN AND I HAD TO EAT HIM. Arlene was happy with the turnout, but someone pointed out that a recent pro-life rally had drawn a crowd of four thousand to the same site. The Atheist speakers were preaching to the choir. When the gathering began to disband, I caught up with Spike as he moved his walker toward his car. One morning at the convention, Spike had told me of a job he'd once had that had allowed him to deface $3.5 million every day, crossing the word "God" off the money. I wanted to speak with him because he was the man who had been the first to discover that the O'Hair family had been kidnapped, who had wandered into the house and realized that something wasn't right. I asked him to tell me the story. Spike neatly converted his walker to a stool and planted himself down with the capitol as his backdrop.

"The real story?" he said. "Not the one we told everybody?"

I was confused. Spike revealed that the Atheists had changed the facts of how they had discovered that the O'Hairs had been kidnapped. "The story that there was food on the table and all that, that you've probably heard? It's not true. That was a little rumor started by me." Knowing that O'Hair would be attacked by the press, the Atheists had manipulated the story just as the press had manipulated them. Spike had been in touch with the O'Hairs all the while they were missing. They'd been controlled by the kidnappers as the money was being converted into gold coins. It turned out that Spike had been arranging an appearance for Madalyn on the Phil Donahue show the day she was murdered. But no one, not even the Atheists, knew for sure that they had been kidnapped until the murderers confessed. Arlene had told me that Waters and his accomplice had eventually admitted to tying Madalyn up and forcing her to watch them rape her granddaughter before they killed them all.

At first, Spike had seemed glad to reveal what he knew, but now he was thinking better of it. "Madalyn O'Hair never wanted a biography done of her," he said. "And I agreed before she was kidnapped that I wouldn't be involved in one." He tricked his stool back into a walker and moved away.

I was alone on the pathway. It was spring, and the day's stiff wind distributed the scent of trees in bloom. Suddenly, everything I'd come to believe about Atheism had been thrown into doubt. Could an Atheist really not be a member of the VFW? Could you really argue that Akh-en-Aton was a monotheist when he too was a kind of god? Was there really a tape of George H. W. Bush disparaging Atheists somewhere in Iowa?* Was Thomas Paine a deist? Did Vanini really die at the stake? The page the Atheists had stolen from religion told them it was okay to rewrite history, that it was fine to manipulate opinion. Eddie Tabbasch had told them that it was justifiable to fool people, to mislead so as to win. It was the very policy that had marginalized Atheists for as long as anyone could remember. Should they be blamed for trying to cheat as well?

The capital was clearing out, but it had been even more deserted earlier when Arlene and George and I had first arrived to set things up. The streets had been silent except for public transportation. I'd taken a walk around the deserted capitol building. Here, the separation of church and state amounted to an empty street: five major denominations of Christianity (Baptist, Episcopalian, Lutheran, Methodist, Catholic) sat adjacent to the capitol, their architecture as bold as advertising. I set out to knock on some doors for reaction to the march. The Methodists had their wedding, the Lutherans and Baptists were gone, and the Episcopalians were preparing for an interment—I caught an annoyed rector just as he was vesting up. "That's America," he said of the Atheists. "They can say what they want."

Across from the Catholic church two guys worked at power-washing a building, and parking meters stood ridiculous vigils beside empty stalls. I tried the church door, expecting to yank against its lock. But it pulled wide and my whole body caught in surprise when I looked inside. A thousand people were gathered for some kind of silent ritual, an army of the well dressed. Far ahead of me, a row of men in gowns took baby steps toward the altar, where a priest waited for them. "It's the ordination of the deaconate," a woman in the lobby told me. It was a promotion ceremony, and it concluded just as I stepped back, a thousand souls rising as one to applaud their own and send that deafening surf down the empty street, toward the capitol of Michigan.

---

*George W. Bush, in his second presidential debate with John Kerry in 2004, said, "But I'm mindful in a free society that people can worship if they want to or not. You're equally an American if you choose to worship an almighty, and if you choose not to." This may have been a slip. The president continued: "If you're a Christian, Jew, or Muslim, you're equally an American. That's the great thing about America, is the right to worship the way you see fit."

1902–1907

———◆———

When James came home from the Gifford lectures he turned his attention to formal philosophy. He longed to leave behind the "squashy public lecture style" and place himself more firmly with the serious scholars who had always been his closest friends. James had said that he would prefer the company of a philosopher with whom he had profound disagreements to that of an acolyte who had adopted his system wholesale; he had more in common with the philosopher. And now he began to worry that he would be remembered only for his popular work as a "'talker to teachers,' 'religious experiencer,' or 'willer to believe.'" He set about crafting a philosophy using, as one biographer described it, Pragmatism as the technique and radical empiricism as the building material. The result would be a realistic pluralism. "I am sure that a book of the systematic sort *can* be written," James told a friend early in 1903, "a philosophy of pure experience, which will immediately prove a centre of crystallization and a new rallying-point of opinion in philosophy."

But whether such a book could be written was a different question from whether James could write it. By the next year he had managed only thirty-two pages of a volume that he believed would run five hundred.

It's easy to make the mistake of seeing James as functionally retired after he came home from Scotland. Even he may have believed it. Life slowed down. He worried about his daughter's social debut, he attended his youngest son's baseball games. He became more active politically. At the behest of W.E.B. Du Bois, he joined the effort to curtail an epidemic of lynchings in the South, and a little later in the decade he offered support to a movement begun by Clifford Beers, a former mental patient crusading to improve conditions for the mentally ill. And all the while James wrote. The volume of his production in the years after *Varieties* was as heavy as ever.

A confession: all biographers pick their spots, William James biographers perhaps even more carefully. My James tends to focus on his middle work, deemphasizing *The Principles of Psychology* and his later efforts to make a philosophy whole. My James is precisely the James that James now worried would be the only part of him to survive. But as I read him, the later swing toward philosophy was a misstep: he was giving in to a tendency for which he had originally excoriated philosophy. If I had made a mistake in thinking that Atheism could cure the sick soul I'd become, James made a mistake in thinking that a new philosophy could change the world. As well, he was capitulating to the critics who had labeled him indecisive. The middle James wasn't particularly interested in origins or endings or answers—he was concerned with where we were now and how we moved forward— and decisiveness too final would have been at odds with the variations at the heart of his belief. Yet for the early years of the new century his opaque philosophy seemed set on offering an answer.

He never did give up the lecture style. He used a lecture series in 1905 to flesh out his ideas, and he published a number of strictly theoretical works between 1903 and 1906 that were eventually collected in *Some Problems in Philosophy* and *Essays in Radical Empiricism,* both of which were printed in book form only posthumously. James considered his system incomplete. Just before he died, he left an instruction on how *Problems* should be introduced: "Call it 'A beginning of an introduction to philosophy.' Say that I hoped by it to round out my system, which is now too much like an arch built only on one side."

In 1904, James spent a good bit of time with his brother Henry, who returned to America after more than two decades (partly at William's urging) to collect material for *The American Scene.* In 1905 James sat at the bedside as one of his colleagues in psychical research, Richard Hodgson, died. Leonora Piper tried contacting the dead man, and though she seemed to be able to cull details from a private conversation between Hodgson and James, James would later describe the SPR material as "*Not* convincing, to me: but baffling exceedingly." Also in 1905, James traveled to Italy to attend a Philosophical Conference in Rome, where he was surprised by the *Leonardo* group that had religiously taken up the call of Pragmatism. Pragmatism had not done much of anything since James had introduced it in 1898, but he had revamped "Philosophical Conceptions and Practical Results," the piece that introduced it, as "The Pragmatic Method" six years later. The mid-1900s bore witness to the growth of a movement. James encountered segments of the philosophy in an entire school of thought in Chicago led by John Dewey, and felt himself echoed by F.C.S. Schiller in

England. Henri Bergson was a new correspondent and confidant in France who confirmed radical empiricism, and even his friendship with Oliver Wendell Holmes seemed to rekindle around aspects of the thinking. James was hopeful. "I am persuaded that a great new philosophic movement is in the air," he wrote to a friend. Pragmatism needed a manifesto, but before he could write it he was scheduled to teach at Stanford.

He arrived in Palo Alto in January 1906 and offered an introductory philosophy course for three hundred students. Alice didn't join him until February. It was in this interval that James reported the near-mystical conversation experiences that sounded so much like Scientology's auditing to me. These were exacerbated, his more cynical biographers have claimed, by the sentimental shift of thinkers in old age. James may or may not have been touched by the "more" within himself, but regardless, once Alice joined him, he was ready for prophecy again. On February 25, 1906, he delivered "The Moral Equivalent of War" to a large university assembly, arguing that what man needed was a substitute for his martial spirit. James overtly predicted Pearl Harbor when he described Japan's ambition to control the Pacific Ocean. He warned: "But there is no reason to think that women can no longer be the mothers of Napoleonic or Alexandrian characters; and if these come in Japan and find their opportunity surprises may lurk in ambush for us."

Generally James placed himself square in the "anti-militarist party," but blind pacifism was no solution to the problem, he claimed. To ignore man's militarism was to overlook both nature and history. But how could we exploit what we knew of our nature, how could we produce our utopias while acknowledging the military spirit? The solution anticipated the Peace Corps:

> If now—and this is my idea—there was, instead of a military conscription a conscription of the whole youthful population to form a certain number of years a part of the army enlisted against Nature, *the injustice would tend to be evened out, and numerous other goods to the commonwealth would follow.*

God provided a case in point almost at once. A few weeks later James was shaken out of bed by the Great San Francisco Earthquake, which took down all the chimneys at Stanford and leveled a good deal of San Francisco in three-quarters of a minute. Two months later he was back in Cambridge acting as a correspondent for *The Youth's Companion*. The quake, he wrote, had begun as a musical crescendo, then

> *everything that was on anything else slid off to the floor, over went the bureau and chiffonier with a crash, as the* fortissimo *was reached, plaster cracked, an awful roaring noise seemed to fill the outer air, and in an instant all was still again, save the soft babble of human voices from far and near.*

He described the event with the same kind of excitement he might have reported at the table rumbling of a séance. During the commotion, his thrill was teleological.

> *I felt no trace whatever of fear; it was pure delight and welcome.*
> "Go *it*," *I almost cried aloud,* "and go it *stronger.*"

Those he spoke to in the wake of the earthquake seemed to support the hypothesis that that personification of the quake, giving it intent and malice, was the natural reaction to such an event. What was surprising to James was the sense of community that emerged—people seemed joyous, somehow, in the immediate aftermath, and strangers sought one another out to talk about it.

What he found when he rushed to San Francisco was precisely that battle against Nature he had prescribed in his lecture:

> *It was a strange sight indeed to see an entire population in the streets, busy as ants in an uncovered ant-hill scurrying to save their eggs and larvæ. Every horse, and everything on wheels in the city, from hucksters' wagons to automobiles, was being loaded with what effects could be scraped together from houses which the advancing flames were threatening.*

The city experienced minor looting, but the petty crimes were far outweighed by the disaster's tendency to identify natural leaders and caregivers, who came to the fore as though called. A sense of unity predominated:

> *The cheerfulness, or, at any rate, the steadfastness of tone, was universal. Not a single whine or plaintive word did I hear from the hundred losers*

whom I spoke to. Instead of that there was a temper of helpfulness be-
yond the counting.

It is easy to glorify this as something characteristically American. . . .
But I like to think that what I write of is a normal and universal trait of
human nature.

After the summer, once the excitement of the experience faded, James
found that he was enthusiastic to produce his Pragmatism book. This
would be his real philosophy. The project spilled out of him beginning in
September 1906, and he finished in time to deliver the Lowell lectures in
mid-November of the same year.

If James was right to say, as he had to his father, that life mainly expresses
but a single note, then that note for James was not sick souls or over-beliefs
or the automatic sweetheart. That note was somewhere inside *Pragmatism:
A New Name for Some Old Ways of Thinking.*

He began with a discussion of the dilemma of philosophy. We were
stuck, James said. On the one hand science had taken such a hold of the
imagination that our children were "almost born scientific"; on the other,
religious philosophy either was "radical and aggressive" or had "the air of
fighting a slow retreat." James claimed to have something different and
wholly new to offer his audience, and at moments he nearly assumed the
pitch of a snake-oil salesman: "What *you* want is a philosophy that will not
only exercise your powers of intellectual abstraction, but that will make
some positive connexion with this actual world of finite human lives."
Pragmatism would prove a solution for the dilemma, he said, a synthesis
that could "remain religious like the rationalisms, but at the same time . . .
preserve the richest intimacy with facts."

Again, Pragmatism was defined by its method and its theory of truth.
The method of Pragmatism was to look on facts as tools of measurement.
Instead of asking what a thing's origin was, ask what difference it made, or
might make. What was its "cash value"? James's critics have spent a good bit
of time punishing him for his money metaphors (one claimed they revealed
latent greed), but what he was really doing was extending a metaphor in-
herent in the language. We say that we "pay attention," or that James's critics
made him "pay" for his word choice. Ideas find "purchase" when they are
correct, and we "buy" them, or accept them, only when they have "worth,"
or when there is an intellectual "payoff." James was returning to the initial

definition of currency as value, since warped into the cruder "cash." The Pragmatic method sought to evaluate ideas on that level. Once this was accepted, James said, "the centre of gravity of philosophy must therefore alter its place."

The lectures applied the Pragmatic method to a number of standard metaphysical problems, demonstrating how it "unstiffened" them without relying on any particular doctrine. Pragmatism naturally led to a pluralistic view. This view could acknowledge a potential future in which all thinking might very well be condensed into an ideal system, but until then Pragmatism was also able to accommodate a world that was still imperfect, and might always be so. A close inspection of this imperfection led to the second part of Pragmatism, its truth. It was now apparent that the existence of

> *many widely differing systems [of thought] obliges us to overhaul the very idea of truth, for at present we have no definite notion of what the word may mean.*

James asked, "May there not after all be a possible ambiguity in truth?" This point might well be the note that speaks most directly to James's work as a whole. It had been building over a lifetime, receiving input from a wide variety of sources. Benjamin Paul Blood, a mystic who had exchanged letters with James for many years, once wrote to him:

> *Truth* must *be a correspondence. All about us is arbitrary overgrowth, in expression; and the route to truth is a backward path—a retracing to the unsophisticated simplicity of diviner days. There* must *be a true expression—the true for itself, of the in itself. To deny it is to deny First Principle, and leave all to chance.*

And James's brother Bob had once written from a sanatorium:

> *I see it every where—among all denominations. When a religion makes you more tender to Everyone and everything it must be for you at least the true religion.*

When James translated it all into logic, describing it for himself, truth became an action, took on a verblike potential:

Truth happens *to an idea. It becomes true, is* made *true by events. Its verity* is *in fact an event, a process: the process namely of its verifying itself, its veri-*faction. *Its validity is the process of its valid-*ation.

And later:

Truth for us is simply a collective name for the verification-process, just as health, wealth, strength, etc., are names for other processes connected with life. . . . Truth is made, *just as health, wealth and strength are made, in the course of experience.*

James offered Pragmatism's method and its definition of truth as a mediator between the cult of science and timid religions, between "crude naturalism" and "transcendental absolutism." The world, he argued, needed a religion that could address the universe as it stood, incomplete and evolving, "growing in all sorts of places, especially in the places where thinking beings are at work." A religion that could identify the common thread binding together people of clearly different needs. James worried at the end of the talks that Pragmatism appeared irreligious or atheistic. To correct this impression, he harkened back to *Varieties:*

I can not start upon a whole theology at the end of this last lecture; but when I tell you that I have written a book on men's religious experiences, which has on the whole been regarded as making for the reality of God, you will perhaps exempt my own pragmatism from the charge of being an atheistic system.

Not only was God possible in James's Pragmatism, but so, with its flexible truth, was a polytheism that was the original form of religion and that "mankind has only imperfectly and vaguely sublimated . . . into monotheism."

James delivered the Pragmatism lectures once more, the following year. The second series, at Columbia University, drew an audience of more than one thousand. Between the two courses, James taught his final class at Harvard, in January 1907. A few months later, he wrote to a friend that the freedom was

too good to be true. To be alone with truth and God! es ist nicht zu glauben! *What a future! What a vision of ease!*

Goddess

—◆—

The whole history of witchcraft and early medicine is a commentary on the facility with which anything which chances to be conceived of is believed the moment the belief chimes in with an emotional mood.

—William James

To communicate with Mars, converse with spirits . . .
Describe the horoscope, haruspicate or scry,
Observe disease in signatures, evoke
Biography from the wrinkles of the palm
And tragedy from fingers; release omens
By sortilege, or tea leaves . . . all these are usual
Pastimes and drugs, and features of the press:
And always will be, some of them especially
When there is distress of nations and perplexity
Whether on the shores of Asia, or in the Edgware Road.

—T. S. Eliot

1. Merry Meet

It was still a day before Uncle Draggi would arrive, and a day before Merry-Meet, the national meeting of the Covenant of the Goddess, or CoG, would officially begin, but already witches were convening in the conference rooms of a casino hotel in Reno, Nevada, and already Kirk White, the founder and academic dean of Cherry Hill Seminary, a learning institute for neo-Pagans, had a problem: he was trying to arrange the tables in the room so that they would form a circle, but the room was rectangular and so were the tables and together it was a riddle beyond Pagan ken. "We're right at that moment when we're going to have to start hiring lawyers, talking to politicians," Kirk had told me, as people milled around the room and the witches got their coffee. "But how do you keep Paganism from simply reflecting the mainstream?"

A sense of momentum can help new religious movements grow, and just about every new religious movement that begins to record its own expansion finds a way to argue that it is the fastest-growing movement to be found. But Wicca had the sanction of the Atheists' ARIS study, which had tallied 8,000 witches in 1990 and 134,000 in 2001. Of course, the numbers might mean anything: after a decade of growing tolerance, existing witches might have been more willing to acknowledge their faith. In either case, the Covenant of the Goddess, the largest organization of solitaries and covens in the world, was feeling the strain of success: they were having a hard time just keeping up with coven applications. What often drew people to faiths like Wicca was the fact that they were small and far outside the mainstream. CoG had attempted to grow without the bureaucratic consequences of strict organization. William James had anticipated this moment in his boiled-down narrative of a religion's life: this was when groups "got strong enough to 'organize' themselves, [and] became ecclesiastical institutions with corporate ambitions of their own." I'd already seen how this could derail a religion and send it whirling off to what James called second-hand automatisms, but the Wiccans were trying to do it in a better way. They were trying to organize around the pluralism that James's Pragmatism promised. The breadth of belief within Wicca stretched from atheism through monotheism to duotheism and polytheism. In attempting to incorporate it all, Wiccans were building what James had described as "a plurality of individuals, with relations partly external, partly intimate, like and unlike . . . yet keeping house together." And the problem—Kirk White's problem—was that organization tended toward the rigidity that had sent many witches outside the mainstream in the first place.

Kirk was a tall, boyish man with a mess of curly dark hair. He surveyed the rectangular tables and jammed his hands onto his hips. "Part of my lecture is that we don't want to wind up with all our pews facing forward," he said, "and here we are with all our pews facing forward."

He gave up finally, and I took a seat beside Bryte Unicorn and Firedancer, two middle-aged witches from Florida. The casino setting for MerryMeet was a concession to CoG's consensus-based decision-making process. They'd borrowed this from the Quakers but prided themselves on arriving at as many as thirty unanimous decisions in two days at annual meetings, as opposed to five or six decisions in a week for the Quakers. An old sticking point was money, though—any attempt to raise dues risked losing covens by the cauldronful—and as a result, at least according to some, CoG couldn't afford to do much besides exist and hold MerryMeet. CoG plotted by economy (hence the casino setting), and it took imagination to understand the room as suitable to a religion of nature worship: the cosmic splatter of the casino carpeting was meant to disguise stains, but you could choose to read its stars stuck mid-twinkle as a mood of otherness. The mirrored ceiling might be sky.

Behind me sat Lady Circe and a man named Fred. The witches around the room, when Kirk conducted a survey, turned out to be from Texas, Oregon, Vermont, Michigan, and California. The meeting was about Pagan pastoral counseling, and the poll emphasized Wicca's growth through festivals and the Internet. "I've done seven weddings this spring," Kirk said. "And only one was someone I knew beforehand. Paganism is becoming a service-based thing."

He asked how many professional counselors there were in the room and two people admitted to training. Then he asked how many people wound up doing counseling anyway. Everyone raised a hand. "As soon as you say you're a witch or wear a pentacle," Kirk said, "you assume a level of responsibility. The message here is that all Pagan leaders are counselors."

The meeting was structured—to the extent that any meeting of witches could be structured—to address Wicca's collision with the society from which it had sought refuge. The witches referred to those they counseled as "patients." "This is about how not to have a malpractice suit," Kirk explained. Just how literally the witches took the idea of magic kept popping up once the lecture turned to ethics and values. One woman got a big laugh with a story about an artist who had asked her to summon a demon so he could paint it. "Well, which demon do you want me to raise?" was the punch line. When the laughter faded, the witch said, "It's not my business if he wants to summon a demon, but it is my responsibility to tell him that it's a very dangerous thing to do." This time, no one laughed. As a group we decided that it was okay to put an astral light over the head of a rapist, but a hex was really going too far. Kirk, sitting on a table at the front of the room, wanted to back up and talk about values, as distinguished from ethics and morals. But by then the witches had decided that it was time for a break, and it took only a few seconds for the motion to be unanimously approved throughout the room. Kirk was helpless. The witches made for the bathrooms and the cookie table.

Opening ritual wasn't until tomorrow, but MerryMeet had begun.

2. UNCLE DEAR

Earlier in the summer I'd traveled to Seattle to meet Uncle Draggi and attend a Wiccan solstice celebration. I'd posted a letter on a CoG website, hoping to find a solitary practitioner cut from a fairy-tale mold. I found Draggi instead.

Wicca is less a religion that emerged from nature than one attempting to reconnect with it. It's a reaction to a Christianity painted as patriarchal and linked to an increasingly industrial and impersonal civilization. By emphasizing the feminine spirit, Wicca hopes to hark back to early Goddess-based cultures in tune with the natural world; but its modern founders are all men and Wicca itself tends to thrive in cities. So it's really not an accident that its convention wound up in a casino hotel or that the Pacific Northwest, and Seattle in particular, would become one of its hotbeds. The city of Seattle, I thought, might itself be construed as accidental. Downtown was altogether too close to the industrial tidal flats where cranes for cargo ships stood like petrified behemoths, and a lack of civil imagination in the city had made possible the corner of 206th Street and 206th Street, as though no one had ever thought it might get so big. Nostalgia was impossible in Seattle; the evidence of the old just made it seem neglected. If urban blight had helped to create a spiritual void that keyed the search for alternate religions, perhaps this was why Seattle also held an annual summer solstice parade and festival.

Even James had been bleak on Seattle. In 1898, on the trip west that introduced Pragmatism to the world, he stopped in Seattle for one night. The journey over on the Canada Pacific railroad had transfixed him for an entire day, he wrote to Alice, and that night he planned to spend a pleasant evening reading Melville. But coming into the city was another matter. Fires had devastated the land outside town, and "the houses and stations on the way are of completest hideousness and poverty, and this poor Seattle, with a couple of streets of fine business blocks, is surrounded by rawness unspeakable."

Uncle Draggi lived off a strip just north of the city where insurance agents advertised rates on marquees as if they were bingo nights and a giant habitrail outside the McDonald's facilitated children's malnourishment. An odd collection of properties lined the road: paintball centers, holistic health stores, baseball-card shops, auto dealerships, graveyards. It was easy to question the American trajectory when it became apparent—as it did for me while visiting eight religious movements and traveling to all the regions of the country—that America was now best characterized by this random sprawl, a creeping homogeneous bereftness. Stopped at a red light, I watched two Islamic women in burkas wander into a dollar store and thought of James's "cash value." Here the reverse seemed to apply. America *was* a dollar store, and even a single pass through Seattle marked off the steady devaluation of the spirit, the slashed price of the soul.

Uncle Draggi had worked as a bookkeeper until a few days before I arrived. He'd been let go. He was a compact, pudgy man pushing sixty who seeped a lingering optimism and innocence, though he'd never reacted all that well to authority, which was probably why he'd been fired. He'd been a solitary Wicca practitioner for thirty years, but arguably he'd been a witch even longer, he told me. He was cooking up a Vietnamese sauce for the solstice when I arrived; he was a Vietnam vet. His wife, Lynn, was home. Her weaving machine took up a good deal of their front room, and one wall was booked over with Draggi's library of Eastern philosophy. Draggi had a big scraggly beard of kinky gray hairs, and every time I saw him, at least one part of his outfit was combat fatigues. The fairy tale in which Draggi was the witch had never been written.

Although the blades of Satanists were necessarily sharp, the ritual knives of witches, the *athames* they used to carve sacred space, were as dull and symbolic as a finger. Draggi took me first to a small beach where he and a few others came to cut circles sometimes, slicing off a pocket of sanctity and invoking various gods and goddesses. For some Wiccans, cutting a circle involved drawing down the moon—the process by which a priestess actually became the Goddess for a time. The little beach was adjacent to a lush, undevelopable bluff, though there were train tracks between the water and the hills, and that combination of industry and nature, the ducks and vines and trees and the light slaps of water in a sprinkly evening, seemed to demonstrate what Draggi was trying to tell me about why he was a witch. "You're not separate," he said, meaning everything, everything around us. He had a habit of slipping into the second person when he talked about himself. Seattle worked for Wicca, he said, because it sat at a confluence of mountains and ocean. He agreed when I suggested that the rural loneliness that helped form the traditions from which Wicca had emerged were echoed in the languor of modernity.

Draggi had been raised on his grandparents' farm, a lonely childhood with his father in a German POW camp and his mother employed in the war effort. As an infant, he once fell down a set of basement stairs. His grandmother claimed he was unconscious for only a moment, but Draggi remembered it differently: he came to and perceived a kind of portal to a bright, other world. Before the door a beautiful woman sat on a stool. Even when Draggi segued into fantastic stories, he remained a calm and articulate man, speaking slowly to get it right. "Now, granted," he said, "I'm one year old. How am I going to know if she's beautiful? Well, she was beautiful—leave it at that." He climbed into her lap, had a talk. Then she made him an offer. He could go through the door, where everything was bright and wonderful, or he could return to the world and do something for her. Draggi chose the latter course and was upset when she disappeared. He remained angry until he realized that she would always be there, and it turned out she returned occasionally even now. They still had wonderful talks.

I followed Draggi around for a couple days before the solstice, giving him a chance to tell his story. We'd hit moments like this, moments when he would report events that required emotional investment in the supernatural, and I would realize how far I'd come in my Jamesian journey. I'd felt like a sick soul among the Atheists, but in hanging out with a solitary witch I felt less alone. I didn't accept Draggi's vision as particularly acceptable for myself; but I didn't need to reject him either. If I had begun my study as one of the deadly respectable clerico-academic-scientific types—who, according to James, tended to ignore the likes of Draggi—now I had been shaken from that house-of-cards faith; I had seen the way in which the old idol of hypothesis verification was its own over-belief, the way it had divvied all of us up into a babble of scientific cants and lingos, had made us fanatics blind even to our own fanaticism, unhappy and seeking, desperate to try anything that tasted like truth. America itself was the sick soul, a divided consciousness, a bifurcated society struggling to climb free of its cold womb. How *could* you tell another what would ring true to the hot place of their consciousness? Not long after he returned from delivering *Varieties* in Scotland, James wrote in a letter, "But I am intensely an individualist, and believe that as a practical problem for the individual, the religion he stands by must be the one which he finds best for him, even though there were better individuals, and their religion better for them." I understood at least this much now, so when Draggi jumped into the deep end of his faith, I jumped with him.

He told me of his childhood. He had been a kid alone on a farm. "To me," he said, "my playmates were the wind, the trees, the bushes, the little bugs and animals, things like that. I could see them, talk to them—we would have some interesting conversations. To me, this was normal." Nor was it unprecedented; Draggi's grandmother was a routine Christian, but his grandfather could see into the future. "It was no big deal—it was just what he did." Draggi became interested in mythology and fairy tales, though sometimes some part of him knew that the stories he read weren't correct, that it hadn't happened that way. He began to experiment with ritualized behavior, unusual ponderings of the moon, more elaborate talks with his friends, drawing arcane symbols in the dirt. He worked a variety of odd jobs before enlisting in the army at eighteen. He said he had been Special Forces, but he wouldn't be specific about what he'd done, even when I reminded him that the thirty-year gag on secret information had expired. More than once, he had been caught performing his private rituals on guard duty, he said, and sometimes he had found it difficult to hold his tongue when the little folk warned him of an ambush. He reported an exchange he once had with his sergeant: "'We don't want to go this way because there's an ambush down there, and over there.' 'How do you know that?' 'Well, that little guy standing over under that bush told me.' 'Uh-huh. You been drinking that weird hooch?' Yeah okay. I been drinking my weird hooch. And sure as shit, just down and around, there's an ambush. So what do you do? I tried to shut up. Sometimes you can't. You have to say something. And then you're weird. And everybody looks at you strange. So now you're lonely again. Being a loner in the service is not a good thing to be."

Draggi remained lonely until he was discharged and stumbled across a copy of *Green Egg*, an American Pagan publication from the seventies whose open editorial policy amounted to a kind of pluralistic anarchy. But now Draggi knew he wasn't alone. He returned to Seattle and studied with an elder there, in a class that ran weekly for a year and a day by tradition. He tried school, worked a few jobs, spent a year in Japan. People became witches for different reasons—sometimes rebellion, sometimes politics. Draggi was a solitary, he said, because he hadn't encountered anyone with reasons similar to his own. Wicca is a religion of distinct traditions. A witch can be initiated into more than one "trad"—Gardnerian, Dianic, New Reformed Orthodox Order of the Golden Dawn, and so on. There are hundreds. Draggi claimed his tradition as Hindu-Zen Celto-Stregheria, which described both his travels and his ethnic heritage, and which, he admitted, put off a few of his brethren. Even among witches he was a little lonely.

On the solstice, Draggi was scheduled to man a Vietnam veterans booth at the festival in Fremont, Seattle's Greenwich Village. A few hundred tents made an impromptu mall a couple of blocks down from the parade route. Draggi and a few other vets stood around looking haunted. The festival was mostly a forum for crafts, but there were religious and pseudoreligious organizations there as well, promoting services or agendas: the Freemasons, some fundamentalist group with a giant flow chart detailing moral decay, a guru leading chants in a tent. I wandered over to watch the parade. There were really two parades. One was the official parade; the other was a band of exhibitionists who preceded it. A man dressed like the pope with a makeshift cherub attached to his ass rolled around on a ten-speed. Sequined nuns slunk by, black dresses slit to mid-thigh. A naked man marched up the street with a proud and perfect erection. He was just the advance scout.

Eventually a battalion of naked bicyclists, giggly and none of them particularly attractive, coasted by, and we, the crowd, tittered like sixth graders hearing the words for genitalia spoken aloud for the first time.

Some Wiccan traditions have a history of ritual conducted in the nude, which they call "skyclad." Mid-twentieth-century accounts tell of witches smearing bear oil over their bodies to keep themselves warm during winter rituals, and of elderly witches succumbing to the cold anyway. But that wasn't what was happening at the Fremont Solstice Parade. Ritual as performance was a common explanation for the disintegration of religion—I'd seen that too—and a parade was a precise hybrid of ritual and exhibition. The parade wasn't a rejection of religion at all; rather, it was a desperate lunge toward religious foolishness.

It's probably apparent that I wasn't in the hottest of moods for my time in Seattle. James had opened my mind, but now I was having trouble figuring out how to self-identify. I was kind of stuck. If Draggi was a Hindu-Zen Celto-Stregheria witch, then should I be described as a Judeo-Christian ex-Catholic Jamesian Secularist? My collision with religious movements hadn't converted me to anything, but James had taught me that there was no mode of thought that was not ultimately a belief system. The great side effect of consciousness was metaphysical quandary, and however one chose to address the attendant dilemma of curiosity—even if to reject it—was the definition of religion. Now that my old answers had been challenged, I was back at theological square one. The Fremont Solstice Parade might have reflected the confusion of my own mind: the goofball excuses for commentary, those silly ways of reacting to the world, ritual reduced to titillation to distract us from the vast industrial void we had constructed around us.

Back at the booth, Draggi was distributing hugs to people who'd had relatives in wars, Vietnam or more recent—it didn't matter. I didn't tell him about my mood. We left for the solstice celebration early, which would be held at the Independent Order of Odd Fellows, another of those pseudo-religious organizations whose hall stood on one of the Seattle strips measuring decline. Draggi and I arrived early. The meeting center was a broad open space decked out with nineteenth-century accoutrements—padded seats rimming the room, a trinity of thrones, candleholders spaced along the walls—that made it ritualistically multifunctional, a courtroom/sanctuary that could take a potluck in a pinch. The solstice celebration was a Covenant of the Goddess event, organized by the Seattle Local Council, which meant that witches from a number of different trads would participate and that the ritual itself would be sort of generalized so that no one felt excluded. It was all part of that fine line Wicca was walking these days as it tried to organize.

The witches trickled in with dishes for our meal. I met a man named Marshall, who looked like an accountant but had been doing astrology for forty years. He called Seattle a Scorpio city and a kind of purgatory. Another man, named Gwythion, appeared, covered with long dark hair and swarms of tattoos and piercings, dressed in a kilt and using a cane. No one paid him much mind. Dwayne was the entirely average-looking man who would lead the night's ceremony—he was of a shamanistic tradition, and he agreed to let me record it only after I acknowledged that any account of such a thing would be subjective. Modern witches have always had an odd relationship with the press. Kirk White would later tell me that Cherry Hill Seminary taught an entire class on how witches should handle the media. A woman named Zanoni, a thin, small sexy grandmother of a witch, approached me and said, "You're not gonna put any gossip in that book of yours, young man, or you're gonna wish you had a broom that can zoom!"

I sat down with Zanoni. She was renowned for having been among the group in the seventies that originally formed CoG. I asked her what her trad was, but she had been initiated into several. "It doesn't matter," she said. "They all got a piece of the puzzle. Don't none of us got the whole answer." Like Draggi, Zanoni had been a witch her whole life, and had done witchy things even when she was a girl: raising tables, seeing deceased people, knowing who was about to show up. When the Space Shuttle *Challenger* exploded, one of its female astronauts appeared to Zanoni and pleaded, *I'm not done.* Zanoni replied, "Calm down, lady. Now, who the hell are you?" She waved at the memory. "It took me three days to get rid of her."

The kitchen filled with the kind of standard middle-aged witches who would go to MerryMeet and a barrage of the teenagers who were threatening the fabric of Wicca with their numbers and untested enthusiasm. We made a circle around the table before we ate, to acknowledge the animals and plants who had given their lives for our meal. We thanked the Goddess who had given of her body, the God who had given of his energy. "Blessed be," we all said.

After we ate, Dwayne gathered us in the main hall for ritual instruction. The ritual was the last of a quartet of ceremonies he'd written linking mind, body, spirit, and heart to the corresponding seasons. Summer was the heart, he said. He passed around a jar of small plastic stones. We each took one. During the ritual we would approach Dwayne and offer the stone, sort of an imitation opal, as that part of our heart that we were willing to return to the community. He would offer us a stone in return, and then we could offer these to one another. He reminded us of his shamanistic tradition. "I'd like us to circle up and do an energy raising at the beginning," he said, "but don't be freaked out if you don't see me calling quarters. This is not just about this community here tonight. I am basically your symbol, your gateway, your doorway to commit feelings back to your community, whatever it is."

He dismissed us to the kitchen while he prepared the room, whispering incantations and rubbing his hands over the walls. Gwythion disappeared into a bathroom and came out wearing just a robe—he was Gardnerian probably, and the robe was a skyclad compromise. We formed a line to reenter the hall. Someone started in with a drum, tapping out a slow marching beat, and a young woman who sort of controlled the room's sexual energy—she wore a hat and slinky top of matching red and a long tight skirt—censed us all as we walked in, a kind of spiritual frisk or massage, splashing us with smoke. Marshall put his hands together and bowed his head as he waited in line. Zanoni stood behind me, and even though I didn't really feel anything I turned once and caught her passing her hands over my spine, palms an inch from me, either casting a spell or sculpting whatever energy I was giving off. The girl in red smiled dearly at all of us, and we each fell in love with her in turn. The circle filled in.

We chanted for a while, a kind of group groan shifting between the note of the men and the note of the women, and when we were done Dwayne instructed us to let the energy go and run. His talk turned more delicate now, less whisper than careful speech, and someone began a gentle rhythm with a rattle as we took turns approaching Dwayne to deposit our hearts back into the jar. Every so often Uncle Draggi hit a little bell at the end of the room. Dwayne kissed everyone on the forehead and wrapped them in an elaborate hug, a hug that tried to return to the origin of hugs, an attempt to displace the sterile, ritualized hug of the secular world, a hug that had all the value of a sudden embrace intended to alleviate grief or trauma. Dwayne closed his eyes for everyone and held them deep in the folds of his arms. When it was my turn, I felt his lips on my forehead and heard him breathe twice. "I give you my heart," he said, "and another to return to your community. Go in peace."

I sat down. The witches crisscrossed the circle, offering their hearts to one another. One woman silently slipped a stone into my hand, and I walked over to Uncle Draggi to give him mine. Zanoni sneaked up behind me again when I returned. She gave me her stone.

"I put a good charge on this," she said.

"I already got one."

"It doesn't matter. I was told to give this to you. I charged it with specific gods of writing."

When everyone had been hugged, Dwayne spoke again. "My path has longed to come here," he said, "and my lineage is long as well. Many here have come long paths in their own time. We all have community—take what you've received here as a reminder into your daily lives. Blessed be."

But no one moved. "I don't think we're done yet, Dwayne," Zanoni said. We tried singing a few songs, but because Wicca was a young religion its music and its lyrics sometimes had an adolescent quality, or it too often recalled the sixties, when Wicca began its American boom. The songs we tried weren't quite catchy enough to get past a chorus or two. Someone suggested that we all bless Dwayne, so we began that, lining up again to kiss Dwayne's forehead. Then some magic happened, I think. The girl in red sat up and suddenly hit the notes of a one-lyric song (*"We are opening up in sweet surrender / To the luminous love light of the One"*), and somehow the sexy trill of her voice and the boldness of her delivery approximated the mood of the room well enough so that after just a single chorus others started to pick it up. As we each took an extra turn with Dwayne, the song grew into fugue and harmony, and whoever had the rattle kicked in with a rapid beat, so that suddenly it was danceable, and before long people were doing that as well. The magic was that at some point Dwayne's ritual had become effective. It was all still kind of juvenile in its way, but this was the coda to Dwayne's symphony of ceremony, and, just as William James had written of witchcraft, I could feel belief chiming with an emotional mood. The limbo of Seattle, the endless pageantry of pop America—it was all distant from our crafted bubble of music and acceptance. I liked getting kissed by Dwayne; I liked kissing Dwayne. This was the nature of pluralism, this was the variety within Wicca finding its common denominator and letting it resonate. A single voice rang out and others joined not to simulate it but to harmonize with it, commentaries not simply ironic or in protest but celebratory and complimentary, until what was achieved could be neither proved, nor described, nor denied.

The next day Uncle Draggi took me to a spot across Puget Sound from Seattle and we watched the massive ships creeping into port and the gargantuan cranes hefting shipping containers into deep holds. Draggi mused that he had been fired from his job on a day that was both Friday the thirteenth and a full moon. He shrugged.

I decided to make him my pastoral counselor. I told him about my mood, my problem with self-identification. I admitted that even though I'd felt something at the ritual—energy, whatever—I was still having problems with the literalness of Wicca, with all religion. Should one sign on to other peoples' gods or goddesses just because they seemed to work? Was Draggi really seeing little people? Had the woman who visited him as an infant been the Goddess? For James it was just this, the accounts of interaction with the divine, that made religion compelling, but when it came to what I believed the clerico-academic-scientific part of me still poked through the tissue in my mind. I wanted Draggi to admit either that he was signing on to visions born of imagination or that his demons were evidence of dysfunction. He wasn't fazed. He posed a simple question or two, and then asked whether there could be a legitimate value distinction between, say, his life and mine when our paths had come to intersect at this time, this place, this bench. Then he talked about the Goddess.

"I've thought about this on more than one occasion," he said, "and for reasons I would have a hard time articulating I don't know if I could make a case that this was the Goddess. Someone else might just say that's my guardian angel. Or the Virgin Mary. Or a deva. To me, it's irrelevant. This entity took on a form that I could see and understand. Am I seeing little people like they show up in Disney? In some cases, yes, literally. Sometimes, it's nothing more than"—he pointed to a shrub at the edge of the sound—"okay, that bush there, that tree. Down at the bottom, on the left, next to the trunk, I could say there is a creature there, standing thus high, it looks like this, I could take out a pencil and damn near sketch the thing. Other times, I look over there and perceive this creature, but I don't see it with my eyes. I don't see a thing. The eyeballs are not reacting or perceiving in this fashion, but in some cases I can damn near see them."

It wasn't really a complete answer, but he left it at that. I asked him one more question: what his name meant. He chuckled.

"It's very simple. I happened to see it in a dance-performance handbill. *Draggi*. Aha, I said, that's my name. Little by little I became known as Uncle Draggi because I'm this kindly old man. A few years ago I found out what the hell *draggi* means. It's sort of embarrassing, but screw it. Turns out in the Slovak languages *draggi* means 'dear.' As in Dear John. So all this time I've been known as Uncle Dear."

3. The Circle Is Cast

At MerryMeet, the witches made a routine of arriving an hour late for almost everything. People called it Pagan Standard Time.

The Goddess of Wicca may vary from coven to coven, but a common image was the Triple Goddess. The Triple Goddess bound together the three aspects of the lives of women—maiden, mother, crone—and was a concept based on a variety of pre-Christian idols unearthed in Europe in the twentieth century. In the general appearance of modern witches, the three aspects of the Triple Goddess tended to express as long wild hair for the maiden, a matronly bulk for the mother, and delicate reading glasses for the crone. An average witch walking around MerryMeet—some of them sneaking off to play slot machines between events—might have presented with two of the aspects regardless of age: a young, shiny, heavyset woman with short hair and square-framed spectacles, or a rail-thin older woman with a gray mane down to her knees but wearing those same glasses. For the most part, people at MerryMeet called one another by their magical or Craft names, if they had one. And everyday reality was called the mundane world, that place where we used our mundane names and worked our mundane jobs.

Uncle Draggi arrived the morning of the opening ritual. It took the organizers a while to get ready, and some alternative healing broke out near the escalator's fire doors, witches applying various practices to one another. Eventually, more than a hundred of us filed into a large room and formed an oval connecting four small curtained booths. Witches waited inside. We began the ritual by individually reciting, *The circle is cast, hand to hand,* and taking one another's hands around the room. Then the first officer of CoG was introduced. His name was Finn. He was a witchy-looking older man with flowing gray-dark hair, a tendency to wear open shirts to show off a still-tight chest, and bare feet so full of hammer toes they recalled cloven hooves. He stood on a stool in the middle of the circle as the witches in the booths emerged in animal costumes and performed tribal dance routines to music appropriate to the four elements: wind, fire, water, earth. In a normal Wiccan ritual, a circle was opened at the beginning of the ceremony, then closed at the end, and covens differed on what to do with the energy that resulted. One could sacrifice it or use it to cast a spell. But now we ended the ritual without closing the circle—it would remain open until a ceremony at the end of the weekend.

I sat with Draggi for a while as Grand Council prepared to convene, Finn and several other CoG officers taking positions behind tables on a dais and representatives of the various covens spread throughout the room. The witches would voice approval of measures by "twinkling," wriggling their hands in the air in a kind of silent applause. "Check one, check one," said a witch testing the microphone. CoG had a total of 135 covens in sixteen Local Councils and 100 solitaries; 385 witches had clergy credentials, which meant they could work in hospitals or prisons. The exact number of total witches was difficult to calculate because covens were entitled to complete secrecy and could number as few as three witches or as many as twenty. A tally when the room came to order revealed thirty-nine covens represented. It was a quorum. The room twinkled.

Modern witchcraft began in Europe, mainly Britain. Sensational attention the movement received early in the twentieth century claimed that witches punished during the Inquisition were practitioners of a religion that had survived the pagan purge at the beginning of the Middle Ages. The number of witches burned at the stake was first estimated in the millions, a solid foundation of persecution upon which to spin yarns and establish a tradition. More copious Craft research eventually whittled the number down to forty to fifty thousand and revealed that the label *witch* probably didn't apply to those who were persecuted. The stereotype of witches still prominent today—sacrificing babies, flying on brooms—came from a book written in 1486 by a pair of monks. The book was called *Malleus Maleficarum,* or *The Witch-Hammer,* a document commissioned to justify ongoing persecutions. It's probable that the book's authors borrowed from reports of South Asian practices, and it's even possible that some pagan practices, particularly fertility and quasi-medical rites, had managed to persist in eastern Europe. Yet *The Witch-Hammer* dramatically overstated its case, entirely misrepresenting the phenomenon it claimed to record.

Belief in witchcraft was once considered un-Christian—Charlemagne had once decreed that those who burned witches should be put to death in turn—but at the end of the fifteenth century, as had happened with the Devil, the policy shifted and it became heresy to *not* believe in witchcraft. The attempt to eradicate a tradition that had never formally existed kick-started the modern movement. Wicca was born of bad press. Even the word *coven* came from a sensational account of an alleged witch in 1662.

There are accounts of medieval groups dabbling in occult imagery, but modern witchcraft definitively traces its roots back only a couple hundred years. Craft historians cite a number of forces recognizable in the modern movement. The first included Freemasonry and secret societies, originally powerful craft guilds that became more pagan as their influence waned. It was originally thought that Freemasonry evolved from witchcraft, but later research agreed that Wicca borrowed both the structure of Freemason ceremonies and its reputation for secrecy. A second influence was "cunning folk," rural men and women in England who were practitioners of what would now be called alternative healing: acupuncture, homeopathy, herbalism, and the like. Cunning folk kept books of remedies that gave them an aura of knowledge and education. Some of them used their reputations to offer special services, either placing curses or preventing them. The cunning folk with the most malicious reputations tended to be female, but they had never been known to work in groups or covens.

Finally, the beginning of the nineteenth century saw a movement toward a single Goddess figure, and an acceptable God as well. The same longing for a connection with the natural world that sent some to classical literature and Druidry led others to archaeology and images of powerful goddesses. The pre-Christian figurines of the Triple Goddess triggered speculation on prehistoric Goddess-based cultures, and the many pagan goddesses who came later—Anath, Isis, Aphrodite, Ishtar—were interpreted as demotions of an earlier Great Goddess figure. Inventive archaeology suggested that the Great Goddess had found spectacular expression on Malta, and finds in India pointed to a supreme proto-Shiva figure. As modern witchcraft began to emerge, the Goddess underwent a process of synthesis, a monotheistic return. The Goddess drew on the Bible, where "Wisdom" was personified as female, and borrowed aspects of Diana, Aradia, and the Great Whore of Babylon. She was understood as both creatrix and redeemer, was sometimes characterized as a muse who operated through dreams or altered states (certain early Christians would describe the Holy Spirit as feminine), and eventually ascended from an association with Earth to an association with the moon, its stages of waxing and waning representing the maiden, mother, and crone. For some Wiccans, there would be a God as well: Pan, who reemerged in literature around the turn of the century as a patron of the forbidden. Pan wasn't patriarchal, and he did not threaten the Goddess's individuality. Eventually he became Wicca's "Horned God," the male aspect for covens that preferred gender balance and duotheism.

Paganism acknowledges a lineage through nineteenth-century Spiritualism—mediums and such—and James biographers have hinted that James's vision of psychology could be measured through the growth of the kind of pastoral counseling Kirk White was teaching. The history read like a succession of forked paths. James's *Principles* triggered a break from abstraction and metaphysics in psychology, the first split separating German laboratory science from French theories of the unconscious. This latter path split again, one route headed toward person-centered psychology (Carl Rogers) and psychoanalysis (Freud and his disciples), and the other (with which James would have been more sympathetic) toward pagan healing practices and magic. Later in life, James warmed to the work of Gustav Fechner, whose "Earth-Soul," a conscious planet, was source material for a variety of theories in neo-Paganism, the most popular being Gaia, a new name for a living Earth.

Groups like the Hermetic Order of the Golden Dawn and Aleister Crowley's Ordo Templi Orientis served Craft historians as the evolutionary link between Freemasonry and Wicca, but working covens of witches, in forms recognizable today, could be traced back only as far as the 1920s. Even for this, all the evidence was anecdotal. Wicca had established its origins firmly only after the death of Crowley in 1947 and the repeal of British witchcraft laws in 1951. The old law, the Witchcraft Act of 1736, had made both practicing witchcraft and accusing someone of being a witch illegal—a kind of overkill solution to the Inquisition. The new freedom of the 1950s paved the way for Gerald Gardner, a Conradian figure who had worked for years as a customs inspector in Malaysia. On returning to England, Gardner became, as much as its prophet, Wicca's first public relations specialist. Gardner brought to Wicca experience in Freemasonry, Spiritualism, Buddhism, and tribal magical practices, as well as a comprehensive knowledge of the ceremonial Malaysian knife, the *keris*. This last served as the model for the *athame*.

Details of Gardner's immersion into Wicca are sketchy—he claimed that nude rituals conducted by covens that now bear his name actually came from a coven into which he had been initiated in the 1930s. This coven, it was said, had once performed ceremonies to put a curse on Adolf Hitler, but close details of whom Gardner associated with are sometimes demonstrable as outright invention. At first, Gardner was seen as the likely heir to Ordo Templi Orientis when Crowley died, but he eschewed it in favor of a more distinct witch religion. He had written a novel in 1940, *A Goddess Arrives,* and another in 1949, *High Magic's Aid,* and when it was legally viable he published *Witchcraft Today* and *The Meaning of Witchcraft* as nonfiction, posing in the first as an anthropologist who had stumbled across an ancient witch tradition. Even earlier he had taken a greater step: as soon as the Vagrancy and Witchcraft Acts were repealed in 1951, he announced a witch religion to the press, based on rituals he had been collecting and writing for several years. Wicca quietly tapped into a growing countercultural mood.

Gardner's work—and the work of those he included in his coven—gave Wicca much of its basic shape. He introduced the *Book of Shadows,* a kind of coven log to record sabbats and esbats, though he may have simply offered names for practices already in place. Magic was refined into two categories: high magic included rituals and ceremonies with the mystical goal of interaction with the divine; low magic encompassed operations meant for specific effect, usually medicinal, though many applications were meant to cure loneliness. Wiccan ethics emerged with a slightly modified Golden Rule: "Do what ye will and ye harm none." The "Crede" could be traced to a number of earlier statements, themselves marking a curious religious evolution: in *Varieties,* James quoted Saint Augustine as saying, "If you but love [God], you may do as you incline"; in the sixteenth century the French novelist François Rabelais wrote, "Do as thou wilt because men that are free, of gentle birth, well bred and at home in civilized company possess a natural instinct that inclines them to virtue and saves them from vice"; Aleister Crowley believed that Rabelais had predicted him and radicalized the line in 1904 with "Do what thou wilt shall be the whole of the law." Wicca resolved it, finally, with the wholesome caveat "and ye harm none."

If not a prophet, Gardner was at least Wicca's singularity; when he died, in 1964, the religion exploded into chaos and civil war. Personalities in conflict simply split off from one another and began new covens with new practices. The many traditions of Wicca began to appear, their success often measured by the amount of media attention they received. Witchcraft in the United States can be traced back as far as the Church of Aphrodite, active on Long Island in 1938, and there are rumors of groups in the Ozarks in the 1940s. The most significant change Wicca experienced in America was its absorption into women's spirituality and feminism. Women-only Wiccan traditions emerged and endured. By the 1970s the United States was the center of global neo-Paganism. The movement was still immature— a witch couple created "unicorns" by surgically relocating the antlers of kid goats, and once there was a group effort made to levitate the Pentagon—but even as it rode an emotional wave of need and belief a headier undercurrent of research began to swell. Isaac Bonewits, an ex-Druid all-purpose neo-Pagan, dropped the bombshell that really there was no surviving witch tradition; there was only "the myth of the Unitarian, Universalist, white witchcult of Western theosophical Britainy." And new interpretations of the idols that had once suggested the Great Goddess now acknowledged that there might not have been a Goddess at all.

Wicca was forced to mature. It became apparent that its original expression was at least in part the result of a reaction to conservative repression, though the movement had long since been co-opted by liberalism. The history it hoped for didn't exist, and what history it did have wasn't particularly flattering; Gardner was eventually discredited. Witches themselves got used to the idea that theirs was a young religion, and what belief there was became more sophisticated. Prominent male Wiccan leaders died off, and more and more the movement was led by women. Rituals became more overtly an effort to connect with nature, and magic was described as useful self-delusion. Pluralism, tolerance, and a celebration of variety of belief became common themes for Wiccan writers.

James had once described the media as the organ and promulgator of a state of mind in which Americans were "smitten with utter silliness." He warned that such a media could result in "a new 'dark ages' that may last more centuries than the first one." But the Wiccan strategy of press manipulation eventually got a handle on that as well: more fair-handed representations of witches as members of a nature-loving religion wended their way into newspaper accounts and television shows. The Goddess had been dispelled just as Wicca caught on, yet she remained in a less literal form. A Wiccan theologian described the Goddess as real "because human energy goes into making Her real. . . . She is a metaphor because, great though she may be, She is finite, like any other human concept, whereas reality is infinite."

4. BEN FRANKLIN IN DRAG

I sat in on Grand Council for a while with Uncle Draggi but eventually left to attend a crowded talk on CoG history. I squeezed in between the Queen of Flamfoo and a quiet, effete man called Baldr the Bold. CoG, too, had been born of bad press. In the early 1970s Northern California teemed with Pagan groups, and an unflattering newspaper article made some of them wonder whether they should unite and form a bureaucratic wing to deal with legal matters. The meeting, held in someone's living room, had in the retelling an aura of a council of great leaders. Many came simply to ensure that a federation wouldn't try to define *witch* too narrowly. At the same time, they had all seen Pagan groups collapse under too much diversity. The surprise was that they did in fact have things in common, and on summer solstice 1975 thirteen founding covens formed the original Covenant of the Goddess, with bylaws borrowed from a Congregationalist system. The only requirement was that a goddess appear somewhere in a coven's theology. They did not define *witch,* and they openly acknowledged that practitioners outside the Covenant were witches, too, and that all were entitled to secrecy. They worked out the system of Local Councils, the Assemblies of Solitaries, and the decision-making processes.

MerryMeet proceeded something like a convention—Grand Council was the main focus, but there were a number of activities happening as well. Witches were free to come and go as they pleased, each working through the complicated schedule to attend whatever applied to their trad. On the second day someone finally opened the vending room, where witches could buy books, handmade brass *athames,* tourmaline pendants, and ritual gear. Some believed the vending room was the only reason Merry-Meet even existed anymore. "I don't know a Pagan who wasn't born to shop," one witch told me. "Where else can you buy your fancy wares?" What became apparent as MerryMeet hit stride was that its pluralism had a downside: the span of Craft research ranged from the original sensationalism to the more recent serious scholarship. The most prominent Wiccan history had grown into rigor and accountability, but there was another stratum of witch writers who still believed all the disproved theories of goddesses and ancient cults. If pluralism was really to be possible, then both the shysters and the scholars had to be included in the program. This was precisely the charge that had been leveled against James's Pragmatism: "These pragmatists destroy all objective standards . . . and put foolishness and wisdom on one level." And the truth was, Wicca thrived on those old theories; they were still its best draw.

In the morning I went to a workshop by the popular Wiccan writer M. Macha Nightmare, who said, "I'm an obsessive networker—I'm having a love affair with the Pagan world!" She told us about her new book, *Witchcraft and the Web*. We talked about issues like what a witch should do when a twelve-year-old asks for spells in a chat room, and whether there was anything to the claim that you could feel energy from a cyberritual. From there, I went to another book presentation, this by a young man delivering a talk on pre-Christian gods. His main point seemed to be that ancient sacrifices were actually the ritual slaughter of food. I headed back to Grand Council just as they were summing up some Internet-related matter. "You'll have to talk to the Web witch about that," the first officer said.

Uncle Draggi leaned over and told me that he had started a commotion a little while earlier when he got up and asked a question about the delivery of mail. The U.S. Post Office refused to deliver to magical names, it seemed. Draggi was often frustrated with Grand Council because he was a bookkeeper and recognized the inefficiency of their accounting practices. Now, the meeting moved on to matters of expansion. Questions cropped up. How could a CoG member who wanted to recommend a new coven do so for a coven whose rituals were entirely secret? What should the standard be for a witch who claimed to have self-initiated? Just then, Draggi passed me a complete handwritten review of the dinner we'd shared the night before. He was bored. The rough draft was still over on his side of the table.

From there I went to a workshop on the Har Hou, a French sabbat dance from the seventeenth century. The class started late, of course. "We don't have time to cast a formal circle or go hand to hand, so we'll just say it's there," the instructor said.

The Har Hou song had proved effective for healing, for trances, and for raising the Cone of Power. The Cone of Power was how Wicca described the energy of rituals, a kind of phallic holdover from the early days. The song had some simple French lyrics and we held hands to spin around in a circle, speeding up and slowing down as directed. We sang and did a grapevine step with normal hand-holding—no pinkie holds, no basket weaving—and pulsed in and out, making our circle tighter and tighter as we accelerated and pressed our bodies together. Some of the heavier witches had to bow out as the pace became feverish, and when we could go no faster the instructor brought all of us to the center of the circle, where we stood in a tight pack and twinkled our arms over our heads, looking up at the mirrored ceiling, which reflected the fake sky of the carpet. The witches laughed and twittered at all the energy. Or, rather, the laughing was the energy. The diversity of Wicca reared again as we dispersed and the witches differed on what to do with the feeling. Some bent down on one knee to touch the ground and return it to the earth. One witch walked by me, smiling and strong, and said, "No ground. *Keep it in me.*"

The serious Craft historians got their chance that night. A Berkeley coven gave a featured presentation. Several witches who were also academics had been conducting meticulous research in an attempt to restore Gerald Gardner's reputation. A portion of Gardner's papers had wound up in a special collections library in Toronto, but a large chunk of his work had been sold to Ripley's Believe It or Not, and Ripley's wouldn't let the witches touch it. Only the joke was on Ripley's. When its workers collected the goods, they missed an old book that had slipped behind a filing cabinet. Gardner had once spoken of losing the original manuscript from which he had drafted his first *Book of Shadows,* a claim that had seemed suspicious at the time. But now the lost text turned out to be just this book, *Ye Bok of Ye Art Magical,* definitive proof that there had been active covens before Gardner delivered witchcraft to the press. The presentation was an overview of the cross-referencing of *Ye Bok* with other early texts.

In the morning, Grand Council turned postmodern when someone made a motion that MerryMeet disband itself. The room hit on an accidental Cone of Power with the energy of anxiety. Not everyone agreed that a casino hotel was a good setting for nature-worshipping witches. Uncle Draggi leaned over and whispered, "Roughing it is coming to mean room service." An idea was floated to piggyback the national meeting on a Pagan festival. MerryMeet's main organizer got up to report that this year's event looked like it would actually turn a profit—the casino was partly responsible for this, she said, and besides, Reno had a thriving community of witches, and how else would they have gotten access to the wisdom present in this room? Someone finally put forth a countermotion to preserve MerryMeet. The witches twinkled.

I missed more events than I attended: a lecture on Dionysus; a speaker comparing Western witches to Kali worshippers in India; a demonstration of sacred cooking; and "Dancing in the Dark," a trance event that locked its conference-room door and posted a sign telling people to keep an open mind. Before the main ritual on Saturday night—a living tarot reading that would tell the future of the Covenant—I had time to attend "Witchcraft at the Crossroads," a lecture by Wiccan writer Raven Grimassi.

Grimassi was opposite the Berkeley coven on the Wiccan research spectrum. He was the author of nine books celebrating the mythical witchcraft of pre-Christian Europe. MerryMeet organizers wouldn't slander him openly, but they did smirk and suggest that maybe not all Wiccans approached research in the same way.

Yet Grimassi's lecture was packed. The small room they gave him was hot with witches even before he arrived. Grimassi was a short, jowly man with long hair and a black suit. He looked a little like Ben Franklin in drag. He started with the joke that people usually thought he was going to be a woman but this was the best he could do in this incarnation.

"A lot of people have gone mental in witchcraft," he said. He told us he was still a believer in real magic. Just as we have inherited our genes, he said, so have we inherited a spiritual DNA. He intended to teach us how to access our inner cauldron, and he told us that witchcraft was three thousand years old instead of fifty. A good example of magic, he claimed, was giving someone the middle finger. It was the use of a symbol to alter the consciousness of another person. Grimassi called magic "joo-joo."

James had spent much of his later years articulating and rearticulating Pragmatism, but he never did find a good argument with which to defend his pluralism against the charge that it lacked an absolute standard. "One cannot say this of pluralism," he admitted.

> *Its world is always vulnerable, for some part may go astray; and having no "eternal" edition of it to draw comfort from, its partisans must always feel to some degree insecure. . . . This forms one permanent inferiority of pluralism from the pragmatic point of view. It has no saving message for the incurably sick soul.*

But Grimassi did have a message, and he began to deliver it now with an alternate history of witchcraft. He argued that the "crossroads" spoken of in olden times was actually more like a Y-intersection. Witches, he said, tended to gather in such spots because that was where joo-joo happened. He was gearing up to the use of a prop, an ornate witch's broom leaning against the wall behind him. He brandished it. With a little imagination one could see a broom as a Y-intersection, he said. He explained the broom to us, taught us the proper way to stick it between our legs so as to "fly," which really just meant knowing who you were and what you wanted. There was a whole broom symbolism. The staff was made of ash and represented the bridge between worlds in Nordic tradition. The switch was birch and was a connection to the spiritual underworld. And the wrap was made of willow and stood for a witch's psychic ability, tying the two together.

"The way you empower the broom is by becoming the root," Grimassi said, and he demonstrated a kind of broom meditation that I recognized at once as a variation on Rhiannon's Druidic tree meditation. Grimassi was a plagiarist! But the crowd didn't seem to mind. He had the switch of the broom facing down, and someone asked him whether it wouldn't be easier to stir one's inner cauldron with the switch facing up. Grimassi said that actually it was a little harder that way because the switch wound up hitting you in the face. He demonstrated this, waving the broom around like a weapon. Then he moved to summary. The broom is a way to get back to the rootedness of the witch, he said. Witches are stewards of nature on this side, and elves and fairies do the same thing on the other side.

"The Goddess, Gaia," he said, "who we all know is conscious, remembers that time when she was venerated. Now she is sick with pollutants. She is calling to us: where are the people who remember me?"

Back up at Grand Council they were looking forward rather than back. Draggi revealed that he had been scolded—told to shut up and sit down—when he finally couldn't take it anymore and complained about bookkeeping matters. "CoG is becoming more *Animal Farm*-esque," he whispered. "Everyone is equal, but some people are more equal. It hacks me off."

The Berkeley group began presenting again. Wicca was spanning the globe. They announced that they were working to protect an Asian city that had retained paganism until the twelfth century and was threatened by a dam project. And they gave a report on the effort to have Wicca represented at the 2004 Parliament of the World's Religions in Barcelona. The first Parliament of the World's Religions had been held in 1893 in Chicago. For a historian writing about the event, the date was significant precisely because it preceded *The Varieties of Religious Experience* by almost a decade.

The 2004 Parliament would host more than one hundred traditions. The Berkeley group was excited. "The thing is," the presenter said, "when you hear about us without all the devil-worship baggage attached, we sound fucking wonderful."

5. THE SUICIDAL MOOD

Just before the living tarot display, I asked a witch if she thought it would be okay to record it. "You'd have to get the permission of every Pagan in there," she said, nodding as though she had imparted an important but pretty basic piece of information.

The living tarot was put on by a San Francisco theater troupe, actors, some of them witches, depicting characters representing each of the twenty-two major arcana of a standard tarot deck. The delivery was determined randomly. The lead witch, who'd organized the show, asked us to ground and center, then drew out an *athame* to cut a circle around us charged by water and earth. She beckoned the old ones. An oversized tarot deck was brought down the center aisle, and we all held hands so that we could all say we had touched them. The actors appeared, dressed ornately and parading through the room fashion-show style, then taking up poses in a group. The audience drew the cards, the lead witch called out the name, and the corresponding actor came forward for a brief monologue.

It started well enough. The Empress suggested possibility and bounty. The Devil and the Sun hinted at temptation; the Moon promised guidance. Temperance advised wisdom between extremes, and the Magician was ambiguous as he made a glass of water turn red for some reason. Strength offered fortitude, the Hanged Man admitted that sacrifices would be made, and the Tower spoke of change and reconstruction with concern about foundations. Judgment warned of days when decisions would come back to haunt us, World indicated new beginnings, the Wheel of Fortune told of the seduction of luck. Death was the gateway to transformation, and Hierophant claimed that the voice we heard from without was actually a voice from within.

It was about then that Death, returned to his spot in the back, sneezed audibly, making his Grim Reaper headgear teeter. The audience's digital watches made for a cricket's interval at 8:30. But that wasn't really what made us anxious. The problem was that the Fool was still up there. No one wanted him to be the final card, the card that would tell us what the year had in store for CoG. Beside me, Uncle Draggi was getting nervous.

Star told us to look to the heavens for guidance. The Emperor lured us with patriarchy, but the Hermit, a woman dressed as a homeless person, countered with wisdom from unlikely sources. The Lovers suggested unpredictability, and Justice emphasized balance on narrow paths. The Chariot lent determination, and the High Priestess reminded us of her resilience and of the power within. All of which was fine—except that the worst had come to pass. The Fool was the only card left, the final outcome of the reading. "Oh, boy," Draggi said. The Fool was adventurous and passionate, yet indecisive and flighty. His egotism could result in chaos.

"The circle is complete," said the lead witch with her knife. "Let her message guide us in the coming year."

James wrote in "The Will to Believe":

> *Now, when I speak of trusting our religious demands, just what do I mean by "trusting"? Is the word to carry with it license to define in detail an invisible world, and to anathematize and excommunicate those whose trust is different? Certainly not! Our faculties of belief were not primarily given us to mark orthodoxies and heresies withal; they were given us to live by. And to trust our religious demands means first of all to live in the light of them, and to act as if the invisible world they suggested were real. It is a fact of human nature, that man can live and die by the help of a sort of faith that goes without a single dogma or definition. The bare assurance that this natural order is not ultimate but a mere sign or vision, the external staging of a many-storied universe . . . this bare assumption is to such men enough to make life seem worth living. . . . Destroy this inner assurance, however, vague as it is, and . . . often enough the wild-eyed look at life—the suicidal mood—will then set in.*

Draggi appeared shaken after the morning ritual in which the new year's CoG officers were introduced and we released the elements and promised them that we would see them again. Most had written off the previous night's tarot reading, in part because it was revealed that somehow we had started pulling cards at the wrong date. "The folly of the gods is higher than the wisdom of man," someone explained. But that wasn't what was bothering Draggi. I stood next to him as the circle was closed and held his hand, but he didn't tell me what was wrong until later. He had wanted to speak to Raven Grimassi, who had once written about Italian witchcraft, Stregheria, part of Draggi's private trad. Draggi had wanted to challenge him on a number of points. But Grimassi was more equal than Draggi. He had stayed at MerryMeet only long enough to deliver his lecture. By the closing ritual, he was gone.

The witches dismissed themselves through the casino. I followed Draggi around as he said good-bye to a few friends, and by the time we headed off to the elevators he was crying. I was headed up to my room; he was headed down to the airport shuttle. We stood before the mirrored elevator doors. I wanted to hug him the way Dwayne had hugged me, or at least say something that had William James's cash value. But I didn't know how. The down elevator came first. Draggi wiped an eye, shook my hand, and said, "Take care, guy." When the doors closed before him I was left with an image of myself where he'd stood.

1907–1910

Neither a reputation for illness nor the photographs of William James match written descriptions of his character at all.

James wore facial hair his entire life, beginning in his teens with a thin mustache that lent him a sinister look. Later, a fatter mustache tugged on his upper lip, and James frowned through his twenties. By thirty he had grown the beard that defined him, trimmed along the sides but furrier and wedge-shaped in and around the lips, proof that he had founded not only the science of psychology but the look for its practitioners as well. James was never photographed smiling. In early adulthood his eyes were soft, his skin unwrinkled. He looked intelligent, but fragile and vulnerable. By the time he was a parent his hairline had begun to recede over a heavy forehead, pouches had formed beneath eyes rimmed with wrinkles, and vertical gray streaks striped the thick pear of the beard. He was generally photographed either sitting as if for a painting or in some kind of pose meant to make him look willful and hearty. In later images he could look positively cruel. Only one image hinted at his character: James reclined on a lounge chair at a bath, a hat tipped forward to shade his eyes and a book propped on his stomach. Spying on him while he was reading was perhaps the only way an age of slow shutter speeds could manage a candid shot of William James.

Descriptions of his personality came mostly from his students, who tended to focus on his nervous energy and enthusiasm. "Even in such details as the contour of the beard and the little fillip in the parting of his hair," one account claimed, "there was something expressive of intentness. To see him was never to forget what it means to be alive." James lived an active life—he valued ruggedness and the outdoors—and a visitor to one of his classes once claimed that he looked more like an athlete than a professor. He reportedly used humor freely in the classroom, and by all accounts—

and in direct contrast to his photographs—he eschewed professorial authority entirely. He permitted students to help him think through and consider theories. John Jay Chapman recalled that James's mind was "never quite in focus . . . you were thus played upon by a logic which was not the logic of intellect, but a far deeper thing, limpid and clear in itself, confused and refractory only when you tried to deal with it intellectually." Most found his informality welcome and inspiring. Some considered him disorganized and unserious.

Even as James approached old age he was comfortable in debates with much younger philosophers. In *Experiment in Autobiography,* H. G. Wells told a story that has often been repeated as an emblem of James's irreverent spirit. Once, while staying with Henry James in England, William learned that G. K. Chesterton was visiting just next door. Chesterton was a much younger author and thinker whom William believed to be a convert to Pragmatism. William wanted to get a look at him, and went outside to prop a gardener's ladder against the fence so he could peer over. Henry was scandalized, and the two fell into a row about it until Wells took William into town.

A photograph of Josiah Royce and James at Chocorua sometime after the turn of the century shows James playfully chastising Royce ("Damn the Absolute!" reads a caption) while Royce sits on a brick wall like a contented Santa. Royce admitted to being casually jealous of James's lingering youthfulness. James would undoubtedly have kept up his strenuous hikes had his heart not continued to bother him. He could be playful in the language he used to talk about his heart distress, but the trouble had been consistent since his fateful hike in 1898, and worsened markedly after he delivered his Pragmatism lectures. *Pragmatism* appeared in June 1907; James traveled with Alice for a time in its wake. By November, sales of *Pragmatism* appeared strong. A year later, however, the numbers had fallen off, and James worried that its failure meant that a companion volume, *A Pluralistic Universe,* based on the Hibbert lectures he delivered in 1908, would also perform poorly.

Given at Oxford, the Hibbert lectures were an opportunity both to take Alice back to England and to continue the dialogue on truth kicked off in *Pragmatism,* a debate that preoccupied the world of philosophy for a time. James clarified his position in a brief talk, "The Meaning of the Word Truth," delivered at Cornell, but Pragmatism would ultimately prove to be just as impotent in generating universal agreement as any philosophical system. The debate over Pragmatism's notion of truth—the basic motivation behind *A Pluralistic Universe* and *The Meaning of Truth: A Sequel to "Pragmatism,"* which appeared in October 1909—amounted to a worldwide hashing out of James's body of work. Or at least that's how it felt to James.

He wrote the Hibbert lectures in the first few months of 1908, delivered them at Oxford in the spring, and traveled through Europe until October. He was delighted when Columbia put out a tome of collected papers, *Essays Philosophical and Psychological,* in James's honor. He wrote detailed notes of thanks to each of the contributors. What some eventually began calling the "Pragmatic controversy" may have first troubled James when reviews of the *Essays* began to come in. Bertrand Russell, in particular, seemed not to get the gist of the thinking. James told him so. James had made a practice of sending copies of his books to his wide range of correspondents, and as reaction to *Pragmatism* and its truth began to trickle in, it became clear that though he had always prided himself on clarity of expression he was not making himself understood now. This was because either Pragmatism's truth was too obscure or his listeners too obstinate in their support of older views. They grasped that truth meant experience agreed with reality, but they were reluctant to climb on board with the notion that the knower was complicit in the known, a necessary creator of it, in fact. The problem was not simply that Pragmatism's truth was obscure. No one was sure what Pragmatism was. Was it even a philosophy? Was it a system? James had called it a method, but what did a method have to do with a fact? The resistance that James encountered, and that he did not live to see resolved, was at least in part a function of his having given birth to a thing his contemporaries could not even name, let alone embrace.

The heart of Pragmatism's truth, at least for James, was that it generally made one more forgiving. With it, pluralism became an actual possibility. In short, once one believed in the possibility of many truths the fruits of religion were made available to everyone. Too much singularity, in either truth or a Christian God or a Hegelian Absolute, lent itself to fragmentation and division. "I now say," James wrote in his conclusions to *A Pluralistic Universe,* "that the notion of the 'one' breeds foreignness and that of the 'many' intimacy."

From 1907 until he died James could call a number of prominent thinkers either comrade or disciple, yet as his truth was vivisected by critics he could not help but fixate on those he had failed to convince. Just before *Pragmatism* appeared, F.C.S. Schiller told James that the world of 1907, thanks to him, was far different from that of 1897. James replied,

> *I can't recognize the truth of the 10 years change of opinion about my*
> *'will to believe.' I don't find anyone—not even my dearest friends,*
> *as [Dickinson] Miller and [Charles] Strong, one whit persuaded.*

A few months later, he wrote to Strong,

> *But my persistent failure to get myself understood of late is breeding in*
> *me a sort of despair as to whether there's any use in discussion, or*
> *whether any philosopher will ever get himself understood by anybody.*

And to Russell, he wrote,

> *It makes one despair of human "understanding" to find men on the*
> *whole as similar as you and myself—similar in our ideals & purposes,*
> *I mean,—so unable to get together in our formulas.*

It didn't help that James was still publishing materials related to the Society for Psychical Research; he was being assaulted on that front as well. James instructed Hugo Münsterberg to ignore a 1909 attack on *The Principles of Psychology* that characterized the book as a work for beginners and James himself as the "spoiled child" of American psychology. Münsterberg and James appeared to reconcile some of their old differences over the matter ("I don't like the notion of Harvard people seeming 'touchy'!" James wrote), but James was quite hurt when Münsterberg turned around and published a paper damning the SPR. A "monumentally foolish performance," James said.★ In old age it appeared that James, like a chicken with a vent bleed, was about to be set upon by those thinkers who were not of his brood. Even Charles Peirce was unimpressed with *Universe:* "I thought your Will to Believe was a very exaggerated utterance, such as injures a serious man very much; but to say what you now do is far more suicidal."

★James's revenge on this front would come only posthumously: Münsterberg was eventually discredited entirely when his ties to Germany were shown to run disturbingly deep; eventually it was suggested that he had been acting as a spy for the German government.

To Henry James, William put up a more valiant front in describing the performance of *Universe:*

> *My own Oxford lectures are making a success. I don't mean* sales, *as yet, but everyone to whom I have sent the volume seems immediately to have* read *it (!) and they mostly write such vehement protestations against it, that I feel sure it is* original, *and that the puddle is being stirred and the toads forced to jump about.*

Henry, who took great delight in *Pragmatism* and *Universe* both, offered a reaction to *The Meaning of Truth* more in keeping with James's acolytes:

> *I find it of thrilling interest, triumphant & brilliant, & am lost in admiration of your wealth & power. I palpitate as you make out your case, (since it seems to me you so utterly do,) as I under no romantic spell ever palpitate now; & into that case I enter intensely, unreservedly, & I think you would allow almost intelligently. I find you nowhere as difficult as you surely make everything for your critics. Clearly you are winning a great battle & great will be your fame.*

The beginning of 1910 found James in relatively good health. After half a century, he was still writing in a journal, though he had taken up the abbreviated method of a few comments on his work and daily habits, and a word about his health. His entry for January 11 read:

> *68 years old to day!*
> *Wrote.*
>
> *good day*

Biographers have often noted that the health of Henry and William James tended to seesaw. When one felt well, the other suffered. This captured both the differences of their thinking and the evidence of their intimacy. It was Henry James who initiated the final phase of William's life. Several months before, Henry had begun to exhibit symptoms similar to William's aortic distress. He had improved for a time, but after he completed the prologues for the twenty-four volume New York Edition of his collected novels and stories he suffered a major collapse. Just a few weeks after William's birthday, Henry wrote, clearly distressed:

What happened was that I found myself at a given moment more &
more beginning to fail of power to eat through the daily more marked in-
crease of a strange & most persistent & depressing stomachic crisis: the
condition of more & more sickishly loathing food. This weakened & un-
dermined & "lowered" me, naturally, more & more—& finally scared
me through rapid & extreme loss of flesh & increase of weakness &
emptiness.

Both Henry and William suspected that the collapse was at least in part
the result of a too strict adherence to an eating technique devised by a man
named Horace Fletcher. The technique was the excessive chewing of one's
food, and Henry had been "Fletcherizing" for years. William had originally
recommended Fletcher to Henry, and Fletcher was quoted as a healthy-
minded quasi-Buddhist mind-curist in *Varieties*. To William's mind, Henry
had simply overdone it, and his illness was probably more in his head than
his body. William first sent his son Harry to care for his uncle, but decided
to go himself not long after, partly because of Henry's affinity for Alice.
The Jameses left for England in March 1910. They found Henry in a weakened state, but William was sure the ailment was nothing more than a nervous breakdown.

A few weeks after their arrival, Henry began to improve and William
himself began to feel weary. He left Henry and Alice in London to seek his
own cures. He made for Nauheim in mid-May. He could feel his sclerosis
accumulating—the arteries of his wrist were perceptibly hardened—and
even brief social contacts became a strain. He was relieved when a test
gave him a diagnosis of aortic enlargement: the relief was that it wasn't just
nervousness continuing to plague him. Henry and Alice joined him in
June. Henry was yet incapacitated enough that William answered his letters
for him to within a few weeks of William's death.

Late in June, William responded to a paper from an old student. He described his effort in replying as "pretty good for a brain after 18 Nauheim
baths," and if the letter was not the last significant intellectual lunge James
made, it was certainly close. It was also the last time he addressed the question of God. He was unimpressed with the student's work, feeling that it
brought too much levity to a weighty subject:

To tell you the truth it doesn't impress me at all, save by its wit and eru-
dition, and I ask you whether an old man soon about to meet his Maker

can hope to save himself from the consequences of his life by pointing to the wit and learning he has shown in treating a tragic subject. No sir, you can't do it,—can't impress God in that way. So far as our scientific conceptions go, it may be admitted that your Creator (and mine) started the Universe with a certain amount of "energy" latent in it, and decreed that everything that should happen thereafter should be a result of parts of that energy falling to lower levels. . . . Until someone hits upon a newer revolutionary concept (which may be to morrow) all physicists must play the game by holding religiously to the above doctrine.

The Jameses decided to bring Henry to Chocorua for the coming winter. The threesome left Nauheim in July, heading first through Switzerland. Henry and William were both in poor condition and lamented the burden they put on Alice.

Henry later called their journey home "a dismal chronicle of suspense and pain." William seeped away on the sea voyage and the trains that took them back to Chocorua. Henry steadily improved. Back in New Hampshire, William's feet swelled as his heart choked. Alice was reduced to feeding him milk to keep his stomach moving. "I can't stand this again—Cruel, *cruel,*" he told Alice, and he instructed her to go to Henry when his time came. She would. James died after a week at Chocorua, in his wife's arms, listing under the spell of morphine. He was photographed once more, and a cast was made of his face.

James's critics have spent the last hundred years suggesting that he was indecisive. It is James's last great joke that his biographers can't decide what happened to his body. He lay in state for four days. After that, there is a pluralism of possible scenarios. James was cremated and his ashes spread in a creek near Chocorua. James was buried in a small cemetery in Boston, where there is a stone with his name. Or James was cremated, then buried.

Sources disagree.

Dog

I firmly disbelieve, myself, that our human experience is the highest form of experience extant in the universe. I believe rather that we stand in much the same relation to the whole of the universe as our canine and feline pets do to the whole of human life. They inhabit our drawing-rooms and libraries. They take part in scenes of whose significance they have no inkling. They are merely tangent to curves of history the beginnings and ends and forms of which pass wholly beyond their ken. So we are tangent to the wider life of things. But, just as many of the dog's and cat's ideals coincide with our ideals, and the dogs and cats have daily living proof of the fact, so we may well believe, on the proofs that religious experience affords, that higher powers exist and are at work to save the world on ideal lines similar to our own.

—William James

The feeling of religious devotion is a highly complex one, consisting of love, complete submission to an exalted and mysterious superior, a strong sense of dependence, fear, reverence, gratitude, hope for the future, and perhaps other elements. No being could experience so complex an emotion until advanced in his intellectual and moral faculties to at least a moderately high level. Nevertheless, we see some distant approach to this state of mind in the deep love of a dog for his master, associated with complete submission, some fear, and perhaps other feelings. . . . Professor Braubach goes so far as to maintain that a dog looks on his master as on a god.

—Charles Darwin

1. Two-Top Mountain

I waited for Brother Stavros in the lobby of the Cambridge Hotel in Cambridge, New York, up above Albany, near the Vermont border. "You can always tell the monks when they come into town," the hotel's desk attendant told me. "They don't wear any garb, but you can tell. It's in their eyes."

The monks of New Skete were well known for two reasons: among the Orthodox Christian community in America, they were controversial for the manner in which they practiced Christianity, and among the public they were famous for raising German shepherd dogs. An extensive dog-breeding program had helped give the monastery its livelihood, spawning book, video, obedience-training, and dog-biscuit businesses as well. The monks' website announced that they had incorporated dogs into their version of Christianity, and the videos included monks delivering lyric speeches that spoke to the connection: "Precisely because they are living creatures, dependent and vulnerable, dogs continually take us outside of ourselves, which is the fundamental moment of being human, and the only way to find God."

A mastery over wild beasts had helped give monks prestige when monasticism began to emerge in the centuries immediately following Christ, but the monks of New Skete, I would learn, weren't so keen on drawing the connection between dogs and faith in person. Their success had backfired to some extent, and they had inadvertently won the reverence of dog lovers the world over who forced canines into relationships that the monks found to be unhealthy. Now the monks were quietly trying to have it both ways. A book they had written about their faith, *In the Spirit of Happiness,* treated the dog program almost as an afterthought. I had a cynical theory: that spiritual guidance and obedience training weren't as different as they seemed, and that the connection between dogs and God went deeper than even James or Darwin had suspected. But I wasn't sure if the weeklong retreat I would take to New Skete would afford me the opportunity to test it. As with Wicca, new religious movements sometimes encourage journalistic contact, but the monks' dog books, *How to Be Your Dog's Best Friend* and *The Art of Raising a Puppy,* had been so wildly successful that they didn't really need the attention. They didn't need me. To be honest, I wasn't sure why they were letting me come at all.

Stavros picked me up in a truck, and I waited for him while he stopped someplace to load up a few plants and soil for a spot on the grounds he was finally filling in. Stavros was a short man with a thin beard, and in the monks' videos he tended to dress in clothes that made him look like a train conductor. He was one of the founding members, one of the men who had broken away from Byzantine Friars in the 1960s with Father Laurence, New Skete's abbot. Stavros had been at the monastery for forty years. He was thoughtful and quick to giggle and talk politics, and the desk attendant was right: there was something about him—not serenity, not certitude or contentedness. He felt like a man not without sin, but perhaps without regret, a man who did not look back on a lifetime of avoidable mistakes. He took me the long way through Cambridge, a perfectly quaint little New England town, and up a hill to a defunct hospital whose parking lot afforded a view of the region's bright green pelt. We were in New York, but Stavros could point to a hill in Vermont, and even closer was Two-Top Mountain, just behind the monastery, which the monks had described in their book as looking like "beautifully proportioned breasts along the eastern horizon."

"That there," Stavros said, "is ours."

The monks' land was tucked behind the town, and the monastery itself was tucked inside the land, on the far side of those breastlike hills. We drove the four miles up into the monastery, dropped my bags at the guesthouse, and picked up Father Bruce, a man from a Carmelite order in Niagara Falls who would be my fellow retreatant for the week. Bruce was typical of the modern breed attracted to monasteries: he had come to religion late in life, having already had a career and a marriage before he became a widower and attended seminary at fifty-two. Stavros gave the two of us a tour of New Skete. We walked up the road from the guesthouse, alongside the monastery's graveyard, a wide grassy space and curving row of stones where monks and relatives were buried, climbing up past the puppy kennel toward the main house.

New Skete had two churches, and it was tempting to use the difference between them to measure the success of the dog program. Transfiguration was the original church, a small structure in the middle of a circular drive before the main house, a little like a log cabin topped with elongated golden bulbs that were supposed to recall Russian onion domes but really looked like big bowling pins. The monks used it now only to say the hour, a midday worship chore. The new church, Holy Wisdom, sat behind it, much larger and generally more rectangular and grand in appearance. Inside, all of its furnishings were beautifully carved, made of zebrawood or ash, its walls were splendored with saints haloed in gold leaf, gorgeous rugs spilled over gorgeous floors, and in one spot near the back of the church there was a tiny mosaic tile from sixth-century Constantinople that Stavros said "gets the Greeks all atwitter." Stavros liked walking us through the sanctuary, and he knew every facet of it, every stone and painting and detail and story. In services, Stavros was the deacon, which meant he was a kind of liturgical handyman, preparing the censer, controlling the lights, always on the move with details to attend to. After Holy Wisdom, he took us down to the main house, most of which was off-limits. This was the cloister, the monks' living space. It was now that I realized that I had pretty much been all over New Skete and I hadn't seen a dog.

We went to the dining room for an informal lunch, and here I began to recognize faces from the dog videos: Brother Christopher, the lead obedience trainer, a monk not yet fifty but with more than twenty years at New Skete, and Brother Marc, whose manner, more than anyone else's, spoke of a kind of powerful intellectual draw. A humble philosopher, he would quietly monitor your meal and take your plate when you were finished.

Then Bruce and I were dismissed back to the guesthouse, which was attached to the gift shop, where they sold icons and dog biscuits and bookmarks with quotations that again drew the parallel between dogs and monks. Bruce and I split off to separate dormitory-style rooms. I slept for a while on a bunk bed, alone in a room for six. Then I came outside again into the lush flesh of the land, the electric prattle of insect hordes, and the trilly exchanges of birds. The monastery felt quiet and deserted but smelled fertile and new. The leaves of the trees were all young and alive in a warm May wind, and flashed their fresh undersides like schools of fish darting through columns of refracted light. I heard a dog bark, up behind the main house. The cloister. At first, it was the cinematic bark that described the silence around it, that proof of quiet. But then another dog barked. And now more joined in to make it cacophonous and echoey against the close hills, and the birds took off, and the insects resumed their invisible wait, and the dogs' raucous song owned the pocket behind Two-Top Mountain.

2. Lazarus

The schism between Western and Eastern Christianity began to form, really, only a few generations after a vision inspired Emperor Constantine to adopt Christianity in A.D. 312. Before the fourth century ended, the East had a system of patriarchs and Constantinople had claimed equality with Rome because it had the relics of Saint Andrew. Early in the Holy Roman Empire basically everyone agreed that a literal reading of scripture meant that Christ must be both fully human and fully God, but where he came from and how he got that way remained up for grabs. Great Councils were called to decide the question, but a rift began to form even as the Trinity emerged as a compromise, Father, Son, and Holy Spirit. While everyone agreed that the threeness of the Trinity was really a way of comprehending a larger oneness, lines of disagreement formed over which of the three derived from which or who came from what, and when. The Nicene-Constantinople Creed explained that the Holy Spirit *proceeded* from the Father, but the West changed the phrase to the Father *and the Son* in the sixth century, slipping in an etymology that was never ratified. It wasn't until Charlemagne that alternate Christian civilizations, separated by space and language, became truly apparent. East and West set about molding themselves politically to distinct predicaments; the chaos of the Middle Ages in Europe favored the emergence of strong leadership in the West, while various wars and sackings helped create a less centralized system of jurisdictions based on nationality in the East. Competing missionary efforts each translated the Bible and branched out into the world. The icons of the East—a practice that flourished for hundreds of years and made the divine more accessible to the laity—were banned by the West in 726. The pope continued to believe that he controlled all of Christendom, while the Greeks considered him primary but not supreme. Disagreements, slights, and failed attempts at reconciliation culminated in representatives of the pope marching boldly into a church in Constantinople to excommunicate the East in 1054.

Differences between East and West can appear superficial—leavened versus unleavened bread, two or three fingers used in making the sign of the cross, icons or no icons—but true differences run deeper. Grossly put, the East strikes outsiders as individualistic but vague in its tendency toward mysticism, while the West is specific but outrageous in its literal reading of the Bible. In terms of God himself, the East believes that man can aspire to at least some abstract form of godness (*theosis*), while the West insists on the reduction or humility of man in relation to God's greatness. It wasn't until the Fourth Crusade, when Christian-on-Christian violence shocked even those who had suffered under Muslims, that the schism found its real cement.

Orthodoxy first came to Russia before all of that. Prince Vladimir of Kiev, the story goes, sent envoys abroad to survey the prayer practices of a variety of nations. He was seduced by the beauty of the Greek liturgy, and married the sister of the Byzantine emperor. Orthodoxy in eastern Europe rode storms of domination by Mongols, Turks, and Communists, occasionally flirting with reconciliation with the West as a tool of survival. But the Orthodox community would retain a unique sense of itself: it added ten extra books to the Bible and once declared Latin baptism entirely invalid. Moscow became the "Third Rome" in mid-millennium, at a time when one third of the land in Russia was owned by monks. The influence of spiritually potent leaders in monasteries, called abbots or startsy, helped bring Orthodoxy to laypeople, and access to a strong spiritual father made joining the monasteries attractive. A number of abbots earned renown through the nineteenth century, including a Father Joseph of a settlement called New Skete, named for the original desert Skete in northern Egypt. Joseph advocated the practice of inner prayer, the repetition of the Jesus Prayer, a Christian mantra that was characteristic of Orthodoxy.

Continuous political upheaval meant Orthodoxy needed to remain flexible, sometimes involuntarily, in its relationship to the state. Peter the Great dismantled the patriarchy, creating the Holy Synod in its place, and when the patriarchy returned in 1917 it was immediately suppressed by the Bolsheviks. Not all of the Orthodox community agreed on how to weather Soviet unbelief—some ran, adding to the dispersion of Orthodoxy through the world, some capitulated, and some went underground to create what was known as a "catacomb church." Orthodoxy prides itself on the fact that despite all the upheaval, the basic character of the modern liturgical service would still be recognizable to those who first devised it.

In 1794, an Orthodox mission established a firm footing in Alaska and survived the transition when the region was sold to the United States in 1867. The twentieth century saw an infusion of Orthodoxy into the United States, with an Orthodox population approaching three million. In 1965, ceremonies in Rome and Constantinople claimed to heal the split between East and West, but like all the old disputes over bread and fingers, the act was largely symbolic and differences remained deeply entrenched.

The history of New York's New Skete began almost immediately thereafter, but had deeper roots. As early as the 1940s, a group of Byzantine Rite Franciscans had been working with Eastern Rite Catholics displaced from eastern Europe to prepare for missions back into Russia once communism failed. The jostle of Vatican II, which basically set out to make mass more accessible, triggered dialogue inside the group as to whether it should tip more East or West as a result. The group's leadership disagreed with its majority. Father Laurence, then young and charismatic, decided to leave the Franciscans, taking Brother Stavros and Brother Peter and Brother Marc and others with him on a journey that at first had no clear destination. They headed north. Laurence had accumulated a number of friends in a kind of intermonastery network, and a group of Benedictines helped set them up, first in a hunting lodge in western Pennsylvania. Six months of solitude gave them the time they needed to prepare for going it alone, a gang of philosophy majors still unsure how they would make a living. They bought their first property in Cambridge, restoring a broken-down farmhouse along a well-traveled road, and stayed there until it became apparent from gawking trespassers that a cloister on a thoroughfare was not a good idea. When the acres near Two-Top Mountain became available, the monks voted to risk it, taking shop classes at local schools to learn how to build a monastery from scratch.

Laurence was typical of an Orthodox elder, learned and thoughtful, to all accounts proficient in guiding the monks' spiritual journey, a presence that could just as easily praise right efforts at the spiritual life as discourage missteps. The monks tended to want to explore the lifestyle of the Christian East, and though they would eventually be accepted into the Orthodox community it did not prevent them from remaining distinct, even a bit shocking. They called themselves Orthodox Catholic, a Christian oxymoron. Their idea of God was entirely abstract and Eastern; the language they used to describe God didn't seem to require a literal entity, yet they insisted that God was real even as they argued that that reality was kind of secondary—and they were more than willing to acknowledge the Bible as ancient literature. At the same time, they decried gross understandings of asceticism. The repetition of the Jesus Prayer, they argued, was just as likely to interfere with one's spiritual growth if it was repeated mindlessly.

Working with animals got the monks into trouble long before the dog program came about—a 1971 *Life* magazine story about New Skete distorted their message when a photographer ran a shot of a monk slaughtering a pig. By then, monasteries' historical association with agriculture had been replaced with stereotypes of more "innocent" professions: furniture making, crafts. More recently, visiting bishops had commented disapprovingly on the monks' continuing association with breeding; the dogs' sexuality was presumably too close for comfort. The makeup of the New Skete community proved controversial as well—in 1969, the monks had been joined by a group of nuns who had undertaken a similar cross-country journey of faith. The nuns of New Skete built a separate complex four miles from the monastery and ran a cheesecake factory. They helped with the dogs as well. A decade later the community added a house for "companions," married couples, just down the hill from Holy Wisdom and Transfiguration.

The monks' first German shepherd dog was simply a pet, and ran away early in the history of the community. They replaced the dog, and their first foray into breeding was merely an extension of the farming they'd been doing for some time already. The program grew by word of mouth, and if the occasional bishop found the idea of monks and breeding distasteful, the public had just the opposite reaction. The program was a success even without publicity.

In the mid-1970s, a New Skete bitch accidentally rolled over onto her litter, smothering a puppy by mistake. Brother Stavros found the dead pup a few minutes later and managed to revive it with a kind of impromptu CPR, something the monks did often during whelpings. It was unusual at so late a stage, but the puppy came back. They named the dog Lazarus. New Skete dogs were already high in demand, and Lazarus sold to an editor at the Little, Brown publishing house, who suggested that the monks write a book about the program. *How to Be Your Dog's Best Friend* has remained in hardback for twenty years, and with *The Art of Raising a Puppy*, published in 1991, the monks were closing in on a million copies in print.

3. Prodigal Dogs

"Our dogs, for example, are in our human life, but not of it," James wrote:

> *They witness hourly the outward body of events whose inner meaning*
> *cannot, by any possible operation, be revealed to their intelligence—*
> *events in which they themselves often play the cardinal part. . . . Take*
> *[a] case which greatly used to impress me in my medical-student days.*
> *Consider a poor dog whom they are vivisecting in a laboratory. He lies*
> *strapped on a board and shrieking at his executioners, and to his own*
> *dark consciousness is literally in a sort of hell. He cannot see a single re-*
> *deeming ray in the whole business; and yet all these diabolical-seeming*
> *events are often controlled by human intentions with which, if his poor*
> *benighted mind could only be made to catch a quick glimpse of them, all*
> *that is heroic in him would religiously acquiesce.*

The James family, in general, loved dogs, and this was perhaps James's way of contending with the fact that as a young man he had participated in laboratory experiments involving the partial removal of dogs' brains. He had worked this passage through first in a letter to his brother Bob, where he suggested that the story of the vivisected dog might serve theologians well as a kind of parable. James family letters and lore have more than their share of dog incidents: one account that tells of a sixteen-year-old James trying and failing to train a greyhound pup bleeds into the mythology of his relationship with his father. ("'Never, never before did I so clearly see the utter & lamentable inefficiency & worthlessness of your character,'" James quoted Henry Sr. on the matter.) As late as 1909, thirty-five years after his "parable," James lent his name to an anti-vivisectionist movement. In the years in between, he filled letters to his children with puppies sketched in various poses of recline. He once wrote of a dog called Dinah to his son Aleck, aged nine:

> *I was so glad to see your noble handwriting and hear good news of*
> *you and your wife Dinah. I feared she might have had some accident*
> *happen to her, for pups have such uncertain lives. I care for you & her*
> *equally; and you must care for her more than for yourself, for she is*
> *your better self,—dein bessres Ich—and more loving faithful devoted*

to you than you *can ever be to any living thing. You are like a God to her.*

I didn't see an adult dog for a few days at New Skete, and after the first evening of vespers and the first morning of matins I realized I hadn't seen Father Laurence either.

The prayer schedule was posted inside the guesthouse, in a kind of family room with heavy wooden couches thrown over with huge pillows and afghans soft as fur. Fans of decade-old copies of *Smithsonian* sat beside the cigar box for the recommended nightly tithe, and on bookshelves were copies of New Skete's old in-house magazine, *Gleanings*. One afternoon, thumbing through it, I discovered a poem called "Obedience Training," written by Brother Job, the monk who had been in charge of the dog program at its inception:

> *I used to think I ran*
> *Because of bitches in heat. . . .*
> *I'm the original prodigal dog.*

Brother Job had been killed in a car accident in the seventies, and was buried in the graveyard just outside the guesthouse. The accident might have ended the dog program right there, but Brother Christopher took over, digesting everything he could find about dog training. Now all the monks were experienced in obedience training and whelping. There were currently nine monks at New Skete, about a dozen nuns, and a few folks at the companions' house. The dog business kept the monks busy: they each had one or two dogs in their care, and they had cut off the list of people waiting for puppies at one hundred. They charged fifteen hundred dollars per puppy, but could have gotten much more. Some dogs went to police academies or into training for service for the disabled, and some stayed at New Skete to produce more puppies. The monks cared for the dogs—mostly bitches—only as long as they were fertile and capable of producing offspring. Then they were retired, donated to families for their old age. Apart from working with the dogs themselves, the monks kept busy with their collateral businesses: the gift shop, the dog biscuits, and high-volume mail-order work.

The nuns held matins down at their own facility, but every evening they would come up for vespers. Often as I trudged up to Holy Wisdom from the guesthouse a van full of nuns zipped by me, cheating the hill. Before the service began they all milled about in the dressing room, putting on robes over street clothes and solemnly entering the rectangle of thrones that surrounded Holy Wisdom's ornate lecterns with their giant ribboned Bibles. The service would begin with bells from the bell tower down by the main house. Sometimes, I was told, the dogs set to howling from the cloister when they heard the heavy jangle.

Brother Stavros stayed hidden for the first part of vespers, manning the lights, and when the first singing came he was there to supply that electric epiphany, bringing them up slow as the chords resolved so that it seemed the music shed the light, the beams flaking away from a resonant hum. In the monks' book *In the Spirit of Happiness,* Brother Marc had spoken of the ability of music to charge, to energize, and James had once said, "Music gives us ontological messages which non-musical criticism is unable to contradict." Sister Ann was the community's musical director, and to begin each song she daintily hit a note on a harmonica and hummed an arpeggio, conducting with a motion like throwing a dart. One man told me that New Skete might have developed an entirely unique musical tradition. In it you could hear the influence of Baptist revival and African chant, then suddenly it might echo a barbershop quartet or South American folk music, and at some services the influences seemed to mingle, segueing into an overlapping tangle of prayers, chants, chords, words, held notes, phrases, glory, Lord God, a confusion that achieved a deep magnetic synthesis that might have been able to bend spoons, shatter glass, or shrivel disease. This was what the monks had in their book called "first fervor," or "God's initial favors," what they would acknowledge was actually quite common: a form of sexual arousal at the onset of prayer's joy, a kind of theological foreplay. It was an immature reaction, really, a beginner's mistake as one fell in love with God. Christian mystics predating the schism had characterized their union with the divine in near conjugal terms, and I, too, must have experienced something like first fervor in basking through those initial services. The music felt like a tuning fork held close to the chest so that it resonated in the integrity of your skeleton. The community sang in English, and sometimes the translations seemed a little silly as they prayed for people to travel safely through land, air, sea, and space, or noted the seraphim with their six eyes and many wings, or chanted the resurrection: *God is risen from the dead, conquering death by death, and on those in the grave restoring life.* But the monks had noted that the word *enthusiasm* meant filled with the breath of

God, and that's what I experienced at the music, enthusiasm, engorgement, and I felt like a piano in tune, adjusted to the touching jack of the song. Still, the incense, when Brother Stavros and Brother Christopher moved into the iconostasis to spray the icons with smoke, settled me down. It was heady stuff. Stavros followed along as Christopher puffed it out—perhaps that's why Stavros favored the clothing of an engineer—the two of them choo-chooing along and the clouds of incense hanging behind them, thick as thunderheads. In those quiet moments the coo of pigeons crept inside the church. Then came the readings from the Bible, which were also delivered in a kind of song—*lectio divina*—prose disguised or layered over with an antimelodic delivery, a random musical zigzag to make familiar stories dimensional and new. One reading told of Lazarus, and of the dog that was the first to approach and lick his wounds, but the connection for the community was only incidental. Then suddenly, it seemed, it was over, and Stavros brought me a piece of bread, and my back hurt from standing so long, and my legs hurt as well, but my chest felt tight and strong, and my cheeks were fat with tears. I swore I was a little high from the incense, but maybe it was just the effect of beauty. Ultimately, the services triggered a kind of loneliness because it was clear that I could watch the community but not truly participate in it. And to be honest, after the services, the monks kind of ignored me.

Coffee was as important a ritual as wine at New Skete, and after matins the monks gathered in the dining room in the main house for an informal breakfast. I took meals with them regularly, and on my second night we all dined at the companions' house. It took me a couple of days to realize that the monks were keeping me at arm's length. They didn't know what I wanted to write about the dogs, and, I eventually learned, they were unsure about what I would write of Father Laurence.

Laurence was gone. After he had led New Skete for thirty years, the monks had gone behind his back to ask a bishop for permission to have him removed. "We retired him," Brother Stavros told me, inadvertently using the word for bitches who outlived their fertility. What exactly happened with Father Laurence would always remain a mystery to me. I knew that the years that had passed under his guidance had witnessed a gradual movement away from the strict religious life of habits and seclusion. Writers on Orthodoxy have suggested that civilization's move away from agricultural society changed the terms of the relationship between pastor and flock. More specifically to New Skete, Orthodoxy was becoming more individualistic, encouraging change, which didn't lend itself to the old tradition of powerful spiritual fathers. It was tempting to speculate that the training of dogs had revealed something too rigid in the process that had created New Skete. They'd been spiritually trained, but now that the place was up and running, they no longer needed an alpha male, a leader of the pack. James's religious narrative concluded with that moment when a religion was passed on to adherents and "the faithful live at second hand exclusively and stone the prophets in their turn."

I was told that in his old age Laurence had simply become difficult to handle, and in fact was thought to be suffering from a disorder of some kind. The monks had let him go with an offer to pay for any medical treatments he may need. The parting was tumultuous, and several monks had left the community as a result. Father Laurence was now staying with a relative in Connecticut. Rumor had it he was already accumulating new followers.

Laurence's story helped work out a larger question I had about New Skete. Poised as they were between Eastern and Western Christianity, the monks were unusual, but was it really fair to label them a new religion and set them alongside Atheists and Druids and Satanists? It wasn't that they had become a cult of personality, as was true of so many of the movements I had visited—just the opposite may have been the case. They had begun in mainstream religion as the result of a powerful personality, but their movement and their journey had taken them in another direction and now they had become something genuinely new. If a community was a highly organized pack, then the monks had taken even that definition to a more perfect state. They had evolved to a point where they no longer needed personality as their mortar. The structure was standing all on its own.

Which is not to say that they rejected administration with a voice in charge. The monks had initiated a system of "prior"-ship to replace the abbot, a revolving system of leaders chosen by vote. The current prior was Brother Luke, and it was Luke I saw on my third day at New Skete, walking his dog at dusk in the wide grassy expanse alongside the graveyard. A dog! Just up from a nap, I hurried out to encounter the first adult canine I had seen. But by the time I got outside Luke was already headed back toward Holy Wisdom, edging around the garage. The other side was the cloister.

I began a pursuit. The whole idea of the cloister was beginning to piss me off a little. In some of my initial talks with Stavros, he had insisted, in distancing New Skete from the world's canine fundamentalists, that dogs were not transcendent beings. But why, then, I thought, were dogs allowed in the main house? Why did the monks keep personal dogs at all? Why were the dogs allowed in the cloister, while I was kept outside? I knew that, historically, aspirants to monasteries were sometimes made to wait for a period of time, even days, to demonstrate patience and purity of motivation, but I was beginning to think the monks were jerking my chain. The New Skete puppy books, I reminded myself, included cute little tests for personality, and the best puppies were not the ones that were wholly subservient but those who showed some degree of spiritedness, a willingness to fight back a little. I followed Luke but did not call out to him. Behind the garage was a road leading behind the main house, the gravel butting up against one of the breasts of Two-Top Mountain. Luke strolled casually along, throwing a rubber toy for his bitch. She did not see me for a time. When finally she glanced back, the two of them froze. The dog made a line for me, a growing speck moving so fast she barely seemed to touch the ground. Luke lowered his head, disappointed that I couldn't follow even simple rules. The dog might have leapt for my throat, but pulled up to greet me instead.

"Did Stavros explain that the cloister is off-limits?" Luke said, when he'd retraced his steps.

Yes, I said, and lied about not knowing where it began exactly. It was a little odd that Luke was the prior—he had been at New Skete only for nine years, young by its standards. Yet there was a pattern: New Skete's original residents had a kind of complacency, a tendency toward silence and capitulation, while its younger members were more willing to speak their minds. The spirited puppies had taken charge. Luke pointed me back toward the guesthouse.

In the morning, after matins, Stavros asked me to help him move some rocks around. He had planted the shrubs he'd purchased when we met, and placing the rocks would finish off the landscaping. We loaded long bits of a flaky sediment into a two-wheeled cart.

"People who studied these mountains," Stavros said, "decided this range might once have been as high as the Himalayas. This stuff—it's schist, not yet slate. It was the very inner part of the mountain."

If there was a lesson there, he decided to leave it mystical. He said we would talk soon about what I would write about New Skete, the dogs, and whether it was possible to grasp the lives of monks from a weeklong retreat. After the chore was complete, back down at the guesthouse, I wondered if I didn't have it all wrong in comparing a monastery to a dog pack.

The monks fed me regularly and took my plate when I was done. They put me to work when they needed me, and I was thrilled to do it because it meant they were finally paying attention to me. Otherwise, I stayed in the guesthouse, and if I strayed too far they scolded me. *They're not the dogs,* I thought. *I'm the dog.*

4. WELTANSCHAUUNG

Before heading to New Skete, I had accumulated a bunch of news clippings on the goofy associations people sometimes made between their dogs and their spirituality. In my hometown there was a Blessing of the Animals ceremony, which included dabbing pets' foreheads with holy water. In Connecticut, two dogs were married in a formal ceremony before their owners mated them; the bride wore a garter on one paw, and someone slapped a little top hat on the groom. "I love it because it's silly," someone was reported as saying. And in Vermont, a folk artist's brush with death inspired him to build a place called the Dog Chapel, where it was possible to celebrate "the spiritual bond we have with our dogs, a place that would be open to all dogs and to people of any faith or belief system."

Stavros promised to let me get my hands dirty with the dog chores, and the monks finally started to open up. I learned that Stavros's dog, Nikki, was down in the puppy kennel for the time being because she was in heat and it drove the males crazy to have her around. Brother Marc's bitch, Oka, was pregnant and they were waiting for her temperature to drop, indicating the onset of labor, though she was carrying only one puppy and a one-puppy litter was so rare that the monks had seen it maybe twice in thirty years. Brother Peter offered to let me help at the puppy kennel one day. Peter was a chubby, quiet man who looked back happily on his life at New Skete, but admitted once in passing that if he could have had another go he might have liked to try the companions' house. We cleaned the adult cages first, Nikki's and three others, and then we tended to a litter that was just about grown. The monks played classical music for the dogs twenty-four hours a day, and we listened to "Ode to Joy" and "Flight of the Bumble Bee" as we gave the puppies medicine hidden in a cream like molasses, Peter checking for descended testicles in the males and tucked vulvas in the females. Then Peter put Nikki and one of the males into a room they used for mating. The dogs ran in circles, flirting. "She's nearing estrus," he said, calculating the best time to artificially inseminate her. "If she lets him mount, it means she's even closer." When Peter stepped outside for something, I sneaked back over to play with the puppies. They came running forward to the fence, hair slicked back like little mobsters, climbing over one another so that they made, together, a little cloister of puppiness, their sighing a kind of pure teleology.

In the afternoon, Brother Christopher let me follow along as he did obedience training with dogs that had come to New Skete for a longer retreat than my own. The obedience program lasted a month and consisted of daily work on four core training principles. Christopher was animated and friendly but had something of the cranky Jesuit about him as well. He had once been a Trappist monk in Iowa, but now he acknowledged a weakness for the books of Tony Hillerman. He was one of only two or three monks at New Skete who had also been ordained as a priest. During services, Christopher was hugely expressive, his eyebrows popping and bobbing as though finding the fresh and unexpected in songs he'd sung a thousand times.

Christopher brought out each dog for twenty minutes of sit, stay, and heel drills, and we walked back and forth chatting. Christopher tended to doubt that I could learn much about being a monk in a week at New Skete. I tried out one of my theories on him: was the tendency of dog fanatics to anthropomorphize their dogs analogous to the tendency of Western Christianity to anthropomorphize God? "Definitely," he said. He argued that people who preferred the company of dogs must have a problem with their conception of people. "I'm a celibate," he said. "So touching a dog, petting a dog—that has a particular value to me. But that's not the reason to have a dog." The difference between the monks and that odd branch of their clientele, I thought, was basically the same as the difference defining the East-West schism, the former more esoteric and considered, the latter more aggressive and literal.

The nuns invited me to dinner. Their complex was a vast cheesecake factory as perfect as something in a fairy tale, and if the monks up the hill with their informal breakfasts of cereal were a little like a collection of bachelors, a faint Seven Dwarfs scenario of clumsiness lacking a woman's touch, then the nuns were an army of godmothers, guardian angels floating about and protecting one another and the monks as well. The nuns seemed to have less to hide than the monks, and Sister Helen, young and bold and buxom, showed me their whole comfy spread: the library, the plant nursery, the music room, the exercise room with donated ski machines, the icon-production workstations, and the giant kitchen for the baking of cheesecakes, with their thirty-pound cheeses and their 115-cake oven. The nuns had only two adult dogs in the house at the moment, but one of the litter in the puppy kennel was earmarked for Helen.

Meals were never just meals at New Skete—each was a feast. We gathered around a long solid table near windows that looked out over thick forests. After our prayer, one of the nuns hit me with a quotation from William James. New Skete apparently had mixed feelings about James—*In the Spirit of Happiness* had quoted him, critically, as saying "Religion is what happens to us in our solitude." They were a community, so they didn't exactly agree with him.

The quotation was taken out of context, but it hardly mattered: the nuns had opened the main vein of the modern criticism of *Varieties*. James had focused too heavily on the individual experience, the argument went, devaluing the group. Critics and biographers fell to either side of the question. On the one hand, James was criticized for an inability to appreciate the collective itself as amounting to a "religious connection." On the other, he was defended for offering up a notion of self and reality that permitted "communality of the profoundest sort."

James wasn't so far from New Skete as the nuns thought. Their community took an approach to asceticism—strenuous but not exaggerated—that James had celebrated and described as "the profounder way of handling the gift of existence." But more directly, he had in fact reached out to organized religion. James himself had often attended church services, and when he finally granted membership to institutional religion in *Varieties,* he sounded as though he might be describing the service at New Skete:

I promised to say nothing of ecclesiastical systems in these lectures. I may be allowed, however, to put in a word at this point on the way in which their satisfaction of certain aesthetic needs contributes to their hold on human nature. Although some persons aim most at intellectual purity and simplification, for others richness is the supreme imaginative requirement. When one's mind is strongly of this type, an individual religion will hardly serve the purpose. The inner need is rather of something institutional and complex, majestic in the hierarchic interrelatedness of its parts, with authority descending from stage to stage, and at every stage objects for adjectives of mystery and splendor, derived in the last resort

from the Godhead who is the fountain and culmination of the system.
One feels then as if in presence of some vast incrusted work of jewelry or
architecture; one hears the multitudinous liturgical appeal; one gets the
honorific vibration coming from every quarter.

Of institutional religions James worried that the "acute fever" of a single
mind experiencing religion would fade to a "dull ache" of tradition and habit
for those who simply followed. But New Skete's experience, rather than
thinning, seemed perfected in the growth of its community, and even they
owed something to James, I thought, as some part of him, handed down,
had helped them edge through the narrative of religious life without losing any of the fervor. Before I came to New Skete, I'd wondered whether
Father Laurence amounted to one of James's genius figures, and since he
was gone I thought I would never really know. But at dinner, the conversation kept gravitating to Laurence, as to a succulent rumor.

"Before," one nun said, "there was a hierarchy. The monks. The nuns.
The companions."

"And the dogs," someone said.

"Yes! And sometimes the dogs were even higher on that scale."

There was some nervous laughter—the older nuns stifled it, stuck in
their habit of complacency, and it was the younger nuns who seemed to
want to press on.

"It was a form of abuse—I think it was," said Sister Helen. "It wasn't at
all like what's happened with the Roman Catholic Church, but at heart the
issue was the same: the priest is always right."

5. HUMANS IN OUR FULLNESS

Finally, a few of the monks agreed to take time out from their chores for a
conversation in a conference room in the main house.

"We're reluctant to speak specifically about dogs and their relationship
to our spiritual lives," Christopher began, "because we so easily get catego-
rized as 'dog people,' with dogs as the center of our spiritual lives. That's
not the case at all. At New Skete dogs play an important role, their own
role. They evoke things from us that are unique. We talked yesterday about
people making idols of their dogs—I recognize this in many of the clients
we've dealt with. It's easy for human beings to anthropomorphize their
dog, but in doing so they dishonor the relationship."

"What happens," Peter said, "is that the dog becomes a surrogate friend or child. Scripture says the animals are created for man's use, and that's basically what animals, dogs, did—they worked together with people to live. Now they're given new roles, guiding the blind, locating people underwater, they can anticipate seizures. But has the dog helped my spirituality? I'd never say that directly."

"Spirituality has to do with the whole," Christopher said. "Each part of life is connected. The dogs are an important part of our life here, and they touch on certain issues that stimulate spiritual growth. Dealing with a creature of a different species puts you in touch, intuitively, with life. That life is suffused with mystery."

"It's analogous to ecology," Stavros said. "Spirituality is a kind of cosmic ecology, seeing the connectedness of everything. That's where the animal fits in. It's expecting too much of a dog to ask it to be a surrogate person or lover. It's doing a disservice to the dog to fool yourself into thinking that's filling your need. That's a type of sickness. People want a thing to fill their need, instead of working with each other. That's what we do as brothers in the monastery, try to work on interacting with each other in the best possible way."

"Here's an image many people have," Christopher said. "You come home from work, you open the door, and there's the dog, and it's saying, 'This is the high point of my day, you coming through the door.' Now as a pure gift, that's a beautiful thing. Where else do we experience a relationship that's so affirming? It's so honest, so guileless. But I can't take it too seriously. I can't allow that to, in a certain sense, have me become the God. The God that the dog worships. That becomes preposterous."

In a number of sections of *In the Spirit of Happiness*, the monks had compressed their personalities to a generalized "seeker" figure whose wanderings could speak for all of them. Watching them cooperate now recalled that: the speeches, even as they sometimes came close to interrupting one another, bled naturally from one to the next. Until, at least, Brother Marc leaned forward. There was nothing pretentious about Marc, even as his quiet intellect commanded a room, and when he spoke, effacingly but gorgeously, his face ran through a range of expressions, as though he experienced the effect of his words even as he composed them.

"Well," he said, "I'm just going to verbalize what I'm thinking—bear with me. One thing that comes to mind is that with the vast changes in the conception of what marriage is, theologically and sociologically, and the immense changes in the family and the mass exodus to the city in the last one hundred and fifty years, say, I think individuals have become alienated from the matrix of earth and nature that we naturally arise from. We're living an artificially divided, fragmented life. As individuals, like grains of sand, rubbing against one another, but not really becoming a part of one another. And when we meet up with dogs, who totally accept us just the way we are, we like this because this is what a human being should be able to have from society. We've lost that. We should be able to come to our village, to our extended family, and no matter how good or bad we are, be totally accepted. We don't have that anymore. So the dog comes to carry the weight of all this need we have. And unless we recognize it, it will become neurotic. Through sociology, through psychology, and we believe through spirituality, we need to come to a new intimacy with one another.

"Monastic life has always been agrarian. Contemplative monks were always attached to the land, growing their own food. And monks have always been closely related to animal husbandry, to use an old term. Animals were a vital part of human life until a hundred years ago. But then it starts to break, that split from animal life happens. And now we're missing it. So we use cats, turtles, goldfish, ferrets, birds to make up for this connection that we need to exist as human beings in our fullness. But to place too much on that relationship overburdens it and can lead to abuse. And now, as monks, intuitively, without maybe even reflecting on it, we've come to find that the dog has been able to fulfill this balance in our life to some extent. They are not just producers for us, but companions in our lives."

"We talked before," Christopher said, "about people who misinterpret what we're doing here. On the one hand you have those individuals who are offended that we are involved in dog breeding, that somehow it's like kinky sex. But that reflects a total misunderstanding of spirituality."

"Even natural sex," Marc said, "is frowned upon with this type of spiritual value."

"Yes. And then you have the other pole, which sees a spiritual dimension present in our relationship with the dog. But that's all it is. These individuals are turned off from faith and project onto us a perspective that isn't there."

"Not only that," Stavros said, "but it's also—these animal-rights people. Well sure, it's horrible when people abuse animals. But when that becomes a person's sole bent, I think that same passion causes you to overlook where you might be abusing other human beings."

"When we were farming," Peter said, "we raised animals, and took them to the slaughterhouse. Eventually we learned how to slaughter them ourselves. Eventually, you start picking up the idea that this animal, you raise it, you feed it, you slaughter it—it dies so you can live. There is a spiritual aspect to it."

"It's not purely economic," Christopher said. "That's one of the things we focus on. We say something about dogs that is not sentimental or romantic, but something rooted in experience that anyone who is just a little bit reflective can connect with. If I respect the dog, then that same discipline affects the network of relationships in my life. How can I respect the dog as a dog, and then all of a sudden treat you—"

Marc couldn't resist the pun. "Like a dog."

"—like a thing. I can't, if I'm going to be consistent."

I asked kind of a complicated question based on James and Darwin. If the difference between man and God was a kind of discrepancy, and the same was true of the relationship between dog and man, then didn't a dog-man relationship say more about the man-God relationship than about people's relationships with one another?

"I think so," Marc said. "Radical Christians would say we serve no one except God. But they don't deserve the authority they believe they've been given. We do have authority, among ourselves, and with animals. But when you work with animals, you realize that authority does not mean manipulation. Authority means precisely service. This is what the good news of the Gospel was. The experience of authority, helping others, being in charge of and responsible for animals, teaches what we believe God is like."

"That's the paradox of the notion of incarnation," Stavros said. "When Jesus, as a real human being, lives among us, and shows that he accepts all of us, he makes the acceptability something that we welcome. You have to accept being acceptable to God. And if you get close to a dog, you see the joy that the dog receives in experiencing your intimacy. In a sense, it's spirituality turned upside down."

"A democratic relationship with a dog is a formula for disaster," Christopher said. "A good relationship is necessarily hierarchical. Dogs function best when there's a clear understanding of hierarchy in the pack. A dog will try to nudge up in the hierarchy, but as soon as it reaches its limit, it finds its proper place and functions well in that position. This is where its true nature blossoms—when the human being helps the dog become what it can be, and the human can only do that by assuming, in a kind of crass way, that he knows what's in the dog's best interest. But it's not despotic, it's not tyrannical—it's hierarchical. And that's the way the human being truly expresses love for the dog. So when you apply that to our relationship with God, you realize that simply because it's a hierarchical relationship doesn't mean it demeans the human being. It raises it. It's like leaven. The whole nature of human existence is that it's raised."

I asked whether the idea of God at New Skete was unique in any way.

"It depends on your understanding of unique," Stavros said. "My relationship to God is unique because I am a unique person. So I would say unique only in that very limited way. Otherwise we would be a sect."

"It would really be presumptuous," Christopher said, "to say we have a unique vision. However, I do think that in our effort to live with each other, all seeking God, mixing the human and the transcendent in such a palpable way—people have remarked about that. The hallmark of any true monastic life is the integration of all of life into one movement: the spiritual life touches on washing dishes, cleaning hallways, singing in church, picking up puppy shit. We get all sorts of visitors here, friends who are atheists, friends who are of totally different religions, but who come to appreciate what they find here. Because of the dogs. But not ending at the dogs. The dogs become, in a way, the midwife to a deeper perception of what the monastery is."

6. WHELPING TO BACH

It wasn't really the monks' fault that their products were pitched to dog lovers they didn't necessarily approve of. Those who had interpreted New Skete's message strictly in terms of dogs included those book editors and filmmakers who pushed them to wear their Sunday robes for the camera and walk their dogs along a rigorous hiking trail in the shadow of Two-Top Mountain, something I never saw the monks do on their own. The monks had become a kind of product. The fact was, the population at New Skete was aging, and the hiking trail would have been too tough for most of them.

I took the trail on Saturday afternoon. There was a map in the guesthouse, but I found my way by scanning for red spray-paint splotches on the trees, faint in the forest's overwhelming green. The original Skete was an ascetic's desert, but the newer one was rich with bloom, its floor sprouting thousands of primordial fernlets. I walked far enough so that even the racket of the dogs in the cloister faded and the birds felt safe enough to go on with their calls. Mountain ash stood all about, white and crisped, strips of their curly bark littering the forest floor like spilled scrolls. I let an orange salamander twist between my fingers, and I paused at a giant oak, once split by lightning, repaired with a decade's growth, its self-surgery visible in the accidental cross-section of its trunk.

When I came back to New Skete a few of the nuns had a puppy litter out with their dam—they were all playing together near the puppy kennel. Brother Christopher was doing obedience training outside the guesthouse again, and Ambrose and Stavros were working in the kennel. Elias minded the store. I came in from the forest, headed back toward Two-Top Mountain, and the dogs started their clamor again, a call that hit the suggestive hills and rode down across the flat, sexy belly of the world.

On Sunday, my last day at New Skete, there was a special service for a funeral. A woman arrived to inter the cremated remains of her first husband in New Skete's graveyard, and she brought her second husband along to help her grieve. I didn't like the looks of them. She was put together with hose and a pudding skin of makeup and her hair was dolled up like the white remnant of something burned, the crispy mantle of a camping lantern. Her husband—the live one—looked as though he had left his best days on a high school football field before struggling through law school at his daddy's alma mater. They sat fidgeting as the monks and nuns chanted for the dead man to go to green pastures and still waters. I didn't believe they were getting it.

The services at New Skete were open to the public, and one of the local parishioners was an older man named Charlie who came every day and helped out with some of the church housekeeping; when candles sank low he milled about and replaced them. One day after matins he stopped me and offered his vision of New Skete. "It's another world," he said. "The monks, they're in *this* world. But they're not *of* it." It was exactly what James had said of dogs, but in reverse. And actually, in getting to know the monks—hearing them call each other Chris or Pete or Stash, short for Stavros; or hearing them call canine scat "puppy poops"—I was beginning to think the reverse was more true: the monks were of this world, but not really in it. The world felt far away at New Skete, and I kind of liked it that way. Wicca and Uncle Draggi had hinted at energies, but the monks had seduced me in ways the other groups I'd visited hadn't at all, and I was pleased to be at a remove from that American trajectory with its casino faiths and theaters-cum-sanctuaries. My journey and study had accidentally re-created Prince Vladimir's search for a faith. I was getting used to days bookended by prayer, scheduled moments of contemplation. When dogs gathered, they sniffed and greeted and measured one another, and I began to think that among people it was just such simple intimacy that had been lost. I felt close to the monks simply because I had watched them perform rituals, because I had caught myself humming their songs as I showered in the guesthouse. The God at New Skete was a backward glance to a time when communion was natural and possible, more than sharing a swig of wine and a slice of cooked bread. And now—this couple. They were not of our pack, I thought.

But if the monks agreed, they didn't show it. There was a meal after the service, and the couple was embraced just as everyone else was embraced, and we all sat in rooms in the common area of the main house, and the monks told funny stories of liturgies gone bad—bishops whose pants fell down during services, bishops caught wearing their pajamas during services, hierarchs prone to sudden liturgical eccentricity. This was followed by stories of the occasional mayhem that resulted from the dog program— tales of nuns panicking with their shoes caught in the jaws of Staffordshire terriers, Jack Russells who disappeared for weeks into the forest, dogs who chased lights, dogs who chased monks up onto tractors, dogs whose owners were insane. We all laughed, and then one of the monks spoke quietly with the woman whose husband had died, and she cried at last. Before I went down to the guesthouse for the night, Brother Christopher stopped me and said, "So, now do you think you understand the life of a monk?"

Oka's temperature dropped at two A.M. Marc knocked on my door so I could watch him whelp his bitch. He handed me a flashlight and we navigated the pure pitch of the night back up to the puppy kennel. Oka was lying in a plastic tub in a whelping room, a heat lamp pointed down at her. There was an equipment tray ready with a suction bulb to clear the puppy's airway, and dental floss to tie off the umbilical cord. Music played in the background, choir boys shrieking prayers, and the puppies yelped for a while when they heard us come in. Oka looked worried. It was her first lit- ter, Marc said, and she wasn't quite sure what was happening. The one-puppy litter was an economic quandary for New Skete—the single dog would take a great deal of effort to raise, and would be far less efficient than a multiple litter. Litters generally consisted of six to eight puppies, sometimes as many as thirteen, and it wasn't uncommon for two or three to die in the birthing process. The first and last had the hardest time of it, Marc said. "Sometimes, they've gotten an infection two or three days before. They come out decomposed. They fall apart right in your hands."

Oka was shivering even though it was warm in the room, but Marc was reluctant to turn up the heat—it was the temperature drop that kept her from being lazy. The dog began to tear at a pile of newspapers in the tub, ripping with paws and teeth, answering an ancient call to nest. "Boy, you're fierce!" Marc said, petting the dog and sniffing at the air over where she stood. "Yes, you are. You're getting into it now."

We sat groggy through the night, waiting for the contractions to begin, Marc telling stories about traumatic whelpings, about intubating puppies whose dams did not produce milk properly, about resuscitating entire litters that came out not breathing. Marc had read once of an old practice of giving a martini to women who resisted labor, and sometimes he gave his dogs a dish of beer to settle them.

"I feel something," he said, kneading Oka's abdomen. "Maybe it's just your last meal. I don't feel it kicking. I hope it's alive."

He helped Oka tear the newspapers for a while, but paused at one sheet that had a picture of John Paul II on it. "Oh, the pope!" he said. He moved to tear it again, a literal schism between himself and the pontiff, then thought better of it. He tossed it back into Oka's bin.

Peter arrived around five A.M. with coffee. It was time to inseminate Nikki. He prepared a large syringe, and Wagner's "Bridal March" played as he readied her for the injection, lubricating a gloved finger and stimulating Nikki's vaginal canal to trigger the peristalsis that would move the sperm into her. Once he was done, the monks began to worry about Oka; the contractions had begun, but she seemed reluctant to push. They speculated that the puppy, because it had received all the nutrients of the pregnancy, was too large and might suffocate in the birth canal if it didn't come out quickly. There was concern because matins was not far off and Peter would have to leave.

Oka looked between the two men as they talked, baffled but faithful, for some reason confident that they would help her regulate the painful season.

They gave her a shot of oxytocin to accelerate the labor, then tried positioning her in various stances to move the puppy along. Peter reached inside but couldn't get a grip.

"Grease won't help," he said. "You don't want to make it slippery. I keep feeling the back of the skull."

"No," Marc said, feeling for himself.

"No? There's no feet there, it's not the tail."

"Oh, God. I've got the jaw, I think. It's big, Pete. I don't know if it's going to get through."

"You think I should get Stash? He's got narrower fingers."

"It's really small. The opening."

"I know. I'm afraid to put my finger in there. I keep pushing it back in."

"Come on, girl."

"Jesus, Mary, and Joseph," Peter said.

The strings of some violent concerto climbed rapidly along scales in the background, and I swore I heard a voice from somewhere back in the kennel.

"What's that?"

"Oh, that's just a puppy."

Peter and Marc rested on their haunches for a time; then Pete decided to cut her. He tore open a sterile scalpel head, pinched it, and leaned in behind Oka to begin the work of widening her vulva. Marc held her head and grunted echoes of the noises that Oka made, her face taking on an indescribable dog emotion built of pain and instinct. If she wasn't transcendent, I wanted to argue, then why would she let these men hold her and tear at her, why did she know they meant her no harm?

"I felt the snout coming out," Peter said, taking a break with his hands bloodied. "I went into the canal. I think it's alive, thank God. But I don't know how far I can go with this surgical stuff."

Several more attempts failed, and they considered calling in a veterinarian. Then Peter had an idea. We all climbed into the tub with Oka to hold her upright, enlisting gravity in the effort. I held her up by her paws until my back strained and Oka groaned deeply and jammed her muzzle in under my jaw. Peter cut her until her vulva was wide enough for a fist, and she yelped as he pressed her sex even wider. The puppy finally fell out of her, and Oka collapsed into the tub. We were all jubilant for a time, as Peter quickly tied the cord and snipped it and held up the puppy and said, "Here you are! Little girl!" The puppy was a slimy mound of black, a huge tongue sticking out of a tiny crease of a mouth, its eyes still closed and its body limp as a sock. Oka delivered the afterbirth on her own, a purplish jellyfish. "Now, she can eat that," Marc said, and Oka went for it as the monks tended to the puppy, gobbling it up but getting its fat balloon caught on the lower part of her jaw. I unhooked it with a finger and down it went, and Oka pressed her ears back to look up at the men, for her puppy.

Now the monks realized that the puppy was not alive. It wasn't breathing. They worked to resuscitate it, holding it before them in two hands, performing compressions with their thumbs and pumping air into its lungs by putting their mouths over the whole of its wet face. Oka watched as they passed the limp shape back and forth.

"I don't think it's going to make it," Peter said.

"Keep massaging it."

They tried for ten minutes or so, the music in the background wandering—someone's odd twistings, a maze like a mathematical search over the possibility of arpeggios—until finally resolving on a chord.

"It looked alive but. . . . Come back," Pete said.

"Well, I think that's it."

"Okay. Oh, dear. Well, little girl. I'm sorry."

Peter looked up. He seemed to hear the music for the first time and recognize it.

"Whelping to Bach," he said.

Up at matins a little later I felt an acute need for God, perhaps the first time I could earnestly say I'd felt such a thing. But even that was a little silly. The monks were neither farmers of dogs nor pet owners, and I was reacting like the latter, a fanatic on the verge of tears for a death that had an upside: the puppy would have strained New Skete's resources. I felt New Skete's music in my bones: *God is risen from the dead, conquering death by death, and on those in the grave restoring life.* "And here religion comes to our rescue," James had written,

> and takes our fate into her hands. There is a state of mind, known to religious men, but to no others, in which the will to assert ourselves and hold our own has been displaced by a willingness to close our mouths and be as nothing in the floods and waterspouts of God.

At New Skete, the dogs perhaps healed the schism between people and their need for connection with the world, and maybe New Skete itself healed the schism between Eastern and Western Christianity. But even my tears, building behind my eyes, revealed that I still didn't understand. When the service ended, Christopher approached to ask whether the puppy had lived. I shook my head. He frowned, neither cruelly dismissive nor particularly sad, and headed off to breakfast.

Epilogue

I think it's customary in a project like this one to eventually come to the hope that your effort will trigger a renaissance of interest in your subject. Maybe it's more naive than customary. Regardless, all during my study of James and new religious movements I wondered how the world might have turned out if psychology had followed a doctrine of radical empiricism instead of veering off into psychoanalysis and behaviorism. As fantasy this has its attraction, and perhaps it's enough to note that the world would have been significantly different for following James. But as a lament it's misguided because it's not as though James's thinking has vanished. Rather, he continues to ripple the ponds into which he cast his lines: philosophy, religion, psychology, paranormal studies.

As a religion, Pragmatism failed not long after James died. The academic controversy over its truth petered out. As a philosophy, Pragmatism—though not always James's version of it—has since been championed by the likes of Richard Rorty, John Dewey, Hilary Putnam, Jacques Barzun, and Cornel West. It is invoked in scholarship on jurisprudence and literary theory. The effects of James's thinking pop up more directly—though unattributed—in the work of religious scholars such as Emile Durkheim ("People are more confident because they feel stronger, and they are stronger in reality because the strength that was flagging has been reawakened in their consciousness") and Mircea Eliade ("The myths that projected Jesus of Nazareth into a universe of archetypes and transcendent figures are as 'true' as his acts and words"). A recent book-length study explored James's influence on Ludwig Wittgenstein. Wittgenstein cited James often in his published work, even more in his private notebooks. And some unattributed passages in Wittgenstein are hauntingly close to James. Wittgenstein avoided referencing *Varieties* publicly, but academic sleuthing revealed that he had read the lectures in 1912, recommended them to a student in 1930, and once told Bertrand Russell, "This book does me a *lot* of good." The study's author claimed that Wittgenstein returned to James's work as often as he returned to Saint Augustine.

At the opposite end of the continuum, James continues to fuel the remnants of Spiritualism. In 1901, just before James finished writing the first ten lectures of *Varieties,* he visited a colleague in psychical research, Frederic Myers, as Myers's health was failing. Myers and James had made a pact: whoever died first would attempt to contact the other from the spirit realm. Too saddened to sit by Myers's hospital bed, James remained in the hallway with a notebook, ready to record any message that came. Myers died peacefully, and James left his notebook blank. When James's own time came, he appeared to have better luck from the other side; at least three mediums have since channeled book-length documents from a "control" that claimed to be William James. In 1931, Jane Revere Burke's James claimed that "up to now man has not entered fully into this idea that he is a co-creator with God." Maude V. Underhill's James revealed that he was the leader of a collection of progressive schools in the world beyond death. And the third medium, Susy Smith, eventually became a subject of the Veritas Research Project at the University of Arizona's Human Energy Systems Laboratory. This laboratory—sister to the Society for Psychical Research, which is still in existence—uses a quote from James as its motto and offers the William James Postdoctoral Fellowship in Mediumship and Survival Research. In *The Book of James (William James, That Is),* Smith offers an explanation for why her text doesn't sound a whole lot like James, and then reports him saying, "If you could always maintain your awareness of the fact of your complete oneness with God, your lives would be glorious even before you come over here."

In short, academics quote James without citing him, and mediums cite him without quoting him.

I returned from my last trip to a new religious movement in the spring of 2004. Over the next year I kept tabs on each of the groups I'd visited.

Rhiannon the Druid continues to live in her comfortable shack in Cohasset with her children, Fiona and Jimmy, but the local Druid network has suffered some strain. Some of her work had been plagiarized, Rhiannon told me. The online classes have dried up as well. She blames a lack of dedication. She has since turned to alternative healing of animals and is planning to go back to school to become a veterinary technician. She bought a horse, Faern. Animals heal better, she said, because they aren't clouded by bias against the benefits of acupressure or massage therapy. In Los Angeles, the young actress Ariadne has expanded her animal menagerie with a second pit bull and a variety of other creatures. She continues with acting classes and auditions.

I revisited the Unarius Star Center a day after they celebrated their fiftieth anniversary. Out on the El Cajon strip, one of the lights of 50,000 Books had burned out—now there were only five thousand books. Franklin was at the Star Center, as always, helping clean up after the party. Dottie Millen, he told me, had finally been placed in a nursing home. But otherwise Unarius was thriving, outlasting its failed prophecy, and Franklin was proud that they still didn't have a clear leader among them. One of Ernest Norman's books, *The Truth About Mars,* was selling particularly well, Franklin said, because a pair of mechanical rovers that NASA had landed on Mars were proving everything the book claimed. "We are fortunate that we can maintain our sanity in this crazy world," Franklin told me. "And this crazy world—it's waking up."

The Christian Wrestling Federation went through a second downturn after I broke off from them in Pennsylvania. The wrestling, it turned out, was more important than the message for some of the wrestlers. The personnel shifted. Rob Vaughn/Jesus Freak took a job as a youth minister and decided to go to seminary to get a master's degree in theology. The CWF abandoned the Rock Gym for the more practical CWF Warehouse, and now the ministry soldiers on with some of the old names, Chris Idol and Shiloh and Tim Storm, and a few new ones: Bishop, Apocalypse, the Cross Factor, and Son of Thunder. They've cut back on the travel some, but Rob's website now counts more than four thousand Christian decisions.

Uncle Draggi had been in therapy for post-traumatic stress disorder for several months when I spoke to him early in 2005. He was on pills for depression, but he wasn't sure what they were called. Sometime before, the Seattle Local Council of the Covenant of the Goddess voluntarily dissolved because its members thought CoG had become too exclusive. But as a group they still meet outside the auspices of the Covenant, and last Samhein Draggi designed a ritual that really blew some folks' socks off, he told me. CoG itself has held additional MerryMeets in Fort Worth and New Mexico. They continue to struggle with difficult issues, like what amounts to a two-thirds majority in a coven with only five members. A contingent of a dozen witches attended the 2004 Parliament of the World's Religions in Barcelona, and since then CoG has received queries from witches in Canada, Japan, New Zealand, Australia, and South America.

Life at New Skete has remained largely unchanged, though after I completed my retreat there two of the nuns broke away to form their own group. This left holes in the cheesecake business. Brother Stavros and one other monk now help with the baking, and Brother John has taken over the puppy kennel. Brother Marc's bitch Oka was retired after her difficult whelping and now lives with a family that has been caring for New Skete dogs for more than thirty years. Stavros told me that the dog program is booming. They are taking new puppy orders again after receiving two new studs from Germany. One of them is called James, but I think the connection is accidental. "We suddenly had a big burst of fertility," Stavros said. "It should be a no-brainer. You just need a good stud."

Scientology has continued with its efforts to go mainstream, emphasizing its drug and literacy programs and angling for positive media attention. The press page of its website now lists the date on which L. Ron Hubbard "passed away," and a promotional page for the Scientology primer *What Is Scientology?* describes the book as "No mumbo jumbo. No initiation. No human sacrifice. Just the facts." In 2005 the actor Tom Cruise, who has long given credit to Ron's study tech for helping him beat a diagnosis of dyslexia, raised the profile of Scientology by placing information tents on the sets of Steven Spielberg's remake of *War of the Worlds*. In Germany, Cruise and Spielberg agreed to an interview about the film with *Der Spiegel*. The magazine's interviewer took the opportunity to point out that the German government had placed Scientology under surveillance and that in Germany the religion is considered "an exploitative cult with totalitarian tendencies." Cruise replied that the surveillance was not as strict as it had once been. The interview continued:

DER SPIEGEL: Do you see it as your job to recruit new followers for Scientology?

CRUISE: I'm a helper. For instance, I myself have helped hundreds of people get off drugs. In Scientology, we have the only successful drug rehabilitation program in the world. It's called Narconon.

DER SPIEGEL: That's not correct. Yours is never mentioned among the recognized detox programs. Independent experts warn against it because it is rooted in pseudoscience.

CRUISE: You don't understand what I am saying. It's a statistically proven fact that there is only one successful drug rehabilitation program in the world. Period.

DER SPIEGEL: With all due respect, we doubt that. Mr. Cruise, you made studio executives, for example from Paramount, tour Scientology's "Celebrity Centre" in Hollywood. Are you trying to extend Scientology's influence in Hollywood?

CRUISE: I just want to help people. I want everyone to do well.

After I walked out on the L. Ron Hubbard birthday celebration in Los Angeles, I received almost daily phone calls from the mother church for six months.

As a burst of fanaticism always keys a corresponding gain in unbelief, American Atheists has experienced a dramatic increase in media attention as the conservative right in America has gained steam. Another Godless March, this time on a bitterly cold Washington morning on the occasion of the Supreme Court argument over the Ten Commandments,* drew only twenty-two Atheists but thirty-seven members of the press. Arlene-Marie, from Michigan, laughed at the memory of the scene over her cell phone—she had called me back from the veranda of her boat on the Great Lakes. She said that she herself had done more than one hundred television interviews in the first half of 2005, and that Michigan Atheists were planning their own television program. On a sadder note, Bob Brooks, one of the speakers I had met at the Godless March on Lansing, took his own life in 2004, after an illness. The Atheists comforted him in his final days and offered him advice as to how to execute the act, including suggestions about the kind of shells to use in his shotgun. The note he left, posted on the Michigan Atheists website, was in keeping with the Atheist tradition of near-death proclamations of unbelief:

---

*The Court ruled that Ten Commandment displays were permissible for some public spaces, such as monuments, but inappropriate for others, such as courthouses.

> My death is neither based on courage, nor cowardice. It is the logical con-
> clusion of a rational mind based upon my values and circumstances. . . .
> Cutting my ties to this world is not easy. However, my life belongs to
> me, not the doctors, preachers, or government, all of whom forbid my
> action.

And finally, in California, Blanche Barton continues with her private
education of Satan Xerxes. The boy is now taking fencing and piano lessons.
Up at the Black House of the North, Robert Lang and Diana DeMagis
have been promoted to magister and magistra. They have adopted a Great
Dane, and in 2004 Di gave birth to a daughter, Freyja. Late in 2003, on the
Day of the Dead, I went back to Canada to attend the wedding of Jen and
Magister Michael Rose. The entire Toronto grotto reconvened in the black
dungeon chamber. They asked me to recite a portion of *The Satanic Bible* as
part of the ceremony. I did my best. But when it was over I made a slip that
revealed to everyone that I still had a lot to learn about Satanism. Greg's
girlfriend sneezed.

"Bless you!" I said.

A James critic once quipped that, according to James, if it was useful to believe in the existence of a character such as William James, then "this belief
would be true, even if he didn't exist." James might not have disagreed. But
he would have argued that it was pointless to grub about in the business of
the past, and a mistake to attribute too much to someone who was just a
man. He certainly would not have agreed with the idea of a literary pilgrimage. But that didn't stop me from climbing Mount Marcy—the
mountain that vexed James just before he wrote *Varieties*—a year after my
religious cycle. It was my last James trip.

I have a bad leg, the permanent mark of the accident I described in my
Scientology auditing session, so the climb was difficult, a six-hour ascent
up a creekbed pitched at a forty-five degree angle, generously called a
"footpath." People have been climbing Mount Marcy recreationally since
at least 1837, and the climb has undoubtedly gotten easier since James's ascent. When I finally made the mountaintop I found a ranger on permanent
duty there. He introduced himself as the "summit steward" and warned me
away from fragile alpine plants. He seemed a little lonely. The forests of the
Adirondacks weren't so different from the land around New Skete, and the

range of bulging peaks recalled the crumpled-bedsheet hills of California. A herd of thunderheads levitated just above the summit. I snoozed for a while. On the way back down, leaping from rock to rock, I thought more than once of James's "alpine climber," whose leap of faith demonstrated Pragmatism's truth. Each of my jumps might have been the original inspiration for a metaphor that has lasted a century. I didn't get lost, but like James I was a little queasy when I finally stumbled back to the lodge where I was staying.

If it's customary to hope that a biography might actually come to make a difference in the world, then it's at least tempting to wonder whether a biography would please its subject. James reacted poorly to the one attempt to distill him that was made during his lifetime—he chastised a woman who had tried to capture his thinking, accusing her of rummaging through his work so selectively that she misrepresented him entirely. Working with this incident in mind, I have tried to keep the larger sweep of James's thought at the fore, while at the same time acknowledging the thinking that has managed to survive, those remnants that have proved themselves to have a "cash value" James could not have denied. In this, I have become something of a James disciple. I'm not a convert—even in Pragmatism, there isn't anything specific to convert to—but the lingering effect of James on me has been to soften the confusion of a hacked-apart world, a world perplexed by modernity, a world pluralistic by accident rather than design. The whole deep spread of civilization is a bit less stiff with James in your bag of tricks. If I had started out not knowing whether I was on a spiritual journey, then I have ended the same, though on this end I am a bit less baffled than I used to be.

As to whether James would approve of all this, it's probably best to leave off with one of his contradictions. James was of two minds on the ability of words to capture the essence of anything. On the one hand, Wittgenstein returned repeatedly to James's claim that words had souls as well as bodies. He referred to a passage in *The Principles of Psychology* in which James described the phenomenon of staring at a printed word until it lost its meaning. "Let the reader try this with any word on this page," he wrote.

He will soon begin to wonder if it can possibly be the word he has been using all his life with this meaning. It stares back at him from the paper like a glass eye, with no speculation in it. Its body is indeed there, but its soul is fled.

This implies a kind of faith in words. James eventually argued that while not all words were based in the senses, all had distinct emotions associated with them. Even words like *this, or,* and *and* had meaning and feelings. This made the stream of consciousness possible. "Single words, and conjunctions of words," he wrote of the attempt to describe mysticism in *Varieties,* "[can] bring it in when the mind is tuned aright." On the other hand, James doubted the overall value of words, whether they were contractions, or sensual, or were formed into sentences or books or biographies. In *Pragmatism,* speaking of the promise of words like *God, free-will,* and *design,* he warned,

> *If you stop, in dealing with such words, with their definition, thinking that to be an intellectual finality, where are you? Stupidly staring at a pretentious sham.*

And two years after completing *Principles* he wrote to a friend: "It would be an awful universe if *everything* could be converted into words words words."

Acknowledgments

First, thanks to everyone in this book who shared a story.

Thanks, too, to the battery of folks who helped make this work possible or readable: Giles Anderson, Cat Adams, Cheeni Rao, Alex Carey, Mike Delaney, Carolina Hotchandani, Rebecca Hall, Barbara Kontouzi, Denny Marbourg, Daniel Castilla, Julie Fishman, Mark Szybist, Todd Goddard, Mary Kay Hallman, Lynn Laufenberg, Joe Malloy, Lisa Johnston, Megan Carnes, and Joe Millar.

And worlds of gratitude to all the wise people at Random House, in particular Fleetwood Robbins, Daniel Menaker, Janet Wygal, Amelia Zalcman, Laura Goldin, and my editor, Will Murphy.

Notes

The Devil Is a Gentleman is an act of synthesis conducted in a Jamesian spirit. But one does not write such a book without becoming acutely aware that an act of synthesis is also an act of redaction. If, as James believed, there is danger in a world that suffers from intellectual fracture—which may be the rationale for synthesis—then there is corresponding danger to an artificially edited and compressed version of that same world. *The Devil Is a Gentleman* is not scholarship. It is a literary effort bolstered, as the text suggests in many places, by the thinking of others. Certainly, many of the insights into James's life come from my own reading of his work and his letters. But a good deal, too, comes from James's various biographers, to whom I am deeply indebted. James's radical empiricism suggested that both reality and the perception of reality were valuable avenues of inquiry. Just as James constructed a "composite photograph" of the saintly personality from testimonies and biographies in *Varieties,* so have I made a portrait of him out of his work, his letters, and those subjective, incomplete, passionate biographies that say as much about James as they do about the thinkers who have wrestled with him. Rather than fracture my text with exhaustive footnoting—which might well defeat the purpose of synthesis—I offer a less formal acknowledgment of the following books, which were indispensable in the creation of my James: Gay Wilson Allen, *William James;* Jacques Barzun, *A Stroll with William James;* Louis Menand, *The Metaphysical Club;* Henry James, *Notes of a Son and Brother;* Gerald E. Myers, *William James: His Life and Thought;* Ralph Barton Perry, *The Thought and Character of William James;* Linda Simon, *Genuine Reality: A Life of William James;* Jean Strouse, *Alice James;* Ignas K. Skrupskelis and Elizabeth M Berkeley, editors, *The Correspondence of William James;* Eugene Taylor, *William James on Consciousness Beyond the Margin.*

Similarly, *The Devil Is a Gentleman* is spackled with short histories on various topics. These are intended as backdrop and context for each chapter's narrative, and their value is as much in their consistency as in their contradictions. The exact texts I consulted for each can be found in the notes section, below.

ABBREVIATIONS

Adler: Adler, Margot. *Drawing Down the Moon: Witches, Druids, Goddess Worshippers, and Other Pagans in America Today.* New York: Penguin Books, 1979.
Allen: Allen, Gay Wilson. *William James.* New York: The Viking Press, 1967.
Anshen: Anshen, Ruth Nanda. *The Reality of the Devil: Evil in Man.* New York: Dell, 1972.

Armstrong: Armstrong, Karen. *A History of God.* New York: Ballantine, 1993.

Atack: Atack, Jon. *A Piece of Blue Sky: Scientology, Dianetics, and L. Ron Hubbard Exposed.* New York: Carol Publishing Group, 1990.

Barzun: Barzun, Jacques. *A Stroll with William James.* Chicago: University of Chicago Press, 1983.

BC: James, William. *Briefer Course.* In *Writings, 1878–1899.* New York: Library Classics of the United States, 1992.

Carus: Carus, Paul. *The History of the Devil and the Idea of Evil.* New York: Bell Publishing Company, 1900.

COR: Skrupskelis, Ignas K., and Elizabeth M. Berkeley, eds. *The Correspondence of William James.* 12 vols. Charlottesville: University of Virginia Press, 1992–2004.

Corydon: Corydon, Bent. *L. Ron Hubbard: Messiah or Madman?* Fort Lee, N.J.: Barricade Books, 1987.

DAJ: Edel, Leon, ed. *The Dairy of Alice James.* New York: Dodd, Mead & Company, 1934.

Eliade: Eliade, Mircea. *A History of Religious Ideas.* 3 vols. Chicago: University of Chicago Press, 1978.

Hubbard: Hubbard, L. Ron. *Dianetics: The Modern Science of Mental Health.* Los Angeles: Bridge Publications, 1950.

Jaynes: Jaynes, Julian. *The Origin of Consciousness in the Breakdown of the Bicameral Mind.* Boston: Houghton Mifflin Company, 1976.

Mazer: Mazer, Sharon. *Professional Wrestling: Sport and Spectacle.* Jackson: University Press of Mississippi, 1998.

Miles: Miles, Jack. *God: A Biography.* New York: Random House, 1995.

Morton: Morton, Gerald W., and George M. O'Brien. *Wrestling to Rasslin': Ancient Sport to American Spectacle.* Bowling Green: Bowling Green State University Popular Press, 1985.

MT: James, William. *The Meaning of Truth.* In *Writings: 1902–1910.* New York: Library Classics of the United States, 1987.

Myers: Myers, Gerald E. *William James: His Life and Thought.* New Haven: Yale University Press, 1986.

Perry: Perry, Ralph Barton. *The Thought and Character of William James.* Nashville: Vanderbilt University Press, 1948.

PP: James, William. *The Principles of Psychology.* Cambridge: Harvard University Press, 1981.

PRA: James, William. *Pragmatism.* In *Writings: 1902–1910.* New York: Library Classics of the United States, 1987.

PU: James, William. *A Pluralistic Universe.* In *Writings: 1902–1910.* New York: Library Classics of the United States, 1987.

Simon: Simon, Linda. *Genuine Reality: A Life of William James.* Chicago: University of Chicago Press, 1998.

Smith: Smith, George. *Atheism: The Case Against God.* New York: Prometheus Books, 1989.

Strouse: Strouse, Jean. *Alice James: A Biography.* Cambridge: Harvard University Press, 1980.

Sutin: Sutin, Lawrence. *Do What Thou Wilt: A Life of Aleister Crowley.* New York: St. Martin's–Griffin, 2000.

Swedenborg: Swedenborg, Emanuel. *Concerning the Earths in Our Solar System, Etc.* London: Emanuel Swedenborg, 1758.

C. Taylor: Taylor, Charles. *Varieties of Religion Today: William James Revisited.* Cambridge: Harvard University Press, 2002.

E. Taylor: Taylor, Eugene. *William James on Consciousness Beyond the Margin.* Princeton: Princeton University Press, 1996.

TTS: James, William. *Talks to Teachers and Students.* In *Writings: 1878–1899.* New York: Library Classics of the United States, 1992.

VRE: James, William. *The Varieties of Religious Experience.* In *Writings: 1902–1910.* New York: Library Classics of the United States, 1987.

Wolfe: Wolfe, Alan. *The Transformation of American Religion: How We Actually Live Our Faith.* New York: Free Press, 2003.

Wright: Wright, Lawrence. *Saints and Sinners.* New York: Random House, 1993.

WTB: James, William. *The Will to Believe.* In *Writings: 1878–1899.* New York: Library Classics of the United States, 1992.

Zaretsky: Zaretsky, Irving I., and Mark P. Leone, eds. *Religious Movements in Contemporary America.* Princeton: Princeton University Press, 1974.

EPIGRAPHS

vii "If one could be": Letter to Alice Howe Gibbens James, June 24, 1897, *COR,* vol. 8, p. 279.

vii "I do not know": Joseph C. Millar, "Rivers Green & Not So."

PROLOGUE

xv "a free surrender": Martin Luther, *Commentary on Galatians 3:19,* quoted in Armstrong, p. 278.

xv "Let us weigh": Blaise Pascal, *Pensées,* quoted in G. Smith, p. 182.

xv "The *speculative* interest": Immanuel Kant, *Critique of Pure Reason,* quoted in Collins, p. 189.

xvi "Our faith is": *WTB,* p. 463.

xvi "It is like those gambling": *WTB,* p. 527.

xvi "the risk of being": *WTB,* p. 469.

xvii "The first thing to": *VRE,* p. 105.

xvii "We have the beginnings": *VRE,* p. 389.

xvii "James is our great": C. Taylor, p. 59.

xviii "One can never fathom": *VRE,* p. 298.

INFINITE

3 "Yet how believe as": *VRE,* p. 172.

3 "The Andromedans hear your voice": Denis Johnson, "The White Fires of Venus," *The Throne of the Third Heaven of the Nations Millennium General Assembly: Poems, Collected and New.* New York: HarperCollins, 1996, p. 94.

1. Applewhite

6 Heaven's Gate: This history of Heaven's Gate is compiled from a large number of newspaper accounts of the group from around the time of the suicides. Even more useful was Robert W. Balch's article "Waiting for the Ships: Disillusionment and the Revitalization of Faith in Bo and Peep's UFO Cult," in *The Gods Have Landed: New Religions from Other Worlds,* ed. James R. Lewis.

6–7 "wrong side of" and "that religion and" and "But as soon as": *VRE,* p. 312.

8 "We have a right to believe": *WTB,* p. 495.

2. Fairy Godmother

9 Unarius: Some of the history of Unarius delivered here came from the Unariuns themselves. But also critical was the work of Diana Tumminia and R. George Kirkpatrick, in particular their collaborative paper "Unarius: Emergent Aspects of an American Flying Saucer

Group," which was reprinted in *The Gods Have Landed: New Religions from Other Worlds,* ed. James R. Lewis. As well, Tumminia's article "How Prophecy Never Fails: Interpretive Reason in a Flying-Saucer Group," in *Sociology of Religion,* 59, no. 2 (1998), pp. 157–70, shed light on Unarius's predicament.

11 "And it is equally certain": *WTB,* pp. 562–63.

3. *Homo spiritualis*

16 "Let us play fair": *VRE,* p. 22.

17 "a shuffling and matching": *VRE,* pp. 400–401.

17 "Anything larger will do": *VRE,* p. 468.

5. *Species of Inconsistency*

21 "day of inwardness": *VRE,* p. 308.

22 "the happiness which": *VRE,* p. 77.

22 "A small man's": *VRE,* p. 220.

26 "There are only two ways": *VRE,* p. 197.

27 "confrontation, symbiosis": Eliade, vol. 1, p. 270.

1842–1864

30 "To all appearance": Simon, p. 25.

31 "comparatively *low*": Swedenborg, p. iii.

31 The philosophy Henry Sr. went on: Perry, p. 9.

32 "This is, indeed": *WTB,* p. 485.

33 "Boils are surely": Letter to Henry James, Jr., August 8, 1900, Skrupskelis and Berkeley, eds., *William and Henry James: Selected Letters,* p. 393.

33 "Harry's orbit and mine": Perry, p. 94.

34 "the perfect man": Simon, p. 41.

34 "Why should not a given": Letter to Henry James, Sr., August 24, 1860, *COR,* vol. 4, p. 40.

36 "as many professors": Barzun, p. 20.

OLD ONES

37 "Our lives are": *Memories and Studies,* quoted in Allen, p. 466.

37 "*Fergus.* The whole day have": *Selected Poems,* p. 46.

1. *Rhiannon and Ariadne*

39 "It was full eight inches long": Putnam Camp Log, September 11, 1896, quoted in Simon, p. 259.

42 "Feeling is private and dumb": *VRE,* p. 388.

2. *Tree Meditation*

42 Druidry: This history of Druidry combines material from the following works: Miranda J. Green, *The World of the Druids;* Peter Berresford Ellis, *A Brief History of the Druids;* John Matthews, ed., *The Druid Source Book;* Ronald Hutton, *The Triumph of the Moon;* and Margot Adler, *Drawing Down the Moon.*

43 "preside over sacred things": Quoted in Miranda Green, *The World of the Druids,* p. 10.

49 "bent as we are on": *VRE,* p. 17.

50 "in the natural sciences": *VRE,* p. 24.

50 "Few of us are not": *VRE,* p. 30.

50 "It is certain that": *VRE,* p. 36.

50 "tho't transference being": Letter to Alfred Georg Ludwig Lehmann, October 19, 1899, *COR,* vol. 9, p. 62.

3. Godfeast

53 "William's illness": Allen, p. 135.

53 "No one has a right": Letter to Henry James, Sr., and Mary Robertson Walsh James, April 21, 1865, *COR,* vol. 4, p. 100.

53 "prolonged seasickness will": *VRE,* p. 137.

53 "the application of small blisters": "A Suggestion for the Prevention of Seasickness," *Boston Medical and Surgical Journal* 116, quoted in Myers, p. 370.

54 "the very lightest": Letter to Henry James, Sr., June 3, 1865, *COR,* vol. 4, p. 107.

54 "Ah Jesuina, Jesuina": Letter to Alice James, August 31, 1865, *COR,* vol. 4, p. 120.

54 "There is not a bit" and "in an easy": Allen, p. 116.

55 "mental therapeutics should *not*": *Evening Transcript,* March 24, 1894, quoted in Allen, p. 372.

55 "banded with the spiritists": Letter to James Jackson Putnam, March 3, 1898, quoted in Allen, p. 373.

55 "temporarily useful": *VRE,* p. 449n.

55 "It has bridged the chasm": *WTB,* p. 699.

55 "The future of psychology": Ernest Jones, *The Life and Work of Sigmund Freud,* quoted in Allen, p. 466.

55 "obsess[ion] with" and "American religious" and "Bah!": Letter to Théodore Flournoy, September 28, 1909, *COR,* vol. 12, p. 334.

55 "Eeeny, meenie, miney mo": Allen, p. 471.

56 "If anything": E. Taylor, p. 108.

1866–1878

62 "The idea of people swarming": Perry, p. 77.

63 "I must say": Letter to Katharine Temple Emmett, August 17, 1868, *COR,* vol. 4, p. 332.

63 "whatever letters": Letter to Theodora Sedgwick, August 8, 1874, *COR,* vol. 4, p. 500.

63 "shiver": Letter to Thomas Wren Ward, March 14, 1870, *COR,* vol. 4, p. 403.

64 "the consolation": Perry, p. 82.

64 "I am coming home": Allen, p. 151.

64 "too undeveloped a state": Letter to Henry Pickering Walcott, April 1, 1894, *COR,* vol. 7, p. 496.

65 "I can't bring myself": Letter to Henry James, Jr., May 7, 1870, Skrupskelis and Berkeley, eds., *William and Henry James: Selected Letters,* p. 73.

65 "My first act": see Allen, p. 168, among others.

66 "[my] twin bro": Letter to Henry James, Jr., April 6, 1873, *COR,* vol. 1, p. 193.

66 "At present Harry": Letter to Garth Wilkinson James, November 16, 1873, quoted in Allen, p. 185.

66 "lend life and charm": This is reported secondhand from Alice James in a letter dated July 18, 1889, quoted in Perry, p. 175.

67 the formal introduction of modern psychology: Skrupskelis and Berkeley, eds., *William and Henry James: Selected Letters,* p. 99.

67 "my only wonder" Letter to George Holmes Howison, May 1, 1879, *COR,* vol. 5, p. 50.

68 "To state abruptly": Letter to Alice Howe Gibbens James, September 1876, *COR,* vol. 4, p. 543.

68 "Over the right-hand near mountain": Letter to Alice Howe Gibbens James, July 31, 1880, *COR,* vol. 5, p. 128.

68 "The weather has been": Letter to Alice Howe Gibbens James, September 18, 1881, *COR,* vol. 5, p. 177.

69 "Oh darling": Letter to Alice Howe Gibbens James, July 13, 1882, *COR,* vol. 5, p. 222.

KING

71 "Men who see each other's": "The Function of Cognition," *MT,* p. 845.

1. Jesus Freak

74 "Whoever not only says": *VRE,* pp. 261–62.

75 "Wrestling is not a sport": Roland Barthes, "The World of Wrestling," *Mythologies* (New York: Farrar, Straus and Giroux, 1972), p. 15.

2. The Rock Gym

78 "Seeking but not always finding": Wolfe, p. 65.

78 "The action at the heart": Mazer, p. 103.

78 "it is a duration, a display": Barthes, "The World of Wrestling," p. 21.

81 "In what we consider": Morton, p. 120.

82 "Some of you": *VRE,* p. 236.

82 "violent accompaniments": *VRE,* p. 231.

82 "So with the conversion": *VRE,* p. 237.

3. This Is Not a Show

83 "the art of winning": *VRE,* p. 34.

83 "I am against": Letter to Sarah Wyman Whitman, June 7, 1899, *COR,* vol. 8, p. 546.

83 "for [some]": *VRE,* p. 412n.

84 "Strange as it may seem": Armstrong, p. 27.

84 "if we were forced": Miles, p. 106.

85 "no one can doubt": Barthes, "The World of Wrestling," p. 25.

85 The origin of wrestling: This short take on the history of wrestling essentially combines the work of Sharon Mazer, *Professional Wrestling: Sport and Spectacle,* and Gerald W. Morton and George M. O'Brien, *Wrestling to Rasslin': Ancient Sport to American Spectacle.* The A&E documentary *The Unreal Story of Pro Wrestling* was also a source.

86 "The lust for blood": W. C. Martin, "Friday Night in the Coliseum," quoted in Morton, p. 157.

86 "in every aspect": Wolfe, p. 3.

87 "The weight of the past": Letter to Alice James, December 22, 1873, *COR,* vol. 4, p. 473.

87 "'typically American,'" and "a mind and": Barzun, p. 12 and p. 99.

87 "the spirit of the frontiersman": Josiah Royce, *William James and Other Essays on the Philosophy of Life,* quoted in Myers, p. 456.

87 "James the psychologist": Myers, p. 415.

87 "naked, vacuous": Letter to Henry James, October 10, 1872, *COR,* vol. 1, p. 174.

87 "too greedy": Letter to Robertson James, January 22, 1868, *COR,* vol. 4, p. 262.

87 "callousness to abstract": Letter to H. G. Wells, September 11, 1906, *COR,* vol. 11, p. 267.

87 "God bless the": Letter to Frances Rollins Morse, September 17, 1899, *COR,* vol. 9, p. 44.

87 "American vegetation": Letter to Frances Rollins Morse, April 30, 1901, *COR,* vol. 9, p. 473.

88 "Drop your english": Letter to Henry James, June 6, 1903, *COR,* vol. 3, p. 242.

88 "every individual": Letter to Oliver Wendell Holmes, Jr., May 15, 1868, *COR,* vol. 4, p. 303.

88 "Why drag in": Letter to Théodore Flournoy, July 23, 1902, *COR,* vol. 10, p. 589, calendared; quoted in Allen, p. 432.

88 "You are of all": Letter from Charles Peirce to William James, March 16, 1903, *COR,* vol. 10, p. 213.

89 "a band of devotees": Perry, p. 313.

89 "I am still": Letter from Giovanni Papini to William James, May 3, 1906, *COR*, vol. 11, p. 587, calendared; quoted in Perry, p. 315.

89 "To think of": Letter to F.C.S. Schiller, April 7, 1906, *COR*, vol. 11, p. 198n.

89 "determination to make": *Journal of Philosophy, Psychology, and Scientific Method,* quoted in Perry, p. 314.

89 "You speak": Letter from Henri Bergson to William James, April 30, 1909, *COR*, vol. 12, p. 611, calendared; quoted in Perry, p. 349.

89 "I leave the 'Cause'": Letter to F.C.S. Schiller, August 8, 1910, *COR*, vol. 12, p. 573.

4. The Main Event

91 "Why should you not": Letter to Charles Augustus Strong, August 9, 1907, *COR*, vol. 11, pp. 342–43.

92 "the best man": *VRE*, p. 438.

92 "What do you mean by God?": *Writings: 1902–1910*, pp. 1183–85.

1878–1890

99 "I want you to feel": Letter to Henry James, Sr., September 26, 1867, *COR*, vol. 4, p. 203.

99 "he is just like": *DAJ*, entry for November 18, 1889, p. 57.

100 "exaggerated sympathy": *DAJ*, entry for June 1, 1891, p. 208.

100 "Here lies a man": *DAJ*, entry for June 24, 1891, p. 217.

100 "Darling old father": Letter to Henry James, Sr., December 14, 1882, quoted in Allen, pp. 254–55.

101 "Oh, I have": Simon, p. 180.

101 "Father's cry": Letter to Henry James, Jr., January 9, 1883, quoted in Perry, p. 41.

101 "We are founding here": Letter to Katharine James Prince, December 24, 1884, *COR*, vol. 5, p. 542.

101 "If I may employ the language," *PR*, p. 694.

103 "a force of some sort": Letter to Catherine Elizabeth Havens, June 14, 1874, *COR*, vol. 4, p. 496.

103 "I confess that at times": *Writings: 1902–1910*, p. 1250.

104 "All these things call up a vague": Letter from Henry Holt to William James, November 16, 1889, *COR*, vol. 6, pp. 552–53.

105 "Publishers are demons": Letter to Henry Holt, March 21, 1890, quoted in Perry, p. 188.

105 "*Of course* you": Letter from Henry Holt to William James, April 2, 1890, quoted in Perry, p. 189.

105 "proclaims me really": Letter to Alice Howe Gibbens James, May 24, 1890, quoted in Simon, p. 229.

105 "a loathsome, distended": Letter to Henry Holt, May 9, 1890, *COR*, vol. 7, p. 24.

106 "real world": *PRA*, p. 518.

106 "The prince of darkness": *PRA*, p. 518.

SATAN

107 "Passive happiness is slack": *VRE*, p. 274.

107 "When women bear children": D. H. Lawrence, *Studies in Classic American Literature* (1923; repr., New York: Penguin, 1977), p. 103.

107 "And if we have to declare": Carus, p. 5.

1. The Devil Is a Gentleman

109 "The devil, *quoad existentiam*": WTB, p. 579.

2. *The Black House of the North*

110 "the mother earth is": Letter to Charles Waldstein, July 20, 1887, *COR*, vol. 6, p. 241.

111 "the best fruits": *TTS*, p. 863.

111 "This human drama": *TTS*, p. 863.

111 "the flash of a pistol": Letter to Alice Howe Gibbens James, July 29, 1896, *COR*, vol. 8, p. 177.

111 "The trail of": *VRE*, p. 515.

113 "is the real core": *VRE*, p. 151.

3. *Satan Xerxes*

118 "The ancient saying": *VRE*, p. 74.

118 Devil worship: This short history of the Devil here and on p. 137 compresses theories and thinking from the following books: Paul Carus, *The History of the Devil and the Idea of Evil;* Elaine Pagels, *The Origin of Satan;* Ruth Nanda Anshen, *The Reality of the Devil: Evil in Man;* and Gordon Stein, ed., *The Encyclopedia of Unbelief.*

120 "the most striking": *WTB*, p. 468.

121 "the world is all the richer": *VRE*, p. 52.

121 "As God's image is little": Anshen, p. 130.

4. *Bees Making Honey*

127 "There is nobody": Burton H. Wolfe, *The Devil's Avenger,* quoted in Blanche Barton, *The Secret Life of a Satanist*, pp. 59–60.

127 "often spoken of": *VRE*, p. 84.

127 "are actually formed for his cult": *VRE*, pp. 83–84.

128 "a stroke from which": "What Psychical Research Has Accomplished," *WTB*, p. 690.

129 "The Satanist is training himself": Edward J. Moody, "Magical Therapy: An Anthropological Investigation of Contemporary Satanism," in Zaretsky, p. 382.

130 "a balance of nature": Wright, p. 195.

130 "Action seems to follow": "The Gospel of Relaxation," *TTS*, p. 826.

131 "We can act *as if*": *VRE*, p. 56.

5. *Evil Frankly Accepted*

132 "James taught me": *Sunday Times*, London, April 11, 1926, quoted in Perry, p. 317.

133 "All the evil": Letter to Edgar Beach Van Winkle, March 1, 1858, *COR*, vol. 4, p. 12.

135 "Surely, there is no": *WTB*, p. 599.

135 "so far as he feels": *WTB*, p. 600.

135 "the best simply": *WTB*, p. 608.

135 "in which individual": *WTB*, p. 601.

135 "the actually possible": *WTB*, p. 608.

135 "There is but one": *WTB*, p. 613.

136 "The capacity of the": *WTB*, p. 616.

137 "An evil frankly accepted": "On Some Hegelisms," *WTB*, p. 661.

6. *Birthmark*

137 Historically, there are: See note for Devil worship for p. 118, above.

1890–1898

142 "How well one has to be": Entry for July 18, 1890, *DAJ*, p. 129.

142 "Within the last year": Entry for June 16, 1891, *DAJ*, p. 211.

142 "To him who waits": Entry for May 31, 1891, *DAJ*, p. 206.

142 "I know you've": Letter to Alice James, July 6, 1891, *COR*, vol. 7, p. 177.

142 Alice's biographer: Strouse, p. 326.

142 "Tenderest love to all": Quoted in Simon, p. 241.

143 "Some parts": Letter to Sarah Wyman Whitman, May 28, 1894, *COR,* vol. 7, p. 510.

143 "psychological phase": Letter to Dickinson S. Miller, quoted in Myers, p. 3.

143 "of the fact that": Letter from Henry James III to Elizabeth Glendower Evans, May 25, 1931, quoted in Simon, p. 249.

144 "Plato, Locke, Spinoza": *PRA,* p. 503.

144 "Philosophy has often been": *PRA,* p. 542.

145 "popular in the extreme": *TTS,* p. 707.

145 "have an awful side": Letter to Henry James, May 3, 1903, quoted in Allen, p. 440.

145 "I often have a desire": Letter to Alice Howe Gibbens James, February 15, 1888, *COR,* vol. 6, p. 320.

145 "You write of the 'peace'": Letter to Alice Howe Gibbens James, September 16, 1897, *COR,* vol. 8, p. 305.

146 "remove [him]self": Letter to Théodore Flournoy, August 13, 1895, quoted in Allen, p. 540.

146 "reconcile us": "The Sentiment of Rationality," *WTB,* p. 512.

147 "We ought": "The Will to Believe," *WTB,* p. 478.

147 "'experience' against 'philosophy'": Letter to Frances R. Morse, April 12, 1900, quoted in Perry, p. 257.

147 "You must not leave me": Letter to Alice Howe Gibbens James, January 6, 1883, quoted in Perry, p. 253.

AUTHOR

149 "Every now and then": "The Moral Philosopher and the Moral Life," *WTB,* p. 613.

149 "It is not certain that": Albert Camus, *Lyrical and Critical Essays* (1967; repr. New York: Vintage, 1970), p. 228

1. The Tiny Bridge

151 "the shadow that loyally walks": Jaynes, p. 11.

151 In 1892, he found: See C. Taylor, p. 51.

152 "psychology is not *à l'ordre du jour*": Letter to Oliver Wendell Holmes, Jr., May 15, 1868, *COR,* vol. 4, p. 302.

152 "Here then . . . is the tiny bridge": Jaynes, pp. 104-05.

152 "The mighty themes": Jaynes, p. 226.

153 "The whole long song": Jaynes, p. 277.

153 "great blooming buzzing": *PP,* p. 462.

153 A prominent William James scholar: Jacques Barzun, "Doing Without Knowing," *Times Literary Supplement,* May 19, 1978.

153 "They are products": W. T. Jones, "Julian Jaynes and the Bicameral Mind: A Case Study in the Sociology of Belief," *Philosophy of the Social Sciences* 12, no. 2 (1982), p. 169.

153 "In this period of transition": Jaynes, p. 443.

2. Authors of the Universe

153 "The first poets": Jaynes, p. 361.

154 "When Julian Jaynes speculates": John Updike, *Hugging the Shore* (New York: Ecco, 1994), p. 823.

154 Oates responded more opaquely: See Sharon L. Dean's "Terror and the Bicameral Mind: Joyce Carol Oates's Use of Julian Jaynes in Her Pseudonymous Fiction," *Clues: A Journal of Detection* 15, no. 1 (1994).

154 "If we follow any one": *VRE,* p. 459.

154 "The saints are authors": *VRE,* p. 245.

157 The article had been written by a doctoral student: See Harriet Whitehead, "Reasonably Fantastic: Some Perspectives on Scientology, Science Fiction, and Occultism," in Zaretsky, pp. 547–87.

3. Admiral (Biography I)

161 Lafayette Ronald Hubbard: The biography of L. Ron Hubbard delivered here is a condensed version of that given in *What Is Scientology? A Guidebook to the World's Fastest Growing Religion.*

4. The Preclear

168 "like an actor": Hubbard, p. 648.

168 Hubbard claimed that most engrams: See Hubbard, p. 267.

168 "Psychiatry is seeking to create": *What Is Scientology? A Guidebook to the World's Fastest Growing Religion*, p. 466.

169 "The principle of causality": *WTB*, pp. 567–68.

5. The Sole Source (Biography II)

172 "My quest to understand": Jon Atack, "Scientology, Religion or Intelligence Agency: The View from the Lion's Den," paper delivered at the Dialog Centre International conference in Berlin, October 1995, available at http://www.holysmoke.org/sdhok/atack.html.

172 put forth by the debunkers: This version of L. Ron Hubbard's biography essentially combines the accounts given in Jon Atack's *A Piece of Blue Sky: Scientology, Dianetics, and L. Ron Hubbard Exposed* and Bent Corydon's *L. Ron Hubbard: Messiah or Madman?* Many of the facts are corroborated in a wide variety of media sources, including *Time, Newsweek, Forbes, L.A. Weekly, The Washington Post, The New York Times,* the *St. Petersburg Times,* and the *Los Angeles Times.*

172 "lacking in the essential": Quoted in Atack, p. 80.

172 "the most Thelemic": Letter from Parsons to Crowley, quoted in Atack, p. 92.

172 "Apparently Parsons or Hubbard": Quoted in Sutin, p. 414.

175 "dangerous lunatic": Atack, p. 122.

175 "All men shall be my slaves!": Quoted in Corydon, p. 58.

175 By 1949: See Atack, p. 137.

175 Noted fringe-religion: Gardner, p. 270.

176 "By the end of 1950": Atack, p. 118.

176 "Hubbard was left with": Corydon, p. 318.

176 "passive relaxation, concentration": *VRE,* p. 109.

177 "We should be very alert": Atack, p. 139.

177 "Intelligence we get": Atack, p. 144.

177 "the equivalent of a": Atack, p. 150.

177 "tricked, cheated": Widely quoted (*Rocky Mountain News,* August 27, 1995; *The New York Times,* March 9, 1997; *Time,* May 6, 1991; *60 Minutes,* 1980), but see Atack, p. 330.

177 "face an E-Meter": Atack, p. 147.

178 "the youngsters": Joel Sappell and Robert W. Welkos, "Life with L. Ron Hubbard," *Los Angeles Times,* June 24, 1990.

178 "complete with finance": Richard Behar, "The Prophet and Profits of Scientology," *Forbes Magazine,* October 27, 1986.

179 "remains a threat": Stephen A. Kent, "Scientology and the European Human Rights Debate: A Reply to Leisa Goodman, J. Gordon Melton, and the European Rehabilitation Project Force Study," *Marburg Journal of Religion* 8, no. 1 (2003).

179 "We own quite a bit": Corydon, p. 71.

180 "Mr. Hubbard": Robert Lindsey, "Fight over Funds Divides Scientology Group," *The New York Times,* January 6, 1983.

180 "individuals antithetical": *What Is Scientology? A Guidebook to the World's Fastest Growing Religion,* p. 494.

180 "It's like the *Lord of the Flies*": *The New York Times,* January 6, 1983.

181 "a hasty attempt": Atack, p. 285.

181 *DMSMH* hit the bestseller list again: Mike McIntyre, "Hubbard Hot-Author Status Called Illusion," *San Diego Union,* April 15, 1990. This was also described in "Costly Strategy Continues to Turn Out Bestsellers," *Los Angeles Times,* June 28, 1990, by Joel Sappell and Robert W. Welkos.

181 "In the late nineties, *60 Minutes*": "The Cult Awareness Network," *60 Minutes,* December 28, 1997.

181 IRS whistle-blowers: Douglas Franz, "Scientology's Puzzling Journey from Tax Rebel to Tax Exempt," *The New York Times,* March 9, 1997.

181 One day David Miscavige walked unannounced: Douglas Frantz, "The Shadowy Story Behind Scientology's Tax-Exempt Status," *The New York Times,* March 9, 1997, and follow-up stories on March 19, 1997; December 31, 1997; and January 1, 1998.

6. The Win

182 "easy enuf": Letter to Alexander Robertson James, May, 1900, *COR,* vol. 9, p. 197.

183 "a rather ordinary": Letter to G. Stanley Hall, October 10, 1879, *COR,* vol. 5, p. 65.

183 "a strange mania": Letter to Carl Stumpf, December 20, 1892, *COR,* vol. 7, p. 354.

183 "knocked together": *PRA,* p. 503.

183 "occasionally more *amusing*": Letter to Carl Stumpf, February 6, 1887, *COR,* vol. 6, p. 203.

183 "We should then have": *Writings: 1878–1899,* p. 898.

184 "a voyage of discovery": Hubbard, p. 1.

184 "the very core": *BC,* p. 178.

184 "One might here use": Hubbard, pp. 587–88.

185 "Such religious geniuses": *VRE,* p. 15.

185 "I doubt whether": *Writings: 1902–1910,* pp. 1274–75.

1898–1902

194 "Everywhere they ask": Letter from Josiah Royce to William James, February 7, 1900, *COR,* vol. 9, p. 588, calendared; quoted in Allen, p. 412.

194 "to attempt it": Letter to Frances Rollins Morse, April 13, 1900, *COR,* vol. 9, p. 186.

194 "state of spiritual": Letter to Alice Howe Gibbens James, July 9, 1898, *COR,* vol. 8, pp. 390–91.

195 "But was ever man": Letter from Alice Howe Gibbens James to Henry James, January 13, 1898, quoted in Allen, p. 395.

195 "If you ask what these": "Philosophical Conceptions and Practical Results," quoted in Perry, p. 255.

196 "It seems like a regular": Letter to Mary Raymond, March 2, 1899, quoted in Simon, p. 302.

196 "Although in middle life": Letter to *Springfield Republican,* June 4, 1900, quoted in Perry, p. 246.

196 "The great thing is": Letter to Francis Boott, September 15, 1900, quoted in Simon, p. 302.

197 "the feelings, acts, and": *VRE,* p. 36.

197 "easy and felicitous": *VRE,* p. 53.

197 "belief that there is an": *VRE,* p. 55.

198 "too deeply of": *VRE,* p. 174.

199 "throwing of our conscious": *VRE,* p. 195.

199 "Here if anywhere": *VRE,* p. 239.

199 "I have given 9": Letter to Henry William Rankin, June 16, 1901, *COR,* vol. 9, p. 501.

200 "to steep myself": Letter to C. E. Norton, June 26, 1901, quoted in Allen, p. 426.

200 "By their fruits": *VRE,* p. 26.

201 "How *can* you": *VRE,* p. 300.

202 "they show the way": *VRE,* p. 325.

202 "a touching expression": *VRE*, p. 311.

202 "The counting in": *VRE*, p. 386; I've made slight compressions here.

202 "veracity upon the": *VRE*, p. 387.

202 "absolutely worthless": *VRE*, p. 401.

202 "In prayer": *VRE*, p. 428.

203 "deal with . . . personal": *VRE*, p. 446.

203 "is such a 'more'": *VRE*, p. 455.

203 "a 'god of battles'": *VRE*, p. 437.

203 "was real since": *VRE*, p. 461.

203 "The whole drift": *VRE*, p. 463.

204 "too biological for": Letter to Carl Stumpf, July 10, 1901, quoted in Perry, p. 257.

204 "both God's friends": Letter to Pauline Goldmark, August 1, 1902, quoted in Perry, p. 261.

204 "I actually dread to die": Letter to Sarah Wyman Whitman, August 22, 1903, quoted in Simon, p. 309.

Godless

205 "The cultivator of this science": *VRE*, p. 439.

205 "It is so easy for": Fyodor Dostoyevsky, *The Idiot*, trans. Henry and Olga Carlisle (New York: Penguin, 1969), p. 570.

1. Vanini

206 Giulo Cesare Vanini: The story of Vanini delivered here is a compressed version of that given by Giovanni Papuli in *The Encyclopedia of Unbelief*, ed. Gordon Stein, p. 710–13.

2. The Paine Issue

209 "The more fervent": *VRE*, p. 39.

3. Buzz Aldrin Taking Communion in Space

211 Atheism: This history of unbelief compiles material from the following books: George Smith's *Atheism: The Case Against God*; Gordon Stein, ed., *The Encyclopedia of Unbelief*; and Warren Allen Smith, ed., *Who's Who in Hell*. Also essential were Karen Armstrong's *A History of God*, James Collins's *God in Modern Philosophy*, and Mircea Eliade's *A History of Religious Ideas*. O'Hair's history, in particular the later accounts of her death, includes material from a variety of newspaper accounts.

211 "But it is also": Wolfe, p. 248.

212 "greater than any sin": Quoted in Smith, p. 4.

214 "As to the book": Letter from Thomas Paine to Andrew Dean, August 15, 1806, quoted in Zindler, *The Age of Reason: Part Three*, p. iii.

214 "If it is true": Robert G. Ingersoll, "Mistakes of Moses," quoted in Smith, p. 196.

215 "I need someone who": *Playboy*, 1965, quoted in Warren Allen Smith, ed., *Who's Who in Hell*, p. 817.

216 "I have told Jon": W. Smith, ed., *Who's Who in Hell*, p. 818.

5. Automatic Sweetheart

222 "Assuredly," he wrote: *VRE*, p. 463.

222 But he had previously: *WTB*, p. 543.

222 James's example of the woodpecker: *PRA*, p. 575.

222 "to constitute a knockdown proof": *VRE*, p. 394n.

222 *"That shape"* . . . "another case of fear": *VRE*, pp. 149–51.

223 "We must therefore": *VRE*, p. 38.

223 "automatic sweetheart": *MT*, p. 922n.

224 "Some persons, for instance": *VRE*, pp. 190–91; I've made slight compressions here.

1902–1907

232 "squashy public": Quoted in Perry, p. 273.

232 "'talker to'": Letter to William James, Jr., July 4, 1903, quoted in Simon, p. 329.

232 He set about crafting: Perry, p. 278.

232 "I am sure that a book": Letter to F.C.S. Schiller, April 8, 1903, quoted in Perry, p. 276.

233 "Call it 'A beginning'": A memorandum dated July 26, 1910, quoted in Simon, p. 383 and Allen, p. 469.

233 "*Not* convincing": Letter to F.C.S. Schiller, August 24, 1906, quoted in Simon, p. 343.

234 "I am persuaded": Letter to Pauline Goldmark, February 24, 1904, *COR*, vol. 10, p. 384.

234 "But there is no reason": *Writings: 1902–1910*, p. 1286; I've made slight compressions here.

234 "If now—and this": *Writings: 1902–1910*, p. 1291.

235 "everything that was on": *Writings: 1902–1910*, p. 1215.

235 "I felt no trace": *Writings: 1902–1910*, pp. 1215–16.

235 "It was a strange sight": *Writings: 1902–1910*, p. 1218.

235 "The cheerfulness": *Writings: 1902–1910*, p. 1222.

236 "What *you* want": *PRA*, p. 494.

236 "remain religious like": *PRA*, pp. 500–501.

237 "the centre of gravity": *PRA*, p. 540.

237 "many widely differing": *PRA*, p. 570.

237 "May there not": *PRA*, p. 571.

237 "Truth *must* be a correspondence": Letter to William James from Benjamin Paul Blood, April 30, 1885, *COR*, vol. 6, p. 30.

237 "I see it every where": Letter to William James from Robertson James, November 6, 1901, *COR*, vol. 9, p. 556.

238 "Truth *happens* to an idea": *PRA*, p. 574.

238 "Truth for us is": *PRA*, p. 581.

238 "growing in all sorts": *PRA*, p. 600.

238 "I can not start": *PRA*, pp. 618–19.

238 "mankind has only": *PRA*, p. 618.

238 "too good": Letter to F.C.S. Schiller, May 18, 1907, *COR*, vol. 11, p. 364.

GODDESS

239 "The whole history": *Writings: 1878–1899*, p. 1046.

239 "To communicate with Mars": T. S. Eliot, "The Dry Salvages," *Four Quartets* (New York: Harvest, 1968), p. 31.

1. MerryMeet

240 "got strong enough": *VRE*, p. 305.

241 "a plurality of individuals": Quoted in Perry, p. 295.

2. Uncle Dear

243 "the houses": Letter to Alice Howe Gibbens James, August 5, 1898, *COR*, vol. 8, p. 405.

245 "But I am intensely": Letter to Grace Norton, September 12, 1902, *COR*, vol. 10, p. 121.

3. The Circle Is Cast

253 Modern witchcraft began: The history of witchcraft and Wicca combines material from the following books: Ronald Hutton, *The Triumph of the Moon;* Margot Adler, *Drawing*

Down the Moon; and Mircea Eliade, *Occultism, Witchcraft, and Cultural Fashions* and *A History of Religious Ideas.*

256 "If you but love": *VRE,* p. 78.

256 "Do as thou wilt": Widely attributed to *Gargantua,* 1534. François Rabelais, *Gargantua & Pantagruel,* trans. Jacques LeClercq (New York: Heritage, 1936), p. 142.

256 "Do what thou wilt": Aleister Crowley, *The Book of the Law,* as quoted in Sutin, p. 117.

257 "the myth of the Unitarian": Quoted in Adler, p. 45.

257 "smitten with": Letter to Samuel Delano, July 27, 1903, Skrupskelis and Berkeley, eds., *Correspondence,* vol. 10, p. 282.

257 "because human energy": Quoted in Adler, p. 172.

4. Ben Franklin in Drag

259 "These pragmatists destroy": James is characterizing the criticism himself. See *PRA,* p. 588.

261 "One cannot say this": *Writings: 1902–1910,* pp. 940–41.

263 For a historian writing: See Eric J. Ziolkowski, *A Museum of Faiths: Histories and Legacies of the 1893 World's Parliament of Religions* (Atlanta: Scholars Press, 1993), p. 49.

5. The Suicidal Mood

264 "Now, when I speak": *WTB,* pp. 498–99.

1907–1910

268 "Even in such details": Rollo Walter Brown, *Harvard Yard in the Golden Age,* quoted in Allen, p. 301.

269 "never quite in focus": John Jay Chapman, *Memories and Milestones,* quoted in Allen, p. 301.

270 "I now say": *PU,* p. 776.

271 "I can't recognize the truth": Letter to F.C.S. Schiller, May 18, 1907, *COR,* vol. 11, pp. 364–65.

271 "But my persistent failure": Letter to Charles Augustus Strong, September 17, 1907, *COR,* vol. 11, p. 449.

271 "It makes one despair": Letter to Bertrand Russell, May 14, 1909, *COR,* vol. 12, p. 220.

271 "I don't like the notion": Letter to Hugo Münsterberg, March 16, 1909, *COR,* vol. 12, p. 178.

271 "monumentally foolish": Quoted in E. Taylor, p. 106.

271 "I thought your Will to Believe": Letter from Charles Sanders Peirce to William James, March 9, 1909, *COR,* vol. 12, p. 171.

272 "My own Oxford lectures": Letter to Henry James, May 31, 1909, *COR,* vol. 3, p. 389.

272 "I find it of thrilling interest": Letter from Henry James to William James, October 31, 1909, *COR,* vol. 3, p. 402.

273 "What happened was that": Letter from Henry James to William James, February 8, 1910, *COR,* vol. 12, p. 409.

273 "pretty good for": Letter to Henry Adams, June 17, 1910, *COR,* vol. 12, p. 555.

274 "a dismal chronicle": Letter from Henry James to Grace Norton, August 26, 1910, quoted in Allen, p. 491.

274 "I can't stand": Quoted in Allen, p. 490.

274 James was cremated and his ashes spread: Allen, p. 493.

274 James was buried in a small cemetery: Simon, p. 388.

274 Or James was cremated: *Writings: 1902–1910,* p. 1167.

Dog

275 "I firmly disbelieve": *PRA*, p. 619.

275 "The feeling of religious devotion": Charles Darwin, *The Descent of Man* (1871; repr., Princeton: Princeton University Press, 1981), p. 68.

1. Two-Top Mountain

276 "Precisely because they are living": Monks of New Skete, *Raising Your Dog with the Monks of New Skete,* Atmosphere Entertainment, 1996, tape 1.

277 "beautifully proportioned breasts": Monks of New Skete, *In the Spirit of Happiness,* p. 14.

2. Lazarus

279 The schism between: The history of Orthodoxy delivered here is essentially a compressed version of that given by Timothy Ware in *The Orthodox Church.* Other useful insight is pulled from Karen Armstrong's *The History of God* and Mircea Eliade's *A History of Religious Ideas.*

3. Prodigal Dogs

283 "Our dogs, for example": *WTB*, p. 499.

283 a letter to his brother Bob: See Letter to Robertson James, February 20, 1875, *COR*, vol. 4, p. 509.

283 "'Never, never before'": Letter to Edgar Beach Van Winkle, November 12, 1858, *COR*, vol. 4, p. 23.

283 "I was so glad to see": Letter to Alexander Robertson James, August 7, 1899, *COR*, vol. 9, pp. 19–20.

283 "Music gives us ontological": *VRE*, p. 380.

287 "the faithful live at second hand": *VRE*, p. 308.

4. Weltanschauung

289 "the spiritual bond we have": Stephen Huneck's Dog Chapel, www.huneck.com/shop/catalog/dog_chapel.php

291 "religious connection" and "communality of": see C. Taylor, p. 24, and Myers, p. 350.

291 "the profounder way": *VRE*, p. 330.

291 "I promised to say nothing": *VRE*, p. 412.

6. Whelping to Bach

301 "And here religion": *VRE*, pp. 49–50.

Epilogue

303 "People are more confident": Durkheim, *The Elementary Forms of Religious Life,* p. 350. See also Durkheim's comments on the Arunta on p. 229, as well as a variety of references to *The Principles of Psychology* toward the end of *The Elementary Forms of Religious Life.*

303 "The myths that": Eliade, vol. 2, p. 339.

303 A recent book-length study: See Russell B. Goodman, *Wittgenstein and William James.*

304 "up to now man": Jane Revere Burke, *Let Us In* (New York: E. P. Dutton, 1931).

304 Maude V. Underhill's James: "The Upward Path," an unpublished manuscript, quoted in Smith, p. 15.

304 Susy Smith: Susy Smith, *The Book of James (William James, That Is)* (New York: toExcel, 2000).

304 "If you could always": Susy Smith, p. 23.

306 In Germany, Cruise and Spielberg: *Der Spiegel,* April 27, 2005.

308 "this belief would be": G. E. Moore, quoted in Goodman, p. 15.

309 "Let the reader try this": *PP,* p. 726.

310 "Single words": *VRE,* p. 345.

310 "If you stop": *PRA,* p. 539.

310 "It would be an awful": Letter to Grace Norton, December 28, 1892, Skrupskelis and Berkeley, eds., *Correspondence,* vol. 7, p. 358.

𝔅ibliography

JAMES

Allen, Gay Wilson. *William James.* New York: Viking Press, 1967.

Barzun, Jacques. *A Stroll with William James.* Chicago: University of Chicago Press, 1983.

Boorstin, Jon. *The Newsboys' Lodging House, or The Confessions of William James.* New York: Penguin Books, 2003.

Capps, David, and Janet L. Jacobs, eds. *The Struggle for Life: A Companion to William James's* The Varieties of Religious Experience. West Lafayette, Ind.: Society for the Scientific Study of Religion, 1995.

Edel, Leon, ed. *The Diary of Alice James.* New York: Dodd, Mead & Company, 1934.

Goodman, Russell B. *Wittgenstein and William James.* New York: Cambridge University Press, 2002.

James, Henry. *Notes of a Son and Brother.* New York: Charles Scribner's Sons, 1914.

James, William. *The Principles of Psychology.* 2 vols. Cambridge: Harvard University Press, 1981.

———. *The Varieties of Religious Experience.* New York: Collier Macmillan Publishers, 1961.

———. *Writings: 1878–1899.* New York: Library Classics of the United States, 1992. (Includes *Briefer Course, Talks to Teachers and Students,* and *The Will to Believe.*)

———. *Writings: 1902–1910.* New York: Library Classics of the United States, 1987. (Includes *The Meaning of Truth, Pragmatism, A Pluralistic Universe,* and *The Varieties of Religious Experience.*)

Menand, Louis. *The Metaphysical Club: A Story of Ideas in America.* New York: Farrar, Straus and Giroux, 2001.

———, ed. *Pragmatism: A Reader.* New York: Random House, 1997.

Myers, Gerald E. *William James: His Life and Thought.* New Haven: Yale University Press, 1986.

Perry, Ralph Barton. *In the Spirit of William James.* New Haven: Yale University Press, 1938.

———. *The Thought and Character of William James.* Nashville: Vanderbilt University Press, 1948.

Simon, Linda. *Genuine Reality: A Life of William James.* Chicago: University of Chicago Press, 1998.

Skrupskelis, Ignas K., and Elizabeth M. Berkeley, eds. *The Correspondence of William James.* 12 vols. Charlottesville: University of Virginia Press, 1992–2004.

———, eds. *William and Henry James: Selected Letters.* Charlottesville: University of Virginia Press, 1997.

Strouse, Jean. *Alice James: A Biography.* Cambridge: Harvard University Press, 1980.

Swedenborg, Emanuel. *Concerning the Earths in Our Solar System, Etc.* London: Emanuel Swedenborg, 1758.

Taylor, Charles. *Varieties of Religion Today: William James Revisited.* Cambridge: Harvard University Press, 2002.

Taylor, Eugene. *William James on Consciousness Beyond the Margin.* Princeton: Princeton University Press, 1996.

Wernham, James C. S. *James's Will to Believe Doctrine: A Heretical View.* Montreal: McGill-Queen's University Press, 1987.

General

Armstrong, Karen. *A History of God.* New York: Ballantine, 1993.

Collins, James. *God in Modern Philosophy.* Chicago: Henry Regnery Company, 1959.

Durkheim, Emile. *The Elementary Forms of Religious Life.* London: George Allen, 1915.

Eliade, Mircea. *A History of Religious Ideas.* 3 vols. Chicago: University of Chicago Press, 1978.

Gardner, Martin. *Fads and Fallacies: In the Name of Science.* New York: Dover Publications, 1952.

Melton, J. Gordon. *Encyclopedia of American Religions* 6th ed. Farmington Hills, Mich.: Gale Group, 1998.

Miles, Jack. *God: A Biography.* New York: Random House, 1995.

Sutin, Lawrence. *Do What Thou Wilt: A Life of Aleister Crowley.* New York: St. Martin's–Griffin, 2000.

Wolfe, Alan. *The Transformation of American Religion: How We Actually Live Our Faith.* New York: Free Press, 2003.

Wright, Lawrence. *Saints and Sinners.* New York: Random House, 1993.

Zaretsky, Irving I., and Mark P. Leone, eds. *Religious Movements in Contemporary America.* Princeton: Princeton University Press, 1974.

Infinite

Jung, C. G. *Flying Saucers: A Modern Myth of Things Seen in the Sky.* Translated by R. F. C. Hull, 1958. Repr., New York: MJF Books, 1978.

Lewis, James R., ed. *The Gods Have Landed: New Religions from Other Worlds.* Albany: State University of New York Press, 1995.

Norman, Ernest L. *The Truth About Mars: An Eyewitness Account.* El Cajon, Calif.: Unarius Academy of Science, 1998.

Old Ones

Cunliffe, Barry. *The Ancient Celts.* New York: Penguin Books, 1997.

Ellis, Peter Berresford. *A Brief History of the Druids.* New York: Carroll & Graf, 2002.

Green, Miranda J. *The World of the Druids.* New York: Thames and Hudson, 1997.

Hutton, Ronald. *The Triumph of the Moon: A History of Modern Pagan Witchcraft.* New York: Oxford University Press, 1999.

Matthews, John, ed. *The Druid Source Book.* London: Blandford Press, 1996.

KING

Mazer, Sharon. *Professional Wrestling: Sport and Spectacle.* Jackson: University Press of
Mississippi, 1998.

Morton, Gerald W., and George M. O'Brien. *Wrestling to Rasslin': Ancient Sport to
American Spectacle.* Bowling Green: Bowling Green State University Popular Press,
1985.

The Unreal Story of Pro Wrestling. Produced by Chris Mortensen and Don Cambou.
A&E Television Networks, 1998.

SATAN

Ashen, Ruth Nanda. *The Reality of the Devil: Evil in Man.* New York: Dell, 1972.

Barton, Blanche. *The Church of Satan.* New York: Hell's Kitchen Productions, 1990.

———. *The Secret Life of a Satanist.* Los Angeles: Feral House, 1990.

Carus, Paul. *The History of the Devil and the Idea of Evil.* New York: Bell Publishing
Company, 1900.

LaVey, Anton Szandor. *The Satanic Bible.* New York: Avon Books, 1969.

———. *The Satanic Witch.* Los Angeles: Feral House, 1970.

Pagels, Elaine. *The Origin of Satan.* New York: Random House, 1995.

Satanis: The Devil's Mass. Produced by Ray Laurent, 1970.

Stein, Gordon, ed. *The Encyclopedia of Unbelief.* Buffalo, N.Y.: Prometheus Books, 1985.

AUTHOR

Atack, Jon. *A Piece of Blue Sky: Scientology, Dianetics, and L. Ron Hubbard Exposed.* New
York: Carol Publishing Group, 1990.

Corydon, Bent. *L. Ron Hubbard: Messiah or Madman?* Fort Lee, N.J.: Barricade Books,
1987.

Dianetics Seminar. Los Angeles: Bridge Publications, 1988.

Hubbard, L. Ron. *Battlefield Earth: A Saga of the Year 3000.* New York: St. Martin's Press,
1982.

———. *Dianetics: The Modern Science of Mental Health.* Los Angeles: Bridge Publications, 1950.

———. *Scientology: The Fundamentals of Thought.* Los Angeles: Bridge Publications,
1988.

Jaynes, Julian. *The Origin of Consciousness in the Breakdown of the Bicameral Mind.* Boston:
Houghton Mifflin Company, 1976.

What Is Scientology? A Guidebook to the World's Fastest Growing Religion. Los Angeles:
Bridge Publications, 1993.

GODLESS

Smith, George. *Atheism: The Case Against God.* New York: Prometheus Books, 1989.

Smith, Warren Allen, ed. *Who's Who in Hell.* Fort Lee, N.J.: Barricade Books, 2000.

Stein, Gordon, ed. *The Encyclopedia of Unbelief.* Amherst: Prometheus Books, 1985.

Zindler, Frank, ed. *The Age of Reason: Part Three.* Austin: American Atheist Press, 1993.

GODDESS

Adler, Margot. *Drawing Down the Moon: Witches, Druids, Goddess Worshippers, and Other
Pagans in America Today.* New York: Penguin Books, 1979.

Bonewits, Isaac. *Real Magic.* York Beach, Maine: Weiser Books, 1971.

Eliade, Mircea. *Occultism, Witchcraft, and Cultural Fashions.* Chicago: University of
    Chicago Press, 1976.
Gardner, Gerald B. *Witchcraft Today.* Lake Toxaway, N.C.: Mercury Publishing, 1954.
Hutton, Ronald. *The Triumph of the Moon: A History of Modern Pagan Witchcraft.* New
    York: Oxford University Press, 1999.
Starhawk. *The Spiral Dance: A Rebirth of the Ancient Religion of the Great Goddess.* 1979.
    Repr., New York: HarperSanFrancisco, 1999.
Valiente, Doreen. *Natural Magic.* Blaine, Wash.: Phoenix Publishing, 1975.

Dog

The Monks of New Skete. *The Art of Raising a Puppy.* Boston: Little, Brown and Com-
    pany, 1991.
————. *How to Be Your Dog's Best Friend.* 1978. Repr. Boston: Little, Brown and Com-
    pany, 2002.
————. *I and Dog.* New York: Yorkville Press, 2003.
————. *In the Spirit of Happiness.* Boston: Little, Brown and Company, 1999.
Ware, Timothy. *The Orthodox Church.* New York: Penguin Books, 1963.

About the Author

J. C. HALLMAN, a graduate of the Iowa Writers' Workshop
and the Writing Seminars at Johns Hopkins, has published fiction
and nonfiction in *GQ* and other national magazines. His first book,
The Chess Artist, was published to wide acclaim. Hallman is
currently serving as the Banister Writer-in-Residence
at Sweet Briar College. He can be reached at
jchallman@gmail.com.

About the Type

This book was set in Bembo, a typeface based on an old-style Roman face that was used for Cardinal Bembo's tract *De Aetna* in 1495. Bembo was cut by Francisco Griffo in the early sixteenth century. The Lanston Monotype Company of Philadelphia brought the well-proportioned letterforms of Bembo to the United States in the 1930s.